AUSTRALIAN MOTORCYCLE HEROES
1949-1989

John

Keep the old pecker up! Thought you might like to read about the good old times. Hope it brings back a lot of fond memories. I couldn't have done it without your help

Thanks for everything

Barry

SEPT 94

DEDICATION

To Sema, for her support and encouragement. And to Australia's international motorcycle soldiers of fortune, whose very effort in heading overseas to race established them as a special group. Thank you.
Don Cox

To all those who packed their gear and had a go. Congratulations and thank you.
Will Hagon

AUSTRALIAN MOTORCYCLE HEROES 1949–1989

DON COX & WILL HAGON

ANGUS & ROBERTSON PUBLISHERS

First published in 1989 by
Angus & Robertson Publishers
Unit 4, Eden Park, 31 Waterloo Road
North Ryde, NSW, Australia 2113, and
16 Golden Square, London WIR 4BN
United Kingdom.

© Don Cox & Will Hagon 1989

Designed and produced by
John Ferguson Pty Ltd
100 Kippax St
SURRY HILLS 2010

This book is copyright. Apart from any fair dealing for the purposes of private study, research, critism or review, as permitted under the Copyright Act, no part may be reproduced by any process without written permission. Inquiries should be addressed to the publisher.

National Library of Australia
Cataloguing-in-publication entry
  Cox, Don.
     Australian motorcycle heroes, 1949-1989.
     ISBN 0 207 16207 7
     1. Motorcyclists – Australia – Biography. I. Hagon, Will. II. Title
  796.7'5,0922

Typeset by The Type Shop, Sydney
Printed by Globe Press, Melbourne.

CONTENTS

	Foreword	7
	Preface	8
1.	Continental Circus	10
2.	The Hintons	26
3.	Ken Kavanagh	42
4.	Keith Campbell	56
5.	Bob Mitchell	70
6.	Bob Brown	82
7.	Tom Phillis	92
8.	Jack Ahearn	106
9.	Jack Findlay	118
10.	Kel Carruthers	144
11.	Barry Smith	156
12.	John Dodds	166
13.	Gregg Hansford	176
14.	The Last Privateers	188
15.	Tokyo Express	206
16.	Wayne Gardner	214
	Authors' Dozen	228
	Honour Rolls	230
	Acknowledgments	237
	Index	238

FOREWORD

Grand Prix motorcycle racing has finally made it in Australia, with live telecasts of the grands prix from overseas, and now a grand prix of our own at Phillip Island.

Just watch the sport take off from here now that Australians can see for themselves all the speed, colour and excitement of GP racing. Today Australian riders are able to show they can take on and beat the best from overseas, and do it on their home ground.

It's quite a change from when I went overseas in 1981, as a young rider with a dream of winning the world championship. And, of course, there were plenty of riders before me who pioneered Australian involvement in GP racing. Some were very successful, others not quite so much. But we all had something in common — a love of motorcycle racing and a determination to overcome any obstacle while chasing racetrack success.

When I became the first Australian to win the world 500cc championship in 1987, I felt I was representing the aspirations of all those Aussie riders before me who had striven to reach the top overseas — often without any recognition back home.

Now these riders have that long overdue recognition, through this well researched book. I congratulate the authors, Will Hagon and Don Cox, for their obvious commitment to righting that wrong, and for giving those pioneers their rightful place in Australian motorcycle racing history.

I'm sure an understanding of what has been achieved by so many riders will inspire a new generation of Australian riders to chase the dream of world championship glory.

Wayne Gardner
World 500cc champion, 1987

PREFACE

Eric McPherson gunned his new AJS 7R 350 out from under the trees at Governor's Bridge and into Glencrutchery Road. He had only to clear this corner and it was a straight run of less than 500 metres to complete his second official practice lap of the 61 km Isle of Man Mountain Circuit. His target that lap was a time of less than 30 minutes.

But there was a patch of oil on the road where a machine had crashed a few minutes earlier. There was no warning flag. Eric powered straight over the oil slick. Next moment he was skidding across the road on the backside of his leathers. He hit the kerb feet-first and jarred his spine. He was unable to ride for several weeks. McPherson was very dejected. He was 37 years old and had waited ten years for the opportunity to ride in the event he and his fellow racers considered the pinnacle of motorcycling.

Eric McPherson's first-morning exit from the 1948 Isle of Man TT meeting in no way diminishes his place on Australia's international motorcycling honour roll. He was Australia's first post World War II Isle of Man representative.

In 1949, McPherson tried again. The Auto-Cycle Council of Australia nominated McPherson and Harry Hinton as official IoM representatives. Ballarat rider George Morrison went as a freelance racer. Morrison would later start an Australian privateer trend by painting a kangaroo motif on his racing helmet.

Eric McPherson travelled in Britain and Europe with wife Ruby on an AJS outfit, with his racing machine stowed in the box sidecar. McPherson retired from the 1949 350 TT with mechanical trouble. But in the months that followed he became the first Australian to score points in the new world motorcycle grand prix championships. He finished fifth in the Dutch 350 GP, fifth in the Belgian 350 GP and fourth at Ulster, to claim equal third place in the inaugural world 350 championship. McPherson, Hinton and Morrison also began a post-war boom for Australians gaining works rides.

More than a dozen Australians had competed in the Isle of Man Tourist Trophy races up to 1939, beginning with Newcastle's Dr Les Bailey, who rode a Douglas to 15th place in the 1912 500 TT. In 1946, the Auto-Cycle Council of Australia set up an IoM fund to assist future official Australian representatives. The TT races resumed in 1947 and the first Australian team was selected in 1948. The Anglophile ACCA continued to nominate official Isle of Man representatives until 1971. Oddly enough, it has never nominated or funded official world road-racing championship representatives.

The early grants paid to IoM TT representatives covered their boat fares to and from England. The one-way voyage could take anything from 25 days to six weeks, so riders extended their stay and contested races in Europe. The European scene offered something racing in Australia and the Isle of Man did not — the chance for private entrants to earn a living from racing. European race organisers, particularly those who promoted non-championship international races, paid starting money to attract riders.

Australians who missed IoM team selection were soon tempted to make the trip to Europe as freelance riders. They usually worked two jobs, to save their boat fares and the price tags for new bikes. Australia's private entrants of the 1950s began a grand tradition of riders living on the road for six months a year in former army panel vans, gutted buses or Ford Thames vans, as part of the Continental Circus. The privateer's gypsy life attracted some great characters and produced some amazing stories.

Eighteen months ago, in August 1987, we discussed the idea of a book about Australia's post World War II international racers. The catalyst was the telecast of the Czechoslovakian GP at the new Brno circuit. And Wayne Gardner was poised to win the world 500 championship. We had a hunch that the story of our other world champions and major championship contenders had never been fully told in one publication.

This idea was prompted by the SBS-TV studio guest that evening, Eric Hinton, who recounted extraordinary things his generation of riders did on the Brno public road circuit in the 1950s.

The idea of following the European race season in a van with your motorcycle in the back can seem very romantic from 18,000 km away. The reality is that it is tough, particularly when the results and the money aren't coming, and when homesickness pulls at the heart. But Australians had been leading this existence, largely unrecognised in their own country, for 40 years.

We did not set out to write the history of the world championships 1949-1989 from an Australian point of view. Our aim was to tell the story of the men. The formula for a motorcycle race hero doesn't change. The requirements in talent, determination and courage applied as much in the austere days of 1949, when a 500 race-bike running on 72 octane fuel was lucky to hit 180 km/h, as they do when works 500s can top 310 km/h and spin their rear tyres at the slightest provocation.

But who do you include? Well over 100 Australians have packed their hopes and their bags to try to make a living as a racer in Europe. In recent times we've seen Australians head off to North America or Japan with the same goal. We hope the decision to profile a selection of Australia's 100 or more post World War II soldiers of fortune gives an insight into the struggles, pain, achievement and elation of the whole group. The main criterion was riders who'd spent full seasons racing in Europe.

Australian representative Eric McPherson descends Bray Hill during the 1949 Isle of Man TT.

The selection made, we endeavoured to catalogue as many of our internationals as the sports record books and riders' memories could identify. This list appears as the Honour Roll, Internationals 1912-1988.

The contrast in goals between 1949 official IoM representatives Eric McPherson and Harry Hinton, and 1988 grand prix victors Wayne Gardner and Kevin Magee highlights the dilemma of 1950s and 1960s Australian internationals. It also brings into focus one of the difficulties of assessing rider achievement on world championship results.

McPherson and Hinton, for example, did not leave Australia with ambitions to be world champion. Their goal was to compete in the world's most famous motorcycle race and later to earn a factory ride. The goal for the men who followed them in the next 20 years was the factory ride. And if not, simply to make a living as a motorcycle racer.

There were so many works machines in the grands prix during the bulk of the 1950s and 1960s that private entrants often went to the starting line knowing they were racing for sixth or eighth place. In fact many riders of the period ignored grand prix events to contest non-championship international meetings, which paid better start money. Many riders simply ignored the world championships.

Keith Bryen, a 1950s private entrant and Moto Guzzi team-mate to Keith Campbell for two grands prix in 1957, said privateers had other measures of success than the world championship point-score tables. World championships were titles works riders chased. "Most private entrants never gave the world championships a second thought. The big thing for us was to be the first privateer home. The sign that you'd made it in Europe was to have an international race organiser ask you to ride at his meeting the following weekend."

Nonetheless, to score world championship points was a measure of achievement, because a rider had to be among the leading private entrants to finish in the top six (or top ten after 1969) of a grand prix.

Up to the end of 1988, four Australians had won world championships — Keith Campbell, Tom Phillis, Kel Carruthers and Wayne Gardner. Eleven had won world championship grands prix — Ken Kavanagh, Keith Campbell, Tom Phillis, Jack Ahearn, Barry Smith, Kel Carruthers, John Dodds, Jack Findlay, Gregg Hansford, Wayne Gardner and Kevin Magee. Another 11 have made the winner's dais of a grand prix, by finishing second or third, and 22 more have scored world championship grand prix points for minor GP placings. That makes a total of 44 Australians who've scored grand prix points. It made our choice of riders to profile even more difficult.

Every year of the 40 years of world championship competition has seen Australians "in the points" in at least one class. The United Kingdom, Italy and Switzerland are the only other nations which can make that claim. And the United States has only had regular points scorers in the past decade.

What follows is our selection of 21 heroes. It's not an exhaustive list. Our aim was to tell a story and see it in print at a time when the maximum number of Australians could appreciate the efforts of these men. We hope we've done justice to them in the pages that follow, because these Australians worked hard over the past 40 years to carve a place in motorcycle road-racing's history. For the period 1949-1989 they're our Australian motorcycle heroes.

Don Cox & Will Hagon,
Sydney, March 1989

CONTINENTAL CIRCUS

CHAPTER 1

The concept of an international motorcycle road-racing championship took shape in the 1920s when the French, Belgian, Italian, Ulster, German, Hungarian, Dutch, Austrian and Swedish grands prix were born.

The advent of a regular calendar of grand prix events in the European spring and summer encouraged international riders to contest a number of these races. The group of riders moving from one race to the next was soon dubbed "the continental circus"; British racer turned commentator Graham Walker, the father of Formula One motor-racing commentator Murray Walker, was believed to be the one to coin the term.

The first European championships were not series but one-race affairs. Beginning in 1924, one grand prix each year was granted the title European Grand Prix; the race winner was the European Champion for that year. The first two European championships were held at Monza in Italy. In the next 12 years the European GP rotated between Belgium's Spa-Francorchamps Circuit, Germany's Nurburgring and Sachsenring, Geneva and Berne in Switzerland, Barcelona (Spain), Montlhery (near Paris), Rome, Saxtorp (Sweden), Assen (Holland) and the Cladys Circuit in Northern Ireland. (Australian championships were decided in a similar fashion until 1972, by rotating the venue among the states.)

Every European grand prix of this period offered 250, 350 and 500 solo classes. Some hosts added other solo classes (125, 175, 750 and even 1000) and a 600 cm^3 sidecar class.

The early European championship races were tough events. The road surface was often no more than rolled gravel. Lap distances were up to 30 kilometres and race distances up to 600 kilometres. Some races lasted four hours, with three or four solo classes often run together. Such events led to interesting tactics: a factory team might detail one of its 500 entrants to help its best 350 entry, by riding just in front of him to provide a "tow" on the straights.

An Australian rider, Arthur Simcock, scored second placings in the 1930 and 1931 European championships. Simcock rode an AJS to second in the 1930 European 350 championship at Spa-Francorchamps, behind works Norton rider Ernie Nott. The following year Simcock split the Norton entries to finish second in the European 500 championship, held at Montlhery. Simcock rode a JAP-engined OK Supreme; Tim Hunt won the race, and famed Scottish rider Jimmy Guthrie was third. Simcock later became the London representative of the Auto-Cycle Council of Australia, the country's governing body of motorcycle sport.

The European championship became a pointscore series in 1938. There were eight rounds: the grands prix of Holland, Belgium, Switzerland, France, Germany, Ulster and Italy, and the Isle of Man Tourist Trophy. The Swedish GP was added to the 1939 series, but only seven rounds were run before World War II broke out.

There was no restriction on the method of engine induction for these events. The fuel used was a 50/50 mixture of petrol and the anti-knock agent benzol, so the effective octane rating was nearly 100. The first machines used in the European championship were little more than race-tuned versions of sports machines sold to the public. But within 15 years racing machines had become highly specialised and sophisticated.

The combination of strong competition, laissez faire rules and late 1930s government support to German and Italian factories produced several exotic machines. In 1939, supercharged two-stroke DKWs finished first and second in the 250 championship and won the 350 championship, while in the same year a supercharged four-cylinder, water-cooled double-overhead-camshaft Gilera four won the 500 championship, from a "blown" BMW twin. British factories AJS and Velocette also produced supercharged multi-cylinder machines.

The shape of post-war championship road racing was cast in London in December 1946 at a meeting of the world governing body of motorcycling, the Federation Internationale des Clubs Motorcyclistes. (The title was simplified a few years later to Federation Internationale Motorcycliste.) The meeting voted to limit the fuel used for international road racing to ordinary pump petrol, and to ban supercharging. In contrast, grand prix motor car racing's rule makers didn't restrict fuel until 1958, and they simply waited for supercharged cars to phase themselves out in the early 1950s by allowing capacity advantages for naturally aspirated engines.

The FICM's decisions in 1946 were unusually altruistic, because the nations which proposed the major changes had the most to lose by them. Britain's delegates proposed the restriction on fuel, which hurt their 350 and 500 cm^3 air-cooled single-cylinder engines such as Norton and Velocette more than any other. And Italy's delegates moved the motion to ban supercharging, meaning the pre-war Gilera 500 and 250 fours, Bianchi's 500 four, Moto Guzzi's 500 triple and two Benelli 250s (a single and a four) were all obsolete. Germany's supercharged BMW and DKW machines were also ruled out; they would have been sidelined anyway as Germany was not re-admitted to international motorcycle sport until 1951.

The decision on fuel was a pain for the factories in the late 1940s. The immediate drama was the quality of generally available fuel, commonly known as pool petrol, in 1947. Its octane rating was around 72,

DKW works rider August Höbl leads Australian pair Maurie Quincey (Norton) and Ken Kavanagh (Moto Guzzi) at the start of the 1954 Belgian 350 GP.

compared with nearly 100 for the petrol/benzol blend used up to 1939. (Unfavourable comparisons were drawn with kerosene and heating oil!) The switch to pool petrol affected engines in two ways. Firstly, the reduced octane rating meant that the factories had to lower the compression ratios of existing designs and hence reduce power. The compression ratio of the Norton 500 was reduced from 10.5:1 to 7.2:1. Power fell from 37 kW to just over 30 kW. Secondly, the petrol-burning engine ran hotter and lost power as the temperature rose. However, an experimental water-cooled 500 single built by Norton design engineer Leo Kosmicki for the Vanwell racing car project could maintain 35 kW.

Variations in fuel octane rating and quality produced continuing problems. Australian international Eric Hinton reckoned the difference between the octane rating of fuel in Britain and Europe in the 1950s meant a rider with an engine tuned for lower-octane European fuel was at a disadvantage racing in Britain; a rider who raced only in Britain could run a higher compression ratio.

Poor quality fuel was as much a problem to two-stroke racers in the 1970s as four-stroke racers in the 1940s and '50s. A bad batch of fuel can wreck an engine in a few laps; the culprit is detonation. In scientific terms, when the heat generated by compression ignites the mixture before the spark plug fires, it is called spontaneous combustion. In practical terms, the cylinder head and the top of the piston can look as though they have been attacked by a diamond-toothed rat!

The European championship was revived in 1947, as a single race meeting, allocated to Switzerland, and in 1948 to Northern Ireland. The championship series was resurrected for 1949. And with the series came a new title: World Championship. So motorcycle road racing had world championships a year before grand prix cars.

Australian rider Eric McPherson (AJS) scored points in three of the five races of the inaugural World 350 Championship. With a fourth and two fifth placings, he claimed equal third in the championship pointscore. Italian riders and machines claimed the first world titles in the 125 and 250 classes, while British riders and machines won the first world 350, 500 and sidecar crowns. The first world champions were Nello Pagani (Mondial 125), Bruno Ruffo (Moto Guzzi 250), Freddie Frith (Velocette 350), Les Graham (AJS 500) and Eric Oliver/Denis Jenkinson (Norton 500 sidecar).

The pointscore system was based from 1949 until 1977 on a rider's best scores from half the total number of rounds plus one (ignoring fractions). So if there were ten races, six counted; if there were seven races, four counted. Since 1977 all rounds have counted, which means that a mechanical failure is more critical in motorcycle championship racing than in car racing. The first five finishers scored points in 1949, and an extra point was awarded for fastest lap. From 1950 to 1968 the first six placegetters scored points. From 1969 until 1987 the first ten finishers scored points. In 1988 the first 15 finishers scored points.

In 1949 there were four solo classes, 125, 250, 350 and 500 cm^3, and 500 cm^3 sidecars. A championship for 50 cm^3 machines was added in 1962, and changed to an 80 cm^3 championship in 1984. The 350 cm^3 championship was discontinued at the end of 1982, after being a recognised class since the 1911 Isle of Man TT. Two world sidecar championships were run in 1979.

Australian riders have won world grand prix championships in four solo classes: Keith Campbell (350cm^3 in 1957), Tom Phillis (125 cm^3 in 1961), Kel Carruthers (250 cm^3 in 1969) and Wayne Gardner (500 cm^3 in 1987).

The FIM sanctioned a short-lived series for Formula 750 machines, known as the FIM F750 Prize from 1973 to 1976 and the World F750 Championship from 1977 to 1979. Australian riders John Dodds and Jack Findlay won the FIM F750 Prize in 1974 and 1975 respectively.

In 1977 the FIM sanctioned world championships in TT Formula One, TT Formula Two and TT Formula Three. The TT formulae were classes for motorcycles with production-based engines, with a capacity bias towards four-stroke engines because a two-stroke engine can produce more power for a given capacity than a four stroke. The aim of the TT formulae was to give promoters of circuits deemed unsafe for future grand prix racing, like the Isle of Man and Dundrod in Northern Ireland, a new racing category.

Australia's Barry Smith won the TTF3 title in 1979 and 1981. New Zealand's Graeme Crosby captured the TTF1 crown in 1980-1981. The TTF2 and TTF3 titles have since disappeared. A new World Superbike Championship was introduced in 1988. An FIM-sanctioned endurance racing championship was introduced in 1975 and given world championship status in 1980. Australian riders Wayne Gardner, Kevin Magee and Michael Doohan, and Kiwi Graeme Crosby have won rounds of these championships; Gardner, Magee and Crosby in the endurance championship, Magee in TTF1 and Doohan in the superbike championship.

The grand prix rules for solo motorcycles have remained remarkably constant over the 40 years of the world championships. Significant rule changes, however, occurred in 1958, when full streamlining was banned for solo machines, in 1970, when limits on the number of cylinders and gears were enacted, in 1977, when noise restrictions were introduced, and in 1987, when clutch starts were introduced for all classes.

Another time, another place . . . Start of the 500 cm³ event of the 1955 international meeting at Mildura, Victoria. Front grid row comp

s Dickie Dale, George Crowe, Australian international trio Keith Campbell, Jack Ahearn and Bob Brown, and Albury's Doug Fugger.

THE AUSTRALIANS

World 500 cm³ motorcycle champion and 1987 Sportsperson of the Year, Wayne Gardner brought grand prix motorcycle racing to the attention of the Australian general public. But Gardner was far from being the only Australian motorcycle racer with the ambition, dedication and determination to pack his helmet and leathers and reach for the top in one of the world's most spectacular sports.

More than 40 Australians have figured in world championship grand prix results since the championship races began in 1949; only a handful have done so in car racing. And for each Australian who has scored points in the world motorcycle championships, at least two others have headed to Europe and tried. That commitment alone marks them as a cut above the ordinary, because racing 18,000 kilometres from home is no easy task, particularly when, for most of the Australians who tried, the effort was self-funded, self-managed and conducted on self-prepared machines.

Australia, with 58 world championship grand prix wins to the end of 1988, ranks ninth in the world according to the total number of grands prix won, behind the United Kingdom, Italy, West Germany, Spain, Switzerland, the United States of America, Rhodesia (Zimbabwe) and The Netherlands. The country has also produced two winners of the FIM Formula 750 Prize (forerunner of a world F750 championship), John Dodds in 1974 and Jack Findlay in 1975, and a twice winner of the world TT Formula Three championship in Barry Smith. Five Australians have won TT races at the Isle of Man: Ken Kavanagh, Barry Smith (four times), Kel Carruthers (twice), Jack Findlay and Graeme McGregor (twice). And Australia has one of the best riders never to win a world championship, Gregg Hansford. He was the 1978-1979 runner-up in the 250 class, and won ten 250 and 350 grands prix.

These achievements have not been without sacrifice. The public road circuits used for racing on the Isle of Man, and in Northern Ireland and Europe in the 1950s, 1960s and 1970s were unforgiving. Keith Campbell and Tom Phillis were killed within a year of winning their world crowns. Five other Australian motorcycle road racers were killed overseas during the period 1953-1961, when Australia nominated official teams for the Isle of Man TT. Two more riders, Les Kenny and Ken Blake, have since been killed racing at the Isle of Man.

Accidents on other public road circuits left two Australian champions of the 1970s, Ray Quincey and Warren Willing, with permanent disabilities. Gregg Hansford's motorcycle racing career was also ended by a serious accident.

The efforts of Australian racers have been well recognised overseas, but not always in Australia. Keith Campbell won our first world championship

Ballarat rider George Morrison (Norton, No 64) started a post-War trend with the kangaroo motif on his helmet. The race is the 1950 Belgian 350 GP.

Maurie Quincey in action at the Isle of Man. A serious crash in the 1955 TT ended his international racing career.

in any form of grand prix racing in 1957, two years before Jack Brabham won his first world driver's crown. Keith was a hero in many of the European towns which hosted international street-circuit meetings, but his world title seems to have made little impact with the media in his sports-mad home town, Melbourne.

The specialist newspaper *Australian Motor Sports* lamented in August 1958: "Following the sad death of Keith Campbell, there were several columns on the front page of one paper, and a full page in a weekly sporting paper. It does seem a terrible shame that a man must lose his life before gaining any recognition in our newspapers."

Motorcycle races have drawn large crowds in Australia for as long as the sport has existed. Major road-racing meetings in the 1930s in South Australia and in the 1950s in Victoria attracted crowds of 25,000 to 30,000. One race in Tasmania in 1955 attracted a similar figure — an impressive turn-up when the entire population of the island state was only just over 300,000. Racing in one Australian city, Bathurst, dates back to 1931, yet by the mid 1980s that meeting was under threat due to confrontations between police and sections of the crowd. Fortunately the general media then rediscovered international motorcycle racing in 1986-1987.

Recognition of Australian international achievements has improved with the years, particularly since the advent of televised race meetings. Tom Phillis and Kel Carruthers were finalists in the prestigious ABC Sportsman of the Year award, and Wayne Gardner won it. In 1988, Carruthers was inducted into the NSW sports Hall of Champions, as one of the country's top 200 sports persons of all time. Only three other motor-sport champions made the list: world champion drivers Jack Brabham and Alan Jones, and world speedway champion, Arthur "Bluey" Wilkinson. Carruthers also enjoyed the unique recognition of appearing on a postage stamp — but it was in the Kingdom of Yemen, not his own country.

Unfortunately, many Australian racers who achieved notable firsts or went close to championship honours in Europe, did so without Australia ever knowing. Most Australian motorcycle enthusiasts — let alone readers of the daily sports pages — would not know that John Dodds and Jack Findlay had won the equivalent of a European championship in the Formula 750 class. Even in the 1980s, an Australian ranked 200th in world tennis had a better chance of having his name recognised at home than an Australian in the top ten of world motorcycle racing.

Australians have been competing in international motorcycle races virtually since the sport was born. The Isle of Man Tourist Trophy (TT) races began in 1907. Australian riders S.L. Bailey and H. Regless competed in the TT between 1912 and 1914. A further ten Australian riders competed on the Isle of Man between 1924 and 1939. Among that group of between-war IoM contestants was Australia's first claimant to the description "one of the world's best" — Arthur Simcock.

Simcock was the first Australian to figure in a major international motorcycle championship result. He was twice runner-up in the European championships in 1930-1931. Those championships were decided on the results of one race, which carried the title Grand Prix of Europe. Simcock was second in the 350 class at Spa-Francorchamps in 1930, and second in the 500 class the following year at Montlhery, near Paris. Five years later, Australia's Lionel Van Praag won the inaugural world speedway crown. It was an appropriate result, for the sport had its identifiable beginnings in Australia. Simcock represented Australia at the TT from 1927 to 1933, and later, based in London, he represented Australian motorcycle sport as an official. He was also clerk of the course for the 1961 world speedway final in Wembley Stadium, London, and he died in November 1962.

The world grand prix championships had no sooner begun in 1949 than Australian riders again proved to be among the world's best. Eric McPherson was equal third in the inaugural world

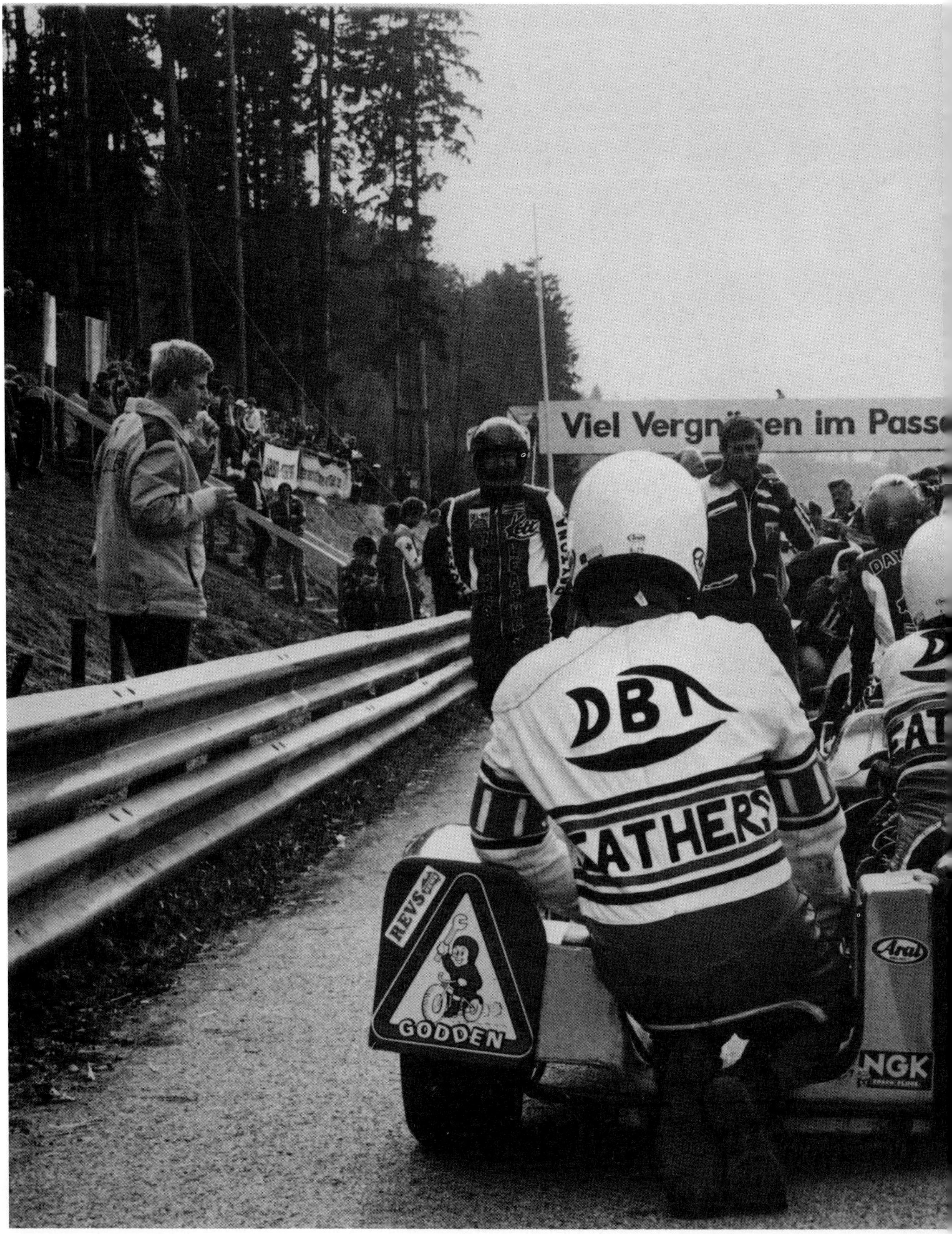
REVS
GODDEN
Arai
NGK

350 cm³ championship. The following year, Harry Hinton held his works Norton back in the run to the flag in the last lap of the Italian 350 Grand Prix to ensure victory for his team leader, Geoff Duke. In 1951 Hinton was favoured to win the 250 TT at the Isle of Man after smashing the IoM 250 cm³ lap record during official practice. But Hinton was seriously injured when he crashed while holding second place in the 350 TT, and he did not race overseas again.

In 1952, Ken Kavanagh became the first rider from outside Europe to win a world championship grand prix. Four years later, in 1956, he scored Australia's first Isle of Man TT victory. The following year, Keith Campbell became the first rider from outside Europe to win a world championship. This pair of Australians also had a unique connection with the Moto Guzzi 500 cm³ V8, arguably the world's most exotic racing motorcycle. Kavanagh rode the V8 in its race debut at Easter in 1956, and Campbell set a lap record in its race swansong in the 1957 Belgian GP.

Tom Phillis was the first Western rider contracted to ride for Honda, and the first to win a world championship grand prix on a Japanese motorcycle. These milestones occurred in 1960 and 1961 respectively, not long after another Honda star, Wayne Gardner, was born.

Australian riders earned many factory rides between 1949 and 1960, first with British companies, then the Italians, and finally with Japan's biggest manufacturer, Honda. The period from Tom Phillis's death, in June 1962, to 1968 was a lean one for Australians gaining works rides, given the number of rides available. Yet in 1969, when the works job market suffered a downturn, Kel Carruthers and Barry Smith held down 33 per cent of the available factory rides. Twenty years later, in 1989, a new record was set for Australians as works riders, with Wayne Gardner, Kevin Magee and Michael Doohan all signed to contest the full grand prix season on factory 500 racers.

Australian riders have achieved many things in the first 40 years of world grand prix championship motorcycling, but none of our world champions has yet defended a crown successfully. For the first half of 1988, Wayne Gardner battled with a Honda which, despite all the best intentions of its designers, was a step backwards from his winning 1987 machine. But even in his moments of greatest disappointment, Gardner knew there would still be two factory Hondas and his crew of four mechanics at the next grand prix. Two of our previous world champions did not enjoy that level of security.

The post-championship blues is yet another

"This is what we came for!" Peter Campbell and passenger Richard Goodwin count down to the start of their first GP at Salzburgring in 1979. They finished eighth.

largely untold story of Australians competing in world championships. Keith Campbell had won the world 350 championship and was actually on his honeymoon when his works Moto Guzzi ride evaporated. Three of Italy's most successful manufacturers met at the end of the 1957 season and agreed to cease grand prix racing; they announced the decision on September 26, 1957. Campbell returned to Europe and rode privately entered Nortons, however he was killed in France in July 1958, during what was intended to be a lucrative last international season.

Tom Phillis's case was quite extraordinary; his story has never previously been published. Phillis won the 1961 world 125 championship for Honda, and he was retained by the Japanese maker for 1962 — he thought to race and win again. But Honda appeared to have had more of a figurehead role in mind. It told Phillis not to win grands prix races, and the first time he looked like winning one he received pit signals to slow down. This was despite Phillis being the only world champion on the Honda payroll. Honda's other world champion in 1961, Mike Hailwood, had signed to ride 350 and 500 cm^3 machines for Italy's MV Agusta team. Perhaps Honda had longer-term plans for Phillis. Maybe it wanted to make sure the machine was seen as more important than the rider. It may simply have wanted a rider from a more important marketplace to win. None of these scenarios explained why Honda then provided the means for Rhodesian Jim Redman to assume superstar status by winning six world championships in the next four years. And what of the rules requiring races to be decided on merit rather than team instructions?

Kel Carruthers' experience with Benelli after he won the firm its first championship in 19 years might have seemed odd — but such are the ways of Italian race teams. Carruthers won the world 250 championship in 1969 despite spending most of the season on the firm's second-string four-cylinder 250. Rule changes for the 1970 season limiting 250 cm^3 machines to two cylinders forced Benelli to concentrate off-season development on the 350. But strikes in Italy that winter hampered the small Benelli development team. Carruthers was home in Australia in January 1970 when word arrived that his new 350-four may not be ready until June. Italian team-mate Renzo Pasolini would again have first choice of machinery.

There was, however, a positive side in terms of Carruthers' long-term career. Kel switched to privately entered Yamahas and went within an ace of successfully defending his 250 crown. He then raced Yamahas in the United States, and within three years he was appointed founding team manager of Yamaha's American team. He has been on Yamaha or Yamaha team payrolls ever since.

THE WORLD OF THE PRIVATE ENTRANT

Works rides are only one side of the story. Until Gregg Hansford, every post-war Australian racer who went to Europe did so initially as a private entrant. The majority completed their international careers as private entrants. Almost all of them became homesick heroes.

The goal most strived for was not, as you might think, a world championship, but a works ride. World solo titles were the exclusive domain of works riders until 1970, when a shortage of works machines in the middle-capacity class gave private entrants a realistic chance of winning.

Kel Carruthers' goal when he went to Europe in 1966 was a works ride. Today he sees a certain irony in the aspirations of up-and-coming racers. "We went to Europe to get a works ride. Now they won't leave home unless they've got one!"

The other great attractions for Australians to race in Europe were the challenge of the world's longest race circuit and oldest race at the Isle of Man, the chance to improve their riding skills by competing every weekend for six months, and, because race organisers paid start money, the opportunity to earn a living in their chosen sport.

Riders of the 1950s and 1960s say there were two races in one in the grands prix — the race for the lead among the works riders and the battle to be the first private entrant home. Australian riders such as Bob Mitchell, Bob Brown, Jack Ahearn, Jack Findlay and Kel Carruthers were proud to claim the honour of best-placed private entrant in a world championship. Mitchell did it in the sidecar class, Brown in the 350 and 500, Ahearn and Findlay in the 500 class, and Carruthers in the 350 and 250 categories.

Racing as a private entrant was not easy. Switzerland's three times world champion Luigi Taveri raced with and met many Australian riders in the 1950s and 1960s, and he saw enough of the conditions under which the Australian private entrants operated to appreciate their determination. "I remember the Australians were very good. Sometimes we riders in Europe thought they were better than we were, but they always had to do it without money. And they put the money they had into their bikes," Taveri recalled. "Today a rider tries to do as much practice as he can. But the Australians in the 1950s and 1960s worried about doing too many laps in practice, so they wouldn't wear their bikes out before the race. They would do the minimum number of practice laps allowed.

"Life was so different for the Australians — they used to live in a little caravan, with a cup of tea and a sausage. My wife and I would go to each race from our home, stay in a hotel near the circuit and come back to Switzerland. But the Australians lived for a

Sydney teenager Tony McAlpine excelled at dirt-track racing in the late 1930s. The sport provided an ideal training ground for road racing.

whole season away from home in a caravan; it was not so easy for them."

Taveri's observation highlights the real problem for Australians racing overseas. During the post World War II period, Australians have always been competitive as riders. The hard part has been putting the package together 18,000 kilometres from home. The actual racing is only part of the equation; other factors always applied. Jeff Sayle, who spent six seasons in Europe between 1978 and 1983, recalled: "When you go away, you've already shown you can race. It's all the other things — living away from home, being short of money, travelling, different countries, different food, learning new circuits, not getting homesick and not having family problems. These days the guys who go away have good sponsorship, so the main thing is not to get homesick."

If you name a problem that can occur racing in Europe, at least one Australian has had that problem. There were the privateer machines with annoying faults, from teeth breaking off the bevels of Manx Norton camshaft drives to the unreliable ignitions of early Yamaha production racers. Other machines, privately entered and works, were simply the right idea at the wrong time, either through lack of development or poor-quality materials. Transporters broke down, too, and caravan frames simply fell apart on rough secondary roads in Europe.

There were hard-nosed border officials, customs officers and race organisers, including a few who reneged on deals. One Switzerland organiser was suspended out of his office window by an irate Aussie until he paid an agreed figure. Others were genuinely helpful. Smart organisers remembered good performances when they issued invitations and start-money offers for the following year — because the good runners attracted customers.

Political and economic factors inside and outside motorcycling affected Australian riders. The Dutch TT riders' strike of 1955 caused four Australians to lose their racing licences for six months. Gregg Hansford's loyalty to the World Series movement in 1979-1980 contributed to his being without a grand prix contract for 1980. Australians were among the first riders to race in the newly created Democratic Republic of Germany (East Germany) in 1956, at the height of the Cold War. The Suez Crisis of the same period caused Tom and Betty Phillis to delay their first trip to Europe by a year. Russia's heavy-handed put-down of Czechoslovakia's reformist Dubcek Government in 1968 meant a frightening time for Australian riders and their families heading west after the Czech GP; they had their vans searched for defectors by Russian soldiers. Today, a rider wishing to base himself in Britain would have to consider the country's immigration laws; Wayne Gardner had to obtain a work permit when he was based there.

But for all the problems, most Australian private entrants, even the ones who came home broke from Europe, say they would do it again. Many reckon their years racing in Europe were the best in their lives. They were in their twenties and thirties doing something they loved with their mates or families. The fact that much of it was very hard work — long drives, cramped living conditions, indifferent weather — made the enjoyment and sense of achievement more sweet.

Riders of the 1950s put on their best gear and Australian team blazers each Sunday night for race presentations. In later years, riders simply gathered and let off steam after working all week. They made sure that everyone from the Aussie contingent went out and relaxed. In the 1950s, 1960s and 1970s, Australian privateer riders set up camp together at circuits and worked together on their machines, which were usually similar models. It was a spirit soon rekindled when two Australian sidecar drivers, Andre Bosman and Doug Chivas, contested the 1988 grands prix as private entrants.

Jack Findlay, a private entrant for 18 of his 20 European seasons, reckoned the grand prix paddock in his day was like a family gathering. "Once the regulars realised a new rider was there and that he was serious, they'd give you a hand, tell you what to do and look after you a bit," he recalled. "It's not like nowadays, where teams are closetted in their big annexes."

The fact that most private entrants arrived in Europe with minimal budgets prompted many cost-cutting measures. Some were considered part of calling yourself a private entrant, but riders learned the tricks of the game, just as taxi drivers learn shortcuts. Scrounging petrol provided for racing to put in the race transporter was common. Another bit of specialist knowledge was how to avoid border insurance, which over a season amounted to a hefty sum. This activity soon became a game for several free-spirited works riders, even though they could afford it. Barry Smith reckoned that you could not call yourself a grand prix rider until you could talk your way into the pits at Spa-Francorchamps. (The organisers would never provide enough passes for riders and mechanics.)

Private entrants could, however, make money. If the season went well they met their racing expenses, came home for the Australian summer without having to take a job, and bought new bikes when they went back to Europe the following season. The more successful and business-minded riders ended their careers with a nest egg. But the money was nowhere near the sums on offer now that major sponsors and television have come into the sport. A top international private entrant of the 1960s might have ended his career with about as much saved as

THE CIRCUITS From Roads To Tracks

Motorcycle road racing was appropriately named when the world championships began in 1949. Five of the six circuits used for the inaugural world championships were on public roads.

Many international meetings in Europe and Northern Ireland, where Australia's racers of the 1950s and 1960s competed regularly, were also held on street circuits. The exception was the British mainland, where racing on closed public roads was banned from 1903. That law triggered the development of the Isle of Man as a motor racing venue. The post-World War II British solution to this restriction was to use abandoned airbases.

The grand prix road circuits of 1949 were indeed grand. The Isle of Man circuit was 61 km, Assen was 16.5 km of cobblestoned road, Belgium's Spa-Francorchamps was 14.1 km, Berne in Switzerland was 7.3 km and Northern Ireland's Cladys circuit was 26.5 km, of which 11.2 km was one huge undulating straight. The only closed circuit was Monza, built in the 1920s in parkland near Milan.

All these circuits were fast. The slowest winning speed in a 1949 500 GP was 140 km/h by Harold Daniell at the Isle of Man. His works Norton had a top speed of about 190 km/h. The fastest race average was 158 km/h by Nello Pagani's Gilera at Monza. The real speed track of the 1950s was the original sausage-shaped Hockenheim circuit. The lap record there in 1957 was 208 km/h set by Bob McIntyre on a works Gilera 500-four in the rain! Compare that with the final lap record of 220.7 km/h at the 14.1 km Spa-Francorchamps course set 21 years later by Barry Sheene on a works Suzuki 500.

The race distances were tough in 1949. The Ulster 500 GP race distance was 661 km and the race lasted four hours and 16 minutes. The minimum distance for a 500 grand prix was 200 km. The shortest race time of the year was one hour and 16 minutes for a 201 km race at Monza.

Forty years later GP races last between 40 minutes and an hour, but many race average speeds are about the same as Pagani's speed in 1949 at Monza. The machines have three times as much power as Pagani's Gilera, but the circuits have changed drastically. The straights are shorter and there are many more tight corners.

The world championships still use three of the original venues — Assen, Spa and Monza — but in very different form. Assen is a new circuit (built in 1955 and modified in 1984), the new Spa (opened in 1979) retains less than one third of the old circuit and Monza has been shortened, re-aligned and modified with chicanes. The new-look Spa-Francorchamps was by 1984 the longest circuit used for world championship grands prix, at 6.976 km.

The Isle of Man Mountain Circuit, Northern Ireland's 12 km Dundrod circuit (which replaced Cladys in 1952) and Montjuich Park, Barcelona (home of the Spanish GP from 1955 to 1968) are still used for motorcycle racing, but not for world grand prix championship events.

Australia's 1969 world champion Kel Carruthers told the authors: "I liked road circuits because I could apply myself on them. The problem was that safety had to be improved. It's a pity you couldn't take the Dundrod circuit and put it in a field, so it was safe. These days designers build tracks, not roads, with nicely radiused corners. You can't have 'road' racing any longer because it's too dangerous.

"I look back now at Opatija in Yugoslavia and think a guy had to be crazy to race there, because of the stone walls and such. But the shape of the circuit was really good, because it followed the lie of the land."

Carruthers said he found the 22.85 km Nurburgring circuit of the 1960s a more difficult learning proposition than the Isle of Man. "Nurburgring was still narrow when I raced there, with the trees close to the edge of the track so you couldn't see the next corner. There were no barriers — if you went off the road you went into the trees.

The push for increased safety for car racing in the late 1960s/early 1970s led to circuits such as Nurburgring having the trees cut back from the road and safety fences installed. Unfortunately for motorcycle racers, the ribbed steel Armco fencing caused many serious injuries to limbs. Further demands for improved car racing safety in the late 1970s and early 1980s saw new circuits built at Nurburgring and Francorchamps.

But if grand prix circuits have changed, the real revolution of the 1980s has been the end of the European tradition of international races on road circuits. In the 1950s, towns all over Europe would host an annual street-circuit race, either through the town or on the outskirts. France alone had more than 20 such circuits in the 1950s, and Belgium perhaps another eight. Some of the Belgian meetings, such as Mettet and Chimay, were held for 40 years and only disappeared in the early 1980s.

The other major change of the past decade has been that the world's leading riders no longer contest international races unless the race is important to their sponsors. Works riders of the late 1980s have race contracts to the 15 or 16 races of the grand prix season and perhaps two other races in Japan. These riders don't wish to do more meetings. This is in stark contrast to the situation 20 years earlier, where private entrants needed to race every weekend to stay solvent.

Bob Brown and Allen Burt used a gutted 26-seat Bedford coach as transporter and living quarters in 1956.

Keith Bryen and Eric Hinton were placed one-two at the Norisring in 1957. Architecture is from the 1930s . . .

Rosevilla guesthouse, Isle of Man, 1955. Back row (L to R): Allen Burt, Gerald Roberts (Canada), Bill Collett (NZ), Fred Cook (NZ) and Bob Brown. Front (L to R): John Hemplemann (NZ), Richie Thompson and a typically well-dressed Maurie Quincey.

one of today's top three Australian domestic riders collects in one season from his contract, prizemoney and bonuses. This, in part, explains why today's riders do not want to head overseas without works contracts — they make very good money at home.

And the money to be made now overseas is enough for the top few riders to retire on, says Kel Carruthers. "That never used to happen. On the other end of the scale, it can cost so much now that a guy can be ruined financially. When I raced, you didn't spend as much and you didn't make a lot, and if you were any good you ended up with a small amount of profit."

The important requirements for private entrants to make money in the days before major sponsorships were four-fold: to make it through the lean first year and establish your riding credentials with the organisers of international racing meetings; to own two or three reliable machines; to have a paid start every weekend of the European season; and to avoid injury. To a private entrant like Jack Findlay, it was a disaster to have a free Sunday between March and September.

WHY THEY SUCCEEDED

To understand why Australian motorcycle racers succeeded in Europe, you must first look at the domestic scene. It has not always been the most healthy in terms of promotions and crowds, but it has invariably been competitive, with local international series and return visits by Australian internationals helping maintain a high standard of riding.

Now consider what the domestic private entrant goes through to race in Australia. He probably began his career in his teens on dirt tracks, so racing on wet and slippery tracks, and the idea of sliding a motorcycle in the dry is not foreign to him. He is used to maintaining his own machine and driving 1000 kilometres on a Friday night to a race meeting. So he is dedicated, determined and has a working mechanical knowledge.

The nature and variety of Australian circuits has also equipped Australians well for Europe, says Melburnian Barry Smith, whose racing career lasted from the late 1950s into the 1980s. Australian riders are practised at learning new circuits quickly. Since World War II, Australia has had fast public road circuits at Bathurst, Orange, Mildura and Longford; tight road circuits at Victoria Park, Ballarat, and in Western Australia; road circuits with loose surfaces; airfield circuits at Fishermans Bend, Ballarat and Lowood and Mt Druitt; classic grand prix type circuits at Phillip Island and Surfers Paradise; and a cross-section of 2 km to 2.4 km circuits. One of those, Brisbane's Lakeside Raceway, gave riders a feel for English race circuits. In addition to the local circuits, most Australian international riders of the last two decades raced in New Zealand before they went further afield.

The reasons why some riders who looked worldbeaters at home did not click overseas, and some riders who went away as unknowns became successful internationals, are the many factors other than the racing. Some were downright homesick, some lacked that last gram of determination, others missed the helpers they had at home, many were short of money and, sadly, some were hurt before their potential really showed through at international level.

Australians of the 1950s were reluctant to sell themselves. Eric Hinton and Jack Findlay said such a notion was embarrassing for them. Later on, riders began promoting themselves or met people who would door-knock sponsors and teams on their behalf. Wayne Gardner is not ashamed to say he chased team managers around in his early days in Europe; he believed he could do the job, but he needed the bikes to do it.

Of all the post-war Australians who went to Europe, six have settled in overseas and at least another six came home with wives they met either in Europe or while travelling back and forth. The six stayers were all successful.

Ken Kavanagh, Australia's first Isle of Man TT winner, runs a dry cleaning business in the Italian city of Bergamo, home of the modern Marlboro Yamaha Team Agostini. Jack Findlay, whose international career spanned 20 years and included victory in the 1975 FIM Formula F750 Prize, lives in Paris. John Dodds, 1974 FIM F750 Prize winner, lives in Germany. Kel Carruthers, the 1969 world 250 champion, lives in California and works for the team based in Bergamo. Graeme McGregor, our most recent IoM TT winner, lives in Lincolnshire, England. And 1987 world 500 champion Wayne Gardner is now a resident of Monte Carlo.

Perhaps that shows just how much motorcycle racing has changed in 40 years. Racing has been a major sport in Europe throughout those 40 years, and in the 1980s has become a major spectator and participant sport in Japan. Some races in Europe in the 1950s and 1960s attracted crowds which are only equalled today at the traditionally big meets such as Japan's Suzuka and Holland's Assen.

Australians were among the world's leading riders when the world championships began in 1949; three Australians who went to Europe in 1949 were offered works machines within months of arriving. In 1988, the country again had factory teams chasing three riders. The difference today is not so much that Australian riders have finally made it, but that their sport — international motorcycle racing — finally has.

THE HINTONS

CHAPTER 2

SOME Australian families are synonymous with particular industries: Packer, Murdoch and Fairfax with media, Kidman with cattle. And if you look through the past winners at Bathurst you might conclude the Hinton family business was motorcycle racing. Three generations of Hintons have between them won 25 grand prix events in all classes, including sidecar.

The record is remarkable. Harry Hinton, sons Eric and Rob, and Eric's son Tony won grand prix events at Bathurst, and Eric's other son Peter has won a graded race. Harry Hinton, Harry Jnr and Eric all won Australian Championships, and Peter missed an Australian title by a few points. Only one other Australian family, the Osbornes from Geelong, can claim three generations of national motorcycle road-racing success.

Harry Hinton, Harry Jnr and Eric raced in Europe. Rob was an international sidecar passenger, a mechanic for Eric and raced in Indonesia and New Zealand. Peter and Tony Hinton spent their primary school years in the grand prix paddocks of Europe. Tony later boosted the Hinton overseas record to three generations by contesting a race in Japan.

Yet talk to the Hintons today and they're sure the late Harry Hinton Snr never intended to start a racing dynasty.

That Harry raced motorcycles at all was remarkable, because he lost his left eye in a road accident in 1931 aged 20. Yet he raced until 1955, when he was 44. And any image of sons Harry Jnr, Eric and Rob being trained from boyhood to recite the landmarks at the Isle of Man is mistaken. They were far too busy playing tennis on the neighbourhood courts that they helped maintain. Rob at 15 won a junior competition match against Tony Roche, who went on to be a Wimbledon singles finalist.

But motorcycling was so much a part of Harry's world it was bound to intrigue his sons. How could youngsters not be interested when their dad had been a sponsored BSA rider in Australia and a works Norton rider in Europe? In the post World War II days Harry Hinton owned two motorcycle shops in suburban Sydney. The family home at Belfield had a double garage, half of which was devoted to Harry's competition machines. By 1953 the collection included three ex-works Nortons, recognition of Harry's achievements in Europe from 1949 to mid-1951.

Harry Hinton had every reason to be a BSA and Norton man. He was born in the English city of Birmingham (home of both companies) in 1911. He spent his early years in the same section of Birmingham as later Norton Motors managing director Gilbert Smith. Harry emigrated to Australia with his parents soon after World War I and grew up

A pensive Harry Hinton, on his debut at the Isle of Man in 1949.

in the Sydney fringe suburb of Canley Vale. His introduction to motorcycle racing came in 1929, in beach races run by the Western Suburbs Motorcycle Club on Seven Mile Beach, Gerringong.

Hinton was a motor mechanic by trade, but 1931 (the early years of the Depression) found him working as a courier. His company vehicle was a 1930 model Indian Scout with sidecar. It was while riding this machine in the commercial heart of Sydney that Harry suffered his first serious accident. A car pulled out suddenly from a side street on the left and hit the sidecar, sending it careering across the road into a wall. Harry was thrown off, but the handlebar caught his face and nearly tore his left eye out of its socket. The eye was removed in hospital to ensure he retained use of the other eye.

Loss of an eye is supposed to affect depth perception. Yet Harry Hinton's forte in his 1930s motorcycle career was late braking on loose surfaces. In 1949, race organisers at the Ulster Grand Prix demanded he take a sight test. The result showed exactly what Harry had proved on the racetrack — his vision was good.

Hinton's comeback to racing and results in the 1930s proved he had two other key attributes. Tremendous determination and a gift for motorcycle tuning. Harry Hinton made unfancied bikes competitive and competitive bikes even faster. This ability led to another Harry Hinton trait: a fetish for keeping his development secrets secret. Why help the other bloke when he's the one you have to beat, he reasoned.

Harry entered the motorcycle trade when he left hospital. He was soon working in the workshop of Norton distributor Hazel and Moore, reconditioning used motorcycles at piece rates — £2.10.0 ($5) per machine. At 1932 wage levels and with a growing number of Australians walking the country looking for work, an output of two or more reconditioned machines a week represented a healthy pay packet.

By the end of 1932 Hinton owned an overhead-camshaft Norton International 500, which became his race bike. The first Hinton son, Harry Jnr, was born the same year, the second, Eric, in 1934.

Hinton took the Inter Norton 500 to notable wins, including the Christmas Guineas at Schofields. But it seized while he was running second on the Phillip Island Anniversary road races, held on the gravel streets of the island. Harry was able to borrow another Norton and win the 350 race.

In 1933 BSA agent Bennett and Wood accepted veteran racer Tommy Benstead's recommendation and hired Harry Hinton as its number one trade (sponsored) rider. A workshop position came with the ride.

BSA's management was against building outright racers and sophisticated sports models. So the company's push-rod machines had a pedestrian image compared with the overhead camshaft racers and sportsters of rivals like Norton and Velocette, and the innovative Rudge machines. The BSA Blue Star 250, 350 and 500 models Hinton was hired to promote in 1933 were sports versions of the catalogued tourers, mildy tuned at the factory.

But the Bennett and Wood riders, led by Hinton, achieved such strong results riding these machines and the later Empire Star and Gold Star models in open competition that BSA used the results internationally to promote its roadsters.

The race-tuned BSA 350 and 500 accelerated as well as the rival overhead-camshaft racers, but lacked top-end speed and became fragile when ridden hard on circuits with long straights. These characteristics made them ideal for dirt-track racing, where the longest straight might be a quarter of a mile, but put them at a disadvantage on the long

Harry Hinton rode BSAs for local agent Bennett and Wood in the 1930s. This publicity shot, taken in 1936 at Sydney's Centennial Park, shows a Blue Star model.

straights of road-racing circuits such as Bathurst's 11 km pre-1938, dirt-surfaced Vale circuit.

The results prove the point. Hinton and Eric McPherson won many 350 and 500 dirt-track events, but Hinton's best results in these classes at the Vale circuit were high placings. In 1934 he finished third in the 350 race and fourth in the 500, in races won by an AJS and Norton respectively. In 1936 Harry rode a game race to bring a BSA 500 home second, behind Leo Tobin's overhead-cam Norton but ahead of noted 1930s riders Bat Byrnes, Art Senior and Frank Mussett.

The best weapon in Bennett and Wood's BSA armoury was the Hinton-tuned iron-barrelled 250. It was particularly successful on the dirt tracks. Here was a machine which regularly had the better of Tom Jemison's Velocette. Up to 1937, Harry hadn't ridden the BSA 250 at Bathurst, because the 250 and 350 classes were run concurrently. But for the last meeting on the Vale circuit, he rode the 250. The race was more one of attrition than of great dices. But Hinton's BSA went the distance, beating the surviving Velocette by a minute.

The Mount Panorama circuit at Bathurst was opened the following Easter to coincide with Australia's 150 year celebrations. The pressure of the Easter 1938 deadline meant the first meeting was run on a gravel surface. Harry Hinton rode a BSA 500 in the 500 TT, then bolted on a sidecar and won the three-wheel event.

The 1930s trade teams competed nearly every weekend in dirt-track hillclimbs, road races or reliability trials. Road trials for standard machines were very popular in the 1930s. The trials lasted one to six days, with two-day weekend trials being common. The Bennett and Wood BSA team for these events was Hinton, McPherson and Harry Bartrop, later an organiser of the Easter Bathurst meetings.

Bartrop said Harry Hinton had a special party trick to liven up the meal stops of these events. He'd remove his glass eye and pop it into a glass of water just as the waitress arrived. The best time was the breakfast stop after an all-night riding stint. Asked why he was so successful, Harry once quipped it was because he "kept one eye on the road"!

Hinton tried something different again in 1939. He went to England as mechanic for America's 1938 world champion speedway rider Jack Milne, who was a regular visitor to Australia. The trip gave Harry and Vienie Hinton the opportunity to see the Isle of Man TT. Milne's target was the world speedway final. But events in Europe in September 1939 meant it was not held. Harry and Vienie were very nearly caught in Britain when the war started. They were desperate to leave, because they had two young sons at home in Sydney, staying with Harry's mother at Canley Vale. They eventually found berths on the last passenger ship out of Liverpool and came home via America.

The last Bathurst road race for six years was held at Easter 1940. Harry Hinton won the 250 race on his BSA. The only racing for at least the next four years was speedway. Hinton and McPherson used some of the spare time while their road-racing careers were on ice to form the Motor Cycle Racing Club of NSW, which later promoted meetings at Mt Druitt and Oran Park. Harry's third son, Robert, was born in 1944. After the war Hinton opened his motorcycle business in Bankstown and purchased a 1932 works 500 Norton from Hazel and Moore. The company also provided a 1938 350 Manx racer. The move certainly helped his road-racing career. He won the 350 race at Bathurst in 1947 on the '38 model Norton.

The following year was a landmark year for Australian motorcycle road racing. The Australian TT was revived and allocated to Bathurst, and the first Australian team was selected for the Isle of Man TT. Hazel and Moore imported a new Triumph 500 production racer (known as the Grand Prix model) for Bathurst. Hinton won the Australian 350 TT on his Norton and, riding the Triumph, finished second in the 500 race to Frank Mussett's pre-war works Velocette.

Three riders were selected for the first Australian IoM TT team: Mussett, Hinton and Eric McPherson. But business commitments prevented Mussett from returning to the island (where he'd raced in 1939) and Norton Motors couldn't provide machines for Hinton.

Scottish international Fergus Anderson visited Australia in the summer of 1948-1949, with his Moto Guzzi racers. He received a rude shock at the standard of local riders and machines. He didn't win a race. Harry Hinton downed the popular Scot in the 500 races at Woodside (South Australia) and Victoria Park, Ballarat.

The ACCA selected only two riders for the 1949 IoM TT, Hinton and McPherson, the former teammates from the 1930s. A third rider, George Morrison, went as a private entrant. Morrison had become friends with Hinton at the annual New Year's Day road races at Ballarat. Both ordered 350 and 500 Manx Nortons for their European campaign.

Hinton rode at the Easter Bathurst meeting before leaving for England. He won the 250 class on his BSA and completed a hat-trick of Bathurst 350 class wins on his Norton.

Hinton and Morrison sailed to Liverpool on the *Georgie*. They had a fast 28-day trip, because the ship's crew wanted to be home for the running of the Grand National at Aintree! Hinton and Morrison collected their Nortons in Birmingham, bought a two-tonne former army van and set out to see the racing world.

Harry Hinton in full cry at Victoria Park, Ballarat (Victoria) in 1950, on his 1948 model ex-works Norton 500

Harry and George made impressive debuts at the Isle of Man, with their press-on styles and placings. Hinton was 15th in the 350 TT and an exceptional ninth in the 500 TT. Morrison looked set for a top-six finish in the 500 TT, until his frame almost fell apart on the last lap. Eight kilometres from the finish, the float bowl of his carburettor vibrated off the bike. He pushed and coasted the last 8km and still finished 31st. McPherson, in his second TT attempt, retired his AJS in the 350 TT.

Hinton and Morrison made great travelling mates in 1949. Eric and Ruby McPherson usually followed the Hinton/Morrison van in their AJS sidecar. Compared with many later Australian travellers they were almost gentlemen racers. They lived in hotels. If Harry or George had a breakdown during practice, the other would lend him his machine to ensure he qualified. You have to be good mates to lend someone your bike at the expense of your own practice time on a new circuit. At one meeting in Holland, Hinton loaned English Continental Circus runner and later journalist Vic Willoughby a 350, so Vic could collect his start money in the 500 race. Vic told the authors Harry was "a great old fellow", while John Surtees said "Pa Hinton was before my time as a rider, but still one of the biggest characters around".

Both Harry and George were in their late thirties and both mechanically gifted. They needed to be, because the Manx Norton "Garden Gate" frames broke as fast as Hinton, Morrison and the staff back in Bracebridge Street could repair them. The rule of thumb was that if the machine stopped vibrating, then the frame had broken. The two Australian riders did regular all-nighters on their machines.

The Continental Circus that summer took in the Swiss GP at Berne, the Dutch TT at Assen, the Belgian GP at Spa-Francorchamps, and international meetings such as Zandvoort (near Amsterdam), and Mettet and Gedinne in Belgium. Hinton and Morrison became a specialty act in the internationals. At Mettet, Hinton won the 350 race and Morrison the 500, with Hinton second. The following weekend the pair engineered a dead-heat in the Belgian TT at Gedinne! It won them wide publicity as the "wild Australians" and put their starting money at some circuits up to £200 each. This represented half the cost of a new Manx Norton, or 33 times the average weekly wage back in Australia.

Norton was so impressed with the pair's efforts it offered them works machines (a 350 for Hinton and a 500 for Morrison) for the second biggest motorcycle race in the British Isles, the Ulster Grand Prix. The race was held on August 21 on the 26.5 km Cladys circuit, which had an undulating main straight of more than 11 km. The race distance was a brutal 25 laps (662 km) and took more than four hours. Three classes, 500, 350 and 250, started at two-minute intervals.

Norton team boss Joe Craig didn't attend this meeting due to development commitments. He put the works machines in the care of tuner Steve Lancefield, brother-in-law of Norton rider Harold Daniell. Lancefield, according to Morrison, didn't like his two Australian charges and didn't allow them to sit on their works machines until minutes before the race. They had to practice on their own Manx Nortons.

Morrison crashed on the first lap, when the superior twin-leading shoe brakes of the works Norton caught him unprepared. Eric McPherson finished fourth in the 350 class on a works AJS and Hinton was seventh.

Harry Hinton returned home with a prized piece of luggage. Norton gave him Irish rider Artie Bell's 1948 works 500. Harry rode this machine to victory in the 1949 Australian 500 TT on a road circuit at Nurioopta in South Australia. Eric McPherson was runner-up on a Velocette. Tony McAlpine won the Unlimited TT on his Vincent 1000 V-twin, from Hinton and McPherson. Hinton then raced at Ballarat, where he won the Victorian 500 GP. Easter Bathurst 1950 produced Hinton's first win in the 500 class on Mount Panorama, after finishing second in 1946 and '48.

Hinton, McPherson and Morrison were selected as Australia's 1950 IoM team. Hinton, Morrison and bespectacled Londoner Harold Daniell formed the works Norton "B-team" for the meeting. The 1950 TT marked the IoM debut of Norton's new double-cradle frame with swinging-arm rear suspension in place of the plunger-type rear end. Ireland's Rex McCandless designed the frame. It improved

Ace IoM photographer Bill Salmond captured Eric Hinton (Manx Norton) on Bray Hill in the 1958 350 TT.

Harry Hinton (centre) and NSW ACU official Ray White (right) greet Geoff Duke at Sydney Airport in December 1954.

George Morrison, Harry Hinton's team mate in the 1950 Norton B-team at the Isle of Man TT, with his works 350.

handling and ride so much over the old "Garden Gate" frames that Harold Daniell christened it the "Featherbed". The name stuck. For 1950 only the Norton "A-team" of Geoff Duke, Johnny Lockett and Artie Bell had Featherbeds. If a spare was available, it went to Daniell.

Hinton finished tenth in both the 350 and 500 TTs. Morrison suffered a broken chain in the 350 event and finished one place and 90 seconds behind Hinton in the 500. McPherson suffered a broken clutch while leading the Anzac contingent in the 350 race and rode a 358 cm³ AJS to a highly creditable 14th place in the 500 TT. He'd finished a TT at his third attempt.

Harry and Vienie Hinton travelled the Continent together in 1950, while George Morrison shared his panel van with the McPhersons. Hinton and Morrison starred in their first meeting of 1950 on the Continent, at Zandvoort. Harry won the 350 race and George the 500. Hinton followed that up with sixth place in the Belgian 500 GP at Spa-Francorchamps — he was the first Norton rider to finish. It also made Harry Hinton the first Australian to score points in the world 500 championship.

The next meeting, the Dutch TT on the old 16.5 km road circuit at Assen, was memorable for the other two Australians. Harry opened the day by riding his own Manx Norton into sixth place in the 350 race, behind three works Velocettes and two works Nortons, but ahead of another works Norton and the entire AJS works team. George Morrison crashed on the first lap of the race while trying too hard on a brand new tyre. He sustained a broken leg and did not ride again in Europe.

The Dutch 500 TT of 1950 has gone into Norton history as the black day when the entire works team either crashed or withdrew with tyre failures. The team's experimental Dunlop tyres shed their treads.

The retirement of the works Nortons left a trio of Gilera fours in front, chased by a very determined Harry Hinton on his private Norton. At half distance Hinton was two-and-a-half minutes behind the third Gilera ridden by Carlo Bandolira. But the race still had eight laps and 55 minutes to run. Hinton responded with a great ride. He set fastest lap at 153.7 km/h and passed Bandolira with three laps remaining to take third place. Eric McPherson finished fifth on Morrison's Norton. New Zealand's Sid Jensen was sixth on a Triumph.

Hinton continued to impress in the Swiss GP, which in 1950 was held in Geneva on a section of concrete motorway. It was wet and the road slippery. Harry finished seventh in the 350 GP. He fell during the 500 race after colliding with works AJS Porcupine rider Ted Frend, with whom he'd been dicing.

Hinton was recalled to the works Norton team for the Ulster 350 GP. Eric McPherson again rode a works 350 AJS. The race was another four-hour epic. The works Velocettes were still the machines to beat in the 350 class. But Hinton and McPherson disputed third place until McPherson suffered clutch trouble. He lost ground, but retained fourth place. Hinton finished third.

Norton retained Hinton for the season's final grand prix at Monza. He provided value as a mechanic and rider. There's a romantic view of Joe Craig and the Norton Motors race shop (which some say he ran like the secret service) that it was the repository of all knowledge on air-cooled, single-cylinder two-valve motorcycle engines. Sure, Craig and his team extracted impressive power from such engines, but there were times when a practical Antipodean could provide fresh input. The 1950

Harry Hinton finished third in the 1950 Ulster 350 GP on a works "Featherbed" Norton. Compare the chassis with Morrison's 1950 TT mount (previous photograph).

Harry Hinton (works Norton) and Eric McPherson (works AJS) duel for third place in the 1950 Ulster 350 GP.

works Nortons were prone to carburettor flooding. Hinton reasoned it might be because the carburettor float bowl was mounted from the bottom. During practice he borrowed some welding equipment, added a bracket to the frame of his works 350, and mounted the float bowl from the top. The modified bike was a rocket, so the works mechanics performed a similar modification to Geoff Duke's machine for the race.

Duke told the authors: "Harry Hinton was a good friend, a fine rider and a clever engineer. While he was in Europe you could never discount his presence. He had a very quick works Norton in that race at Monza. Every time he passed me on the straight, he'd tow Les Graham's works AJS past as well. But Harry did the decent thing on the last lap and allowed me to win. Les was second and Harry finished third."

Hinton had gone within a second and a half of Australia's first grand prix victory. He achieved fastest lap. His works ride was assured for 1951.

Harry Hinton won the 500 and Unlimited races at Bathurst in 1951, then sailed to England to lead new Australian IoM team-mates Tony McAlpine and Ken Kavanagh. Harry had three machines — two works Featherbed Nortons and Maurice Cann's 250 Moto Guzzi. The Guzzi had taken Cann to second place in the 250 TT in 1950, just two-tenths of a second behind Benelli rider Dario Ambrosini.

TT practice week saw Hinton consistently in the top three on the 350 leaderboard. Some mornings he was fastest. But the performance of the week came on the Thursday. Harry, in his third ride on the 250 Guzzi, lapped a full minute under Ambrosini's 250 lap record. Ambrosini's time was 27 minutes 59 seconds, Hinton's time was 26 minutes 56 seconds, an average speed of 135.5 km/h or 84 mph.

Hinton went into race week as favourite for the 250 TT and a strong contender in the 350 and 500 races. By the end of race week, fellow countrymen like McAlpine were convinced he'd never race again after a huge accident in the first race, the 350 TT.

Harry began the 350 TT in style. Geoff Duke broke the lap record from a standing start, to lead Hinton by 33 seconds. Another works Norton rider, Johnny Lockett, was third. Duke increased his lead to a minute after two laps, and Hinton stretched his advantage over Lockett to 19 seconds. A quarter of the way into lap three, Hinton crashed heavily at Laurel Bank (the corner where Tom Phillis was killed 11 years later).

Harry Hinton with his 1951 IoM TT "practice bike" — a standard Manx Norton 350. Hinton was seriously injured a few days later, when he crashed during the 350 TT.

Harry was pitched down the road on his left side and received multiple breaks to his left hand and arm, and splintered his left kneecap.

Harry's son Eric is convinced the accident was triggered by what engineers call stiction (literally sticking friction) when a rear suspension unit was on full extension. It was a common enough problem with suspension units at that time. The effect would have been to change Harry Hinton's machine without warning from one with rear suspension, capable of absorbing bumps, to one with a solid rear end. It would then have only taken one bump to catch Harry unprepared, by bouncing his rear wheel off the ground and slewing the bike sideways.

Hinton spent two months convalescing on the island. While he was there he helped tutor young Keith Campbell for his Isle of Man debut in the Manx Grand Prix. In mid-August 1951 Harry accompanied the Norton works team to the Ulster Grand Prix. Ken Kavanagh had been given Hinton's place in the team.

According to Ken, Hinton saved the team from embarrassment at that meeting. Rain began falling a few minutes before the start of the grand prix. Hinton rushed onto the grid and pushed handkerchiefs into the front brake air vents of the Duke and Kavanagh Nortons. A Hinton boot ensured the handkerchiefs stayed in place. The race had barely started when many riders found their brakes waterlogged and near useless. But Duke and Kavanagh had no brake troubles. They finished one-two after a diabolical four-hour wet-weather ride.

Most people thought Harry Hinton's racing days were finished, but not the determined Harry. Early in 1952 Norton Motors sent him the works 350 ridden by Kavanagh at Ulster. Harry returned to racing at the Easter Bathurst meeting. He won the 350 race on the ex-Kavanagh machine, then bolted in his 1948 works motor and won the 500 event.

For 1953 Norton Motors sent Hinton the rolling chassis from Ray Amm's works 500 (the engine went to New Zealand), so he could contest two classes at a meeting without switching engines. He also built a special 250 cm³ Norton. The 250 special carried Hinton to victory in the 1953 Australian 250 TT at Longford, Tasmania. He also finished second to Maurie Quincey in the 500 TT and third in the Unlimited.

But perhaps Harry's finest moment was Bathurst in 1953. He was the first man to win four races in one meeting at Mount Panorama — 250, 350, 500 and Unlimited. Harry Hinton crashed during practice for the 1954 Bathurst meeting and was unable to race. But in 1955, aged 44, he won the 350/500 double. Harry had his last race at Mt Druitt in July 1955. He passed his machines on to sons Harry Jnr and Eric, who were already making their names on home-built Norton Featherbed copies.

Harry took a keen interest in his sons' careers and joined them in Europe for a while in 1958. In 1959 he built Eric's Australian 250 TT winning mount from a 1935 model works New Imperial.

Harry Hinton died in 1978, aged 77.

THE SONS OF HARRY

Eric Hinton gazed into the distance from the railing of the *SS Orcades*. He had been watching the Indian Ocean for a couple of weeks. The 28,472 tonne Orient liner was one day out of Aden. It was mid-April 1959 and 25-year-old Eric was on his way to the race tracks of Europe. In the past three months he had won the New Zealand 250 TT, the Australian 250, 350 and 500 TT races at Longford, in Tasmania, and the 250 race at Bathurst.

Eric's attentions were divided between home and Europe. His wife Kate was in Sydney, expecting their first child. Eric's brother Harry Jnr and most of their international racing mates were competing in the traditional European season opener, the Imola Shell Cuppa d'Oro (Gold Cup) meeting.

Eric Hinton and Harry Jnr prepare for the 1957 IoM TT. The full-bin Rimond glass fibre fairing was made in Melbourne.

Presentation night for the 1957 Villafranche international. L to R: John Hemplemann (NZ) Horst Kassner (Germany), the Hinton brothers and John Anderson (NZ) with his girlfriend.

Hinton's thoughts were broken by a message from the *Orcades'* radio officer. Harry Jnr had crashed heavily at Imola. The big-end of his Norton had broken as he shut off for a fast corner. The bike had cannoned off a chain-wire fence and back onto the track, striking Harry in the chest. He was in hospital with severe chest injuries. Vienie Hinton was flying from Australia to be with her eldest son.

Eric tried for a flight from Aden to Italy. There was none, and on-going effects of the Suez crisis meant he couldn't leave the ship at Port Said and go to Cairo. He was stuck on the ship until it docked in Naples. Eric caught the train from Naples. It was now a week since the accident. Half an hour after Eric arrived at the hospital, Harry Hinton Jnr died of pneumonia. The nurses had given Harry Jnr ice to stop his lips drying out. It's believed he developed pneumonia from sucking the ice.

Harry Jnr's death changed the racing career of his brothers. Eric says he never raced ten-tenths again, "except for one day at Oran Park in 1962, when I had a ding-dong battle with Jim Redman". Robert, who was 14, was encouraged to continue with his piano lessons and his tennis, a sport where he had genuine promise. He only began racing — as a sidecar passenger — when he went away to Europe with Eric in 1965.

Eric flew to England and sold Harry Jnr's equipment for his wife Fay, who was expecting the couple's first child. His problem now was to find a fare home, and the easiest way he knew of doing it was to race. "It was better than working in a factory for six-and-a-half pounds a week," he said.

So for the next four months, Eric raced. He volunteered and was chosen as a stand-in Australian Isle of Man TT rep.

There were several highlights and a couple of huge disappointments. Eric built one 500 Norton out of parts from three bikes (his own and fellow Australian Ken Kavanagh's) in the pits at Sachsenring, for the non-championship East German GP.

Eric was leading the race by 37 seconds from Rhodesian Gary Hocking (the gun rider of the early 1959 season) when the bitza Norton broke its camshaft drive bevels. He set a lap record which stood until the East German GP became a world championship round in 1961. The following week Eric won the non-championship Czech 500 GP at Brno, beating Hocking and top Englishman Dickie Dale. He also finished second to Geoff Duke in the non-championship Swiss GP at Locarno, which was Duke's last motorcycle race.

In August, Eric had a taste of British production machine racing. He teamed with Scotland's Bob McIntyre on a Royal Enfield 700 twin for the Thruxton Nine-Hour race. Hinton recalls it was a fast machine with poor handling.

"We had to sit up on the petrol tank to stop it from wobbling on the straights. But it was quick. Bob gave us a lead of two laps in the first hour. Then we had ignition trouble, but I went out and put us a lap in front again. The primary chain broke, so we replaced that. Then Bob fell off," Eric said.

At Monza, Eric Hinton was in line for a works ride on the East German MZ two-stroke 250 following a recommendation from August Balthasar, the promoter of the St Wendel international meeting in Germany. "That was my one chance of a works ride. It could have been good too, because the MZ 250 was quicker than my 500 Norton. But then Mike Hailwood's dad Stan 'The Wallet' got in the way.

"It was strange, because the morning I was supposed to test the MZ, I ran into Mike at the hotel. He was only 19 then. Mike said that you couldn't afford to let friendships get in the way in this

Eric Hinton (Norton 500) flies at Ballarat in January 1959 — graphic shot by Melbourne's Charles Rice.

business. Sometimes you had to be ruthless. It didn't matter how you got a bike, as long as you got it. Two hours later, my MZ test was off and Mike was trying the bike, because Stan was able to promise MZ he would sell 200 MZ road bikes at his shops — Kings of Oxford. Then Mike didn't like the bike, he stuck to his Mondial 250. But my chance of a ride was gone. The thing that hurt most was that Tommy Robb (an Irish rider) came and told me my test was off — not MZ.

"I rode my 500 Norton at Monza. I was running fifth when the rear brake broke. Then I went back to England and won the Aintree Gold Cup, which gave me enough money to fly home. I didn't go back to Europe until 1965," Hinton said.

Harry Hinton Jnr was two years older than Eric. He shared his dad's slight build. Eric was 12 kg heavier. It meant Harry was more suited to 350 riding and Eric to 500s. Both completed apprenticeships with a tractor manufacturer to become toolmakers. Harry Jnr was the first to start racing. He rode dirt track and Miniature TT (dirt circuits with right- and left-hand corners).

A racing family — Harry Jnr and Harry Snr at a road-race meeting in New South Wales in 1952.

Harry Jnr crashed a Norton 500T at one such meeting at Mudgee in 1952 and sustained a compound fracture to his leg. The injury blunted his racing career for two years, allowing younger brother Eric to leapfrog him. Eric won his first national title in 1955, Harry Jnr in 1956.

Eric had not set out to become a motorcycle racer. He rode a motorcycle to work, but his sporting aspirations lay in soccer and cycling. In November 1952, when Eric was 18, his dad asked him to ride at Castlereagh airstrip on a Norton 500T he'd tuned. Eric reckoned the bike was so quick he fell off three times and still finished third in the race.

Encouraged by that effort, Eric then borrowed an ES2 Norton frame and a 350 engine, which his father tuned. He won a 350 clubman race at Orange, then bought the machine for £50. In 1954 the Hinton boys built up a pair of budget-priced Manx Norton copies. They had Featherbed replica frames, built in their spare time at work, and Norton engines modified by father Harry. The wheels and tanks were genuine articles, bought from international rider Tony McAlpine.

The Hinton brothers also created an odd piece of Australian motorcycle history. They rode a Norton International 500 in the second and last of the Mt Druitt 24-Hour races. It was eliminated when the bike caught fire. They also competed in Mt Druitt 125 sprint events on racing Lambretta motor scooters, brought to Australia by Lambretta importer Sam Jamieson. The difficulty in push-starting these machines helped Eric keep his weight down. "But they should have been good. Later we realised the problem was our lack of knowledge of two-strokes. They just needed a re-bore to make the piston rings seal."

When Geoff Duke visited Australia in 1954-1955 he saw the sons of his former team-mate Harry Hinton race in the clubman events at Bandiana army base (near Albury) and noted Harry's tutorage in tuning and tactics. In fact, Eric beat Duke to win an all-in handicap race at the end of the day.

Duke wrote in *Motor Cycling* on his return to England: "Eric Hinton won the 500 clubman event with plenty in hand, as I found out to my cost later in the day. This serious young man has the makings of a top-flight rider, despite his youth. He is already way out of the clubman class, riding with more finesse than many of Europe's experienced riders."

When Harry Hinton retired from racing in July 1955, he passed his pair of works Nortons to his sons. They soon made use of the improved machinery. Eric won the 1955 Australian 500 TT held on a road circuit at Southport, Queensland in October. In the Australian 350 TT, the result was Eric Hinton first and Harry Jnr second.

Eric Hinton's two Australian titles won him selection in the 1956 Australian team for the Isle of Man. Jack Ahearn, Bob Brown, Keith Campbell and Tony McAlpine had been suspended for taking part in the 1955 Dutch TT riders' strike, so Eric's team-mates were Keith Bryen (who'd raced in Europe in 1953-1954) and Barry Hodgkinson.

"Selection in the Isle of Man team was a real boost to a rider's finances. You received £100 when you left Australia. That covered my boat fare to England on the *Orcades*. The ACU of Great Britain paid you another £100 when the TT finished. And you received £150 when you came home at the end of the season. Coming home was part of the deal. It meant you brought back new machines, technology and much-needed spare parts, and kept up the standard of local racing," Eric said.

Hinton teamed up with another Sydneysider, Richie Thompson, who'd raced in Europe in 1955

Eric Hinton in the 1956 German GP at Solitude, riding an NSU Sportmax, the best 250 available to a 1950s privateer.

and therefore knew the ropes. They bought a three-tonne Ford van, already set up as a transporter-cum-campervan, from the suspended rider Jack Ahearn. Eric also bought Jack's full streamlining. Eric's new Manx Nortons were not ready for his European race debut at Imola that Easter, so he rode Thompson's Matchless G45.

"It was a frightening race. Dick's G45 kept cutting onto one cylinder then back onto two in the rain. Ken Kavanagh rode the Guzzi V8 in that race with no goggles. After the race I flew to England, collected my Nortons and came back to Europe with Keith Campbell, who had a Cadillac and a five-bike trailer. We raced at St Wendel in the Saar region of Germany. I won the 350 race from Keith. Then Richie and I went to the NSU factory at Neckarsulm, where I collected an NSU 250 Sportmax. Only about 23 were made — you had to be a national champion to get one. It was a very competitive 250 in 1956."

Hinton made a real impression in the next month. He was third in the non-championship Austrian 350 GP, which was run in the rain on a section of autobahn linked by cobblestone entry and exit ramps. The following weekend he was second in the 250 class and the first 500 Norton rider home in the Floreffe international in Belgium. "That was a sad meeting. Fergus Anderson, whom I'd met when he came to Australia in 1948-1949, was killed when he crashed a BMW into a telegraph pole.

"Our next meeting was the North-West 200 in Northern Ireland. After practice, the Girling reps gave me a replacement set of rear suspension units for the NSU. I had a real battle in the 250 race with Sammy Miller, the trials ace, for most of the 200 miles (320 km). Late in the race my bike started handling very badly, as if the rear axle had broken, so I stopped. Then Sammy crashed. We both restarted. Sammy won and I was second. Afterwards I discovered my problem had been the suspension units. They were over-damped. So Girling paid me the equivalent of first-place money.

"From Ireland we went straight to the Isle of Man and started practising. I did 95 laps of the course before official practice started. At first I used a borrowed road bike, then I paid £5 and road-registered my 350 Manx Norton for a week. The secret was to learn where you were going. I had some good teachers: Ken Kavanagh, Geoff Duke, Bob Foster (the 1950 world 350 champion) and Dickie Dale. Ken and Dickie saved me 20 seconds between Rhencullen and Ballaugh Bridge (about nine kilometres) by showing me where to go.

"Knowing where you were going was the key. You had to do lots of learning before official practice started, because the best you could do during the official practice sessions was four laps per morning. I reckoned I knew the course pretty well. I would have finished fifth in my first TT (the 350) but my Norton broke its conrod full bore in top gear and put me in hospital with facial injuries," Hinton said.

Hinton's itinerary for the next two months highlighted the dilemma of the private entrant in Europe. Should he contest world championship grands prix, where the start money was low but there were trade reps to supply equipment and factory team managers to impress, or should he contest the international meetings which paid better start money?

"The next two grands prix were the Dutch and the Belgian. They were the ones which seemed to count for factory rides. But the Dutch were only offering £25 start money, so Richie and I went to an international meeting at Schleiz in East Germany. We were among the first guys from the West to race there after the war."

Hinton in the next month rode at Mulhouse in France and the Alsace Hillclimb, where he won three classes and set a 250 class course record; and the non-championship Swedish GP at Hedemora, where he finished third to Keith Campbell and Briton John Hartle. He then contested the West German GP at Solitude (near Stuttgart), the Senigalia international in Italy and an international street-circuit race in Ville Franche de Rounergue, France.

"I won the 350 race there and had a great battle in the 500 race with Pierre Monneret, who had a four-cylinder Gilera. I tried so hard to stay in front of him I eventually grounded part of the frame and crashed. I was paralysed for two days, but still rode at Sachsenring in East Germany the following weekend. I must have been keen," Eric confessed.

"We went to Brno in Czechoslovakia next. It was a 17 km track, and the tar was so shiny from spilled diesel fuel you couldn't tell if it was wet or dry. I was second to Franta Stastny's works Jawa in the 350 race, then fell off and broke my arm in the 250 race.

There were four of us, Bob Brown, Hans Baltisberger, Horst Kassner and me, racing nose to tail on our NSUs. It started to rain on one side of the course. Bobbie slid off, then me, then Baltisberger. But Kassner stayed on and won.

"That crash and the trip to hospital afterwards were the beginnings of my becoming a more sober rider. The hospital staff set my arm without anaesthetic. One nurse asked if it hurt! I said 'yes'. She said, 'The man next to you won't feel anything, he's dead.' They had Baltisberger laid out next to me. Such callous people. Hans was a nice guy. He was a concert pianist and a top motorcycle racer.

"I took the NSU back to the factory and they said: 'Mr Hinton, nothing on this machine is any good'. They didn't salvage one part, but they fixed it for nothing."

Home for the summer of 1956-1957, Eric teamed with brother Harry Jnr for an assault on the local racing scene. The most important meeting was the 1956 Australian TT, held at Mildura on Boxing Day. Eric reckons his brother's ride in the 350 TT that day was perhaps the best of his career. "Harry had the works bike Norton had sent out to dad in 1952, and the international riders had 1956 Manx Nortons, but he blew us into the weeds." Harry Jnr won the 350 TT from Eric and Maurice Quincey. Eric spent the Australian 500 and Unlimited TTs fruitlessly chasing Keith Campbell's works Guzzi 500 single.

In February 1957, Eric Hinton and Harry Jnr sailed for Europe on the *Orcades*. They took with them some of the first glass fibre fairings made in Australia, neatly styled from the wind-tunnel tested full-bin Moto Guzzi design. They used Eric's van from the previous year, until they wrecked it en route to the Isle of Man. Eric was again a member of the IoM team along with Bob Brown and newcomer Roger Barker. They each bought two new Nortons. Eric's machines were former Norton team machines from 1956.

Before the TT the Hinton brothers raced at the traditional early season internationals, including Imola and St Wendel, where the 350 race produced a Hinton one-two and the 500 race a win for Eric. Harry Jnr had a disappointing Isle of Man debut. He crashed at May Hill during practice, broke his collarbone and therefore could not race. Eric sent a telegram to Harry's fiancée Fay, giving her the bare details. It read: "Harry Fell Off May Hill Broke Collarbone." Fay is supposed to have asked: "Who is May Hill?"

Eric, however, had his finest TT ride in the Silver Jubilee 350 TT. He was fifth, behind four men on Italian works machines — Bob McIntyre (Gilera), Keith Campbell (Guzzi), Bob Brown (Gilera) and John Surtees (MV Agusta). Another good result in the 500 TT looked likely until the last lap.

"The 500 TT was extended from seven to eight laps

Eric Hinton's best IoM result was in 1957. He rode a Norton to fifth place in the 350 TT, behind four works Italian machines.

that year (486 km) to mark the 50th birthday of the Tourist Trophy races. My Norton ran out of brakes coming into Ballacraine on the last lap. Ballacraine is a road junction. There's a road going straight ahead to St Johns, but the circuit takes you to the right. In those days there was a pub on the outside of the corner. There was a rope across the escape road, with a marshal to lift it if required. He was looking the other way when I arrived, so I had to try to get around the corner. I didn't make it. I crashed through the front door of the pub and broke the frame. There was nothing else to do but have a drink," Eric explained.

Eric and Harry concentrated on international meetings for the remainder of the European season. IoM team-mate Roger Barker died of heat exhaustion in a race in East Germany early in July 1957. The Hintons bought his van to replace their wrecked transporter.

"We were doing 20,000 km a season in vans that had top speeds of 80 km/h. Some weeks you could spend three days driving from one race to the next, from Sweden down to Italy, for instance. We tried all sorts of things for transport. At one stage we bought a big Buick from Bob Brown and put the bikes on a trailer."

On the track, the Hinton brothers were among the leading private entrants on the international scene. "At Schleiz in '57 we were third and fourth in the 500 race, behind two works BMWs. We were among the few Norton blokes who could trouble the 500 Beemers." They were also among the first Norton riders to obtain five-speed gearboxes, made in Sweden by Torsten Aagard.

Eric and Harry sailed for Australia a few days after the Italian GP, the traditional European season finale. During the voyage they learned Moto Guzzi, Gilera and FB Mondial had withdrawn from racing, leaving compatriots Keith Campbell, Keith Bryen and Bob Brown without works rides.

It was an eventful summer in Australia. Harry Hinton Jnr married Fay. In mid-December at Mt Druitt the Hintons had their first battle with a shy Sydneysider named Tom Phillis, after they'd been up all night fixing crash damage and gearbox damage to Harry's bike. Phillis would join them in Europe in 1958. On December 29, the Hintons won three Australian TTs at Phillip Island. Eric won the 500 race from Harry Jnr and Bob Brown (on a BMW). Harry Jnr won the 350 TT on his Norton, after a titanic struggle with Ken Rumble, and the 250 TT on Eric's NSU. Eric was selected in the Australian IoM team for 1958, along with Bob Brown and Jack Ahearn.

Harry Jnr was at a loss to know why he was not chosen for the IoM team after finishing first or second in most races that summer.

Harry and Fay Hinton sailed for England in February 1958 with an almost unknown Victorian rider named Jack Findlay, who would spend the next 20 years racing in Europe. Eric stayed on to contest the Easter Bathurst meeting. He won the 500 race and had a healthy lead in the 350 race when his spark plug came loose. Eric then flew to England, an endurance test of 36 hours of vibration in a turbo-prop Bristol Brittania.

Eric opened the season by winning the British Motorcycle Racing Club's 250 Championship at Silverstone on his NSU, beating Derek Minter and Bob Brown. The win was soured by having to butcher the bike's aluminium fairing to satisfy scrutineers. Eric and Harry then had more adventures at St Wendel and Hockenheim.

"The St Wendel race organiser, August Balthasar, gave me a racing pushbike, for putting in a special effort. The plug lead came off the NSU early in the 250 race. I stopped and fixed it by biting through the insulation of the plug lead and wrapping the wire around the spark plug. I got going, unlapped myself and finished runner-up, half a second behind Ernst Degner. Another time I won a painting at a race in East Germany.

"Harry sold his Norton 350 at Hockenheim and bought an old Velocette with girder front forks. Everybody laughed until he qualified fifth fastest on it. Hockenheim then was still a super-fast track with big looping corners at both ends. There were no barriers between the track and the pine forest. The racing direction was anti-clockwise, the opposite to today. During the 250 race the sump plug fell out of my NSU. The bike just turned right and speared off into the pine forest, between the trees. I broke both ankles without falling off the bike. The crash made the television news back in Australia. I still practised for the TT, ten days later."

Eric had finished in the first dozen in three TTs, his highest placing being seventh in the 250 TT, held on the Clypse Circuit. Harry Jnr finished 27th in the 350 race, after his Velocette threw its chain. Harry Hinton Snr was on the Isle of Man to see his sons race, then joined them on the road for a few meetings.

"At Assen I lent Harry Jnr the NSU. He was running third in the 250 race behind two works MVs when the bike blew its head gasket. My brother and I qualified well for the 500 race, but Derek Minter tried a late braking move on the first tight corner and five of us fell down, like dominoes. I ended up in one of Assen's safety ditches with a bent frame. Two Ferodo trade reps, Alex Wise and Lennie Walker, loaned me the hydraulic jack and spare axle from their van to straighten it.

"Mid-season 1958 was a difficult time. Harry and I were contracted to Dunlop, but Avon was coming up with better tyres. Dunlop had good compounds, but it seemed those compounds were only going to Bob McIntyre. By Assen, we were among the last riders still on Dunlop. After the meeting we told the Dunlop blokes if they couldn't give us the same tyres they were giving Bob Mac, then we'd go to Avon.

"Harry and I went to Schleiz the next week, rather than the Belgian GP. The Schleiz organiser offered us £130 each, compared with 30 at Spa. We had to balance our economic survival against the chance of a works offer. It you raced at all the little meetings you could make good money — maybe £3000 in a season. That was pretty good in the 1950s. But you had to be seen at the grand prix to impress the factories."

Eric's best result in the second half of 1958 was in the non-championship Grand Prix of the DDR (East Germany) at Sachsenring. He finished third, behind Swiss rider Luigi Taveri (Norton) and Franta Stastny's works Jawa.

Luigi Taveri still has fond memories of Australian privateers, as typified by the Hintons. In fact he was genuinely surprised that Eric Hinton was never given a works ride. In 1988 he told the authors: "I remember the Australians always not having enough money. They had to race without a proper budget. The Hintons thought it was more important to have fast bikes than nice-looking bikes and nice clothes."

Eric Hinton returned home at the end of the 1958 season. Harry Jnr and Fay Hinton stayed in Birmingham. Harry Jnr died in April the following year. His son Greg was born two months later. Eric completed the 1959 European season, then flew home for good — or so he thought at the time.

Eric and Kate had a son, Peter, in November 1959. Peter was named after Geoff Duke's son. They had a second son, Anthony, in March 1961. Eric's race efforts in the 1960s were relatively quiet, compared with the 1950s. He won the Australian 250 TT at

GEORGE MORRISON The Mate From Ballarat

George Morrison had a lot in common with Harry Hinton — the same trade, similar business interests, the same entree into motorcycle sport and, because they were born in 1911-1912, the same interruption in the prime of their racing careers — World War II.

Morrison and Hinton were fine riders and memorable characters. During 1949 they travelled together in Europe, and generally amazed people on the Isle of Man and across Europe.

Morrison and Hinton staged a dead-heat in a race at Gedinne in Belgium. It was George's idea. He told Harry that if they played smart, they could both collect first prizemoney. "We still had a lot of fun, and the result gave us good drawing power," George said.

George Morrison was born in Melbourne in 1912 and completed an apprenticeship as a motor mechanic with the Mobil Oil Company. He caught the racing bug in 1932-1933, while on assignment for Mobil in Adelaide. George helped a motorcycle dealer prepare test machines for beach racing. He couldn't afford to road-race, because a gallon of methanol racing fuel cost the equivalent of a week's pay, so he bought a Douglas motorcycle in 1934 and went grass-track racing. After winning a few races, George bought a Velocette 250 and switched to scrambles racing, winning 46 events.

Morrison moved to Ballarat in 1936 and opened a motorcycle dealership. The first road races held in Victoria after the war were at Victoria Park, Ballarat. Here Morrison became friends with visiting Sydney rider Harry Hinton. George was not selected for the 1949 Australian Isle of Man TT team, but his international performances that summer soon made a mockery of that non-selection.

Morrison and Hinton created an immediate impression on the Isle of Man. Other riders pussy-footed over the first-gear jump at Ballaugh Bridge and through the right-hand corner that follows. Harry and George took the jump with a rush, sending both wheels well off the ground, and almost brushed the wall with their handlebars as they took the right-hander. "They all thought I was mad," George said. He finished 27th in the 350 TT. In the 500 TT he won plaudits for his riding and his tenacity:

"Halfway around the Isle of Man course there's a village called Kirkmichael. The corner coming into the town is a long, sweeping bend which we could take at about 90 mph. On the outside of the corner was a footpath, about three feet wide, then a low stone wall. During the races people would sit along the wall.

"British roads have low-melting point tar, so it won't crack during the winter. The temperature that day was up around 90 on the old scale, and so, unknown to me, the tar started to melt.

"The first time through Kirkmichael, my bike started to creep across the road. I couldn't work out why. The next thing the bike hit the gutter on the outside of the corner and bounced up onto the footpath. Fortunately, the footpath was concrete, so I had some grip. I didn't back off! There were about 40 spectators sitting along the top of the wall, with their legs dangling in front.

"When I took off down the footpath, the blokes and ladies just flopped backwards over the wall to miss my handlebars. There were legs and bloomers everywhere. I rode the footpath until I was lined up for the next corner, then aimed back into the middle of the road and waved back to say thanks for getting their legs out of the way. The Poms thought I was Superman to do that and not back off!"

Morrison moved into top-six contention in the next six laps. He was duelling with New Zealander Sid Jensen (Triumph). But George's Norton was literally falling apart underneath him, the frame broken in five places. He pushed and coasted the last eight kilometres to finish 31st.

Morrison returned to the Isle of Man in 1950 as a selected Australian team member. Norton hired Morrison and Hinton for the TT, as members of the "B-team", with Londoner Harold Daniell. Morrison pushed home 64th in the 350 TT, after his drive chain broke, and finished 11th, one place behind Hinton, in the 500 TT.

Morrison opened his 1950 European season by winning a 500 international race at Zandvoort. He followed that up with 14th place in the Belgian 350 GP. McPherson was eighth and Hinton 11th. Morrison made an indifferent start in the Dutch 350 GP. He was running about 20th and trying to improve his position when he crashed. The injuries sustained finished his season prematurely.

Morrison then headed home to Australia, via America. "While I was in San Francisco, I met a bloke who'd read about my exploits in Europe and wanted to sponsor me. In 1952 this bloke paid my expenses to go back to America and ride his Manx Norton at Daytona, where the track was half beach and half road.

"But the Yanks were cunning. The AMA (American Motorcyclist Association) wanted an American to win Daytona on a Harley-Davidson or an Indian. They said I would have to do a Novice race and a Junior race before I could have an Expert licence and ride at Daytona. I won a Novice race at Stockton, California and a Junior race at Dodge City, Kansas. But my three-month entry visa ran out before the Daytona race," he lamented.

Bathurst in 1960 on his NSU, to give him two successive 250 race wins at Mt Panorama, and to take the family's Bathurst tally to 20.

But in 1965, Eric developed the itch again. He headed to Europe with brother Rob, then 20, who acted as mechanic. Eric's equipment was a pair of 1957 model Nortons and a Ford Thames van. Any aspirations lanky Rob had towards racing had been stifled at home. But once in Europe, he soon found a part-time job as sidecar passenger for George Auerbacher. Eric made a point of speaking to the hard-driving German about looking after his new ballast. But Rob seemed to revel in being away from home in the grand prix paddocks of Europe. Eric candidly says he "didn't do very much in the 1965 season". His one world championship point-scoring finish was at Imatra, Finland. Eric was sixth in the 350 race, behind three works machines and two fellow private entrants.

But Eric made enough money to encourage him to try again in 1966, with the family. Many racing friends were in Europe that year, including Jack and Betty Ahearn, Kel and Jan Carruthers, Jack Findlay, Mal Stanton, Len and Jill Atlee, Kevin Cass and John Dodds. Eric's boys are now four and five years old, old enough to handle life on the road. Team Hinton's gear expanded to include a 17-foot Sprite caravan and two Bultaco machines, a 125 and a 250.

The single-cylinder two-stroke Bultacos were competitive machines at the time. But they had quirks which nearly drove Eric and Rob to despair. Breaking crankshafts and primary drive chains were the most common dramas. At one meeting in Finland in 1966, Eric blew an engine during practice, repaired it just in time to make the start, rode the entire race in the rain, then had the crankshaft break on the climb to the finishing line. Eric's best GP result of the year was on his Norton 500. He was sixth in the Czech GP, behind compatriots Findlay and Ahearn.

For 1967 Eric found another potentially good racer which was flawed in small areas — the new 250 Kawasaki A1R rotary disc-valve twin. "That bike was almost there. The first time I rode it I told Rob we really had something. It was the fastest private 250 in practice for many races, but something always went wrong. The three races it finished, at Mettet, Montlhery (near Paris) and Wunsdorf (near Hannover), it scored a first, a second and a third. The Mettet result was Kawasaki's first international race victory. The trouble was there were no parts, Phil Read used to lend me carburettor jets from the works Yamahas!"

Eric continued to race in England and Europe in 1968 and 1969. He worked through the winters in England. In '69 he bought a Yamaha TD2 250 through his father's old friend Jack Milne in the USA. That bike took Eric to sixth place in the Belgian GP at Spa, behind four works machines. Eric said the bike, in standard form, was almost as fast as Kel Carruthers' works Benelli at Spa. "At the end of the year someone finally told me the little tricks that would have made the Yamaha a winner," Eric said.

But learning then was too late. Eric had decided to come home. Wife Kate was surprised by the decision. "We finally had the van Eric wanted, the caravan he wanted and the bikes he wanted, and he decided to stop. But the four years I was there were an experience not to be missed. Most of the Australians there were in our age group, so we formed a tight group. Life on the road with two children was no trouble. It was real adventure and an education to them. Eric still tells his apprentices they should go and see the world.

"Before I met Eric and his family I knew nothing about motorcycle racing. In fact I didn't understand why Eric wanted to race until I saw the racing in Europe. When you saw the scene and the crowds in Europe you could see why people tried so hard," Kate said.

Eric Hinton continued to race in Australia until the early 1970s. He built some interesting machines, including three-cylinder 500s, made by grafting an extra cylinder onto a Yamaha 350 twin. Rob Hinton took up solo racing when he returned to Australia. He was a particularly confident rider on the Mount Panorama circuit at Bathurst. In 1975-1976 he won three Australian GPs there, riding a bike built up by Eric. Rob's mechanic, a railway fitter named Mick Smith, later went to Europe as a race mechanic and in 1987 was appointed manager of Team Honda Australia. As Smith described it: "Eric knew all about motorbikes. He taught Rob, and Rob taught me."

During the late 1970s Peter and Tony Hinton took up motorcycle racing, initially junior dirt-track events. The gun rider when they started travelling to junior races in Canberra was a kid named Wayne Gardner. Tony Hinton won the Australian 125 GP at Bathurst in 1984 and the Australian 500 GP at Bathurst the following year. Peter Hinton missed an Australian Road-Racing Championship by a few points in 1983, after withdrawing from one round with a flat rear tyre while running second to Tony.

Some racers of the 1950s are envious of modern-day grand prix riders for the money they earn, but not Eric Hinton. He's pleased that the riders, led by Americans such as Kenny Roberts, demanded improvements. "In my day you could never get the riders to band together. We tried a couple of times, but the English weren't committed and many of the Europeans were able to race and hold down regular jobs, so they didn't worry about being paid poor money."

KEN KAVANAGH

CHAPTER 3

Probably no Australian rider has been so successful so soon after his arrival in Europe, made as much money, lost most of it in unfortunate investments and then been as forgotten in his home country as Thomas Kenrick Kavanagh.

Ken Kavanagh was prepared to try just about anything, including the most fearsome of all racing activities — he had been a sidecar passenger for noted rider Keith Rattan, as well as doing well on his own account, riding solos. He had considered going to Europe in 1948 as an Australian speedway test rider, but it was not until 1951 that he first headed to the Continent as a member of the 1951 Australian Isle of Man team.

In his first season in Europe, Kavanagh scored four major places in world championship grands prix: two second places on the notorious 26.5 km Cladys Circuit at Ulster, a second at Monza, and a third at Assen. He finished fourth in that year's world 350 championship despite not doing all the rounds. Even more impressive was his debut performance on the Isle of Man. He was running fourth at his first attack on the bewildering and daunting 61 km course when he suffered machine trouble. Although he won an IoM TT, he had generally poor luck there, finishing only five times out of 17. Eventually, in 1956, he won the race, and to Kavanagh the result was magical. "The Island was the ultimate. Nobody cared about the world championship in those days," he recalled.

And no wonder. The 350 cm³ and 500 cm³ TTs at the IoM were raced over 425 km, seven laps of the world's longest and least forgiving racing circuit.

In eight years in Europe, Kavanagh was a works rider for four different factories. He was the first Australian to win a world championship grand prix and a Tourist Trophy race at the Isle of Man. It was against the odds that Kavanagh even made the 1951 Isle of Man team. He was a replacement for the original Victorian selection, Maurie Quincey, and Kavanagh made good use of the chance. Indeed, if there was anything for which Ken Kavanagh is remembered, it is that he chased chances with singular determination, and he seldom let them slip.

At his first Isle of Man TT in June 1951, he was sounded out for a possible works Norton ride by crusty team boss Joe Craig. The approach had been prompted by no less than Geoff Duke, who that year won both the 350 cm³ and 500 cm³ world championships. Duke spoke enthusiastically to Craig about the potential he saw in Kavanagh. "On his day, Ken was the fastest of all the Australians I raced against," he recalled.

"Ken had a top ride in the 1951 Ulster 500 cm³ grand prix at Cladys. He led by miles at the end of the first lap and was finally second to me after a very long and tiring race. It rained cats and dogs for 200

Ken Kavanagh, Moto Guzzi works rider and winner of the 1956 Isle of Man 350 TT.

miles," Duke said. The torture, noise, cold and danger of that race lasted four-and-a-quarter hours. Not only was Kavanagh second in that one to Duke, he was second to him in the 350 as well.

The Ulster 500 GP that Kavanagh won at Dundrod in 1953 was also an exceptional ride. Riding a works Norton single, Ken passed Duke on a factory four-cylinder Gilera while he was in the pits with clutch problems. The Australian went on to win, at 144 km/h average speed, in a rain-lashed race that lasted two-and-a-half hours. Just three weeks later he was given a taste of a Moto Guzzi 250 at Monza. He lost a lap-and-a-half trying to get his machine to fire at the start of the race, but then he lapped nearly a second faster than the race winner Enrico Lorenzetti. In the final grand prix of the season, he finished second to Lorenzetti at the tight and hilly Montjuich Park street circuit in Barcelona.

That put him in a privileged position: he had ridden for two factories in one season. Apart from the compliment, it made Kavanagh realise what he had been up against on Nortons. He had discovered what private Norton riders probably feared for a long time — that a Guzzi 250 was as fast as a Norton 350. As a works Norton rider in 1952-1953, Kavanagh was fifth and then fourth in the world 350 cm³ title, and fifth and then third in the 500 cm³ championship. After he joined Moto Guzzi full time in 1954,

Geoff Duke (right) and Ken Kavanagh finished one-two in the 1951 Ulster and Italian 350 GPs.

he was fourth in the 350 championship for the next two years and third in the 500 in the 1954. Overall he won four 350 cm³ world championship grands prix, of which one was the 1956 Isle of Man TT, the first win by an Australian at the Isle, more than 40 years after the first attempt. Kavanagh still remains one of only five Australians to have won there, with ten Tourist Trophy races among them. More Australians have been injured and more killed at IoM than have won races there.

Ken Kavanagh was always serious and professional about his racing at a time when motorcycle racing to most people, even those good enough to win, was still only an amateur sport. Because of such an attitude, fellow riders, Australians and others, are divided in their opinions about him — some like him, while others found his driving ambition and commitment unsavoury. But opinions mattered little to Kavanagh, and he was never afraid to take on the big names — on or off the track. Fortunately he kept well out of trouble on the track, while many of his contemporaries were injured or killed.

But he was no stranger to trouble off the track, even in his early days. Ken's father hated motorcycles, so when he found out that his son had become an apprentice with Melbourne trade and sporting identity Col Sampson, who was one of the founders of the Hartwell Motorcycle Club, the youngster was thrown out of the family home.

"I lived rough on Station Pier at Port Melbourne for a few days," Ken recalled, "but when I started to look increasingly scruffy at work, Col asked what was wrong and eventually I told him. He often used to sleep in the workshop himself, but he'd just been married and had moved into a home. He let me sleep in the workshop."

Kavanagh's start in motorcycle racing goes back to when he joined the large and very active Hartwell Motorcycle Club on February 7, 1944. His first outing was a combined Hartwell/Oakleigh scramble at Dandenong Creek, where he won the newcomers race. He then raced at the Jordanville scramble, and was again successful. At the first post-war, road-race meeting at Victoria Park, Ballarat, Kavanagh, on Col Sampson's Ariel, fought neck and neck with fellow Hartwell club member Jack French in the ten-lap Clubmans TT. Reports described it "as one of the highlights of the day, with the two riders racing shoulder to shoulder with each other, flat out along Gillies Street at 160 km/h. It left the crowd gasping." Kavanagh was bested by French that day, but he won the all-power Victorian "A" grade scramble championship at Templestowe, described at the time by an entertainment-starved public as "the best ever meeting in Victoria."

At the Bonnie Vale Miniature TT, Kavanagh was one of six riders who won or ran second in every event on the program. At Rowville circuit on Australia Day, 1949, a five shilling entry fee gave riders a crack at £100 prize money. Kavanagh, Ron Hunter and Alan Johnson were too good for the famous Scotsman, Fergus Anderson, whose immaculate 7R AJS could not challenge them on the treacherous ball-bearing surface. Anderson was one of a number of European riders, including Geoff Duke, Dickie Dale, Giacomo Agostini, and Rob McElnea, who came to Australia with fine reputations but found that local machinery and riders were very hard to beat on home base.

It was a propitious meeting, for Anderson was later to ride for Guzzi with Kavanagh. They became team-mates in the Moto Guzzi factory team, and Anderson later became Guzzi race team manager and the first man to ride, and crash, the fabulous Guzzi V8. And that in its first test session.

At Fishermans Bend later in 1949, Kavanagh was fourth in the 500 TT. Still mixing dirt with road racing, a few weeks later he won the "A" grade race in an open scramble at Campbellfield. At Darley in 1950, Kavanagh defeated Maurie Quincey in the 500 TT. At the South Australian TT in October, he was second in the 500. And at a combined car and motorcycle meeting at Ballarat airstrip, Kavanagh dominated. All of this was happening with an MSS Velocette and then the first down-under, post-war Manx Norton.

Kavanagh's big chance came when he was chosen with Tony McAlpine and Harry Hinton as a member of the Australian team for the Isle of Man in 1951. The first Victorian choice was Maurie Quincey, but because of business commitments he decided not to go. Kavanagh was first reserve, but it still made him the fourth member of a three-man team. However Ernie Ring, who Ken considered a better rider than he, was the one dropped.

Kavanagh arrived at the Island with plenty of experience and success behind him in most branches of the sport. He well knew that if he let this chance slip, there might never be another. More than most Australians faced with the almost impossibly confusing track, he did it just about right — firstly, he didn't crash, and even more impressively, he was quick. It was the start of a remarkably successful first continental season.

One comment made about Kavanagh at that time was that "he was the best of a generally bad bunch". Most Australians at Isle of Man made the mistake of riding too fast too soon, while many of those they were racing were perhaps not as good but over a period of years they had learned the IoM as they had learned to race. It was impossible for any rider to learn the place properly in a matter of a few weeks, especially trying to travel really fast. And when a race lap took nearly half an hour, the number of laps a rider could do on a road bike at slow speeds learning the place was obviously limited.

Harry Hinton had been injured during the 350 TT, leaving the Norton team one rider short. Norton race-team boss Joe Craig offered Kavanagh a works bike, but Ken refused it, saying he thought his Manx was fast enough. Moreover, he would not have time to practise on it, so he felt he would not have made the best use of its better brakes and speed.

Ken finished the first lap of the 500 in ninth place, and he worked his way up to fourth before an oil tank burst on the last lap, resulting in a non-finish. Two weeks later he raced his Nortons at Thruxton circuit in England. He finished second to Rhodesian Ray Amm in the 350 race, but pushed hard enough in the 500 for Amm to crash — that gave Kavanagh his first race win in Europe. Amm, along with British rider John Surtees, was considered by Maurie Quincey to be fairly wild in his early days. While Surtees smoothed out when he got faster bikes, Amm remained on the wild side and was eventually killed at Imola, in his first ride on an MV Agusta, in a 350 cm^3 race being led by Kavanagh.

Two weeks after Thruxton, Ken won both the 350 and 500 races on a Manx Norton Featherbed at Tarare circuit in France. He was beaten only by Duke on a works Norton at Ulster and in the 350 cm^3 Italian world championship GP at Monza. Later, Kavanagh was third in the 350 cm^3 world championship race at Assen, behind the AJS factory pair of Doran and Petch. The Australian then went to the 13 km long Schotten circuit, northeast of Frankfurt, for Germany's first international post-war meeting. *Motor Cycling* magazine said of him: "In the 350, Kavanagh dominated throughout, his graceful style making an excellent impression. But he really earned the crowd's appreciation in the next event. On his 500 Norton he was third to Germany's top riders, Georg Meier and Walter Zeller on BMWs".

Now was the time for Kavanagh to ride works bikes. For the 350 and 500 world championship races on the Dundrod circuit at Ulster, Ireland, Geoff Duke, who had recommended Kavanagh for the more powerful, harder-revving machinery, was the Norton team leader. There was only two lengths between Duke and Kavanagh when they finished first and second in the 350 race, and he backed up Duke equally well in the 500 cm^3 GP, their Nortons taking the two top placings ahead of the reigning 500 champion, Umberto Masetti, on a four-cylinder Gilera.

Kavanagh had done superbly well in his introduction to European circuits and world championship road racing. He returned to Australia in late October. At his first race meeting, armed with two new Manx Nortons at Ballarat Airstrip, he cleaned up. They were the first models in Australia with the double-cradle frame, known as the Featherbed. In 1952, Kavanagh went to the usual New Year's Day meeting at Ballarat, but not to the Bathurst Easter meeting — he was keen to get back to racing in Europe.

Back in England, Kavanagh won the 350 and 500 races at an international meeting at Boreham Wood, making him a British Champion. He also won both races on the 7.3 km track at Hedemora, in Sweden. At the Isle of Man, Kavanagh looked a certainty for fourth place in the 500 TT, which would have been the best performance ever by an Australian. But his primary chain broke at the Bungalow, more than six kilometres from the finish. Luckily, much of the track after that was downhill, so he pushed and coasted home to finish 32nd and collect a bronze replica for finishing within a percentage of the winner's time. His best lap had been an impressive 145 km/h average speed.

In the earlier 350 cm^3 race, "Last Lap" Kavanagh had equally bad luck. After being sixth for the first four laps, he moved up to fourth, before an exhaust valve broke at Kirkmichael on the last lap. His non-finish affected two team results: Norton appeared to have the team prize in the bag, with Duke and Reg Armstrong running one and two ahead of New Zealander Rod Coleman on a factory AJS; it would also have won Australia the team prize, as Ernie Ring, now in Europe, went especially well to finish eighth. Sydney's Tony McAlpine had trouble with almost inoperable rear springing, which gave him a difficult and slow ride to 23rd place.

Although it was again a good performance by Kavanagh, it seemed that he was not riding as fiercely as previously. Was this due to the responsibility of being on a works Norton and having to be more certain of a result? Or was Kavanagh under team orders, as was to occur in other races that season?

But there was little to worry about on that Isle of Man night. At the prizegiving there was an uproarious reception for Kavanagh for his perseverence in finishing. He, Ray Amm, and Rod Coleman were treated like film stars, pursued by a continuous stream of photographers and autograph hunters. Australian and New Zealand flags flew proudly from the first floor window of Rosevilla, the Australian team headquarters in Douglas. But Kavanagh was celebrating with the Norton team at Castle Mona — his future lay more with Norton than a bunch of happy colonials.

Yet that future took an interesting turn later in the year at the German GP on the Solitude road circuit. "Half the 11.5 km track had recently been resurfaced, making it very slippery with a hot sun and lots of traffic on it," Kavanagh wrote in August 1952 to the *NSW Motorcyclist* magazine.

"Rod Coleman (NZ, AJS twin) crashed and was concussed, Milani had broken his collarbone crashing his Gilera, and his team-mate Masetti had also been off. Amm was taken to hospital with a broken leg and three cracked vertebrae. We (the Norton team) were already minus Geoff Duke, after a crash a week earlier at Schotten, in which he broke a toe and dislocated an ankle.

"So it was up to Reg Armstrong and me to fly the Norton flag. We decided I should try to win the 350 race, and he the 500. If he did that, Norton still stood a chance of winning the 500 cm³ world championship.

"Our main rivals, Jack Brett and Bill Lomas, both on AJSs, crashed, with Brett bringing Lomas down. That left Reg and me out on our own, able to suit ourselves. On the last lap, as planned, I took the lead. The joy of those last few kilometres down towards the finish, to my first grand prix victory, was sensational. Then as I came out of the last corner with the chequered flag just 200 metres away, I froze. I just broke up and shut the motor off. In a flash Reg was by, winning by a wheel. Once more I was second!"

So to the 500 race, the one that Reg Armstrong was to win because of the championship position. "I led from the start, with Reg second," Kavanagh said. "But by the end of the second lap, he had Les Graham (the first world 500 cm³ champion) on an MV only three seconds behind him. So they gave the panic signal, every man for himself. I rode as I've never ridden before, building up a 90-second gap on Les and 20 seconds on Reg.

"That continued until three laps from the end, when it was obvious Reg was safe from any threat from Graham. Out came the signal I was dreading: return to original plan. I was pretty dejected — having to wander around those last few laps waiting for the rest of our merry band to catch up. We resumed our original positions about three kilometres from the end and Reg went over the line first, for his second win of the day.

"When they left me out front for so long, I'd thought and hoped I was going to be allowed to win it. But that's the way it goes. Races are for the good of the marque, not the individual."

That remark remained pertinent to much of Kavanagh's career.

Although Armstrong was then leading Masetti by three points in the championship, he was six points behind at the end of the season. If Kavanagh had been allowed to win the Solitude race, he'd have finished in fourth place in the championship instead of sixth. Things finally came right for Kavanagh at the next world championship race, in Ulster. He and Ernie Ring, who had finished sixth in the German 350 race, both finished one place better than previously — Kavanagh was first, Armstrong second and Ring fifth.

The next year, 1953, saw Kavanagh's Isle of Man ambitions come closer to fruition. The opposition was tougher and his machinery at a greater disadvantage; even Geoff Duke left Norton at the end of 1952 for Italian Gilera, although they did not have a 350, only a 500. In the 350s, there were two very fast but not reliable three-cylinder, two-stroke German DKWs, two four-cylinder MVs and a lone Moto Guzzi for Fergus Anderson.

Although Les Graham's MV retired with a slipping clutch, and the early leader, Rod Coleman's AJS split a tank and retired, Kavanagh still did not win. He hit the lead in a fight between his and Ray Amm's Nortons, but with a record 147.8 km/h lap, Amm hit the lead and won by seven seconds. Both riders were faster than Duke's 1952 race record.

A big dampener on the result was that another Hartwell club member, former Tasmanian Geoff Walker, was killed in the same race. A magnificent headstone was erected to his memory on the island. The accidents continued in the 500 race. After missing the 350 event, Duke fell in the 500. Worse still, Les Graham was killed on the second lap on the fast run down Bray Hill. Kavanagh was initially sixth and had progressed to fourth by lap three, before retiring with yet another engine problem. In the end, despite hefty multi-cylinder opposition from MVs and Gileras, the winner was Ray Amm on a single-cylinder Norton.

The season was a vindication of Duke's move to Gilera. Following Masetti's second title on a Gilera in 1952, Duke took the first of his three successive 500 cm³ titles in 1953. The Italian fours took the first two places in that year's championship, ridden by Duke and Armstrong. Kavanagh was third on a Norton, ahead of Milani on another Gilera.

The big highlight for Kavanagh was the 500 cm³ race at Ulster. It was one of those races that so impressed Duke, and so it should have, for Kavanagh beat Duke with both guile and skill. He was the first Australian to beat Duke in Europe.

Kavanagh and Jack Brett on Nortons had been

faster in practice than Duke and Armstrong on the Gileras, but according to Kavanagh, "We didn't put much store in that. We thought they'd clear out from the start and that we'd be working hard to decide third place."

Kavanagh had a drama on the warm-up lap with a slipping clutch, but another was fitted with just minutes to spare before the start. He was about fourth away, but was second to Duke within half a lap. As the race was nearly 390 kms, and Ken was scheduled to refuel at half-distance, there was no urgency to stop Duke pulling away, which he did at around three seconds a lap.

"I wondered whether Geoff was in trouble, when around lap ten his lead steadied at 23 seconds for two laps," Kavanagh recalled. "It wasn't a big enough lead to cover for possible problems during a pit stop. We're generally looking for a one-minute margin as being comfortable in such conditions.

"I was to refuel on lap 16 and decided I'd make it even better than my usually quick stops. I reckoned, all going well, that I would catch up on Duke on his pit stop, as he would have to take a lot of fuel for the Gilera and so would be stationary longer than I.

Placegetters in the 1953 IoM 350 TT. L to R: fourth-placed Jack Brett (Norton), winner Ray Amm (Norton), runner-up Ken Kavanagh (Norton) and third-placed Fergus Anderson (Guzzi). Norton team boss Joe Craig is at Amm's left.

"Two laps before my stop, I decided to pile on the pressure, just to measure Duke's reaction. In the first lap I picked up two seconds, so I decided to hold my hand, leaving the charge until after the pit stop.

"I screamed into the pit with everything locked on. I threw my goggles away before I reached the Norton pit, so we had one less thing to worry about. The tank cap was open, the hose in. I grabbed the new goggles from the mechanic's shoulder. By this time I was off the machine, had made sure it was in first gear, pulled back against compression and retarded the ignition, ready for the push start.

"I looked into the tank. For some reason it was still half full, so I took on no more than a gallon and I was away, stationary for no more than ten seconds. At the end of the lap, I was signalled that Duke was leading by 45 seconds, but with his pit stop still to do. Then, joy upon joy, the sky darkened. I knew if it rained, I'd have 'The Duke' tossed.

"I held the gap at 45 seconds, waiting for Geoff to stop. Then, on the 19th lap, as I hurtled past the pits at 200 km/h, I saw someone pushing a Gilera to start. I could see the crowd going mad. I kept thinking, 'Am I in the lead or was that only Armstrong?'

"I waited patiently for confirmation at the end of the lap, but at the Hairpin three kilometres before the lap's end, I looked up the approach leg and there, braking, was a Gilera. On the rider's helmet was painted not the shamrock of Reg Armstrong, but the Lancastrian red rose of 'The Duke'. I was really in front!

"As I tore past the pit area again, I was signalled plus seven seconds. The three mechanics and Joe Craig and Artie Bell were jumping up and down. I did everything I knew. I two-wheel slid the Norton through third and top gear bends, I scratched it out of gutters and bounced it off walls. For three laps, I could see Duke coming into the Hairpin and I began to wonder 'Who will fall off first, him or me?'

"Then down came the rain, and I was never so happy. It was in my goggles, my boots, down my neck. It hurt my face but I pressed on harder. The poor old Norton slithered all over the place, but it did the trick. The gap opened up: eight seconds a lap for two laps. Then 'The Duke' gave it away.

"The rain stopped and the roads started to dry, but even though I slowed down a bit I still gained around three seconds a lap until the finish. Then it was all over. Before I knew it I was being congratulated by a host of officials and receiving the victor's laurels from the Prime Minister, Lord Brookeborough." Ken Kavanagh was well pleased with his victory — and on family ground, in Ireland, to be sure.

After Gilera cleaned up in the Swiss Grand Prix, with no chance of winning the world championship, Norton and AJS decided not to compete at Monza, where their speed disadvantage was even more pronounced. That gave Kavanagh a valuable break, for it prompted Moto Guzzi's Fergus Anderson to ask Norton's Joe Craig if Kavanagh could ride a 250 Guzzi at Monza — they wanted all the help they could enlist, to aid their title chase against the German NSUs. This was eventually agreed to, but his presence did not help the team effort very much.

Kavanagh's 250 Guzzi refused to fire at the push start and he lost a lap and a half on the field. Although he then lapped faster than the leader Lorenzetti, he was black-flagged after six laps. "I was quicker there on a 250 Guzzi than I'd ever been on a 350 Norton," Kavanagh recalled. It was a sobering reminder of what Norton riders were up against. But things went better at the next championship meeting, the final for the season on the tight, hilly Montjuich Park circuit at Barcelona. Riding a 250 Guzzi, Kavanagh led the race but was ordered yet again to slow down — to let Lorenzetti win. Kavanagh came in second and Fergus Anderson third on two of five Guzzis racing.

There was no 350 race in Spain, so the Guzzi team used their 350s in the 500 race. In pouring rain, Kavanagh led the field, which included some 500 multis, until his magneto became waterlogged. His team-mate, Fergus Anderson, went on to win, also on a 350.

Ken Kavanagh pushes his Norton to the finish of the Isle of Man 500 TT in 1953, after losing his drive chain.

Before that, Kavanagh had kept busy by racing at Scarborough and, most impressively, at Silverstone. The Gileras romped away at Scarborough, but Silverstone, a circuit Kavanagh didn't like, was very different. Although only team boss, Joe Craig, and Norton chief executive, Gilbert Smith, knew, it was likely to be his last ride on the official Nortons. "Naturally I was keen to do a good job," Kavanagh said, "to finish off the two-and-a-half-year association the same way as I'd started.

"Silverstone's fast and slow corners are good, but the surface was absolutely without grip, owing to its continuous use for car racing over many years. Although Duke was one person who did like it, on his second practice lap he got a full lock slide on the Gilera and was dumped on his face. The Gilera then bounced on the back of his hand, so he was in no shape to race the following day.

"As Ray Amm was still out of action, the works Nortons were for Brett, me and John Storr in the 350 race, with Surtees replacing Storr in the 500. I was untroubled to win both the 350 and 500 preliminary races and the 350 final," Kavanagh said.

However, the 500 was a harder task. "I was slipstreaming Dickie Dale on the Gilera four, which was a thousand revs down on its normal maximum. On the tenth lap, as we banked into Stowe corner at around 145 km/h, the Gilera locked up and went into a slide across the road in a heap. I was brought down, too, but in a flash picked up the bike and was off up the road, playing at scramble racing. By the time I'd regained control, Derek Farrant on an AJS twin was in the lead.

"I toured around for a couple of laps to make sure the Norton was in one piece, then when I decided everything was okay I passed Derek to win. In the 350 race, I broke Duke's record by a second, but in the 500, after the do with Dale, I was more subdued. Even though, I was only 0.2 second outside Surtees' record."

It was after this meeting that the legendary engineering chief of Moto Guzzi and the designer of the V8, Ing Giulio Carcano, offered Kavanagh a full works contract for the 1954 season. Norton and AJS were on the verge of pulling out of racing, so there really was not much to decide — he went to Guzzi. Their light but not especially powerful 350 singles dominated that class, winning five GPs to two each for Norton and AJS. In the sidecar class, the BMW boxer (horizontally opposed) twins were giving the Nortons a hard time. They won three races each but BMW won the championship, the first of an unequalled 14 in succession.

The 500 cm³ class was even tougher on the legendary British marque. Gilera won the first race of the season in France, although a Norton with Ray Amm aboard then won at IoM and Ulster. The cruel twist to that was that rain shortened the Ulster race below the minimum distance required for a world championship race, so it did not count for the championship. But it would not have made much difference — Duke then went on a rampage, winning the next five GPs in a row. Kavanagh was second to him at Spa and second in the final race of the season to Dickie Dale, as he took MV's only 500 win of the season.

But as was usual in those days, there was plenty of riding to be done in other than world championship grands prix. Kavanagh raced and won at Pau, France, in early April. It was his first race as a member of the Moto Guzzi team. Fellow Victorian Keith Campbell was third. Former protégé Bob Mitchell was sixth in the sidecar race.

Then, it was on to the Isle of Man. Further sadness occurred with yet another death, of Laurie Boulter, who was touring IoM with Kavanagh. It happened two days before practice was due to start, when Boulter's attention was diverted and he hit a parked car at 50 km/h.

"Last Lap" Kavanagh had a big schedule in front of him at IoM: 250, 350 and 500 cm³ TTs. He retired from all three. In the 250 he did not even complete a lap before his Guzzi stopped, after refusing to fire until he was second last away. The 350 was better, for a while. The two Guzzis of Anderson and Kavanagh were first and second, with Ray Amm's Norton a few seconds back in third. When Anderson went out, Kavanagh led and then battled with Amm. But Kavanagh's engine expired on lap four. His compensation was a new lap record, an impressive 18 seconds below the previous. The best result for an Australian was by Gordon Laing, who was sixth, while Jack Ahearn was ninth, a second ahead of Maurie Quincey, with Keith Bryen 13th. Kavanagh dropped out of the 500 race after only two laps. The race was run in conditions so foul that it was stopped only two laps later, three short of full race distance. The track was awash with water, and thick clouds loomed over the high points of the treacherous track. Even the winner, Ray Amm on a Norton, crashed.

Then followed the Belgian Grand Prix at Spa; it was a meeting of mixed emotions for Kavanagh. He won the 350 race in which Victorian Gordon Laing was killed. Fergus Anderson was second on a Guzzi, only after Kavanagh had fought so hard with Amm's Norton that its clutch disintegrated. Maurie Quincey was ninth, Ahearn tenth and Keith Campbell 12th. Kavanagh's winning speed was a new record of 163.7 km/h. The 500 was not so simple against the almost unbeatable combination of Duke and Gilera. Kavanagh was kept busy, again with Ray Amm, and then with Louis Martin on a four-cylinder Gilera. But Kavanagh went well to split the two Gileras and take second place.

One of the biggest meetings of the year, the Dutch TT at Assen, was a reversal of Kavanagh's pleasing first and second at Spa. His 250 was no match for the flying NSUs, although he did beat one of them to be the highest placed Guzzi in fourth place. He did not start in the 350, and he retired with handling problems in the 500. The 250 race was won by German Werner Haas, who won the championship, retired from racing and then died in an air accident the following spring.

The Gileras of this era were so good that when Geoff Duke persuaded the factory to take them out of mothballs several years later, to take on the mostly private machinery racing, they were still the bikes to beat. So Duke did not have much trouble winning the Italian 500 GP at Monza. Kavanagh was sixth, just ahead Ray Amm on his Norton. But in the 350 race, Kavanagh was third, just 0.01 of a second behind team-mate Fergus Anderson and Lorenzetti, all on Guzzis.

It was about this time that Anderson, a columnist for *Motor Cycle* magazine in England, as well as being a race rider and then team manager, wrote frankly about "team orders, as they affected me and Kavanagh this season (1954) with Moto Guzzi.

"If you want a first-class example of why the majority of the factory riders think the individual World Championships should be discontinued, then you need only to consider the happenings in the 350 cm^3 class this year as it concerns Ken Kavanagh and me. Months before the Dutch GP, it was decided that to avoid tiring a rider out by running him in three classes at Assen (it is not the riders who think they tire!), Ken would ride the 250 and 500 and that I would ride the 350 and 500.

"Before the Belgian GP, we agreed between ourselves that Ken should be first and I'd be second. I jokingly made the condition that if he won he should not let the factory talk him into riding a 350 in the Dutch. That was exactly what was suggested, but too late. The factory then wanted me to win at Solitude, but I talked them out of that, pointing out that if we could take first and second, we should get 14 points and they would have their eggs in two baskets. However neither of us finished.

"Came the Swiss event and once again the orders were Anderson first, Kavanagh second, and there was no valid argument against this. Then it was hoped I would win again at Monza, with my long-suffering team-mate again, if necessary, waiting for me as he had at Berne (in Switzerland). Ken and I work well together and given the chance, we could share what honours are going without any differences.

"The evil of the present championships is that harmonious working is made virtually impossible," Anderson wrote.

Things have changed a little, in that very few riders now do more than one class. And there are probably fewer team rankings and team orders now than there were then. The difficulty of riding, and particularly sliding, the current bikes, especially the 500s, means rider ability counts more than instructions from the pits. But it does show that Ken Kavanagh could and probably would have won more races, world championship and otherwise, if he had been allowed to race on his merit. Anderson also said in the same story that Kavanagh was often only allowed to win when retirements had left him as the only team member still with a healthy machine.

In May 1955, Kavanagh's constant sparring partner, Ray Amm, was having this first ride for MV Agusta, on a 350 in a non-championship race at Imola. Amm was in second place behind Kavanagh when he crashed on the first lap on a slow corner

Ken Kavanagh rounds the Governor's Bridge hairpin, en route to winning the 1956 IoM 350 TT for Moto Guzzi.

and died of head injuries.

Until Kavanagh's first IoM win, the 350 in 1956, his beat result was second to Ray Amm in 1953. But he gave Guzzi a win, in a time of 2 hrs 57m 29.4 secs, at an average of 144 km/h. It was a brilliantly judged race by Kavanagh, having come through the field after several early leaders retired. His final lap was also his fastest, at an average of 150 km/h.

The IoM competition was traditionally fierce. Englishman Bill Lomas had left AJS to join Guzzi, replacing Fergus Anderson, who had been killed earlier in the season at Floreffe. So Lomas was out to win, although he had John Surtees on an MV to contend with, as well as some treacherously wet roads. Lomas shot off at a tremendous rate, leading from the first lap and increasing his lead from 25 to 31 seconds by the end of the third lap. Then Surtees had a charge, reducing the lead to just 15 seconds. By then Kavanagh was third, 49 seconds behind. He got no message to close up, so he stayed at about that gap until the sixth lap when Lomas's Guzzi expired. Surtees now had to refuel, but Ken had a big tank, enough for 423 kilometres non-stop.

Carcano was timing gaps at Quarter Bridge and passing them on by phone to the pits, while Lomas's dad was near the Gooseneck. On the sixth lap, Kavanagh got to within two seconds of Surtees' MV and must have had a good chance of taking him on the seventh and final lap. But a rushed fuel stop that didn't fully top the tank saw Surtees run out of fuel at Stonebreaker's Hut, 16 kilometres from the finish. So Kavanagh went on to win.

Despite what it must have meant to him, Kavanagh donated the original of that trophy to the Hartwell Motorcycle Club in Melbourne, for its annual Most Outstanding Road Racer award. The trophy has been in good hands. It was first given in 1977 to international Maurie Quincey's son Ray, and has since been awarded to the likes of Paul Lewis, Barry Smith, Steve Trinder, Glenn Middlemiss and Chris Oldfield, all of whom have won an Australian championship.

After being a works rider for Moto Guzzi, and being one of only a few riders to experience perhaps the all-time exotic machine, the 500 cm³ Guzzi V8, Kavanagh fought with them over a cure for handling problems. He wanted a derivation of Norton front forks, but this did not sit too well with the Mandello company. So he left them at the end of 1956, only to have a briefer, more tempestuous time with MV. Kavanagh said, "The only time I rode an MV was at Barcelona, where they didn't want me to ride. So I barrowed Carlo Bandirola's bike, after John Surtees' parents refused to let me use his."

Things got worse for Kavanagh at Imola. "After practice, Domenico Agusta didn't want me to race unless I could guarantee a win. With Geoff Duke, a six times world champion there on a four-cylinder Gilera, I said I couldn't guarantee that, although second should be fairly definite. He offered me £3000 not to ride."

When MV failed to enter Kavanagh for Isle of Man, he then sued them for hindering his career. All of which did not do much for his two-wheel racing ambitions in 1957. So, in 1958, he switched to car racing, in what was to be a two-driver project with Australia's first world motorcycle champion, the 350 champion in 1957 on a Moto Guzzi, Victorian Keith Campbell. But Campbell was delayed getting customs clearance for his car and was killed only a couple of weeks later in a non-championship motorcycle race in France.

Kavanagh went car racing on his own, in some top machinery, a lightweight works 1957 Maserati 250F, ex-Juan Fangio and Harry Schell. Kavanagh bought it in 1958 and raced it for a year in Europe, South America and England. "I went to South America, returned and was sixth at Syracuse. At Aintree, in

Ken Kavanagh recorded Australia's first world championship GP win at Ulster in 1952, on a works Norton.

England, I retired with water pump trouble. And it broke a conrod in practice for the Belgian Grand Prix, so it was a non-starter."

Then came Goodwood in England in 1959. "On a wet track I came spinning into the pits backwards," Kavanagh recalled. "People were injured, and I decided that my car racing career was over."

He returned briefly to motorcycle racing after that, in Europe and Australia, before retiring, aged 36. He had, for around 15 years, done most things on two wheels: speedway, scrambles (now known as motocross), hill climbing and top-level road racing. It is a tribute to his riding that he achieved what he did, without hurting himself, in an era when death and injury were dreadfully common. And he might have won more races but for the system of having a lead rider, pre-race team orders and priorities on race results.

Kavanagh's worst injury was two stitches to his face in 1959. He was riding a 125 Ducati at Imola when its sump plug unscrewed and spilled oil in front of the rear wheel. "I got into a massive tank slapper, sliding about on the oil," Ken said. "It was like skating on ice. When I crashed, my goggles dug into my face. It was the only time I was ever hurt."

Riding that Ducati was part of a Kavanagh plan to import and distribute Ducatis in Australia. The crazy thing is that, if he had achieved that, he would no doubt be better remembered, and something of a hero to the passionate supporters of the marque, than he is now through his racing successes in the world championships.

With the withdrawal of most of the Continental factories from racing at the end of 1957, and after his 1958 car-racing stint, in 1959 Kavanagh was back where he started — on a 500 Norton. But, he was also prepared to try something different, and rode a 125. The 125 class that year was hotly contested, with East German MZ, Italy's MV Agusta, and Honda all competing. Swiss rider Luigi Taveri and several other notables including Mike Hailwood, were on Ducatis. Of seven races in that year's 125 cm^3 world championship, Kavanagh was fourth, and the second of four Ducatis at Ulster in a race won by Hailwood. It was Ken's best Ducati result. Rhodesian Gary Hocking and East German Ernst Degner were second and third on MZs. He had two fifth places, at Spa in Belgium and Kristianstad in Sweden, and was sixth at Assen. Kavanagh's 500 cm^3

Ken Kavanagh won the 1955 Dutch 350 GP on a Moto Guzzi, but was out of luck in the IoM event (pictured).

season was not as good. He finished in the top six only once, at Hockenheim where he was fourth, behind fellow Australian Bob Brown who placed third.

Kavanagh had asked Ducati to develop a twin overhead camshaft 250 twin — virtually two 125 singles grafted together. He had persuaded Castrol to put some money into the project, and he added a not insubstantial £2000 of his own money. But the Castrol/Kavanagh project faded when millionaire motorcycle dealer Stan Hailwood, father of Mike, started contributing considerably bigger lumps of money to the Italian factory.

Kavanagh now left Europe for Australia in late November, to race over the 1959-1960 Christmas and New Year period. He took with him a brace of bikes: 125 and 250 Ducatis, 350 and 500 Nortons. He had last raced at home in the summer of 1951-1952 as a Norton factory rider.

By now he was rumoured to be earning in the region of £5000 annually, as Australia's most successful and highest paid racing motorcyclist.

The 1959 IoM 125 TT was held on the Clypse Course Kavanagh is pictured on a works 'desmo' Ducati. Ken was now 35 years old and considering retirement.

He was entered for Phillip Island on all four bikes, and after eight years in Europe he was eagerly sought for radio and television interviews. Race previews of the time suggested that the main opposition for Kavanagh "will come from Australia's 1959 IoM reps fresh from a successful season of racing in England and the Continent — Eric Hinton, Tom Phillis and Ron Miles."

In ideal weather, Kavanagh made a good start and, although he was briefly overtaken by Eric Hinton he went on to win the 125 race. It was the only race in which he finished. In the Senior "A" Kavanagh slowed with faulty contact breaker. At Fishermans Bend, in a two-day combined car and motorcycle meeting for the Victorian TT, Kavanagh won two titles on the first of two days of racing. And a big crowd on the second day saw his 223cm^3 Ducati victorious. A little later, at the Australian Grand Prix at Longford in Tasmania, Kavanagh also rode his 125 Ducati to victory, while Eric Hinton on Ken's 250 Ducati also won.

By 1960 the Japanese, headed by Honda, were active in international racing following their growing success in road bikes and the decline of the British industry. It didn't suit Kavanagh. "Australia hadn't signed a peace treaty with Japan when I left

Eric Hinton and Ken Kavanagh in the pits at Brno, 1959. Hinton helped Kavanagh with his Nortons that season.

in 1951, so we were technically still at war. I wasn't interested in racing for them, so I retired."

A further reason for his retirement from a brilliantly successful career as a works rider for Norton, Moto Guzzi, MV Agusta and Ducati was that he had been through the full horror of Bob Brown's death. He was in the pits at the Solitude road circuit outside Stuttgart, Germany, when Brown failed to come around. Ken visited him in hospital, heard the doctors describe the hopelessness of his condition to Bob's wife, and then helped relatives organise affairs, including shipping the body back to Australia.

Kavanagh had seen the same sort of thing with Ray Amm. As well Dave Bennett was gone, Derek Ennett was killed on the last lap of the Ulster GP on Ken's bike, and Kavanagh was uncomfortably close to both Laurie Boulter and Harry Hinton Jnr when both were killed in separate incidents.

Death and serious injury were fairly common occurrences in those days, so riders were fairly good at blotting the risks from their minds. If they were no good at being cold and dispassionate about it, they did not last long themselves. But for someone like Kavanagh, whose record was better than most at staying upright, such constant tragedies must have weighed heavily. So, at 36 years of age, one of Australia's better achievers at motorcycle racing retired.

Kavanagh's next trip back to Australia, from the northern Italian town of Bergamo that has been his home since 1960, was in 1981. "It was my 30th year of being away, my mother's 80th birthday and the 50th anniversary of the Hartwell Club, so I thought it was a good time to come back and have a look," Kavanagh recalled. Except for a fuss by Hartwell Club, and an appearance at Winton circuit, it was a fairly low-key visit.

It is a curious coincidence that another Australian motorcycle racer and now race engineer, former Sydneysider Kel Carruthers, lives within 15 kilometres of Kavanagh in another part of Bergamo. Carruthers is based there six months of the year, living in a motor home at the back of Giacomo Agostini's Marlboro Yamaha workshops, fettling bikes during the world championship season. Not only had these two Australians not met during the first ten years they had lived in the same city, they had not even spoken on the phone. In 1988 they got together for the first time, and Kavanagh went to visit Carruthers in his workshop.

Kavanagh has long been away from the race business. Although he was remarkably successful, many aspects of his sporting, business and personal

First place, Spa-Francorchamps, 1954, for Moto Guzzi.

life have been clouded by problems and disappointments. The short, stocky man now living in an apartment with a few mementos of a safe and winning racing career around the lounge room, running a dry-cleaning business, while driving around in an old Citroen, in a sense has shielded himself from his setbacks. He has long since abandoned Australia — or perhaps it abandoned him — but he has been compensated with a typically warm Italian family of three children. Another son, Peter Tighe, of his first marriage, to whom he has spoken on the phone but never met, lives in Australia.

Strangely, nearby, another world motorcycle hero of the 1950s lives out his days, much like Kavanagh, far from the fame and glory that was once a large part of his life.

Umberto Masetti, the second ever world 500 cm^3 champion in 1950, pumps petrol in an Agip station back down the autostrada. "What an end," Kavanagh said ruefully, "for a world champion, pumping petrol at a service station. But then I iron trousers in a dry-cleaning shop. I suppose there's not much difference."

There was a poignancy in his voice that was, somehow, not surprising. He was a man who gave his all, and now there are few people left who really know just what he achieved.

55

KEITH CAMPBELL

CHAPTER 4

It is said talent only takes you so far in sport. Getting to the top also requires determination, application, intelligence and a willingness to make sacrifices. Keith Campbell, Australia's first world motorcycle road-racing champion, set out unaccompanied to the Isle of Man before his 20th birthday. That was in 1951. He returned to Europe in 1952 and worked for another four years to earn a factory ride, after fighting injury, mechanical woes, the usual privateer's financial troubles and even a six-month suspension for taking part in a riders' strike.

Campbell reached the top rung with a works Moto Guzzi ride at the end of 1956, and won the world 350 title in 1957. Then a joint decision by three Italian factories took away the 25-year-old Melburnian's ladder. Moto Guzzi, along with world 500 champion manufacturer Gilera and 125/250 champion FB Mondial, withdrew from grand prix racing. Campbell was the first world motorcycle road-racing champion from outside Europe, and Australia's first world champion in any form of tarmac motor racing. He was two years ahead of car racing's Jack Brabham.

Keith was the youngest post-war Australian road-racer ever to head unaccompanied to Europe, and he still holds the record as Australia's youngest world motorcycle road-racing champion. Keith Campbell in 1956-1957 displayed two key attributes which Kel Carruthers had 12 years later and Wayne Gardner had in the build-up to his championship year. When Campbell was offered a works machine in July 1956, he made best use of the opportunity. And when, in mid-1957, he inherited leadership of the Moto Guzzi team, after injuries to two team-mates, he was equal to the challenge.

Keith started in five rounds of the 1957 world 350 championship. He retired from the first with gear-selection problems, finished second to an acknowledged great TT rider (Scotland's Bob McIntyre) at the Isle of Man, beat McIntyre to win the Dutch TT at Assen, and won the Belgian and Ulster Grands Prix to clinch the championship with one round remaining. Campbell also put in some record laps on arguably the most exotic grand prix 500 cm^3 racer of all time, the Moto Guzzi V8. But reliability problems with the V8 meant his only finish in the 500 championship in 1957 was at the Isle of Man on a Guzzi single.

Geoff Duke and John Surtees, winners of four world 500 titles each in the decade 1951-1960, both reckon the Guzzi V8 would have been the 500 to beat if Guzzi had continued to develop and race it in 1958. News of the Italian teams' withdrawal broke late in September 1957, three weeks after the final round of the world championships and eight days after Campbell's wedding on the Isle of Man. Campbell, Guzzi team-mate Keith Bryen, and Gilera rider Bob Brown (the latter two from Sydney) had lost jobs they'd slogged hard for in Europe.

Keith Campbell and his new Manx bride Geraldine spent the summer of 1957-1958 in Australia. He talked with elder brother George about doing one more race season in Europe, then retiring and investing his 1958 earnings in Melbourne real estate. Campbell and Brown returned to Europe in 1958 as private entrants, riding British single-cylinder machines. They couldn't hope to win grands prix against the works four-cylinder MV Agustas but as proven front-line riders they could expect top-rank starting money in the international races. Campbell was a crowd hero and leading drawcard at non-championship meetings in France. Keith Bryen, meanwhile retired from racing and remained in Sydney, where he still lives.

After three rounds of the 1958 world 350 championship Campbell was third on the points table. He was the best-placed private entrant, behind MV Agusta pair John Surtees and John Hartle, thanks to third placings in the Belgian and Dutch GPs. Keith went one better in the Belgian 500 GP. Riding before 150,000 people, he split the MV pair and finished second, having averaged 182 km/h. British newspaper *The Motor Cycle* said of the two results in Belgium: "No rider came through the meeting with more glory than did Keith Campbell ... the Commonwealth may be proud of a rider whose skill is so pre-eminent, whether factory-backed or not."

But Keith never made round four of the championships. He went to a French international meeting on a tight street circuit at Cadours, near Toulon, on Sunday, July 13, won the 350 event, then crashed to his death after striking an oil patch on the first lap of the 500 race. The oil had been dropped during the intervening sidecar race. Keith Campbell was 26. He had proved, in an all-too-short career, that he was a man of considerable determination.

Keith was an aggressive rider — people who were not didn't become champions. On a couple of occasions he passed riders on the grass verge. But Keith Campbell's Australian international racing contemporaries remember him as a good bloke off the track — likeable, sincere and with a keen, dry sense of humour. Those close to Keith reckon he was a bit of a comic — in fact some of his quips would remind enthusiasts from the 1970s of Graeme Crosby, another very successful Antipodean road racer.

George Campbell reckons his brother's laid-back style was the key to his popularity. "Keith was a nice guy — the sort of fellow who had no enemies and smiled even when things were bad. He was relaxed and never got huffy."

Another part of Keith's charm was a combination of being outwardly disorganised, so he was one of

Keith Campbell receives his trophy for second place in the 1957 IoM 350 TT — his best finish on the Island.

the boys, but inwardly organised, so he was one of the top boys. He was criticised by some internationals because of the scruffy appearance of his bikes and riding gear. But the priority was how the machinery performed, not how it looked. "First things first," Keith used to say.

Keith Campbell may well be better remembered in Europe than in his own country. For example, he won more Swedish Grands Prix than Australian championships. His world championship was big news in Australian motorcycling, but he received little "ink" in the general media until he was killed. Australian television was still in nappies in 1957 and Keith's sister-in-law recalls he appeared just once on the box. Even the world championship grand prix record books don't tell the full Campbell story. Keith won three world championship 350 grands prix in 1957: the Dutch, Belgian and Ulster. He won three Swedish GPs in 1956-1957 (the 350 twice and the 500 in 1957), but that event was not made a world championship round until 1958. In 1955 Campbell won the 350 Finnish and 500 Czech GPs. Those events were not included in the world titles until 1962 and 1965 respectively.

But it wasn't just the grands prix where Campbell shone. By 1956 Keith was a leading private entrant. In 1954 and 1956 he owned three Nortons, so he had the luxury of a spare machine. The reason Campbell could afford £1400 sterling worth of racing machinery, even when he was under suspension from grand prix racing, was his success rate in international meetings.

Keith was a crowd hero at the many non-championship race meetings in France and Scandinavia, meetings which were bread and butter to privateers. He made his money by entering these meetings, often in preference to racing for minimal start money in world championship events. Some riders would enter a couple of grands prix events a season just to stock up on oils and auxiliary parts from the trade representatives. Campbell as a private entrant won on now-forgotten street circuits like Finland's Runsala and Tampere (where the road surface varied from tarmac and cobblestones to gravel), Sweden's Hedemora, Belgium's Seraing, Holland's Tubbergen, and the French circuits of Agen, Albi, Bourg-en-Bresse, Clermont-Ferrand, Moulin and Vesoul.

Bob Mitchell, the Australian who finished fourth in the 1956 world sidecar championship, says Keith Campbell, was the greatest rider he ever saw on the poor and dangerous surfaces encountered at these circuits, such as diesel-soaked tar, slippery cobblestones, ice and snow.

"Keith was a great rider, but nobody knows how

good — he received little recognition in Australia. He was a lovely guy and a real comic. We called him Shambles Campbells, for his scruffy-looking equipment, or Tweetie, after the cartoon character Tweetie Pie, because he always wore an old yellow jumper under his leathers," Bob said.

Mitchell provided a graphic description of Campbell in early privateer mode: "Keith would arrive at a circuit two or three days later than everybody else, because he'd been up in Scandinavia at one of their little meetings. One year he travelled in a furniture van, another year he drove a big black American Cadillac — with his bikes stacked one on top of another on a trailer. The bikes would be covered in mud from the Scandinavian tracks, which were half gravel.

"We Australians would be working away, and Keith would glide up in his Yank Tank, nose in the air. He'd pull down the window, and ask: 'Excuse me, chaps, wonder if you'd tell me what they're paying for first place here?'

"When it came to the race, Keith might have trouble starting his bike. But once he got cracking, he'd come from behind and go through them," Mitchell said. "I'll give you an example from 1954 at St Wendel, a little street circuit in Germany. The event was called the Grand Prix of the Saarland. There was a difficult corner just near the pits. The road came under a railway bridge and curled into a fairly tight uphill left-hander. The road surface was highly polished, rounded cobblestone, and it was raining!

"The starting line was about a kilometre away from the pits. We heard the roar of the massed start. The PA microphone was near the line, and after the field left we heard one Norton still trying to start. 'Poomp ... poomp-poomp ... poomp-poomp-poomp. Poomp-pa-pa-p-p-ppppp.' That was Campbell. Then the field arrived at the pit corner, all on the tight line, many riders with their feet down, feeling their way. Around the corner they went and up the hill.

"Half a minute later comes the sound of one Norton. 'Vam vam-vam' down through the gears. Under the bridge comes Campbell. Power on and sliding. He's not on the tight line, he's going faster in the middle of the road. He slides the bike right out to the gutter, which he uses to knock the bike into line to go up the hill! And he won. Just brilliant," Mitchell said.

Eric Hinton, another of Keith's contemporaries, said Campbell was a very quick rider when he clicked. "Keith was a top private entrant. Riding in all those little meetings meant he was probably sitting back on a hotel balcony in France sipping champagne when some of the grands prix were on," Eric said. "His tatty riding gear was partly because he was superstitious — like a lot of riders — about falling off if he wore new riding gear. The first time Keith rode the Guzzi V8 one of his old boots fell apart and came off. You can imagine what Carcano (the designer) thought. He's developing this incredible bike and the bloke riding it doesn't want to wear new boots!"

Keith Campbell's grandfather had migrated from Scotland. His parents grew up and met in Mildura, but moved to Melbourne after they married. His father, Evelyn, had no trade, so he bought a furniture removal van. They lived in inner-suburban Prahran and had two sons. Keith was born during the Depression on October 2, 1931.

George Campbell, three years Keith's senior, reckons the way he and Keith were brought up gave them their determination. "We didn't have much," he said, "so we worked harder to win. That was the way we both operated. And when it came to racing we were enthusiasts, racing for the love of it. You had to be an enthusiast to risk your life for little silver cups."

Keith left school at 14 in 1945 and was apprenticed as a mechanic in Melbourne's motorcycling heart — Elizabeth Street. Later, when he set his mind on motorcycle racing, he quit the trade and took a job as a welder with appliance manufacturer Electrolux, working for piece rates. Evelyn Campbell was disappointed with Keith's decision to quit an apprenticeship mid-stream. But he later gave his son a couple of hundred pounds towards his international career.

George Campbell, who later became an architect, started racing in his late teens and introduced his brother to the sport, taking him to races as mechanic/helper before he was old enough to hold a licence. Indeed, George recalls racing an ex-army Royal Enfield which Keith bought before he had a licence.

Keith would, according to his brother, have a shot at anything. He entered his first open race meeting at 17, in June 1948. Keith rode his solid-frame AJS 500 to the Moroney's Hill scramble, removed the headlamp and road number plates, raced (and scored one third placing), re-fitted the accessories and rode home. But, despite two race wins at later meetings, Keith soon decided scrambling was the proverbial mug's game. Over the summer of 1948-1949 he rode his AJS at Victoria Park, Ballarat, in the loose-surface road-race at Rowville and at Fishermans Bend. His best finish was a fourth in the open 500 event at Rowville.

Inspired by road racing, Keith bought a new Velocette KTT 350. He took the Velocette to Bathurst for the Easter 1949 races and crashed trying to stay with Harry Hinton and Lloyd Hirst through the Mountain. That crash, and a couple more at Nurioopta in South Australia, made 18-year-old Campbell think more deeply about his riding. He was trying to outride his experience. Around this time Keith also thought about tuning his own machine. He made his own cams for the Velo, using a small bench grinder. The first set had so much overlap it caused blow-back through the carburettor. But he had to learn somehow.

Campbell rode steadily at Bathurst in 1950, then went home to Victoria and won the 350 race at Darley. After that win he sold his first KTT Velo to his brother and bought a better one from gifted South Australian rider/tuner Les Diener.

The Campbell brothers continued road racing in South Australia, Victoria and New South Wales though 1950-1951. At the Darley races in November 1950, for example, Keith was a close second in the 350 race to fellow Velocette rider Maurie Quincey, while George Campbell won the Clubman's race on a Matchless. Keith had more success at the Ballarat airstrip races, but crashed and sustained a leg injury on some loose gravel at Victoria Park, Ballarat, on New Year's Day 1951. He was sidelined until Easter.

The Easter Bathurst meeting of 1951 may well have been a landmark for Keith Campbell as a road racer. The meeting attracted the best field of local riders since the war, on the country's most testing circuit. Eric McPherson was back from three years in Europe, Harry Hinton was riding at Mount Panorama before heading off to the Isle of Man TT, and Victoria's new hot-shot Maurie Quincey was riding at Bathurst for the first time. Other leading entrants who would later race in Europe included Jack Ahearn, Ernie Ring, Keith Bryen and Jack Forrest.

Campbell finished fifth in the 130 km NSW 350 TT, behind Quincey, Ring, Hinton and Bryen, and fourth (on his Velocette 350) in the 160 km 500 TT, behind Hinton, Forrest and Laurie Hayes. One race report of the meeting refers to Campbell as "the youngest of our brightest stars", another included him in a list of eight riders who would hold their own in international competition. The goal of every ambitious Commonwealth road racer of Campbell's day was to compete in the Isle of Man. Keith was ambitious. Before the Easter meeting he had booked

Preparation for the 1951 Manx GP. Harry Hinton, who was recovering from his 350 TT race crash, gives young Campbell some pointers.

60

his passage to England for a planned three-year stay.

On April 18, 1951, a few months short of his 20th birthday, he and the Velocette left Port Melbourne on the liner *Ormonde* for England. Keith's mates in Melbourne's Olympic Motorcycle Club gave him a shaving set as a farewell gift. It was an in-joke, because young Campbell reckoned at the time he only needed to shave once a month.

Ten years earlier a lot of fit, fresh-faced young men were on ships bound for England and war. But it was a novel idea in 1951 for a teenager with £30 in his pocket to strike out on his own, aiming to race for two or three years on the other side of the world.

Campbell played smart for his Isle of Man debut. He lacked the experience required for the International TT races, so he entered the Manx Grand Prix, a meeting held each September on the 61 km Isle of Man course for riders who had not competed in the TT or international grand prix events. Keith was the first Australian to contest this event. His April departure meant he was in the Isle of Man in time to see Geoff Duke win the 1951 350 and 500 TT races on works Nortons.

Harry Hinton, who was seriously injured during that meeting, spent part of his convalescence teaching Campbell the course. This was no small help, because riding the Isle of Man was all about circuit knowledge. By the Wednesday of Manx GP practice week Campbell was fourth on the 350 practice leaderboard, despite foul weather conditions. Next day he was second fastest. Not bad for a newcomer on a home-tuned 1948-model Velocette, let alone the youngest rider in the event.

Campbell held third position in the 1951 Manx 350 GP at half distance. But two-thirds of the way through the next lap, on the Mountain section, he misjudged a 140 km/h corner in thick fog and crashed off the road into a fence.

Keith was concussed, and sustained a broken thumb and lacerations to his face. He spent two months in hospital then packed up his battered Velocette and sailed home. Campbell years later told British journalist Vic Willoughby he left England because he felt shy!

Back in Melbourne Campbell worked 65 hours a week, panel beating and welding, to save for a second trip to the Manx Grand Prix. He took two machines — his Velocette 350 and a second-hand Norton 500 which his father helped finance. Two of his motorcycling mates from Melbourne, Bob Edmonds and Len Tinker, also went.

K. R. Campbell was fourth at the mid-way stage of the 1952 Manx 350 GP, before a tardy refuelling stop dropped him to sixth. The Velocette's magneto gave trouble in the second half of the race, so he could not regain the places lost. Bob McIntyre, a later rival for the world championship, won the race.

Keith also had trouble with the Norton in the 500

Campbell, aged 19, leaps Ballaugh Bridge on his Velocette KTT 350 during the 1951 Manx GP. He crashed later in the race after missing a corner in thick fog.

race. "It just about fell to bits," he reported. "Both the petrol and oil tanks split and the rear springs broke, so the machine was almost uncontrollable from the second lap onwards." But with characteristic determination he coaxed the bike home in 14th position.

There was no return fare to Melbourne this time. Campbell spent the winter working on the Norton production line with Melbourne clubmate Gordon Laing, who'd crashed and broken his leg while practising for the 1952 TT. The bleak winter in Birmingham was an experience Campbell would sooner have forgotten. He hated the cold, and thereafter welcomed each New Year in Australia, even though it meant finding the fare and watching ocean crawl past for 12 weeks each year.

Campbell and Laing joined the Continental Circus in 1953. They travelled in an ex-RAF four-wheel-drive Ford Blitz ambulance. It looked a sight — "a butterbox on huge doughnut tyres," according to Keith Bryen. "They could only just fit in four bikes (Keith's Velocette and Norton, and Gordon's two Nortons), so they slept on a board above the bikes. Whenever you opened the back doors, washing basins, oil tins, clothes, spare parts and tyres fell out," Bryen said.

Campbell's debut season with the circus was more enjoyable than his first Isle of Man efforts. He scored a 350/500 double at Vesoul in France, won on the Norton 500 at Tubbergen (Holland) and Agen in

France, and took the Velocette 350 to a victory at Seraing and a second place at Circuit des Frontier (both in Belgium).

Keith Bryen recalls the time Campbell crashed mid-season and injured his back. A local hospital put him in plaster from neck to groin. That was no good for Campbell — he'd been offered a start in the following Saturday's Dutch TT and he needed the money.

"Keith sat on the Velocette in the Assen paddock and tried to reach the handlebars. He hacksawed away bits of the plaster until he could. The next morning I found the remains of a cast behind the toilets," Bryen said. Campbell raced at Assen and one week later finished 12th in the Belgian 350 Grand Prix.

At the end of the season Keith freighted his now-venerable bikes home to Melbourne and sold them. Four weeks later he was back on a ship bound for England, where he'd ordered two new "short-stroke" Manx Nortons. A typical privateer's short-stroke 350 Manx produced 25 kW at 7000 rpm, and the 500 some 34 kW at 6500 rpm. They weighed a hefty 142 kg, because they were designed for the rigours of the Isle of Man course.

Campbell's efforts in 1954 resulted in elation, pain and heartbreak. He started the year with two Nortons and his Velocette. Keith converted the Velo to a 250 and rode it to third place at Pau, in France, behind new works Guzzi rider Ken Kavanagh. Keith then duelled with diminutive Swiss rider Luigi Taveri in the 350 event. The next time Campbell and Taveri contested a meeting, at Clermont-Ferrand, they scored a victory each. Taveri became a works MV rider within 12 months and later won three world titles with Honda.

Keith's successes continued at St Wendel, where he scored a win and a third placing. By this stage he'd swapped his Velocette for a second Norton 350, which became a spare bike — a real luxury for a private entrant. Campbell had some teething troubles with his new Nortons. Then, at the Isle of Man, he fell during a practice session and broke bones in his left hand. Another rider had crashed and oil had leaked from his machine onto the road, bringing the Australian unstuck. Keith was once more in Nobles Hospital at Douglas. He missed the TT and the Ulster Grand Prix. Three weeks and two major meetings had passed without him earning a penny.

By the Belgian Grand Prix, early in July, Keith was prepared to risk riding with his hand in plaster. He repeated his 1953 result, finishing 12th in the 350 GP. Immediately after the race Campbell learned that his 1953 travelling mate, Gordon Laing, had been killed in a crash on the second lap, after rain hit one side of the 14 km course. But Campbell and compatriots Ken Kavanagh, Jack Ahearn and Maurie Quincey still had the 500 race to contest.

Whatever Campbell's feelings going into the 1954 Belgian 500 GP, the race was a breakthrough in his career. He finished fifth on his private Norton single, behind two works Gilera fours, Kavanagh's works Guzzi and McIntyre's works AJS. And that was with one wrist in plaster.

Successes in international events in the second half of the season boosted Campbell's race earnings. By season's end he had added a second successive double victory at Vesoul, and third places at Mestre (Italy) and Gijon (Spain) to his "bag" for the season.

Keith sailed home for the southern summer with his motorbikes. He wanted to rebuild them before the New Year, when world 500 champion Geoff Duke would race the locals on his works Gilera 500 four. Campbell closed 1954 with a Boxing Day double victory and new lap record at his parents' old home town, Mildura. Six days later he won the Victorian 500 GP at Victoria Park, Ballarat, from Bob Brown.

Keith's first home-ground clash with Geoff Duke was on January 15, 1955 at Gawler airstrip in South Australia. Duke still remembers this race, for three reasons: the circuit was two centimetres deep in gravel ("which didn't do the Gilera's engine much good"), it was so hot some of the locals suffered heat exhaustion, and Keith Campbell led him for half the 500 race — until Keith's gear lever broke. Campbell did, however, win the 350 race from Roger Barker. The following weekend (Australia Day) at the Army's Bandiana base, near Albury, Campbell was pipped in the Duke-chaser stakes by Maurie Quincey.

The standard of Keith Campbell's performances in Europe in 1955 can be judged by the results he added to his letterhead at the end of the season. The only non-first placing was his superb third in the Belgian 350 GP.

Keith won eight international races, including the non-championship Finnish 350 and Czech 500 GPs. But his third place at the Belgian GP was the prized result because factory talent scouts seemed to regard results at Assen and Spa-Francorchamps most highly. Campbell was the only private entrant in the top six of the 350 race at Spa. His Norton split a bunch of works Guzzi singles and three-cylinder two-stroke German DKWs, two of the most innovative machines of the 1950s. Honda borrowed ideas from the DKW in 1982!

He was now "knocking on the door" for a factory ride. But the sport's ruling clique had other ideas. During the Dutch GP, held four weeks after Spa, a group of riders took strike action over the miserly start money offered to private entrants. Australian riders Keith Campbell, Jack Ahearn, Bob Brown and Tony McAlpine, along with New Zealand's John Hemplemann and Chris Stormont and reigning

KEITH BRYEN Guzzi Teammate

Keith Bryen must have wanted to pinch himself at times during 1957. In one season the then 30-year-old Sydneysider rode former works Nortons, works AMC (AJS/Matchless) machines at the Isle of Man and works Moto Guzzis in three grands prix. He was fourth in the world 350 championship.

But the dream run ended abruptly when Moto Guzzi withdrew from grand prix racing in September 1957. Bryen had been called into the team to support Keith Campbell at the Belgian, Ulster and Italian 350 GPs.

Keith and Gwen Bryen flew home to Sydney for the summer. A letter from Moto Guzzi arrived one month later informing Keith of its decision. He was shattered and retired from racing.

Keith Bryen grew up on his father's poultry farm at Wetherill Park, in Sydney's west. The racing bug bit in 1947, when Keith was 20. It was almost inevitable. Keith's mates all owned bikes. Together they founded the Merrylands Motorcycle Club.

Over the next few years he raced a Norton International 500, two BSA Gold Stars, an AJS 7R 350 and a Velocette KTT 350. Then in 1953 he sold up everything, ordered two Manx Nortons through Hazell and Moore, and sailed off to England. "I did the 1953 Isle of Man TT and the remainder of the European season, travelling with Rhodesian Ray Amm, who was a works Norton rider," Keith said. At the end of that eventful year he came home on the P&O liner *Mooltan*, meeting his future wife Gwen on board.

Keith Bryen sold his Nortons in Sydney, but couldn't settle down to a regular job. In March 1954, two weeks into a new job working on heavy machinery, he literally threw down his spanner and announced he was going back to England. Fiancee Gwen would follow, if Keith's season went well.

Bryen collected two new "short-stroke" Nortons in Birmingham and headed for the Isle of Man. Keith's new 350 broke down in the 350 TT, but he placed 11th in the 500 TT. The next meeting was the Ulster Grand Prix. Keith crashed on the first afternoon of practice, breaking his collarbone badly.

He came home, married Gwen, bought a house and tried to live without racing. It didn't work. He went half share in a Manx Norton with Barry Hodgkinson and then he co-rode a Triumph Thunderbird to a class win in the 1955 24-Hour bike race at Mount Druitt.

Then it was off to Europe once more. Bryen rode at Silverstone, St Wendel, Floreffe, Hockenheim and Chimay before the 1956 Isle of Man TT. Keith's best results to that point were a couple of sixth placings at Hockenheim and Chimay. He was 11th in the Isle of Man 350 TT and retired from the 500 TT with clutch trouble.

Keith was still running his Nortons without streamlining, and still having problems with performance and reliability. But the results started to come: fourth in the Dutch 500 TT, second in the East German 500 GP, first in the 500 race at Clermont-Ferrand and second in the 350 event.

But Bryen's 1956 season ended during the 500 race at Tampere.

"A novice rider cut straight across my path when I was flat out in top gear around a big double-apex sweeper. My bike hit a tree 15 feet above the ground. It was wrecked. I slid along the cobblestones. The Finns picked me up, threw me on a make-shift stretcher, then ran along the cobblestones, bouncing me up and down. The nursing staff at the hospital seemed to consist of the patients who could walk! They X-rayed my shoulder. I didn't find the broken ribs until later," Keith said.

Unfortunately Bryen's 1957 began the way 1956 ended, with a crash. Geoff Duke fell on the second lap of the Imola Gold Cup race. Keith cannoned into Duke's horizontal Gilera and fractured his big toe. Duke arranged for the parts to repair Bryen's Norton. And Keith cut away the plaster on his foot with tinsnips to resume racing two weeks later.

Bryen's fairytale run began in the Dutch Grand Prix. He finished fifth in the 350 race and sixth in the 500 on his streamlined Nortons. Two works Moto Guzzi riders, Bill Lomas and Dickie Dale, were injured during the meeting. Their misfortune led to Bryen's works Guzzi rides.

His first factory ride was at the Belgian GP. Bryen came third to old friend and new team-mate Keith Campbell in the 350, and placed second in the 500 race. Bryen waited a fortnight for the next communication with Moto Guzzi, and competed at the non-championship Swedish GP and Norisring international while he waited.

"After Norisring I visited the Moto Guzzi factory, by Lake Como. They booked me to ride the Ulster and Italian GPs, arranged my expenses for those meetings, and matched the starting money I was due to receive for the meetings I would miss — Avus and Villafranche," Bryen said.

At Ulster, Bryen was second to Keith Campbell in the 350 event. But at Monza an ill-handling bike forced his retirement. Bryen didn't know it at the time, but it was the end of his race career. Moto Guzzi retired from racing in September 1957, so Keith Bryen followed the firm out. He became a serviceman at Victa Mowers until retiring in November, 1987.

world 500 champion Geoff Duke, did one lap of the 350 GP and pulled into the pits.

The Dutch Motorcycle Federation, organiser of this financial bonanza of a race meeting, wanted the riders suspended. And at the end of the season the sport's governing body, composed of national federations, backed them. The British Commonwealth riders involved received the longest suspensions. They were forced out of international racing from January 1 until July 1 1956 — the day after the 1956 Dutch GP. The affair probably delayed Campbell's elevation into the works ranks by half a season.

Keith spent a month of the suspension period in Melbourne, where he made up full streamlinings for his 1956 mounts, which he later collected in England. Moto Guzzi teamsters Bill Lomas and Dickie Dale did a race tour of Australia that summer. Keith raced against them at the Boxing Day Mildura meeting, then sat on the sidelines until his departure for Europe on February 1. He collected his new Nortons in Birmingham late in April, along with European debutant and fellow Australian Eric Hinton. Campbell bought two new 350s and a 500. The pair drove straight to St Wendel in Germany in Campbell's 1952 Cadillac, with his five-bike trailer fully loaded.

Campbell had in part circumvented the suspension by obtaining a "non-classic" licence. He could ride at meetings such as St Wendel, but not grands prix. These races gave Keith his cash flow. The St Wendel meeting also indicated that his bikes needed some attention, because not all new Manx Nortons were created equal. Keith finished second to Eric in the 350 race at St Wendel, and later complained to Norton that his new machine was markedly slower than the sister model sold to Hinton.

By July 1956, when Campbell regained his grand prix licence, his bikes were competitive and his riding was sharp. Just how sharp became clear on July 15 at Sweden's fast 7.3 km Hedemora circuit, against a field which included three works Nortons and three works AJS machines. Riding his self-tuned Norton with his self-built aluminium streamlining, Keith won the non-championship 25-lap Swedish 350 GP, beating John Hartle's works Norton by one minute. Eric Hinton was third. Geoff Duke won the 500 race on the works Gilera, but Campbell again embarrassed the British works teams by finishing second.

Campbell had arrived. His talent had at last secured him a works ride. Within a fortnight he was astride a works Moto Guzzi 350 on the starting grid at Senigallia, a medium-length road circuit on the Italian Adriatic coast.

The Moto Guzzi team expected to take the first three placings on this hot, dusty Sunday afternoon. The suggestion put to guest rider Campbell, and works regulars Ken Kavanagh and Dickie Dale, was that they should race for the first six laps, then hold station until the finish. Keith had worked five years for this chance. Even a poor start, due to his lack of familiarity with the Guzzi's coil ignition, wasn't going to spoil it. He took the lead on lap four and made sure he stayed there.

Guzzi hired Campbell again for the Italian Grand Prix at Monza in September. He qualified on the front row for the 350 event, between fellow Guzzi riders Bill Lomas (who'd already clinched the world 350 championship) and Dale. But Campbell's bike developed mechanical trouble four laps into the race. Lomas crashed later in the 350 race and broke his wrist. So Guzzi race engineer Guilio Carcano took a chance and gave Lomas's V8 machine to Campbell for the 500 GP.

Inexperience with Carcano's mechanical marvel meant Campbell again had trouble starting. By the time the V8 fired he was breathing hard and had given the leading Gileras of Duke and company nearly one lap's start. Campbell wasn't fussed. The race distance was 200 kilometres (35 laps) and Keith wanted to impress at the spiritual home of Italian racing. He was soon lapping — on an unfamiliar bike — at the same pace as the leaders. In five laps Keith was tenth. By lap seven, when the Guzzi broke its crankshaft, he was seventh.

Keith celebrated his 25th birthday in October 1956 by signing a works contract with Moto Guzzi. He had entered a new world. Moto Guzzi had the reputation of the factory which cared most for its riders, according to Keith Bryen.

"They looked after you, not the bike, if you crashed. And if you broke a bone they'd put you in a top-class clinic in Italy. The whole operation was impressive — it was a self-contained and aggressive company. Guzzi had a housing estate for the workers, its own power generating equipment and a wind tunnel beside Lake Como," Bryen said.

"The bikes were a revelation after Manx Nortons. When I first rode one of the 350s (in July 1957) I had to remind myself I was on a single. It was so much lighter than a Norton and the centre of gravity was much lower, so it accelerated much more quickly and was easier to handle.

"You didn't have to wrench them down into a corner. You just flipped them where you wanted them. And it had a five-speed gearbox," he added.

Consider the specifications of the new Guzzi 350 that Carcano designed for the 1957 season. In the off-season, Carcano tested Lomas's title-winning 350 against the 1954 model and found it didn't punch as well out of slow corners, so for 1957 he pared 14 kg off his horizontal-cylinder masterpiece, bringing the weight down to 97 kg. He increased power by 2 kW to 28 kW, but with improved

Keith Campbell was supported in the 1957 world championship by compatriot and Moto Guzzi team-mate Keith Bryen. Bryen is pictured here on his way to third place in the Belgian GP, in his debut Guzzi ride.

tractability thanks to smaller valves than the 1956 models. The 1957 350 Guzzi produced maximum power at 7800-8000 rpm and could be ridden out of slow corners from 4000 rpm with progressive throttle. It could achieve better than 60 mpg in a race, thanks in part to Guzzi's streamlining, which was the best in the business.

Now compare the 1957 Guzzi 350 with the private Nortons Campbell had ridden in 1956 and the Gilera four which would prove his main opposition in 1957. The Guzzi, at 28 kW, had two or three kiloWatts more power than the best privateer Norton 350 of the day, and 5 kW less than the Gilera. The Guzzi and the Gilera each had five gears, versus four in the Norton. Weight was no contest. The Guzzi weighed 97 kg, the privateer Nortons 142 kg and the Gileras 145 kg. And how fast were these bikes? Well, the Gilera 350 in 1957 set a world record by covering 225 kilometres in one hour on the banked oval at Monza.

Keith Campbell fitted straight into the Italian team. He soon looked the part, with a stylish haircut to complement his naturally swarthy features. Off the bike he stood 173 cm tall, and at 70 kg had the same riding weight as Wayne Gardner today. Keith's hobby, now he had a works contract to indulge it, was the same as some of today's leading riders and drivers — model aircraft.

Campbell received immediate fringe benefits from his contract. His "luggage" for his annual trip home in 1956-1957 included a Guzzi 350 and a 500 single for major local races. Keith unfortunately crashed the 350 at the December Phillip Island meeting. Rain penetrated his goggles and he completely misjudged his speed into the hairpin at the back of the pits. He sustained a dislocated shoulder and damaged his thumb. But he turned out at Mildura just over a week later for the Australian TT, his shoulder heavily strapped in adhesive bandage. The circuit was a 6 km triangle of public roads. Keith won the Australian 500 and Unlimited TTs from Eric Hinton (Norton), and upped his own lap record (set in 1954) from 154 km/h to 160 km/h. He narrowly missed out on a cash bonus, posted for the first 100 mph (161 km/h) lap. Campbell's commitment to racing in Europe meant these were the only Australian titles he won.

As Eric Hinton recalls: "It was good racing — we tried hard to beat Keith that day. It was windy and both Keith's Guzzi and my Norton had full-bin streamlining. We were leaning about ten degrees from vertical on the main straight. I'm sure the Guzzi 500 single had less power than the Norton, but it had one more gear and a much better power-to-weight ratio, because it was about 40 kg lighter. Keith just missed the first 100 mph lap. If it hadn't been windy, he'd have lapped half a second faster and done it."

Campbell's first major meeting with the Moto Guzzi team in Europe in 1957 was the traditional Easter Gold Cup race at Imola. He failed to finish. Dickie Dale won the race on the 58 kW, 144 kg Guzzi V8. But celebrations were tempered by injury to defending world 350 champion Bill Lomas, who crashed in the 350 event and broke his shoulder. Keith's next two major races produced two more non-finishes. He retired from the opening round of the 350 world championship, the German GP at Hockenheim, with gear-selection problems. He then qualified fastest on a V8 at the Mettet international in Belgium, but retired from the race when gusty conditions made the fully streamlined machine unmanageable.

The Isle of Man TT was round two of the world championship, and has gone into history as Bob McIntyre's meeting. The combination of the no-nonsense Scotsman and Gilera's 350 and 500 fours produced two victories and the first 100 mph lap. Keith Campbell finished second in the 350 TT, after taking it steady in the first half of the race. Bob Brown finished third on another works Gilera, John Surtees was fourth on the works MV, and Eric Hinton fifth on his privately entered 1956 model ex-works Norton. Campbell was fifth in the 500 TT on a Guzzi single, despite a minor spill. At the finish he was just behind Dale, whose V8 ran on seven cylinders for about half of the eight-lap (485 km) race.

Assen was the next world title round. Guzzi's armoury included four V8 bikes and an experimental 350, which Lomas crashed during practice, sustaining a fractured skull and further damage to the shoulder he injured at Imola. The injuries effectively ended Lomas's career. Responsibility was now with Dale and Campbell. But Dale crashed out of the 350 GP and broke his ankle. Keith responded with a great ride, using the Guzzi single's advantages of lighter weight and a lower centre of gravity to beat McIntyre's more powerful Gilera four.

Vic Willoughby was a great fan of McIntyre. But 30 years later he still tips his hat to Campbell for this aggressive, but thoughtful display using his machine's advantages to the full.

"Bob would gobble up Keith on the straights and clap on the anchors. Keith would brake 50 yards later, dive under his handlebar and just fling it into the corner," Willoughby said.

Guilio Carcano, Guzzi's race engineer, gave Campbell the best V8 for the 500 GP. Again Keith had trouble starting, but was soon closing on race leader Surtees (MV Agusta). Keith was 13 seconds behind and gaining at more than a second a lap with 17 laps of the 27-lap race still to run. Then the V8 bogey struck again — the clutch failed.

Campbell went to the next weekend's Belgian GP at Spa-Francorchamps as Moto Guzzi's number one

Early morning practice for the 1957 IoM 350 TT. Note the covering of dead flies on Campbell's helmet.

team rider and leader in the world 350 championship. During the week Guzzi had hired Keith Bryen to back him up, on the strength of two top-six placings on private Nortons at Assen. Gilera was also hit by injuries. Geoff Duke had been sidelined since Imola and now McIntyre was out with a neck injury suffered when he crashed in the 500 GP at Assen.

The 350 battle was now Campbell and Guzzi versus Gilera's Libero Liberati. Guzzi again had a fleet of bikes: four 500 V8s, a new 350 V8 and two 350 singles per rider. Campbell qualified fastest for both the 350 and 500 GPs, and rode superbly in both races. He averaged more than 184 km/h to beat Liberati by 12.5 seconds in the 350 GP. Bryen put in a real team-mate's ride. He hounded the Italian right to the finish, to take third place, well ahead of Guzzi's 50-year-old test rider Alano Montanari and Bob Brown (Gilera).

The Belgian 500 GP was vintage Campbell, while he lasted. Keith just this once made a good start on the V8. He fired past Liberati and Surtees to lead at the end of the first lap. During the next seven laps Campbell set a new lap record of 190.7 km/h. But he was out of the race at half distance with another crankshaft failure. Immediately after the race Keith and Bryen loaded their 350 race bikes into Bryen's Bedford truck for the trip to Keith's pet Swedish GP meet at the picturesque Hedemora circuit. Campbell was in a surprisingly determined mood for this rain-affected non-championship meeting and easily won both the 350 and 500 races.

Moto Guzzi confirmed its professionalism at the

Keith Campbell stands tall on the Assen dais, after scoring his first victory in a world championship GP.

Victory dais, 1957 Ulster GP. Winner Campbell, runner-up Bryen and a less than gracious third-placed Liberati.

next world championship round, on the Dundrod circuit near Belfast. It sent five 350s for Campbell and Bryen — a race and practice bike each plus a spare. The riders made no mistake. Campbell won and clinched the world championship. Bryen was second and set fastest lap. Liberati was third. He couldn't even manage a handshake for the two Australians on the victory podium.

Keith Campbell and the Guzzi V8 did not even make the start of the final championship round at Monza. He crashed at around 225 km/h, during pre-meeting testing, slid along the track for 200 metres and stopped just short of a safety fence. His injuries, though minor, caused Guzzi to withdraw the V8 from the race. The Guzzi never raced again. Two Australians — Ken Kavanagh and Keith Campbell — had ridden the bike in its race debut and race swansong.

Keith was soon out of hospital and on his way to the Isle of Man, where he married Geraldine Reid, daughter of a Douglas churchman, on September 18. Geoff Duke, who was married to Pat Reid, attended, along with Bob Brown. The next week Campbell, Duke and Brown learned they were without rides for 1958; Moto Guzzi had withdrawn from racing.

The Italian withdrawal prompted two other world champion riders of 1957, Cecil Sandford (250) and Liberati (500) to retire. But Keith Campbell was in a different position. He was young by 1950s racer standards, still improving as a rider, and he knew how to run a profitable private race effort with Nortons. The economics of 1950s racing were a disincentive to "retiring at the top", because the big payments were in starting money. Keith was already a proven drawcard in France. As a world champion he would command even better money.

Keith and Geri Campbell returned to England after a southern summer holiday in Australia to piece together a race effort. He took a trip to Italy to sound out the factories for a machine, but without luck. One report (denied by Campbell) in March 1958, suggested he would buy a Maserati 250F racing car. Later, in fact, he did acquire one. By the Easter meeting at Imola, Campbell had arranged new Nortons through English sponsor Reg Dearden and renovated a second-hand van.

Campbell had put in three classy grand prix performances in the first half of 1958. But perhaps his last race meeting showed where he had made his mark in Europe — with townspeople who turned out once a year for the big local race meeting. The Grand Prix de Cadours was a typical non-championship French international on a tight road circuit. Campbell qualified fastest for the 500 race at 115 km/h and won the 350 race. He led from the start of the 500 race, from compatriots Jack Ahearn and Eric Hinton. But during the first lap Keith rode over

Campbell's wedding day, September 18, 1957. L to R: Keith and Geraldine Campbell, the Rev Reid (father of the bride), Pat Duke (the bride's sister) and Geoff Duke.

oil spilled during the sidecar race. He crashed heavily and died of a fractured skull. The sport's governing body later ruled sidecar events must run after all solo events had been decided.

Keith Campbell was 26. His ten years of competitive motorcycling proved he had the classic attributes of grit, perseverance in the face of setback, and the confidence and ability to grasp an opportunity when it was offered.

The two greatest riders of the 1950s rated Campbell highly. Geoff Duke said he didn't have too many duels with Keith, but remembered the 1958 Belgian 350 GP was quite a "ding-dong battle" because he, Campbell and Derek Minter raced wheel-to-wheel for an hour. The deciding factors were that Minter almost went down the slip road at La Source hairpin on the very last lap, and Duke was geared taller, so he lost out as the trio accelerated from La Source to the finishing line. "Keith was a very determined rider, and more consistent than another fine Australian rider of the 1950s, Ken Kavanagh," Duke said in 1988. "He really tried hard on that day at Gawler airstrip."

John Surtees agrees with the assessment of Campbell's determination. "Keith was a very clean and tidy conventional stylist, and quite aggressive. I thought he was more of a 350 rider than a 500 rider, but then all the Guzzi riders were, because the 350 had a steady development program," Surtees said. "Keith was a good goer, and didn't make a habit of falling. He was killed in an extremely unfortunate accident."

BOB MITCHELL

CHAPTER 5

Bob Mitchell is unique among Australian sidecar racers. He is the only Australian sidecar driver who has made the winner's rostrum in a world championship sidecar race, and the only one who has finished in the top four in a world sidecar championship.

Bob Mitchell and former Melbourne schoolmate Max George finished third in 1955 in the Dutch Sidecar Grand Prix, and fifth in the German GP at Nurburgring. The following year Mitchell and his English passenger, Eric Bliss, were third in the Belgian GP, and fourth in the Isle of Man TT and Dutch GP. They were fourth overall in the 1956 world sidecar championship.

That the 25-year-old Mitchell achieved these results when BMW had a factory team of 45 kW fuel-injected, twin-cylinder machines, and the top British riders had works Norton engines, was even more noteworthy. For Bob was a private entrant and used a self-tuned Manx Norton engine which produced 36 kW at best.

British motorcycle journalist and former sidecar passenger Mick Woollett wrote that Bob Mitchell would have been world champion material on a BMW, or if the 1957 title had been an all-privateer affair. Australian solo riders of the day, including Tony McAlpine and Eric Hinton, agreed.

BMW had approached Mitchell late in 1956 with an offer to join its team for 1957, but a change in company racing policy shattered Bob's hopes. BMW withdrew from racing, but let the 1956 works drivers retain their machines for 1957. Bob's chances of winning the world title without equal equipment were virtually nil, so he packed up and returned to Australia with his English wife, his baby son, and his Norton 500 outfit.

Mitchell was "hot" after three seasons racing in Europe. He whitewashed the locals for ten months, then retired from racing. A run of 21 local victories in 1956-1957 included the 1956 Australian Unlimited and 600 cm^3 Sidecar TTs at Mildura, the Australian Unlimited and 600 cm^3 Sidecar Grands Prix at Bandiana, near Albury, and both sidecar classes at the 1957 Easter Bathurst meeting. He is the only driver since World War II to win the Bathurst Unlimited sidecar race on a single-cylinder machine.

Bob Mitchell's introduction to motorcycling began in 1946, when he rode his pushbike to the Jordanville scramble in Melbourne. The main event produced a dogfight between Ken Kavanagh and Jack French, who rode shoulder to shoulder in the main straight, digging furrows in the track with their converted road bikes. "In the corners they elbowed one another in the ribs, like sprint cyclists," Bob recalled.

Mitchell, then 15 and a student at Caulfield Technical School, was mightily impressed. He organised bicycle scramble races among his mates, who carved out a track near Bob's home in suburban Glen Iris. Mitchell also began riding over to the nearby suburb of Hartwell and "hanging around" outside Sampson Bros workshop, where Kavanagh worked.

Young Mitchell became such a fixture outside the workshop that Kavanagh began taking him to race meetings. Then Col Sampson decided Bob might be more useful inside the workshop than blocking the doorway, so he drew up indenture papers for a five-year apprenticeship, went over to the Mitchell home and ended Mrs Mitchell's dreams about her son becoming a doctor.

Sampson Bros was a highly regarded motorcycle workshop and Ariel dealer. It was a thriving business because the 1940s equivalent of the delivery van was a motorcycle with a box sidecar. The shop was also the spiritual home of the Hartwell Motorcycle Club. First-year apprentice pay was about 30 shillings ($3) a week, but Bob didn't mind. He was happy to work 60 hours a week if some of those hours were on his idol's race bikes. Col and Roddy Sampson trained Mitchell so well that he was Apprentice Motorcycle Mechanic of the Year in 1951. He collected the award from Victoria's Governor, Sir Reginald Dallas Brooks, in Melbourne Town Hall.

Mid-way through Bob's apprenticeship, he bought the first BSA Bantam to arrive in Melbourne. The 125 cm^3 two-stroke commuter bike doubled as his scrambler — with the lights removed. In 1949 Mitchell helped one of his workmates, Norm King, out of a temporary financial squeeze by buying Norm's project bike, a race-prepared Ariel 500 with a Norton gearbox. Bob borrowed £60 from his mum for the purchase. The machine came with a sidecar, but Mitchell put that aside for the moment — his priority was solo scrambles. He fitted a high-compression piston to the Ariel and tuned it to run on alcohol.

Bob's switch to sidecar racing sprang from a suggestion by old schoolmate Jim Hocking to fit the unused sidecar to the Ariel. Mitchell already had an insight into sidecar technique from Col "The Fox" Sampson, who scrambled on outfits, and through his once-a-week duty as Sampson Bros' spare parts courier. Col Sampson now taught Bob race tactics.

"The firm had a big Harley 10/12 with a box sidecar," Mitchell recalled. "Every Wednesday I'd drive it from Hartwell in to the centre of Melbourne to collect bikes and parts. On the way back, when the sidecar was loaded, I'd detour through The Boulevarde (Melbourne's famed hack road) to practise my riding technique. It was good fun. I could get the sidecar wheel a foot off the ground when the box was loaded."

Mitchell and Hocking did some test runs in a paddock, then entered the Keilor scramble. In their

Bob and Jean Mitchell at a dinner in Melbourne with Hartwell Club president Allan Johnson (left).

first race they split two of the stars of the day, until alcohol spilled from the tank into Mitchell's eyes. The Mitchell/Hocking team then tried road racing, with more success. The circuit was Darley, near Melbourne, and the event was the B-grade sidecar over six laps. Mitchell was last away after tangling with another outfit at the start, but he raced through the field to win by half a lap.

Bob soon perfected a technique of throwing the outfit sideways before right-hand corners, so he could drive under other outfits on the exit. This sliding practice and his scrambles skills would prove invaluable on the wet and slippery roads of Europe's street circuits, where smoothness counted heavily. When Mitchell returned from Europe in 1956 his control was so smooth, it was difficult to pick the points where his slides began and ended.

When Ken Kavanagh came home after racing in Europe in 1951, he found his former protege was the coming man of Victorian sidecar racing. Ken talked Mr Mitchell snr into buying his son a late-1940s "garden-gate" Manx Norton. Kavanagh supplied some special camshafts for the engine, and Sampson Bros added a sidecar, complete with bodywork modelled on photos of world champion Eric Oliver's Norton outfit. Oliver's Watsonia sidecar had a window in the nose fairing — now, so did Mitchell's.

Within six months of buying the Norton, Mitchell won his first Australian title, in the newly introduced 600 cm^3 sidecar class. The 1952 Australian TT was held on December 26/27 on the new six km Little River circuit at Werribee, west of Melbourne, and the 600 Sidecar TT featured a three-way battle between Mitchell, and established stars Bernie Mack and Laurie Fox. Mitchell was third going into the last corner, a hairpin bend, but he pivot-turned his outfit dirt-track style, snapped on the power and won the sprint to the finishing line. Bob's chances in the Unlimited Sidecar TT, however, were scuttled on the grid. The sidecar collapsed around passenger Hocking's ankles as he climbed aboard — an under-tube had broken.

The peculiarities of Australian racing in the 1950s meant Bob Mitchell's title was back on the line two months later. Host state Tasmania scheduled the 1953 Australian TT for late February on the Longford public road circuit, south of Launceston, a track with a higher average lap speed than Bathurst. Mitchell retained the Australia 600 Sidecar crown and finished second to Frank Sinclair's Vincent 1000 in the Australian Unlimited Sidecar TT. Sinclair's outfit had something special that day: Phil Irving, the engineer who designed the Vincent V-twin engine, had tuned it.

Sinclair was late submitting his entry for the next Darley meeting in Victoria, so he and Irving offered the machine to Mitchell, who won the unlimited race. He continued to ride the machine, and his own Norton 500, until he left for England in 1954, tallying in the nine months from March 1953 the 600 sidecar class at Mt Panorama, Bathurst, the Victorian Hillclimb Championship and nine wins at Darley. He also finished second to fellow Vincent pilot Sandy McCrae in the Bathurst unlimited sidecar race, after some bother with binding brakes.

"Frank Sinclair's bike was a rocket," Mitchell recalled. "Phil's engine seemed to have smooth power right through the range. He told me to rev it to 7000 rpm, and to use more if I needed to. At Bathurst, without streamlining, it did 195 km/h. At Darley it would wheelspin the whole way down the straight — on Bathurst gearing! Riding that bike really boosted our confidence for Europe."

But European sidecar racing was a big step from the Australian scene. Ambitious Australian solo riders could test themselves each summer against returning internationals and any imports, but sidecar racers had no benchmark until they lined up for their first race in Europe.

Jim Hocking could not make the trip to Europe, and he later won two Australian titles as a sidecar

Bob Mitchell and Max George, showing the locals how on the Norton 500 at Ballarat in January 1957.

driver. Mitchell now talked another former schoolmate, Max George, into taking the passenger's role for the 1954 New Year's Day unlimited race at Victoria Park, Ballarat. They won on the Sinclair Vincent. The world sidecar championship, however, was for 500 cm^3 machines, so Mitchell sold everything and ordered a "short-stroke" Manx Norton 500 through Disney Motors in Melbourne. His parents and Ken Kavanagh's wife Joan helped out with the fare to Europe on the aging liner *Oronto*. The Hartwell Club passed the hat for a send-off.

Mitchell and George, both 23 years old, were broke by the time they left Birmingham in April 1954 for their first race meeting at Pau, in France. They had modified the Manx Norton chassis for sidecar racing, and bolted on 1953 world title runner-up Cyril Smith's sidecar frame. Their transport and living quarters was a 3-tonne Bedford truck Sydney rider Keith Bryen had used in 1953 — it cost £50.

Ray Amm, the Norton works team leader, loaned them £25 for the petrol and ferry fare to Pau, and they had to drive at 26 mph (42 km/h) for the last few hundred miles so the petrol would last. There was £60 starting money waiting at Pau, provided they started.

Bob reckoned he chose Pau for his overseas debut because no-one back home would know if they

SIDECAR TECHNIQUE

Bob Mitchell's efforts on a privately entered Norton outfit against works BMWs again proved the truism that races are won by motorcycles and riders, not by specification sheets and test-bench figures.

The flat-twin BMW had an ideal layout for sidecar racing. It also had 45 kW in fuel-injected form to the Norton's 36 kW, one more speed in the gearbox and a weight advantage of perhaps 20 kg. But the Nortons were kept in the hunt because of the European preference for right-hand sidecars. Most race circuits ran clockwise and hence had more right-hand corners than left-handers. A sidecar outfit can take corners faster with the sidecar wheel on the outside, and therefore loaded, than it can with the sidecar wheel unloaded and the passenger fighting to keep the wheel down.

"There were places, however, where riding a Norton against the BMWs was just sad," Mitchell recalled. "Like getting into and out of a downhill hairpin bend. The BMW rider would cut your braking distance by 50 yards going into the corner, because he had three-wheel hydraulically operated brakes and you had cable-operated brakes on two wheels. Then you had to lump the Norton around the corner without slipping the clutch, because it had a fairly high first gear and a powerband of about 1000 rpm between the point where it wouldn't pull and the point where things started to break.

"Meantime, the BMW rider had got around the corner and just pulled up the rise, because his motor ran cleanly from 4000 rpm to over 9000."

"But there were times when the Nortons got legitimately amongst the BMWs, particularly on fast circuits or in the rain. The Norton could not compete with the BMW for acceleration, but it could tramp along quite well once it was wound up to top speed. The advantage we had at Spa-Francorchamps was that the big corners onto the long straights were right-handers, which we could take in big three-wheel drifts," Mitchell said.

"Having the sidecars on opposite sides made for some hairy moments when you were dicing. We'd go into a fast right-hander flat out in a three-wheel drift. The BMW driver couldn't go into the corner as hard, because his outfit was on the other side. But he'd accelerate harder out of the corner. Sometimes you'd almost run over the other bloke's passenger because of the speed difference."

Bob Mitchell (Norton) leads BMW's Willi Schneider at Zandvoort in 1954. It was Mitchell's first victory in Europe.

performed poorly. "We already knew two things," he said. "They didn't give you much practice time and the riding standard at the top was higher than we expected. Before we left for Pau, Max and I had watched Eric Oliver and Cyril Smith race at Silverstone. They were one and two in the world at the time, and they took Woodcote Corner flat in top gear. We went white, because we'd estimated it was a third-gear corner!"

The Pau meeting also taught them a lot more. French driver Jacques Drion sat on Mitchell's outfit and told him he wouldn't finish the race, because his machine and riding position were all wrong. "He also told me — cheeky bastard — to keep to the right when he passed us!" Bob said.

"Seven laps into the 25-lap race I could barely steer because I was so tired. Drion lapped me and we finished sixth. He was right about our outfit. The steering geometry was wrong, our wheels were too big (in diameter), the clip-on handlebars weren't positioned properly, and I needed support under my arms and chest."

Racing every weekend meant Mitchell and George learned and improved rapidly. In the next three weeks they finished fifth at Mettet in Belgium, third in the rain and snow at St Wendel in Germany, and seventh at Hockenheim. Mitchell's fifth meeting was at Zandvoort, Holland, on May 16. The event was decided over three heats, and Mitchell and Belgium's Julian Deronne (Norton) fought out all three, Bob winning the last heat with a well-timed piece of slipstreaming to take the overall win. Australia's ambassador in Amsterdam sent him a congratulatory telegram, but the real message of Zandvoort was back in the field. The BMW team took three brand-new outfits to Zandvoort. "They were faster than our Nortons," Mitchell recalled, "but at that meeting the blokes couldn't ride them properly. Geez, did they go — a man should have woken up!

"The BMW rep said he'd sell me one at a fair price, and Ken Kavanagh offered to lend me the money. But I had no understanding of the BMW. I knew I could put a Norton big-end in overnight. And for the next two years I worked all night putting big-ends in Nortons, while I raced against BMWs which didn't break down."

Mitchell and George pressed on through a very wet European summer, clocking up second places at France's Sombrette and Moulins street-circuit races. At Comminges, in the rain, Mitchell led a class field including Drion, BMW riders Hillebrand and Schneider, and Swiss Norton driver Haldemann, until his goggles filled with water. Then Bob made a mistake: he threw the goggles away and pressed on without eye protection — to finish third.

Bob also contested a couple of the world championship grands prix. He did not finish in the points, but he was the first private entrant home in the Swiss GP at Berne. By season's end, Mitchell had contested 16 meetings; his only crash had been a minor episode in the wet at Feldburg, in Germany, when Max George received a bump on the knee. Apart from maintaining his own outfit, Bob had found time to give solo rider Jack Ahearn a hand with his Nortons. Bob recalled: "It was a highly competitive scene, but we were all terrific mates."

Mitchell and George stayed in Birmingham over the northern winter of 1954-1955. Bob worked during the day in the lube bay of a new service station, behind which was a junkyard with a wooden shed where Bob worked after hours preparing his outfit. Max worked at BSA and spent his spare time building up a 500 Gold Star, which he hoped to race solo.

One day in late 1954, Bob Mitchell and Keith Campbell visited Norton Motors. While they were in the foyer, Bob smiled at one of the secretaries as she walked between offices. He introduced himself to Jean a week later, when he and Keith attended a Norton Motors social club function in the Crown and Cushion pub. Bob cut a suitably dashing figure: compact in frame, fashionable brush-back hairstyle, large blue eyes and wearing his best and only sports coat, which still had dirt from the railings of the *Oronto* on the cuffs. His trump card was, however, his £50 worth of 1937 model Ford V8. Everybody else went home on the bus. Bob and Jean were married in Birmingham in May 1955.

Mitchell bought Cyril Smith's 1954 sidecar chassis for the 1955 season. The rest of the machine was largely as per 1954. Bob still did not have a stream-lining on his outfit. The "word" had it that stream-lining was about to be banned, but the word was wrong. Full streamlining for solos was barred in 1957, but sidecar streamlining was never banned. Meanwhile, Max George's hopes of riding his BSA Gold Star in the 500 solo class came to nothing because he couldn't obtain an international solo licence. So Bob rode the machine at some meetings as a "start-money special". He would qualify, then ride in the race until he found a good viewing position.

Mitchell's 1955 season opened late in April with a fourth place at Dieburg, Germany. The following weekend he snatched second place from old rival Drion on the last corner at Mettet, after slip-streaming Drion's fully faired outfit for the whole race. It was a neat pay-back for the comment a year earlier about keeping right.

"I had my front wheel stuck into the back of his outfit down every straight," Bob recalled. "Drion had a woman passenger, Ingerborg Stroll. She was livid after the race."

Mitchell's results tapered off in the next two months, due to mechanical troubles. He was only finishing every second race. The biggest problem in the Norton motor was the bevel drive to the camshafts, and several Australians lost important races or top-three placings because of it — Keith Campbell, Eric Hinton, Jack Ahearn. "We Colonials had to get the replacement parts posted to us in Europe, at full retail price," Bob said. "At Assen in '55 I came straight in from practice on Max's BSA Goldie, rode out of the circuit and rode off down the highway to Amsterdam airport to pick up new bevels. One policeman on point duty in the Amsterdam suburbs heard the Goldie arriving and stopped all traffic. He waved me through with great gusto. It was Assen fever."

If it wasn't the bevels breaking it was something else; and some of it was Mitchell's fault. Ken Kavanagh had told him that the factory used to fiddle with spacers under the cylinder to get the compression ratio up. So Bob tried to copy-cat that with his own motor. "You'd just get it organised and the bike would go bang. Or there'd be a bad batch of petrol and all the privateers would end up with holes in their pistons and pock marks in their cylinder heads. We were trying to run too much compression. That's why the motors used to hammer out big ends," Mitchell recalled.

"In the middle of 1955 I realised where we were all going the wrong way. Instead of running high compression and retarding the ignition to stop detonation, I went for lower compression and more ignition advance. My Manx went best with that, and the carburettor set up very carefully. To get power from a petrol-burning motor you need the combustion spot on. Once I did that I started getting results."

Classic Mitchell — sliding through the S-bend at Cadwell Park. Passenger Max George has swung in as Mitchell changes from sliding left to sliding right.

Mitchell finished in the points in two of his next three grand prix appearances. He was fifth in the West German GP at Nurburgring, behind the works BMWs of Faust, Noll and Schneider, and Drion's streamlined Norton. Another BMW was sixth. (Faust, Noll and Schneider all won world sidecar championships during the 1950s.) Bob went two places better at the Dutch GP on July 30, using the bevels he'd collected a day or two earlier in Amsterdam. Mitchell finished third, behind Faust and Noll, with Drion and two more BMWs behind him. Norton's works-assisted runners, Oliver, Smith and Pip Harris, all retired with mechanical problems.

Up to this meeting, only four Australians, Harry Hinton, Ken Kavanagh, Gordon Laing and Keith Campbell, had made the winner's rostrum at a world championship grand prix. Mitchell closed 1955 with a third place at Norisring, and a first, a second and a third in three British meetings. After one of those meetings, at Cadwell Park, Bob addressed a crowd of 400 enthusiasts in the Louth Town Hall, Lincolnshire. Unaccustomed as he was to public speaking, he found the occasion daunting.

Bob Mitchell spent the winter of 1955-1956 back in Birmingham. He and Jean had a son, Mark. Bob again worked in the service station and the junkyard shed, where the two main projects tackled were the lowering of his outfit's centre of gravity and making a full fairing. Bob also shifted the fuel tank from the original position, over the engine, down to the sidecar platform. To lift the fuel to the carburettor, he fitted an electric fuel pump and a battery, which sat in the nose of the sidecar. This was advanced sidecar technology for 1956.

Mitchell and George line the streamlined Norton up for a right-hand bend.

Ben Willetts from famed sidecar builders Watsonia helped make Bob's fairing. "It was a beautiful streamlining — all aluminium on a tubular frame," Bob said. "You wouldn't think something so good could come out of a junkyard. The fairing not only improved the aerodynamics, it put more weight on the front wheel, made the outfit steer better, and gave a good flow of air to the engine and front brake. Once we put it on, our bike was almost as fast in top speed as a Rennesport BMW (but not the fuel-injected works bikes). With a good Norton engine, it would do about 200 km/h."

Mitchell needed a new passenger for 1956. Max George had become homesick. According to Bob, Jean Mitchell's presence in the other bunk of the truck during 1955 probably compounded the problem. Max's replacement was to have been Mick Woollett, who at the time combined passengering with part-time reporting. But Cyril Smith had first call on Woollett's services. Eric Oliver came to the rescue by recommending his 1955 "ballast" Eric Bliss, a chirpy Cockney; the going pay for a passenger of Bliss's standard was £8 a week plus £2 a week pocket money when on the Continent.

Mitchell contested four meetings in England early in 1956. He won at Oulton Park on Easter Monday, beating England's best, and he finished second at Brough Airfield, Brands Hatch and Silverstone. The poster for a later Brough meeting featured a picture of Mitchell in the top left-hand corner, because he'd won there in September 1955.

Bob fitted a new engine before he left for the Continent. Norton Motors had, after much haggling, sold him a new Manx 500 power plant. "Norton charged me three-quarters of the price of a complete bike," Mitchell said. "And it was the worst motor I ever raced. It wouldn't pull and it vibrated. We finished fourth at St Wendel, then it broke the crankshaft and blew up while we were practising at Floreffe, in Belgium. And when I say blew up — the engine was demolished. The cambox was split, and the cylinder barrel and crankcases were wrecked. Cyril Smith lent us his spare motor for the race. It was a 1952 works job, a real revelation after the one we'd just blown."

The next day Mitchell had the only big crash of his career. It was raining, which usually helped put him on level pegging with the BMWs. "I was dicing with Schneider for the lead when I confused one of two similar-looking corners," Mitchell recalled. "I arrived at the tight one thinking it was the flat-out one; I threw the outfit sideways just before we hit the gutter and the straw bales.

"We were thrown into the air and landed on our backs. I looked up in time to see Eric land and bounce off the ground. I thought he was dead. Then I saw the outfit wrapped around a telegraph pole and the fairing was wrecked."

Mitchell's fears for his passenger were ended by a burst of broad Cockney: "Cor blimey. 'Ow're we gonna start at 'ockenheim next week?"

At Hockenheim they worked like cut cats to straighten the bike, and they finished fifth, the first team home with no fairing. Mitchell now faced the most hectic week of his career. He had entered for the Isle of Man TT. He had one week to get back to England, find a new motor, repair the streamlining and get his outfit to the Isle of Man.

"We arrived back in Birmingham to find Norton Motors on strike. The spare parts counter was open, but there were no spare motors and not enough bits in the spares department to build one. Luckily, one of the works mechanics, Charlie Edwards, was in. He hunted around the whole building, finding parts here and there. The crankcases weren't even a pair," Bob said.

"But when I put all these parts together, I ended up with the best motor I ever had. It had a wide spread of power and it didn't break. That engine did the rest of the season in Europe and all the races back in Australia until I retired, with barely a spanner laid on it. Fifteen months after I built that motor, Bernie Mack used it to set an Australian 500 sidecar speed record at 112 mph (180 km/h). I still reckon it could have gone faster."

The 1956 Sidecar TT, on the Clypse Circuit, was the only Isle of Man meeting Bob Mitchell contested. He finished fourth, and was the first private owner, behind BMW's Fritz Hillebrand and works-assisted Norton pair Pip Harris and Bill Boddice. It was a fine result by any standard. Yet Bob Mitchell's lasting memory of the meeting was of the officialdom and the attitude that riders should compete in the Island for the honour of it.

"I was on £100 start money for the Dutch GP in 1956, but at the Isle of Man they wanted me to pay to enter. Fortunately Eric Oliver paid for my entry. The works BMW riders were each paid £125 and a Swiss driver who was never in the top six and failed to finish was paid 60," Mitchell said.

"Mr Simcock, the Auto Cycle Council of Australia (ACCA) rep in England, failed to nominate me as an Australian team member, so I missed out on the British Auto Cycle Union's grant of £100, which would have just covered my expenses for the meeting. Simcock later wrote to motorcycle newspapers in Australia saying that I was 'not classed in the top flight of British riders'.

"As an Isle of Man newcomer I had 50 minutes of poorly organised official practice to learn a hazardous 10.7 mile (17 km) circuit. To top it off, the machine examiners pulled us up at the final weigh-in and demanded we cover the inner side of the rear wheel. We had to pinch aluminium teatrays so Ben Willetts could make up the cover!"

Mitchell scored more world championship points

Mitchell finished fourth at his only appearance on the Isle of Man. His passenger was Londoner Eric Bliss.

in the Dutch and Belgian GPs. British newspaper *Motor Cycling* commented on Mitchell's "remarkably good and fast work on the corners" when he finished fourth at Assen. Bob finished behind works BMW riders Hillebrand and Noll, and Cyril Smith, and ahead of four more BMW outfits.

The Belgian GP, one week later, saw a determined Norton effort from Smith, Harris and Mitchell. Smith had a huge lead when he retired at three-quarter distance when he missed a gear and bent the valves in his engine. Noll won for BMW. Harris and Mitchell both passed Hillebrand on the last lap, when the former Luftwaffe pilot stopped momentarily. So the finishing order was Noll, Smith, Mitchell, Hillebrand, then four more BMWs.

Then, late in July, came an offer for Bob Mitchell to join the BMW team. "At Solitude, during practice for the German GP, I got among the BMWs during practice. BMW came to see me and offered me a works ride for 1957. I was so excited," Mitchell recalled. "The BMW reps said I should come to the Frankfurt Motor Show in October to negotiate a fee. But between Solitude and October, the BMW board met and decided not to continue with an official sidecar team. They left the machines in the hands of the existing works riders and allowed them access to the factory facilities. I was heartbroken.

"Mark was born not long after, so I packed up and brought Jean and Mark home," he said. Bob Mitchell had finished the 1956 world sidecar championship fourth overall and the leading private entrant behind Noll, Hillebrand and Harris.

Back home in Australia, Bob Mitchell, with passenger Max George and later Max Woodruffe, and his petrol-burning 500 Norton beat all comers, including alcohol-fuelled Vincents of more than 1000 cm^3. Mitchell won at Mt Druitt, Phillip Island, Ballarat, Bandiana, Fishermans Bend, Bathurst and Wangaratta.

Then the mood changed. "I think I spoiled the party, because some guys stopped entering races," Mitchell recalled. "One day people were writing that my riding was worth the price of admission alone, then people started saying I'd wrecked the sidecar scene, accusing me of having a works engine or an oversized motor, when the limit in most races was 600 or 1300 cm³ ! The Melbourne rider, Lindsay Urqhart, I should say was a notable exception.

"I had nothing more to achieve, so I sold the outfit to Bernie Mack for £600 and retired from racing."

Mitchell spent two years working in Albury for colourful motorcycle racer Doug Fugger. Mitchell even raced a Messerschmidt three-wheeler in a car race. Then, in 1959, Mitchell made a brief comeback as a sidecar racer. Bendigo sponsor Jack Walters even offered to import a new outfit, but Bob rode his 1956 job to wins at Fishermans Bend and Darley, then lost to Lindsay Urqhart's Vincent at Phillip Island. Later that day the Norton broke its connecting rod. Bob rebuilt the engine and returned it to Walters with thanks. By that time Jean and Bob had three children, and his new business, Mitchell-Flannery Motors of Shepparton, was selling the first Datsun motor cars in Australia. He went on to pioneer sales of Toyota passenger cars.

In 1972 he retired from the motor industry and developed a caravan park opposite the Surfers Paradise International Raceway. Never one to remain idle, in the late 1980s he was operating a charter boat on the Gold Coast's waterways.

"The only place on the IoM Clypse Course where the road was more than 12 feet wide," said Mitchell.

Poster for a race at Brough, in East Yorkshire, in 1956, featuring a photograph of Bob Mitchell.

BOB BROWN

CHAPTER 6

Bob Brown was certainly an easy going bloke. He almost missed his first works ride at the 1957 Isle of Man TT by sleeping in! Brown, a Sydney motor mechanic turned taxi driver, had been called into Italy's Gilera team at the suggestion of injured team leader Geoff Duke. But while other riders warmed themselves and their machines for the 5 am practice session, all of the Australians except one were still tucked up and dreaming in the Rosevilla guest house.

One of Brown's compatriots was responsible for setting the "community" alarm clock. Not only had he neglected to do it, he had woken around 4 am and left without rousing the others.

Brown's big day was saved by a voice in the street. It was a Gilera employee calling: "Mr Brown, do you want to ride this motorcycle?" The effect within the guest house was akin to the call "scramble" at an airforce fighter base.

Bob Brown might have been caught napping that morning, but once on the Gilera he gave a typically impressive display. This was only his second meeting on the world's longest motorcycle circuit, his previous Isle of Man mounts being his own relatively pedestrian AJS 7R 350 and Matchless G45 500 twin.

He soon adapted to the two four-cylinder machines, which were some 30 km/h faster and much quicker in acceleration than any road racer he'd ridden. Brown finished third in the 350 TT, behind Bob McIntyre (Gilera) and Keith Campbell (Guzzi), and ahead of John Surtees (MV Agusta).

By tradition, the 500 TT was the biggest race of TT week. The 1957 "Senior" still remains special to Isle of Man fans because it produced the first 100 mph (161 km/h) lap. The race distance had been extended to a gruelling eight laps (486 km) to mark the Silver Jubilee of the Tourist Trophy races. Scotsman Bob McIntyre won and made history with a best lap of 162.75 km/h. John Surtees was second and Bob Brown third.

Gilera employed Bob Brown again for the Belgian GP. Bob finished fifth in the 350 GP, behind Keith Campbell (Guzzi), Libero Liberati (Gilera), Keith Bryen (Guzzi), and Alano Montanari (Guzzi). Then, in the 500 GP, he was the victim of a Gilera team foul-up. Minutes before the start, mechanics found a problem with 500 world title leader Liberati's machine. Brown was already on the grid, with his machine, but the Gilera team manager, Roberto Persi, ordered Bob to give his machine to the Italian rider. Geoff Duke, who was in the pits, was disgusted. Liberati won the race, but was later disqualified for changing machines without official permission. The disqualification gave Australia's Keith Bryen second place and Norton its first 500 grand prix one-two-three since 1952.

Gilera withdrew from grand prix racing at the end

Robert Neil Brown — "as Australian as a shearer in a blue singlet".

Bob Brown (works Gilera 500-four) rounds Creg-ny-Baa on his way to third place in the 1957 IoM 500 TT.

of 1957, along with Moto Guzzi and FB Mondial, thus slashing the number of available works rides. Brown returned to the ranks of private entrants, riding an AJS and a Norton in 1958 and two Nortons in 1959 and 1960. He completed a hat-trick by finishing third in the Senior TT in 1958 and 1959. In 1959 he was third in the world 350 and 500 cham-

83

pionships and was the leading private entrant in both classes.

In 1960 Bob Brown wrote himself into history with another debut works ride at the Isle of Man TT. Drafted into Honda's Isle of Man squad at the last moment, he rode a works 250-four to fourth place in the 250 TT, and became the first Westerner to score world championship points on a Japanese machine.

Six weeks later Bob Brown was dead. He crashed a Honda 250 while practising for the German Grand Prix at the Solitude circuit, and he died four hours later in a Stuttgart hospital. Brown was 30 and had been married for six months. At the time he was third in the world championship on his Norton.

Brown's Honda team-mate and compatriot Tom Phillis later told colleagues that the crash had been triggered by an engine problem. Bob was touring back to the pits because his four-cylinder machine was running on only two cylinders. Phillis said he believed the machine had unexpectedly chimed on four cylinders, catching its rider unprepared and flinging him against a trackside barrier.

Two words keep appearing in descriptions of Bob Brown: popular and stylish. Fellow Australian international Jack Findlay and British journalist Mick Woollett would add a third accolade — professional. "Bob was a really popular bloke and a good rider," said Findlay. "I always hoped I'd have a bit of the style of Bob Brown, because he was professional. He had a good image on and off the bike. He was never scruffy, his leathers were always correct and clean, and he was always smooth and on-line in his riding. It was very important to stay on-line with single-cylinder four-strokes, because the racing line was very narrow and all the private entrants' machines were about equal in power."

Bob Brown was a striking figure: 183 cm (6 feet) tall and well built. He looked as Australian as a shearer in a blue singlet. Bob's travelling mate in 1955-1956, Allen Burt, thought he was typically Australian in attitude too. "Brownie was a good bloke and the best mate I had. He was easygoing, nothing ever worried him, he took things as they came. I didn't see him go off his brain once. Even the Gilera withdrawal didn't worry him. His attitude was, 'Oh well, that's the way it goes'."

Brown was in select company as a rider, both among internationals and compared with other Australians who raced in the days when the term "grand prix private entrant" was synonymous with riding British four-stroke machines. In the late 1950s he mixed it with the best on Nortons: men like Geoff Duke, Keith Campbell, Dickie Dale, Derek Minter, Bob Anderson, Tom Phillis, and young chargers like Mike Hailwood and Gary Hocking.

Brown was selected as an Australian Isle of Man TT representative every year from 1955 to 1960, but he could not ride in the 1956 TT due to a suspension for taking part in a riders' strike at the 1955 Dutch 350 GP. Bob captained the Australian team in 1959 and 1960. He finished in every one of the five 500 TTs he started; that was quite an achievement in the 1950s, when the roads were rough and the races ran to seven and eight laps.

Bob Brown never won a world championship race. MV Agusta always had one or two machines at the head of the 350 and 500 grand prix fields when Bob was at his best on Nortons between 1958 and 1960. In the 1959 Dutch 500 GP, Brown split the works MVs to finish second. In the Ulster 350 GP of the same year, Bob finished second, between John Surtees (MV) and Geoff Duke (Norton). So he shared the podium with the two most successful big bike riders of the 1950s. In races where works bikes were excluded, such as the experimental Formula 1 class in 1959, Brown, too, made it to the winner's dais — in first and second places.

Comparisons across generations are always dicey, because the number of races, the works machines, and tyre companies are never constant. But consider these raw statistics of two top riders who missed out on winning a world championship race. Graeme Crosby in his two best seasons of world 500 championship racing (1981-1982) started in 23 grands prix and finished nine times in the top three (39 per cent). Bob Brown in 1959-1960 started in 11, 500 grands prix and made the winner's rostrum six times (55 per cent).

Robert Neil Brown was born in 1930. His family lived in the Sydney suburb of Canterbury, where he grew up. He took up motorcycle racing while still apprenticed as a motor mechanic. As a clubman competitor he entered all manner of events, mainly dirt-track, and it was there that he first attracted interest with his exciting dirt-track riding style — not least because he displayed this style on a road-racing Velocette KTT 350.

Ron Kessing, his first sponsor, recalled: "Bob was a natural. I reckon he was our best-ever rider. He used to do uncanny things on his Velocette. One day at Wallacia in 1950-1951 he crashed just as I was leaving the circuit. I was so engrossed watching him I drove into a stump! That's when I decided he'd be my next jockey. It didn't worry me that he'd just fallen off — it proved he was human. Up to then I didn't think he was! I approached Bob at a hillclimb meeting at Springwood and told him it was a shame to use a good bike like the KTT on dirt-tracks. When he started riding for me I suggested he join my club, Western Suburbs. He had been with Eastern Suburbs."

Speedway JAP engines provided the power for Kessing's dirt-trackers. The first, a special nicknamed "Boom-Boom", used an ex-army BSA chassis and whatever spare parts Kessing had in stock at his suburban motorcycle shop. The second had a once Alf Hagon-sprung Royal Enfield chassis and a Norton gearbox. Riding his Mark II machine, Kessing said, was a death-defying act. The combination of the grunty JAP engine, the light chassis and the torque multiplication through the gearbox meant it was prone to wheelstanding the moment the throttle was opened.

Brown scored his first significant win on a Kessing special. He beat Harry Hinton's road-race Norton at Mt Druitt when the airfield circuit was still half dirt. The distance Brown lost to the Norton on Mt Druitt's "hill" he regained by aggressive but chanceless riding through the "marbles" at the bottom of the hill.

Bob met his best mate and later European travelling partner Allen Burt during this period. Burt usually rode the BSA framed Kessing machine and Brown the Royal Enfield.

Success on the dirt tracks in Sydney's west brought interest of a sponsor with a top-quality road-race machine. Bob was offered an ex-works DOHC Velocette 350 owned by NSW Velocette and AJS distributor P&R Williams, and prepared by Les Slaughter. Ron Kessing, on hearing of the offer, told Bob to take it. "I told Brownie he might as well go and ride for P&R, because he wouldn't get taken to England riding my stuff," Kessing said.

But the Brown/Kessing association continued off the circuit. Bob drove a taxi cab for Kessing; it was an easier way to make money than crawling under motor cars. A number of motorcycle racers of the day used to drive cabs, including Jack Ahearn and Allen Burt.

Brown rode the P&R Williams/Slaughter Velocette 350 and 250 Velo in the 1954 Australian TT at Bathurst. He finished side-by-side with fellow Velocette rider Ted Carey in the Australian 250 TT, but Carey was awarded the win. The 350 event saw Bob finish second to New Zealander Rod Coleman, who rode an ex-works AJS. Coleman a few months later won the Isle of Man 350 TT on a works prototype three-valve AJS.

The Bathurst results helped Bob gain selection in the Australian Isle of Man TT team for 1955, alongside 1954 team members Jack Ahearn and Maurie Quincey. Bob then ended 1954 with a victory in the Boxing Day 125 race at the new Mildura road circuit, on Wollongong tuner Clem Daniel's BSA Bantam. And, on New Year's Day, 1955, he rode his Velocette 350 to second place in the Victorian 500 GP at Ballarat, behind Keith Campbell (Norton).

The following month Bob Brown and Allen Burt sailed for England. Their contacts with P&R Williams — Brown as a rider and Burt as an employee — meant they ordered Associated Motor Cycle machines rather than Nortons; the choice was a mixed blessing. AMC's racers were the AJS 7R ("the Boy's Racer") and the twin-cylinder Matchless G45 500. The 7R of the day was slower than a Norton 350, but had the benefits of better oil retention, fewer breakages and ease of maintenance. The G45 engine was regarded as fragile, and the chassis was sometimes criticised for being too lightweight in the front end.

Brown and Burt made their overseas debuts in May 1955 in Northern Ireland's North-West 200 meeting. They travelled to the meeting by ferry with their two AJS machines as deck cargo, then took a train to the Port Stewart street circuit. Bob finished second in the 350 race and Allen fourth. The Australian pair then rode their racing bikes, complete with megaphone exhausts, 20 kilometres back to the docks, with police holding up traffic so they would not be delayed at intersections. To the Australians, Burt recalled, this example of motorcyclists being treated as human beings came as a revelation.

Their next meeting, the Isle of Man TT, was very nearly Allen Burt's last. During practice he crashed his AJS into a wall at Crookshanks Corner, near the village of Ramsay. He was in hospital for six months with broken arms and legs. By the end of TT fortnight Burt had been joined in hospital by compatriots Maurie Quincey, whose works Norton had broken a conrod at over 200 km/h, Jack Forrest, with a broken shoulder, and Richie Thompson with a broken foot. Burt spent another six months on the Island, undergoing physiotherapy and regaining fitness. Geoff Duke would often take him for exercises at the swimming pool.

Bob Brown finished both the 350 and 500 TT races. He needed a bit of Aussie improvisation in the 350 class. A pin fell out of the gear lever of Bob's AJS, rendering the gearshift inoperative. Fortunately it happened near a cemetery, so Bob parked the bike

Bob Brown astride the Les Slaughter prepared ex-works Velocette in 1953. L to R: Brown, Slaughter, Eric McPherson and Allen Burt.

85

Allen Burt recovered from his 1955 crash and raced his AJS at the Isle of Man in 1958.

against a fence, found some fencing wire in the graveyard, repaired the gearshift and restarted, to finish 40th. He was 15th in the Senior TT.

With his mate in hospital, Brown set out alone to compete on the Continent. Within two months he had made his mark, in two ways, at the new purpose-built Assen circuit. Bob was one of four Australians who joined a riders' strike in the Dutch 350 GP. He was later suspended for six months. Brown, however, rode the whole Dutch 500 GP race — and rode superbly. The British motorcycle press of the day carried a picture of Bob on his privately entered Matchless G45 twin duelling with one of the works MV fours. He finished fifth, behind three works Gileras and a works MV. Ron Kessing reckoned this result on a Matchless G45 was a marvel.

Brown returned to Australia at the end of the season. He raced in local events until his six-month suspension began on January 1. His results included finishing third on the Matchless to fellow internationals Dickie Dale (Guzzi) and Jack Ahearn (Norton) in the 500 race at Mildura on Boxing Day.

Bob left Port Melbourne for England on February 1 with Keith Campbell, who was also under suspension. Western Suburbs clubmates Brown and Burt were reunited for the 1956 European season, as rider and mechanic. This arrangement suited Brown, because contemporaries reckoned he was a classic example of the adage that mechanics didn't like working on their own vehicles and carpenters lived in houses with windows that stuck. Brown was also considered to enjoy a charmed life with sponsors lending him machines. But then, as Geoff Duke recalled, "Bob didn't crash very often, which helped with works machinery."

Brown and Burt watched the 1956 TT races on the Isle of Man, because Bob was still suspended, then they headed for Europe in a 26-seat Bedford bus which had been converted into a combined campervan and bike transporter. Brown now had three machines, his two 1955 mounts and a new NSU 250 Sportmax loaned to him owned by a fellow Dutch GP striker, Ireland's Reg Armstrong. The NSU single was, in 1956 and for several years after, the best 250 a private entrant could obtain. But the Matchless G45 became the problem child of the trio.

Bob Brown and kangaroo.

Allen Burt recalled fitting eight new exhaust valves in half a season, because the valve colletts used to fly out. He reckoned it was the poor quality material that AMC used, and he said that if they had had time to stop at a machine shop for a day or two they could have fixed the problem.

Within 21 days of Brown's suspension ending, he had piloted his NSU to fifth place in the West German 250 GP at Solitude, behind three works MV Agustas and the NSU of Germany's racer Hans Baltisberger. Brown's next race was the non-championship Czech GP at Brno. The 250 race saw a four-way, all-NSU dice for the lead involving Brown, Eric Hinton, Baltisberger and Horst Kassner.

Hinton's description of the race gave some idea of the conditions encountered by 1950s racers: "Brno then was a 17 km public road circuit. The tar was so dark and shiny from spilled diesel you couldn't tell if it was wet or dry. In the 250 race there were four of us, Kassner, Baltisberger, Brownie and me, out in front, slipstreaming nose-to-nail on our NSUs. Then it started to rain on the back section of the course — and didn't we know!

"Brownie fell off right in front of me. His bike just slid away on a fast bend. I looked around and saw he was waving, to show he was okay. I crashed a few corners later and broke my arm. My bike just slid away too. Three laps later Baltisberger crashed and he was killed," Eric said.

Brown and Burt then faced a long drive and a couple of ferry crossings to the Ulster Grand Prix. Bob's results justified the trip: he was runner-up to John Hartle's works Norton in the 500 GP and finished sixth in the 350 race. Gilera and MV did not contest the meeting, because John Surtees had already clinched the world 500 championship.

Four major Italian factories again competed for world championship honours in 1957. John Surtees reckoned it was like feudal times, with teams of black-clad "knights" doing battle in the names of family-owned factories. There were lots of factory rides in 1957 and a large number of injuries to established works riders. An injured Geoff Duke recommended Bob Brown for rides with Gilera. Keith Campbell and, later in the season, Keith Bryen rode for Moto Guzzi.

Brown had two meetings, the Isle of Man and Belgium, with Gilera. He rode his own British machines in other events. His travelling mate was another great character from Sydney's western suburbs, Richie Thompson, who also raced AMC machines. Brown and Thompson camped by the shores of Lake Lugarno for a week before they contested the traditional European season closer at Monza on September 1. Seventeen days later Bob attended Keith Campbell's wedding in the Isle of Man. Gilera's withdrawal from racing was announced the next week.

Bob's off-season in Australia was notable for one result. He won the 1957 Australian 125 TT at Phillip Island, riding Clem Daniel's DOHC single-cylinder MV. It was the only Australian title Bob Brown won.

Bob Brown raced AJS machines — a 7R 350 and G45 500 — when he first went to Europe in 1955.

Bob Brown finished third in the 1957 IoM 350 TT, despite losing the exhaust megaphones from his works Gilera.

Brown, in his Australian Isle of Man team blazer, accepts his trophy for third place in 1957.

Kel Carruthers, then aged 19, was second on a racing Lambretta two-stroke.

The sport's "Dark Ages" were now about to begin, in 1958, when MV Agusta had the 350 and 500 classes to itself, and only MZ and Ducati troubled it in the smaller classes. The private entrants were now racing for third place in the 250, 350 and 500 races, instead of seventh or eighth as they were in 1957. But the privateer's goal of a works ride was more difficult to obtain, because there were fewer paid "seats".

Bob Brown's mounts for 1958 included an NSU 250 and a new AJS 7R 350. Bob, at the Isle of Man, received one of three developmental Norton 500s with bore and stroke dimensions of 93 mm by 73.5 mm. His transporter was a specially equipped van loaned by Geoff Duke. Brown opened the year's classic racing with a fourth place, just behind young Mike Hailwood, in the 250 TT held on the 17-km Clypse circuit. He was third in the 500 TT. Bob's other world championship point-scoring efforts for the season were all sixth places, in the Swedish and German 500 GPs and the Italian 350 GP.

Bob was home in Sydney for Christmas and New Year. When he flew back to England he took his fiancee, Bernadette Somerville. He now jumped to the top of the private entrants class in 1959. One sign of his success was improved life on the road. Bob followed the lead of European racers and lived in hotels. On the track he concentrated on the 350 and 500 classes, this time riding two Nortons.

Brown finished third in a rain-lashed Isle of Man 500 TT to John Surtees and Alistair King. It was his third 500 TT third in a row. He was also second to Bob McIntyre in a new "Formula 1" event, which was restricted to "over-the-counter" racing bikes. At the next two grands prix, in Holland and Belgium, the Formula 1 races were also held; Brown scored a first and a second.

While Brown was in the Isle of Man, he might have had time to notice a new factory team which had entered a fleet of extremely reliable twin-cylinder machines in the 125 class. It was the Honda Motor Company of Japan.

89

Bob Brown in champion company. He finished second in the 1959 Ulster 350 GP, behind John Surtees (centre) and ahead of Geoff Duke (left).

As the world championship season continued, the story was usually the MV-Agustas, then Bob Brown. At Hockenheim Bob was third in the 500 race to MV's John Surtees and Remo Venturi. At Assen he split this pair to finish a brilliant second in the 500 race. Spa-Francorchamps 500 race saw Brown fourth, less than two seconds behind Geoff Duke (Norton). Bob reversed that result in the next grand prix, taking second place ahead of Duke in the Ulster 350 GP. He was also fifth in the Ulster 500 GP. The season's championship finale at Monza saw Brown third, behind the two MVs in the 350 race, and fourth in the 500 behind the MVs and Duke's Norton.

The world 500 championship positions were: Surtees (MV), Venturi (MV), Brown (Norton), Duke (Norton), and Gary Hocking (Norton). In the 350 class the title positions read: Surtees, John Hartle (MV), Brown, Hocking and Duke. But Gary Hocking was the big winner from the season, in terms of his riding future. MV Agusta signed the Rhodesian to ride 250s and 350s. Its reason, according to scribes of the day, was to break up the Hocking/MZ two-stroke combination that had caused the Italians so much trouble in 1959's 250 championship.

Back home, Bob Brown married Bernadette in Sydney in January 1960. Allen Burt was best man. And Bob hired Clem Daniel, one of his former sponsors, as his mechanic for the 1960 season. The Browns sailed back to England, while Daniel left Sydney in a de Havilland Comet just after Easter. He met up with the Browns at Orly airport, Paris, and they drove south in Bob's van, which carried Castrol and Avon endorsements, to Clermont-Ferrand for the first grand prix of the season.

Bob still had his 1959 Norton machines, and his 1959 form. He was third in the 500 race to Surtees and Venturi, and fourth in the 350, behind Hocking (MV), Czechoslovakia's Franta Stastny (works Jawa twin) and Surtees. Next stop was an international at Hockenheim, where Bob won the 500 race from Ralph Renson and Jim Redman.

Brown and Daniel collected two new Nortons in Birmingham before the Isle of Man. Daniel recalled being taken aback by the condition of the new racing bikes: "They were in a shocking state. It took three or four days to prepare them properly for the races. As we worked on the bikes we had a procession of trade people from Girling, Lockheed and Lucas visit to either service equipment on the bikes or replace it with the proper stuff. With the trade reps we changed the shocks, clutch, brake linings and valve springs, and we rubber-mounted the oil tank. There was even a bloke with a special wooden block and a mallett — he put the dents in the tank for more steering lock," Daniel explained.

"Bob was very well liked by the reps. A lot of the other riders were always 'on the make' trying to get things from them."

Brown's hat-trick of third places in the 500 TT had made him one of the most respected Isle of Man contestants. Early in practice week, Honda approached him to ride one of its new four-cylinder, 16-valve 250s. Fellow Australian Tom Phillis was already booked to ride a Honda 250 and a 125. Brown's machine had been privately entered for Japanese rider Tanaka, and Bob had his first ride on the Honda at Jurby air strip. He reported that the bike wanted to "hold back" on full throttle.

Honda's four-cylinder racers couldn't match the well-sorted Italian machines in that year's 250 TT. Gary Hocking and Carlo Ubbiali were first and second on MV Agusta twins, followed by Tarquinio Provini on the single-cylinder Moto Morini. Bob Brown headed the Honda runners in fourth place, followed by Japanese riders Kitano and Taniguchi. Within a year Honda would catch up and pull away in the 125 and 250 classes. And riders such as

Bob Brown leads Britain's Bob Anderson through the Gooseneck, during the 1960 IoM 500 TT. Both rode Nortons.

Brown, Phillis and Redman would help with that development.

Brown rode his new Nortons in the 350 and 500 TT races; he struck an oil patch and fell in the 350 race, and he finished sixth in the 500 TT after a duel on the road with Bob Anderson. The Australian then used the Post-TT Mallory meeting to readjust to "scratching", before the Dutch GP.

The Dutch organisers refused Bob a start in the 250 GP, even though he'd finished fourth at the Isle of Man. He was not offered a 125 because, according to Daniel, Honda thought he was too big for it. So Brown gave his full attention to his Nortons, with telling effect. The 350 GP saw him finish fourth, behind the Surtees and Hocking MVs, and Bob Anderson's Norton. Then, something unusual happened in the 500 GP: John Surtees crashed his MV. This gave John the chance to watch his rivals in action. Venturi won the race for MV, but Brown rode brilliantly to take second place, two seconds ahead of the number-three MV rider, Mendogni. Surtees later complimented Brown in print for his "impeccable riding".

Brown again headed the Norton runners in the following weekend's Belgian GP. He took third place behind Surtees and Venturi, but ahead of Hailwood and Redman. Bob was now third in the world 500 championship. Honda did not enter its 250s for the meeting. They were reportedly away being modified. The German GP on the Solitude circuit, near Stuttgart, was three weeks away, so Bob rode in a meeting at the Nurburgring track and won a 350 international at Helsinki, in Finland.

From the day he arrived at Stuttgart for the German GP Bob Brown had problems. The race organisers wanted to cut his starting money for the 500 race from £80 to £60, but Bob stuck to his principles and withdrew his 500 class entry. Honda, according to Daniel, said it would make up for the loss of start money. Bob tested the revised Honda 250 in Friday's official practice sessions and told Daniel the machine was unpredictable. "It would never do the same things twice in a corner," Daniel recalled.

That comment was not surprising, given Kel Carruthers' description of the "absolutely awful handling" of his Honda 250-four, which was a replica of the 1960 works racer. The early Honda 250s had an extremely short wheelbase and a chassis which seemed to flex in several directions.

The next morning, Saturday, July 23, Brown took the Honda out again. Solitude was a testing circuit: 11.5 km of public roads. The twisty five kilometres back section alone had 18 corners, some off-camber. *The Motor Cycle* newspaper said: "Among the soloists the consensus of opinion was that the new surface was treacherous even when dry, as a result of a dust film scattered from dried mud deposits."

Bob crashed on the last corner on the back section, sustaining several fractures, including one to the skull. He died that afternoon in a Stuttgart hospital. Reports of the day suggested that Brown had skidded on the dust. But his Honda team-mate, Tom Phillis, said Brown was touring back to the pits with a misfiring engine when it cut in on all four cylinders. It was a rare occurrence — and unfortunately tragic.

Even though he was a very quick rider, he did not throw his bike away very often. Geoff Duke recalled, "The fact that I got him into the Gilera team in 1957 and loaned him my special van for 1957 and 1958 shows how highly I regarded Bob as a rider. Bob went well in the TT. He was third in the 100 mph race which Bob McIntyre won. Bob Brown didn't have as good a machine as Mac in that race — he had a second-string machine."

John Surtees said: "Bob Brown was a nice fellow, and a very good rider. He rode many machines and coped with them all."

Perhaps *The Motor Cycle* said it best: "One of the best loved and most consistent riders of the present generation, Brown was admired for his tremendous riding ability and utter lack of affectation."

TOM
PHILLIS

CHAPTER 7

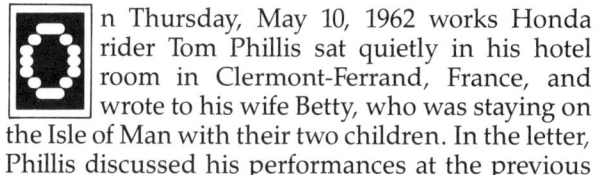

On Thursday, May 10, 1962 works Honda rider Tom Phillis sat quietly in his hotel room in Clermont-Ferrand, France, and wrote to his wife Betty, who was staying on the Isle of Man with their two children. In the letter, Phillis discussed his performances at the previous Sunday's Spanish Grand Prix, in which he'd finished a close third in the 250 race and eighth in the new 50 class.

Tom Phillis was entitled to believe he held a special place in the history of the Honda Motor Company. He was the first Western rider Honda hired and the first to win a world championship grand prix on a Japanese machine. That first Honda victory was at the 1961 Spanish 125 Grand Prix, at Montjuich Park, Barcelona. Phillis in the next seven months won a further five grands prix in the 125 and 250 classes for Honda. He won the 1961 world 125 championship and was second to Mike Hailwood in the world 250 championship. All told in 1961, Tom Phillis scored 15 top-three grand prix positions, an all-time one-season record for an Australian rider.

But Tom Phillis, world champion, wasn't sure what to make of his relationship with Honda when he sat down to write his usual thoughtful letter home that evening in 1962. After the greetings to his wife, he wrote: "As regards the news from Barcelona, I must tell you now in one sentence — I won't be winning any world championships this year. At the Spanish (GP) I had to content myself with an absolute lap record and leading the race until given the frantic 'slow down' from the pits. The 50 is not up to carrying me and that will be (Luigi) Taveri's title anyway, provided he can get it."

Phillis continued the theme later in the letter: "Sorry I haven't written many letters but I spend too much time at the Honda camp looking at and talking about the bikes. I must get out of the habit as it doesn't much matter now, but I still keep feeling I must do my best even when I've been told not to."

This was the last letter Tom Phillis wrote to his wife. He was killed in a race crash at the Isle of Man on Wednesday, June 6, 1962. The only other clue Tom left as to Honda's instructions was in a letter he wrote at the end of May to his old friend and rival Eric Hinton. In that letter Tom said he'd been given a second-string 125 and 250 for the TT. He said Honda's stated aim for him was to wave the flag in 1962 and develop a 350 machine for 1963. But he wanted to win races. Why Honda would want its most experienced rider to run dead was a mystery which died with Phillis.

★ ★ ★ ★ ★ ★

Tom Phillis's world championship made him perhaps the first Australian international motorcyclist to receive general recognition at home. He was the

Thomas Edward Phillis — a quiet man with ability to lead.

first motorcyclist to be a finalist for the ABC Sportsman of the Year, the country's premier sports award, and only the second motorcyclist to be honoured with a civic reception in the Sydney Town Hall (Harry Hinton was the first).

There are motor sport enthusiasts who still recall the sight and the deep-pitched howl of Phillis's post-championship demonstration laps at Sydney's Warwick Farm circuit in December 1961, revving a four-cylinder Honda 250 to the then fantastic figure of 14,000 rpm.

But Phillis didn't only win races and establish records on Hondas. He made his name on 350 and 500 Nortons, and achieved an Isle of Man first for the marque. During the 1961 IoM TT Tom recorded the first-ever 100 mph (161 km/h) lap for a machine with pushrod valve actuation. The machine was the prototype Norton Domiracer, a roadster-based 500 twin Dominator engine slotted into a Manx Norton-type frame.

At the time only six men had recorded 100 mph laps at the Isle of Man, and all except two had achieved the feat on four-cylinder 500s. Phillis finished third in the race, behind acknowledged TT greats Mike Hailwood and Bob McIntyre, both on proven Manx Norton singles. The Domiracer ride gave Phillis his third rostrum position in as many starts at the 1961 TT.

TT aficionados recognised Phillis's two consecutive 100 mph laps as noteworthy because the first 100 mph laps on Nortons had been recorded just one year earlier. Hailwood in that 1961 race made

British-bike history by averaging more than 100 mph (161.86 km/h to be precise) for the entire six laps. Phillis averaged 158.94 km/h for the race, despite some handicaps. His rear tyre rubbed on the swinging arm and he nursed the engine for the last two laps, after damaged pushrods caused it to lose 1000 revs.

Tom Phillis, like Australia's first world motorcycle champion Keith Campbell, really blossomed as a rider in Europe. He won his only two Australian championships at the end of his first overseas season. In the next few years he enjoyed such success at Phillip Island he was known as the circuit's "king".

Tom in street clothes was somehow hard to picture as a racing motorcyclist. He was slightly built (his 66 kg were spread over 178 cm), with dark wavy hair, brown eyes and an engaging grin which rarely left his face. People consistently guessed he was a couple of years younger than his real age. Tom was an outwardly unflappable character, an image heightened by his soft, easy-paced voice, dry humour and unhurried manner in all areas except on a racing bike.

Phillis was by all accounts a good bloke, popular, friendly, yet a touch reserved, and in no way a big-noter. If a group of people gathered around him, as they did, he'd just as likely get them all working on something. He set high standards for himself, and encouraged others to do their best. His relaxed style

Phillis made British-bike history in the 1961 TT with two 100 mph laps on the roadster-based Norton Domiracer.

Tom Phillis, world champion, does a lap of honour at Sydney's new Warwick Farm circuit, on a works replica Honda 250 four.

around the pits was compared with fellow Australian Honda rider Bob Brown, and his quiet popularity and humour with Jack Findlay who, like Phillis, arrived in Europe in 1958. Racing journalists of the late 1950s found Phillis one of the most approachable men in the paddock. Britain's Mick Woollett reckoned Tom was one of his two favourite Australian racers (1950s sidecar racer Bob Mitchell was the other).

"Tom was very modest, a good friend with a good sense of humour. As a rider he was very good. I couldn't split Tom, Keith Campbell and Bob Brown as riders, they were all top-class in the late 1950s," Woollett said.

Six-times world champion Jim Redman, whom Phillis introduced to the Honda team in 1960, wrote in his book *Wheels Of Fortune* that Tom was one of the world's best riders and had a "let the world go by" attitude. Eric Hinton, who had some great races with Phillis in Australia in 1958-1959, said Tom was a typical young married bloke, quiet and shy. "I don't think we ever saw the best of Tom as a rider — that was still coming," Hinton said.

Tom's mechanic in 1961, Bob "Blue" Lewis, described him as a great mate and a great ambassador for Australia in motorcycling. "He helped other people out when they needed it. And he was very mechanically minded. During practice sessions he knew what was wrong with a bike before he pulled into the pits. He had a big input into the Hondas, particularly in 1960."

On the track, Tom Phillis was as dedicated and determined as any. He put so much into the New Year's Day 1962 Phillip Island meeting, in which he won five races against the likes of Kel Carruthers, Trevor Pound and Ken Rumble, he broke down at the presentation dinner.

Thomas Edward Phillis was born on April 9, 1934, and raised in Marrickville, a working-class Sydney suburb. He had an older sister, two younger sisters and a younger brother. To avoid confusion with his father, also named Thomas, the Phillis family addressed Tom Jnr as "Ted". Tom Snr was a dispatch sidecar rider for a large Sydney department store.

Phillis was not a common name. Tom's early scrapbook is littered with clippings referring to T. Phillips (sic). Tom Snr told his son not to worry, but to make the name Phillis famous. Tom Phillis and 1980s Australian Superbike star Rob Phillis are not related. One family has been in Sydney for five generations, the other is from Adelaide and later Albury. During World War II Tom Phillis Snr actually met Rob's father Allan Phillis at a Royal Australian Air Force pay office in Sydney, when both answered to the name Phillis.

Tom Phillis was a bright student. He won a place in a selective high school. His main sporting interest was centred on the banked concrete cycle track at Henson Park, one street from the Phillis home. Tom was the local cycle club's schoolboy road-race champion and a good track rider as well. One night Tom arrived home after a cycle race minus a fair percentage of his skin. He'd dived off the top of the banking to take the race lead and come unstuck. After that, he figured if he was going to lose skin, he might as well do it with a machine that didn't require so much of his energy.

On leaving school, Tom was apprenticed as a motor mechanic. He started motorcycling at 16, by riding errands on his employer's BSA Bantam. Tom Snr gave him some riding tips and took him along

Tom Phillis tries a Honda 250 four for size. The 1961 model produced 31 kW and weighed 104 kg.

for his licence test. Tom bought a rare white-tanked Velocette 350. The Velo was his pride and joy. It lead to the two most important meetings of Tom's life — with future wife Betty and with the man who introduced him to motorcycle racing.

Tom met Betty when she was on her mum's front doorstep, chatting to another motorcyclist. Tom was passing and stopped initially to chat to the motorcyclist. His introduction to motorcycle racing was the product of a chance meeting during his national service period in the RAAF in 1953-1954. A fellow national serviceman, Bob Lewis, was apprenticed to the NSW Velocette agent and had a black-tanked Velocette 350. Lewis reckoned he first talked to Tom to ask him about the white-tanked Velo. They soon became mates.

Tom made his motorcycle racing debut at the Gnoo Blas public road circuit at Orange in 1954. The Phillis family drove from Sydney to watch. But Tom's Velocette failed to complete a lap in the race. Tom's next two races produced two more non-finishes. The fourth race, a clubman race at Mt Druitt, he won.

Phillis put plenty of work into the Velocette. Late 1960s Australian international Phil O'Brien made his racing debut on the former Phillis Velo. He said the bike was quite competitive. The cylinder head had been converted from coil valve springs to hairpin valve springs and it had swinging arm rear suspension in lieu of a rigid rear end.

In February 1955 Tom Phillis married Betty. She was a stenographer at the time, but later became a schoolteacher. They saved together to buy a new motorcycle for Tom's racing, a BSA 500 Gold Star. Tom raced in clubman events for the next two years, learning his craft, not setting the world abuzz. One notable event he contested was the 1955 24-Hour race at Mt Druitt, a circuit built at a disused airfield in Sydney's west. Tom shared a Puch 250 with Roy East and Ray Blackett. They finished 14th, despite a very long pitstop to repair crash damage.

After three seasons as a clubman rider, Phillis reckoned he was ready for a front-line racer. He bought a Manx Norton 500 from 1956 Isle of Man team-member Barry Hodgkinson. It had a full-bin fairing and was tuned to run on methanol fuel (which was permitted in Australia). Tom and Betty planned to set off for Europe at the beginning of 1957, but the Suez Crisis caused them to postpone the trip.

Tom's riding confidence grew in the next 12 months. He finished fourth in the 1957 Easter Bathurst 500 race, behind Jack Ahearn (Norton), Jack Forrest (Rennsport BMW) and Maurie Quincey (Norton). Ahearn, Forrest and Quincey all had international experience and all had won grand prix events on Mount Panorama. This race, and six further racetrack duels during 1957 with Ahearn, greatly influenced 23-year-old Phillis.

Years later Tom said he developed his racing style from what he saw as the best points of Ahearn and Quincey, who had both raced in Europe in 1954-1955. Phillis said early in 1962: "I admired Jack Ahearn's guts. He rode smoothly enough to suit his big frame and I just couldn't pass him. Maurie Quincey taught me style. Quincey's easy and comfortable method of riding a machine was right up to overseas standards. So I split the difference between the two and took it from there."

Phillis won his first open event at Mt Druitt in May 1957. He spent the next six months chasing Ahearn and learning from him. In October 1957 Tom won the 350 race at Fishermans Bend. The following month he won three Queensland titles at the Lowood airfield circuit, near Toowoomba.

The big test was in December at Mt Druitt, when the current international riders returned for the summer. Tom won the 500 "International GP" from Eric Hinton and Ahearn. The result gave Phillis his first burst of publicity and renewed incentive to go to Europe.

Tom and Betty Phillis sold up everything, including Betty's tennis racket, ordered two new Nortons and headed for Europe in 1958. Another international debutant that season was Jack Findlay, while the experienced hands included Keith Campbell, Bob Brown, the Hinton brothers, Jack Ahearn, Allen Burt and Richie Thompson. Many of this crew, including Keith Campbell's wife Geraldine, travelled together on the *Oronsay*.

Phillis began the season well, with four wins at his second overseas meeting at Thruxton aerodrome on Easter Monday 1958. He won the heats and finals of the 350 and 500 events. A few weeks later Tom finished fourth in the 350 international race at St Wendel in Germany (Harry Hinton won the race) and third in the 500. He also rode at Hockenheim and a public road circuit at Salzburg, before heading to the Isle of Man and the Australian riders' home away from home, Rosevilla guest house.

Phillis's TT debut was not the stuff of legends. He played smart and took his time to learn the course. It was so rough in those days he later described the TT as "the world's fastest scramble". But it later became his favourite circuit. Tom's reward for a steady approach was two finishes and two silver replicas for 32nd in the 350 TT and 18th in the 500 TT. Back on the Continent, Phillis's form improved steadily. In July he won the 350 and 500 races at an international meeting at Falkenburg in Sweden. The same month Tom finished third in the 350 race at Cadours in France. Keith Campbell won that race, but was killed a few hours later in the 500 event. Phillis helped get Campbell's van and gear back to England so it could be sold for Campbell's wife Geraldine.

In the next few years Phillis followed Campbell's example and became a regular visitor to Scandinavia. On one visit a Finnish tailor made a suit and sports coat for Tom and used his picture in local advertising.

The story of the 1958-1959 summer season in Australia was Tom Phillis versus Eric Hinton and Ron Miles (Victoria's find of the 1957 and 1958 domestic seasons). It started at Melbourne's Darley circuit in November. Hinton won the 350 race from Phillis. But Tom crashed in the 500 race and broke his collarbone. The 1958 Australian TT was held on Boxing Day, on a street circuit in Albany, Western Australia. Eric Hinton, the 1957 Australian 500 TT winner, had transport trouble and chose not to defend his title. But Tom Phillis and his father made the trip in a small Hillman car.

Tom Phillis Snr described the 4000 km trip across Australia. "The national titles were important for sponsorship and Isle of Man team selection. We rebuilt Tom's motors in the back room at home, then headed west. We had to take the wheels off the bikes to fit them in the trailer.

"We drove day and night, one driving, one sleeping. Tom was uncomfortable either way with his broken collarbone. We had planned to drive to Port Pirie in South Australia, then put the car on the train for the section across the Nullarbor Plain. But when we reached Port Pirie the train was full, so we had to take the dirt road across the Nullarbor. We were on the road for four days!"

But Tom made the trip worthwhile. He rode with his shoulder bandaged to win the Australian 500 TT from Don Leadbetter and Ron Miles, and the 350 TT from Miles. Phillis was third to Miles and Leadbetter in the Australian Unlimited TT. These were the only national titles Phillis and Miles won.

The Phillis-Hinton battle resumed at Phillip Island in January 1959, in the Victorian GP meeting. Tom tailed Eric onto the straight on the last lap of the 500 race and timed his slipstream pass perfectly to win the race by half a length. He was credited with a new lap record at an average of 126 km/h. Tom also won the 350 and 500 events at the Victorian TT meeting, held on February 22 at Fishermans Bend. Eric Hinton did not contest that meeting, but he turned out the following holiday long weekend in Tasmania for the 1959 Australian TT on the 7.5 km Longford public road circuit. A crowd of 30,000 attended.

Hinton beat Phillis by ten seconds to win the 350 TT. But the race of the meeting was the ten-lap 500 TT, as Eric Hinton explained: "I had my dad's former works Norton, with a full-bin front fairing and a tail fairing. Tom had his 1958 Manx with a dolphin fairing. I had a slight top-speed advantage (our two bikes running nose-to-tail were timed at 216 km/h), but Tom would pass me each lap under brakes at the last corner, a virtual hairpin, and lead over the start/finish line.

"After a few laps I realised Tom was using me as his braking marker. So I braked a little early each lap to let him think he had me covered. On the last lap I went past the 300 yard braking marker to about 280, which was as deep as I reckoned I could go and still get around the corner. Tom again braked later than I did. My front brake drum had a turbo extractor fan for extra cooling, so that helped. I made it around the corner; Tom nearly went up the escape road before he sorted things out!

"Tom came along later in the pits and said: 'Hinto, I'll have to go back to school for another 12 months!' He was a good sport. We both bettered Geoff Duke's

Tom Phillis (Norton, No 12) pushes off with works MV rider John Hartle (No 11) in the 1960 IoM TT.

1955 lap record (set on the Gilera four) in that race," Hinton said.

The variation in Australian TT dates meant Tom had held his Australian 350 and 500 crowns for just two months. So he "went back to school" — in Europe. Betty Phillis stayed in Sydney that season and gave birth to a daughter, Debbie.

Tom was a nominee for the 1959 Australian Isle of Man TT team, but he was ruled ineligible for a share of the Australian grant after the ACU of Great Britain gave him a grant as a promising TT rider.

Phillis again bought new Manx Nortons. His performances showed the benefit of a summer's racing in Australia. In May he won the 500 race and finished second in the 350 event at Mettet, one of Belgium's most prestigious international meetings.

In June, Tom finished fifth in the 350 class of the

Isle of Man Formula 1 race, a special event for non-factory machines such as Manx Nortons. He followed that up with 16th place in the rain-lashed 500 TT, two places behind Ron Miles. Tom was forced out of the 350 TT while running 11th when his Norton broke its connecting rod 10 km from the chequered flag in a 425 km race. Fortunately, he was not seriously injured by this mechanical failure.

The 1959 Isle of Man TT marked the world championship debut of the Honda Motor Company. Tom Phillis must have been impressed by the well-built Honda 125 twins, because the entry for the following year's Isle of Man meeting included T.E. Phillis on Honda 125 and 250 machines.

Tom collected more impressive placings in international races on the Continent in the next three months. He was fifth in a Formula 1 350 race at Assen, first in the 500 race at Moulins, scored a second and a third in the 500 and 350 classes at Nurburgring and won the 500 race at Tampere in Finland.

Back in Britain, Tom beat Rhodesia's young star Gary Hocking at Thruxton. He then finished fifth (and scored his first world championship points) in the Ulster 350 GP. The company Phillis finished in was probably more pleasing than the two championship points. The first four were John Surtees, Bob Brown, Geoff Duke and Dickie Dale — two world champions and two former works riders.

Phillis was in top form when he returned to Australia at the end of the season. He won four races (two 350 and two 500 events) at Lowood in Queensland. And won another four at the Victorian GP meeting, held on New Year's Day 1960 at Phillip Island, defeating fellow internationals Bob Brown, Eric Hinton and Ron Miles. Phillis and Hinton shared a new outright lap record. The meeting was one of the first in Australia to be reported on national television.

Phillis that summer became one of the first men to race a Ducati in Australia. At Darley he rode one of the 125s brought over by Bendigo sponsor Jack Walters, and had another battle with Eric Hinton (on an MV). But the little Ducati blew up in the Victorian TT meeting at Fishermans Bend. Ron Miles was the top gun at Fishermans Bend. Phillis was second in the 500 race and crashed (without injury) in the 350 event.

Phillis became a feature attraction at Victorian meetings, particularly the Phillip Island races promoted by the Hartwell Club. The recently introduced NSW Speedways Act had seriously affected road-racing in Tom's home state. There was no licensed motorcycle road-racing circuit within 160 km of Sydney. The Hartwell Club's secretary of the day, Wes Brown, said Tom was always obliging with publicity work for these meetings. In 1961 the club made Tom Phillis an honorary life member.

Over the summer of 1959-1960 Tom Phillis wrote a personal but well-argued letter to the Honda Motor Company seeking a ride in the 1960 season. By February, the story was in print — Tom would ride Hondas at the Isle of Man TT. Tom, Betty and Debbie Phillis headed for Europe with the promise of at least one works Honda ride to supplement his performances on his own Nortons.

Development riding for a company with virtually no experience in classic road racing would not be easy. But a works ride meant prestige and income to a professional rider, and Phillis was in on the ground floor if the Hondas became world-beaters.

Power-wise, the 1960 Honda 125-twin and 250-four were already competitive. The 125 produced 15 kW and the 250 30 kW. It's said Soichiro Honda personally directed design work on the 1960 250 engine, after deciding an earlier version should be scrapped.

The areas which needed development were chassis, suspension, and brakes. These were the areas where Honda needed Western rider input. They knew the circuits and they knew how a machine was supposed to handle on those circuits. The 1960 machines were poor handlers and had problems with ignitions and spark plugs. But each model featured improvements. The riders found the 1961 models were significantly better, and the 1962 issue better again.

One of Tom's first major meetings in Europe in 1960 was St Wendel, where he won the 350 race on his Norton. A week or so later he won the 500 race and was second in the 350 at Helsinki in Finland.

Phillis entered his own Nortons for the Isle of Man 350 and 500 TTs, while Honda supplied his small-bore machines. One of the first things Honda race team manager Kawashima requested from Phillis was a list of the best quality accessories — chains, seats, spark plugs, suspension units — for evaluation. During practice week Honda recruited another Sydneysider, Bob Brown, to ride a 250-four privately entered for Japanese rider Tanaka.

Phillis's Honda debut was hampered by mechanical problems. He was running sixth in the 125 TT until his machine began mis-firing. Tom dropped back to finish tenth. His Japanese Honda teammates filled places six to nine. Italian MV Agusta four-stroke singles took the first three places, followed by a pair of East German MZ two-strokes. One of the MV riders, Luigi Taveri, saw the message: Honda was learning fast. At the end of the season he wrote to Honda's Amsterdam agent and asked for a contract.

Taveri explained to the authors: "The first time I saw a Honda motorcycle was in Switzerland in the mid-1950s. It was not a racing bike and I laughed at it. But in 1959 at the Tourist Trophy we saw Honda racers. The 1959 bikes were not as fast as MV, but

Flying Kangaroos! Tom Phillis and Bob Brown duel on their 500 Nortons at Phillip Island in January 1960.

Phillis checks on the Honda team's preparation at the 1960 IoM TT meeting. The team was garaged in Douglas.

already we could see Honda made nice bikes. In 1960 the bikes were better, and I realised then it was only a matter of time before Honda would be the best. By 1962 the 250 was very good — as fast as a Norton 500. I still ride mine in vintage races."

Mike Hailwood was not impressed so quickly. According to Tom Phillis Snr, Honda asked Tom to sound out Hailwood about riding a Honda. Hailwood said he wouldn't ride a Japanese machine. Mike changed his view within 12 months.

There was another disappointment for Phillis in the 250 TT. His machine developed gearbox trouble on the third lap, while he was in fourth place behind three Italian machines. Tom retired from the race. Bob Brown finished fourth, and so became the first Western rider to score world championship points on a Japanese machine.

Tom's TT week was saved by his Manx Norton 500 (his 350 Norton also let him down). Phillis averaged nearly 98 mph (157.35 km/h to be exact) to place fourth in the six-lap (365 km) 500 TT. Tom finished 48 seconds behind fellow Manx Norton pilot Mike Hailwood, and almost a minute ahead of sixth-placed compatriot Brown. His fastest lap was a fraction under 99 mph.

The result proved Phillis was now a top-flight TT rider. Hailwood recorded one of the first 100 mph laps during this race, riding a Norton prepared by one of the best tuners in England. Yet Tom had finished a two-and-a-quarter hour race less than 50 seconds behind this rising British star.

Phillis crashed and broke his collarbone during practice for the next world championship event, the Dutch TT at Assen. Honda was suddenly short of riders, because Brown had been refused a start in the 250 class and Taniguchi had also crashed. There were plenty of volunteers. But Phillis was good mates with tall Rhodesian rider Jim Redman. As soon as Redman expressed interest, Tom spoke with team manager Kawashima. Within minutes Redman was nominated for a 125 ride.

Tom Phillis's recommendation that day at Assen helped Redman on the road to stardom. Honda was still trialling and hiring riders on a meeting-to-meeting basis. Redman not only stayed and won six world championships, he came to have a large say in the way the Honda team operated in Europe. Luigi Taveri said: "Tom Phillis and Jim Redman were already established when I joined the Honda team in 1961, so I was the outsider. Tom was okay, but Jim was the strong one — he organised the team."

Redman finished fourth in his first race for Honda — the Dutch 125 GP. Honda missed the next grand prix in Belgium, so it could make improvements to the 250s. It returned for the German GP at Solitude. It was a sad meeting for Australia. Bob Brown was killed during official practice, while riding a Honda 250. And there was an eerie postscript. Tanaka, the man Brown had replaced at the Isle of Man, finished third for Honda in the 250 GP, 50 seconds behind the winning twin-cylinder MV.

Phillis recovered from his broken collarbone for the Ulster GP, which drew 100,000 people. The Honda 250s proved more suited to the fast Dundrod circuit than Solitude. MV's Carlo Ubbiali won the race by a bare two seconds from Phillis, with Redman just over a second behind in third place. Tom rode his Norton to sixth in the 500 race, one place behind Redman's Norton.

Honda was so pleased with the 250 result it let Phillis ride a works 125 in some late-season internationals. Tom headed off to Finland, where in one meeting he won the 125 race on the Honda and took the 350/500 double on his Nortons. Back in Britain, Tom beat Mike Hailwood (who was riding a works Ducati 125) at Brands Hatch and won the 125 race at Aintree. These were Honda's first European wins.

Tom Phillis came home at season's end and found a present waiting for him. Honda had built six works replica 250-fours, which the sales department farmed out around the world to help promote the marque. The machine's quoted value was £6000. Honda's annual race budget at the time was a reported £450,000.

The machine caused a minor rumpus when it arrived, because Bennett and Wood had it earmarked for 22-year-old Sydneysider Kel Carruthers, but Tom Phillis was a works rider. Phillis gave the Honda four its Australian debut at Symmons Plains, Tasmania, on December 11, 1960. He won three Tasmanian TTs, the 250, 350 and 500.

Phillis for the second year in a row won four races at the New Year's Day meeting on Phillip Island. He won the five-lap Victorian 250 GP by nearly a minute, then out-ran the Nortons in the 350 GP. But it wasn't just the Honda motorcycle. Phillis switched to Ron Miles' Norton 500 to win the 500 preliminary and the Victorian 500 GP, from Eric Hinton and Jack Ahearn.

Phillis that summer also took a treble at Hume Weir, winning the 250, 500 and unlimited races, with Hinton the runner-up in all three. But the Victorian TT at Ballarat Airstrip produced a reversal for Phillis. Bob West, who'd just returned from a season in Europe travelling with Jack Findlay, beat him in the 500 race by a bare 0.2 second.

Honda signed two Western riders to contest the 1961 world championships: Phillis and Redman. They were given redesigned works 125-twins and 250-fours. Luigi Taveri, who had asked for a place in the squad, was initially given a 1960 model 125. The new works machines had more power, improved ignitions (a real problem in 1960), new carburettors and dry-sump lubrication, so the engine could be set lower in the chassis. The 250 weighed a creditable 104 kg.

Tom Phillis modified his riding style for the Honda 250. He leaned his upper body inside the bike, so he could keep the machine more upright and reduce the risk of the tyres sliding. "Naturally it was a lot safer way of cornering. But my aim wasn't for extra safety, it was to corner quicker than the other fellow," Phillis explained.

Tom took his old RAAF mate Bob Lewis to Europe as mechanic for 1961. Phillis's Thames van carried two Hondas and two Nortons. "Blue" Lewis ended up helping Phillis and Redman with their Nortons and Hondas. Phillis started the 1961 season brilliantly at the Spanish GP on April 23. He won the 125 GP and finished second to MV rider Gary Hocking in the 250 GP. But the source of prime 125 competition was already clear.

Ernst Degner finished second in Spain on the single-cylinder rotary-disc-valve MZ designed by brilliant two-stroke engineer Walter Kaaden. And Mike Hailwood had qualified fastest and led the race until his English-built MZ look-alike EMC fractured its exhaust pipe.

Kaaden's work would inspire race engineers for the next two decades. His machine had the potential to beat Honda's four-stroke twin. According to Mick Woollet's contemporary reports, it was faster in top speed and better under brakes (perhaps because it was lighter). The Honda's strong points were its superior roadholding and acceleration out of slow corners. The MZ certainly had speed. Its winning race averages at the two fastest circuits, Hockenheim and Monza, were more than 158 km/h. In the Hockenheim race, Degner led an MZ walkover. The best placed Honda rider was Taveri, who finished fifth.

But there was a large barrier to Kaaden's development program. MZ was based in East Germany, so he was often hampered by lack of development money, poor quality metals and unreliable ignition components, and a regime which didn't like his race team travelling.

Honda did something around May 1961 which must have puzzled Phillis, Redman and Taveri. The sales department released more works replica 125 and 250 machines to distributors. Phillis and Redman were the longest-serving Honda riders and the men giving the development feedback to the engineers. But now they had to race the MVs, MZs and another fleet of Hondas. No sooner had the new works replicas appeared than millionaire motorcycle dealer Stan Hailwood (whose nickname was "Stan the Wallet") had obtained a pair for his son. Scotland's Bob McIntyre, a master IoM TT rider, also obtained a Honda 250-four.

Phillis replied to MZ's challenge and Honda's scatter-gun tactics the best way he could, with a

Tom Phillis on his way to victory in the 1961 French 125 GP at Clermont-Ferrand, on his Honda twin. He also won the French 250 GP (see chapter opening picture).

double victory in the French GP at the demanding eight kilometres Clermont-Ferrand circuit. He won the 125 class from Degner and Redman, and the 250 race from Mike Hailwood. "Magnifique!" said the French daily press. Phillis also scored successes in international races in May. He won the 250 races at St Wendel and Salzburg, but was narrowly beaten in the Salzburg 125 race by two MZ riders.

The 1961 Isle of Man TT was a Mike Hailwood benefit. He won three races and his machine failed while leading a fourth. Tom Phillis shared the victory dais after all three of Hailwood's wins. But that wasn't all in Tom's TT week. Wife Betty delivered a son, who was named Thomas Braddan Phillis — the Braddan after Braddan Bridge and the village of Kirk Braddan on the TT course.

Hailwood opened his winning treble by taking the 125 TT from Taveri, Phillis, Redman and Schimazaki (all on Hondas). McIntyre led the 250 TT until his Honda ran out of oil. Hailwood won from Phillis, Redman and two more Hondas. Bob Lewis still has Tom's trophy for second place, at an average speed of 96.56 mph (155.37 km/h).

Phillis had entered his own special Norton for the 500 TT. It had a five-speed gearbox and a steering damper, to improve control over the bumps. But during practice week Tom accepted Norton development engineer Doug Hele's offer to ride the experimental Domiracer. Hailwood hounded Gary Hocking's MV until it broke. McIntyre finished second and Phillis third. Tom recorded laps of 100.4 mph and 100.0 mph during the race. After four laps he was running third to Hocking and Hailwood. Hocking retired on the fifth lap, but McIntyre passed Phillis when the Domiracer's engine went off song, so he remained in third place. Hele repaid Phillis by letting him and Lewis rebuild and test engines in the Norton race shop.

Phillis scored his third win of the 125 GP season at Assen. He had a duel with Hailwood until Mike crashed while trying to shake off Tom. The following week Taveri, Phillis and Redman had the race of the season in the Belgian GP at Spa. Taveri won by a clear half wheel from Phillis, with Redman just two seconds behind. Clearly there were no

Honda duel. Phillis leads Hailwood in the 1961 Dutch 125 GP. Phillis won, Hailwood crashed.

team orders. Redman won the 250 race from Phillis and Hailwood.

The 1961 world 125 championship had 11 rounds, so riders would count their best six results. After the Belgian GP, Phillis had scored three wins and two second placings in the first six races, giving him 36 points. Degner's tally at the same stage was 23, from a win, two seconds and a fourth. But Degner and MZ weren't beaten yet. Degner won by 30 seconds in front of a quarter million spectators at his home circuit, Sachsenring. Phillis and Japanese works rider Takahashi were second and third. Takahashi then won the Ulster GP from Degner and Phillis.

The Ulster GP was not a happy meeting for Phillis. His mate Ron Miles crashed to his death during practice. He was sharing accommodation with Tom and using an engine Phillis and Lewis had prepared at Norton Motors. To compound the misery, Tom crashed during the 500 race and was hospitalised for a couple of days with concussion.

The Italian GP produced Degner's third win of the season. Phillis was fourth, behind fellow Honda riders Tanaka and Taveri. Phillis and Degner were now tied on 42 points, because their best six results were three wins and three second placings. The only way either could improve his score and clinch the title was to win one of the remaining two races — at Kristianstad in Sweden and Buenos Aires.

The Kristianstad meeting was dramatic. Degner wanted to win the world championship, but he also wanted to defect to the West with his family. And Suzuki was prepared to help him in return for information on Kaaden's two-stroke development work.

Degner's MZ broke its crankshaft on the third lap of the 125 GP. Taveri won the race for Honda. Phillis was hampered by a misfiring engine and finished sixth. Degner already knew his wife and two sons had crossed to West Germany in the boot of a car. So he waited for the 500 GP to end, drove out of the pits and off to Denmark, where he told border officials he wanted to defect.

Meantime, Mike Hailwood had won the 250 GP, to clinch his first world championship and Honda's first title.

Phillis and Degner had to wait a month for the Argentine GP at Buenos Aires to decide the 125 championship. Degner was loaned an EMC in a bid to win the crown. But political problems connected with his defection complicated getting a racing licence and the bike, let alone making it finish.

Tom was still under pressure. Light rain fell at the start of the 50-lap race. Redman led Phillis for the first 44 laps. There was a battle for the next six laps. But Phillis led where it mattered by a couple of lengths, to take the championship. He also won the 250 GP, to claim second place in the 250 title.

Phillis raced in Chile — another first — then came home a hero. Sydney gave him a civic reception, he was a finalist for the ABC Sportsman of the Year and 15,000 car race fans cheered him at Sydney's new Warwick Farm circuit.

Tom borrowed some Nortons and the Jack Walters' Ducati 125 for his now annual January race show at Phillip Island. For the third year running he won four events. In the Victorian 350 GP, Phillis on a Norton beat Kel Carruthers, who was riding the 1960 works replica Honda 250-four. Tom's only loss on the day was in the 125 GP. Carruthers won that race on Clem Daniel's MV. Later that summer Australian crowds saw two Honda 250-fours in action — Phillis on his Argentine GP-winning machine (shipped from South America) and Carruthers on the 1960 replica. One such meeting was the Victorian TT at Calder, where Phillis won the 250, 350 and 500 races on his Honda 250. His only loss on the Honda was to Ken Rumble, in pouring rain at Hume Weir.

Honda retained Phillis, Redman and Taveri for 1962. They were to contest the 250, 125 and the new 50 cm^3 world championships. The machinery included a new single-cylinder 50, an uprated 125-twin and 250-four, and a 250 machine bored out to 285 cm^3 as a prelude to a full attack on MV in the 350 class.

Luigi Taveri found full Honda team membership a pleasure after his years with Italy's MV. "With Honda, everybody's bike had the same power. But with MV you'd have a big difference and I was never told what the story was," he said.

Phillis began the season in style. He won the 250 race at Imola, with a faster average speed than Gary Hocking recorded in the 500 class. But by IoM TT time Tom was confused as to just what Honda expected of him. Tom's mounts for the season's world championship opener in Spain were a 50 and a 250. The 50 didn't suit his weight and he finished eighth. He was third behind Redman and McIntyre in the 250 race, having been told to slow down after setting fastest lap. The French GP at Clermont-Ferrand produced the same 250 race result, in a blanket finish. Takahashi won the first two 125 GPs from Redman.

Phillis's mounts for the 1962 Isle of Man TT were a 125, 250 and the new 285 cm^3 machine for the 350 race. The fastest laps from the 1961 TT meeting had shown a 250 Honda was only three seconds slower around the 61 km course than MV's 350, which had had little development since John Surtees won three 350 titles on it in the late 1950s. So Honda's 285 machine had potential as a 350 race contender, but its handling was not proven, because the TT was the first round of the 350 championship.

Early in practice week the Honda team was out at Jurby airfield, trying to cure misfires with the 125s and 250s. Meantime, Redman, McIntyre and Phillis all tried the 285 machines during practice. Phillis also did some laps on the new model 125.

Tom's TT week opened on Monday, June 4 with the 250 race. It was a Honda clean sweep. England's Derek Minter won from Redman. Tom Phillis was third, a fine effort given he had to fight his way back after losing five places due to an engine misfire. Ernst Degner won the 50 TT on the new Suzuki, built with the aid of the information he'd brought from MZ. Taveri was second for Honda.

Phillis had two rides on Wednesday, June 6 — the 125 TT in the morning and the 350 TT in the afternoon. It meant Phillis would ride nine laps or 547 km in a day. On the morning of the races, the Redmans helped Betty Phillis take children Debbie and Brad to a nursery, so she could watch from the grandstand. The 125 TT was another Honda walkover. Taveri won from Ireland's Tommy Robb, with Tom Phillis third.

Tom was tired after the race and rested in the back of his van. Just before the next race he kissed Betty, as usual, then turned back for another kiss.

The 350 TT was a potential showdown: Phillis and McIntyre on Honda 285s versus Hailwood and Hocking on MV 350s. Tom was first to push off, followed ten seconds later by Hailwood and a further ten seconds by Hocking. From a standing start, Hocking lapped at 100.90 mph, Hailwood at 100.05 mph, Phillis at 99.22 mph and McIntyre at 98.65 mph.

On the road, this meant Hocking actually caught Hailwood and Phillis by the end of the lap, and that Hailwood also passed Phillis. Maybe it made Phillis

Tom Phillis developed a lean-in style for the Honda 250 four. The venue is Imola in April 1961. The machine is a 1960-model.

even more determined to impress Honda.

Tom Phillis cleared Ballacraine on the second lap. Opposite the grandstand, Tom's pointer on the 100-metre long black scoreboard moved to the letter B.

Minutes later the announcers at Ballaugh, the second commentary point, described the arrival of Hocking and Hailwood — amid the roar of their four-cylinder MV engines. Tom Phillis's pointer remained at Ballacraine. He'd crashed at Laurel Bank, a fast right-hand corner a few kilometres from Ballacraine. Tom died in the ambulance. He was 28.

What happened next was shameful. The last people to hear about injury and death at the Isle of Man are people on the island, because organisers have the idea it spoils the race. Betty Phillis sensed something was very wrong. Yet efforts to find out through race officials (who knew) and the hospital produced no answer. Tom had crashed about 30 minutes into a race which ran over two-and-a-quarter hours. But Betty wasn't told of her husband's death until after the race finished. And then it was Jim Redman who brought the devastating news.

Bennie Pinners, son of the organiser of the annual Whit Monday race meeting in Tubbergen, Holland, was sitting in the grandstand that day, a few rows from Betty Phillis. Bennie has met a lot of racers. He has biographical information on 6000 of them. But he still reckons that afternoon in the Isle of Man grandstand is the saddest thing he's seen in racing.

How would you tell a two-and-a-half-year-old girl her daddy isn't coming back?

English journalist Norman Sharp (left) greets Tom, Betty and Debbie Phillis at London Airport in 1962.

JACK AHEARN

CHAPTER 8

One of the happiest people in Australia when Wayne Gardner became our first 500 world champion was Jack Ahearn, country boy, sometime carpenter, taxi-driver, and used car and motorcycle dealer. But for most of his working life Jack was a professional motorcycle racer. Not in the mould of the now fashionable, colourfully clad factory riders with a small army of support people, spare parts and money, but as a black-clad gypsy, independent and proud.

In 1964 Ahearn put the medal for second place in the 500 world championships around his neck with the pledge "I'll take it off when another Aussie does better". It took 23 years for Wayne Gardner to be crowned and Jack to remove his medal.

Big Jack Ahearn's second place was a great achievement, for the solidly built rider had just turned 40, yet had enjoyed his "best year in Europe, not financially but in results and personal satisfaction." In his eyes and those of his fellow riders, Ahearn was the champion. "We knew we couldn't beat the MV Agustas, so the rider's champion was the best-placed guy behind them."

A single-cylinder 500 Norton like Jack Ahearn used in 1964 put out around 37 kW (about 50 horsepower). More was available, if you could afford a specially prepared one and were prepared to risk blow-ups by revving it to a very busy 7400 revs. Ahearn refused to rev his past 7000 rpm, so he was already sacrificing some power in the interests of reliability. He usually did only the minimum number of practice laps and rarely ran his bike fast on the straights.

"In practices I'd ride it hard around the corners, but knock it off on the straights. It saved the engine until race day and confused the opposition." But perhaps the greater problem was that the British riders, as we shall see later, got the best Nortons.

Count Domenico Agusta's potent, exotic and virtually unbeatable Italian four-cylinder MVs were a different proposition, as was the team's generous race budget. The MV Agusta 500 had a twin overhead camshaft engine pumping out 50 kW (65-70 horsepower) at 10,500 revs. That was a demoralising 35 per cent more than a basic Norton.

To compound its opponents' problems, the MV's power was transmitted through a five-speed gearbox. In accordance with Norton's publicly stated policy that "any gearbox with more than four ratios is a gearbox full of neutrals," the pride of Britain and most privateers had just four ratios. It was the sort of narrow, cosseted thinking that ultimately killed what had been the world's biggest and most esteemed motorcycle industry. The 350 cm³ four-cylinder MV Agusta put out about the same power as most privateers' 500 Nortons.

Anybody not on an MV had no chance of being world champion through the more than 20 years of

Jack Ahearn — oil-stained but happy after winning the 1964 Finnish 500 GP on a Norton.

MV Agusta's 500 cm³ onslaught. MV won 139 500 GPs between 1952 and 1976, plus plenty in other classes, especially the 350. Only in 1988 did Yamaha get within half the number of MV wins in the 500 class. Obviously MV could have any rider it wanted. Add the best rider to the best machine from the factory with the best budget and facilities, and you had a formidable combination.

In Ahearn's case the opposition was considerable; namely the man who would end up with the third best record in the history of motorcycle racing, Stanley Michael Bailey Hailwood. He was nine times world champion, winner of 76 grands prix, plus brilliant performances at Isle of Man, where he won 14 TTs from 1961 to 1979 in five classes on four different brands of bike.

So the tall, crew-cut, laconic Jack Ahearn didn't do badly as runner-up to Hailwood, one of the all-time greats. To do it, he beat another great achiever, Englishman Phil Read, who went on to win seven world championships and 52 grands prix.

In 1964 points were awarded for just the top six placings. Only the best five results out of the nine races could be counted. Because of cost, Ahearn didn't go to the opening round at Daytona in America. He retired from round two at the Isle of

Jack Ahearn (Norton, No 6) chases veteran Swiss-resident privateer Guyla Marsovzski (Matchless, No 38) at Spa.

Man. But he then scored points in the remaining seven rounds. So although he finished tied on 25 points with Read in the championship, Ahearn had an extra four points which he had to drop. It was the epitome of the Ahearn philosophy of always finishing.

His first and only grand prix win came that year, at Imatra in Finland, the second last race of the season.

Jack Ahearn christened the Suzuki 250 four "Whispering Death" when he rode it in 1964-65.

By then Hailwood had won the first six races and Read the seventh. So they didn't go to Finland. In the fifth round of the championship, Ahearn was second to Hailwood at Solitude, a road circuit on the outskirts of Stuttgart in Germany. The difference there between Hailwood's MV and everything else was marked. Hailwood won by two minutes 38 seconds from Ahearn. But Ahearn beat Read by just 0.9 of a second after more than an hour and a quarter of racing.

Ahearn was third at Dundrod in Ireland and Monza, fourth at Assen and Spa, and sixth in front of a massive crowd of around 300,000 people at Sachsenring in East Germany.

Although Ahearn had been an Australian representative at the Isle of Man in 1954, 1955, 1958 and 1962, and had point-scoring placings in the world championships in 1954, 1955 and 1963, his best was still to come. For both Jacks, Findlay and Ahearn, life took on a rosier hue at 40.

"I rode better after 40. The trouble was that I started late, stuffed up by the war," Ahearn said. Indeed, in 1965, the year after his 500 championship second place, it looked as if he'd cap his career with an IoM win. He'd been offered a 250 Suzuki ride, which he denigrated by calling it "Whispering Death." He got the ride "when Mike Hailwood knocked them back (and went to Honda). That four-cylinder Suzuki — the best thing I ever rode — was flying. After days of sorting the thing out so it would do one lap without seizing and then, eventually, six laps, I was passing Honda fours in a straight line. I thought 'this is beaut, I'll give 'em a lap record here'.

"We kicked off by stopping after half a lap, at Ballacraine, to check the plugs. Then I ran in the big ends, the pistons, everything. We spent so much time getting it right. All the time Redman was running round and round on his Honda, but by Friday everything was right. I planned to do one steady lap and then go for it, to show what it could do," Ahearn said. But the plans went awry.

"There was a slippery patch under a tree at Sarah's Cottage. I crashed on it but was in good company. So did Ago (Giacomo Agostini) and Hailwood."

He was also in good company for a while in Douglas hospital. "I was waking up, abusing nurses, generally being a nuisance. I got myself out of there as fast as I could and raced in the 500 race on Friday. My head was hurting so much I had to stand on the footpegs for the whole race (two and a half hours!). Even so I hit one bump that jarred my head and hurt like hell.

Ironically, the winner of the 250 TT was the man whose measure Jack reckoned he had, Rhodesian Jim Redman. The best placed Suzuki was third, with British rider Frank Perris on board. That was despite Jim Redman's and Jack's children painting the works Honda team wheels with sump oil during practice!

Ahearn then went on to the Dutch (fifth, 500 Norton), the Belgian and East German (fourth, 500 Norton) Grands Prix. The Suzuki locked up again and tossed him off in practice for the non-championship French GP. For all the problems with the early Suzukis, Ahearn says the company was lovely to deal with. "They were gentlemen. They appreciated the riders, even bought you dinner. The very opposite of Honda," he said.

"I was concussed in both accidents and finally collapsed on the way to the Ulster. I was taken to Liverpool hospital, where they diagnosed bruising to the brain. I was in a coma for a while, until they drilled some holes to relieve the pressure. That put me out of racing for a couple of months, but it's affected my memory ever since. Even now, I have trouble remembering people's names."

Rather eerily, Ahearn says he blacked out while racing at Amaroo Park nine years later. "I was unconscious during the crash in the Castrol 6 Hour in 1974. I blacked out momentarily, then woke up just before I was flung off. In fact, I jumped off the back of the bike."

That was Jack Ahearn's last motorcycle race. But it wasn't his last motorcycle ride. Ahearn and former international sidecar rider Bob Mitchell got together on road bikes and had a brisk trip down to Sydney to watch another of the Castrol 6 Hour production races. Mitchell came from Surfers Paradise to meet up with Jack at his Lismore home.

Jack says that by the last of his Castrol races: "I was two stone overweight and 50 years old. What I

Jack Ahearn and Melburnian Mal Stanton (Nortons) race before 250,000 people at Sachsenring, East Germany in 1966.

wanted to do was combine me, an A-grader, with a B or C-grader and pass on some knowledge. He'd do the middle stint while I did the bulk of the race at the start and finish. The Norton Commando I used would lope around for more than two hours on a tankful of fuel." And no wonder. Jack was only doing two gear changes a lap. No gearbox full of neutrals here.

Jack's only race on a works machine was in 1958, when former rider Jock West of Associated Motor Cycles (AMC) offered him a ride on one of the famous and successful 7R AJS bikes (a 350) and its 500 equivalent, a G50 Matchless. The latter machine was still experimental. Ahearn gave it its world race debut in the IoM TT, and won the 350 non-championship Austrian GP, before taking the G50 to third place in the 500 race.

Jack's other chance for a works ride was a tryout for Gilera in 1963. The trouble was that he didn't know until later that it was a tryout. On top of that, he was still injured from a crash a month earlier at Ulster. For that Jack had gone fashionable with some very comfortable, ultra-thin Italian leathers. "They offered better looks than they did crash protection," he said. With Sods Law in full operation, Jack gave them a complete workout. "The crash took most of my skin off my back, elbows, shoulders, backside, knees, knuckles and wrists. I was a mess when they put me in the ambulance, covered in bandages but still dripping lots of blood.

"There was a guy in the ambulance who was white as a sheet. He was in dreadful shape. I looked at him and thought he looked familiar. Then I realised, Christ, it's Jack Findlay and he's dead. My first thought was that my bikes were in his truck; how in the hell would I get them to Smith's at Liverpool? Then I saw him move and said, 'You bastard, you're not dead.'

"As Jim Redman was travelling around racing, he didn't need his apartment so he let me recuperate there. I sat for ages in a salt bath. It was agony, but the best way to speed up the healing. It was five weeks later and I was getting itchy to see what everybody was up to, so I went to Monza, just to watch. I'd already had a bootmaker repair the leathers with some good, thick protection sewn on to the arms and elbows.

"I was chatting with Ginger Molloy (a New Zealander), who was also out injured. He said, 'Why don't you start on my two bikes so we can collect the start money and then split it?'

"It seemed like a good idea, but it didn't work very well. A sump plug came loose, I skated around madly on the oil and crashed again. The day after Monza, Geoff Duke told me to turn up and ride the Gilera. John Hartle and Derek Minter were riding for Gilera but both were having trouble with it wriggling around in a straight line. They had several

Jack Ahearn debuted the prototype Matchless G50 in the 1958 IoM 500 TT. He's pictured at the Waterworks II Corner.

versions of the bike there. The way they put it to me was that they wanted my idea of what was wrong with the handling.

"I got into my leathers, with blood dripping into gloves and boots, and went around trying to find out what was causing the handling problems. There were big trucks all around the track with guys pitch-forking hay bales into them. They kept moving around, so you never knew were they'd be and how much of the track they'd be blocking, so I had to be careful. Eventually I reckoned the same as John Hartle, that the fairing was causing the problem.

"What I found out after all this being cautious as I found my way around large trucks, was they were testing me out for a factory ride. Apparently if I'd been a fraction faster I'd have got the ride ahead of Hartle, joining Minter in the Gilera team. If they'd only told what was going on, I'd have made the supreme effort."

And what a bike that four-cylinder Gilera was. "Compared with a Norton the power seemed to go on forever, from almost no revs to as hard as you dared rev it. It didn't suffer at all from mega-phonitis." The exhaust systems on four-strokes in those days, especially single-cylinder engines, were megaphone-shaped, to give added power by utilising the exhaust gas flow in a certain rev-band. Below that they fell into a flat spot. "And you didn't have to slip the clutch to get it out of slow corners," Ahearn added.

The full import of what all Norton riders were up against gradually became obvious to Ahearn. "The stupid thing was that I used to think it was riders who won races. I don't believe it now. Eventually I learned it was really the machine. For the first ten years over there we were virtually racing a 350 against 500s."

Ahearn has two examples to illustrate that. One was the first Norton he raced in Australia in 1953. "That was a factory reject, one they wouldn't sell in England, so they shipped it to Australia. It had cracked brake drums, a stripped and then glued thread on the sump plug. It was leaking oil and didn't have much power." In fact Ahearn's theory was that it wasn't Norton pulling the swiftie, but some of its employees.

"Management probably didn't know what was happening. Some of the employees were collecting old, reject parts, assembling them into bikes for places like Australia and then selling the spare bike. That left them with a nice profit on the British market, totally unknown to the factory."

But when 29-year-old Jack Ahearn saw it sitting there in Hazell and Moore's showroom, he reckoned he had to have it. Jack gathered up 300 pounds, packed a haversack, shoved his foot up the unmuffled megaphone exhaust and rode it away, unregistered, 200 kilometres to its first race meeting at Bathurst. But the brakes gave out in three laps, so Jack sold it and planned to head for England.

He'd first gone racing just after the war, in which he'd been an RAAF trainee pilot. Jack bought a 350 Triumph Tiger 80 to ride in club events. In his first of many races in the Blue Mountains, he won and was promoted to A grade. He took that Triumph to Bathurst for his first appearance there in 1946. It was replaced by a 500 Ariel in 1947. That moved on for a former Freddie Frith KTT Velocette in 1949.

In 1951 he crashed at Bathurst and broke both wrists. "I was double-jointed until then, but they weren't so good after that," he said. One of the most spectacular racing photos from those days shows the unusually tall Ahearn tucked down on a Norton, his chin absolutely on the tank, his elbows tucked in. He must barely have been able to see ahead.

The other Norton experience that convinced him that non-English riders were up against it occurred years later in 1963. He ended up on a bike intended for an English rider, rather than a colonial. Because Jack had borrowed a friend's bike for the 1962 season, he'd left a Manx Norton he'd ordered and paid for at the factory all that year. When he went to pick it up after a season back in Australia in the summer of 1962-1963, it had been sold.

They then gave him his choice of six machines, lined up with horsepower tags on them ready for the Manx Grand Prix in the Isle of Man. All were intended for English riders. "It was so good I bet Reg Deardon £5 that it would do a 100 mph lap. It not only did that; it was the only 100 mph lap done that year on a Norton. It was over-revving in top gear on the Mountain Mile at IoM, where the average Norton was struggling in third." Perhaps Jack Ahearn was happy with third gear on the Mountain Mile. Maurie Quincey's measure of whether a Norton was going properly was that it was actually gaining speed in top gear on the Mountain Mile.

In averaging 100.5 mph (161.9 km/h), it was reported in a later IoM program, "Ahearn surprised the works teams on his 500 Norton, splitting the MVs and Gileras". Prior to that, in 1962, Jack had still been lapping at 156 to 158 km/h on "colonial" Nortons, no less an achievement. As for many Australians in Europe, the availability of money and machinery was the greatest barrier to more success.

Ahearn wasn't impressed with the Norton machinery available to non-British riders. "The colonials — the Australians, South Africans and New Zealanders — were swindled in England. We got the crook, cast-off machines. The good ones stayed in England for English riders. It was no wonder tuners like Francis Beart got good results. They started with better machinery than we could buy and then made it go even faster for those with the money to pay for it.

"I believed in honesty, in integrity — things that don't pay. It's lucky we travelled because I wasted the best years of my life," Jack said. Yet things could have been worse: "Europe was beautiful in the '50s. You could park or camp anywhere. The police were nice. The public was madly enthusiastic, chasing autographs. There were wall-to-wall crowds but it was the organisers who were making the money, not us. We raced every weekend for six months, starting in March. If there was a mid-week hillclimb, we'd do that as well if we could."

Profits for those trying to make a living were modest. "I left Australia in 1954 with ten shillings and came home at the end of the year with £50," Ahearn said. When he left, he only had a ticket to Bombay. "I was in H deck, below the propellor shaft, or so it seemed." His race machine for the season, Jack Forrest's Norton, was stowed aboard. "Betty (who became his wife at the beginning of the next year) gave me ten shillings as I went on board. That went a fair way because Cokes were only threepence.

"The plan was to hitch-bike from Bombay. But a quick look-around soon convinced me that was a hard way to do it. I went back on board, had a long chat with the purser and went all the way to London docks at Tilbury."

That was a high level of enthusiasm, energy and dedication for one who claims: "I wasn't a motorcycle enthusiast. I didn't like bikes. I was a carpenter in Lithgow. I raced bikes only to do something successfully, to get out of Lithgow, make some money and eat. I wasn't much good at anything else." As an only child whose father died during the war, there was plenty of incentive for Jack to start working.

Over 30 years of racing motorcycles, Jack Ahearn proved that he certainly was good at it. He rarely crashed, although his reasoning behind that is a typical Ahearn put-down. "You only crash if you try to win races. I didn't crash because I wasn't trying to win." There's a hilarious account of one piece of Ahearn determination that seems to prove the theory. He won — and crashed — at Feldburg because he was determined to beat another Australian, Victorian Maurie Quincey.

Jack's first aim was to preserve his bike and get to the next meeting. By doing that he met the vital first goal, to earn some money and keep the business assets intact. Trying to win races came next. A more cavalier, less sensible approach, on the circuits on which he raced in this era almost certainly would have seen big Jack in trouble through his long career. He admits to five crashes in his career, although research reveals a few more. Perhaps the severity determines whether or not Jack counts it as a crash. Of the alleged five crashes, Jack says "three were my fault, two the Suzuki's when it locked up". Even with a few more thrown in, Jack didn't do badly in tens of thousands of kilometres of racing over 30 years.

When he was competing in the Castrol 6 Hour production race at Amaroo Park just after his 50th birthday (and his last IoM race) in 1974, Ahearn told the authors: "If you didn't crash or blow an engine (in the 1950s and 1960s), you could buy a new Norton at the beginning of the season and have paid for it with start and prize money by mid-season. You were starting to make money after that."

That was the other, better side to racing up to the 1970s. A privateer may have had no chance of becoming world champion, with a bigger difference between the performance of his bike and that of the factory machines then than now, but he could survive on start and prize money. This has certainly not been the case since the mid-1970s. He didn't need sponsorship to be able to eat and race.

But even then there was some modest sponsorship. Any privateer who reckoned he was going places was proud of the painted signs on his van. Typically they each came with £50 to £100 from companies like Castrol, Avon, Lodge or KLG spark plugs. Modest though they seem, they were usually enough to start the hopefuls on their overseas racing by helping underwrite the cost of a van and leave a few shillings over to get to the first meeting.

When Jack landed in England, he got a lift with a friend to Norton in Birmingham, collected £20 from Castrol and Avon, gathered a plentiful supply of tinned food and was ready for his first meeting, chasing some start and prize money.

Ahearn's opponents will tell you Jack was as hard to beat as any of the professionals in Europe, almost all of them younger than he was. Eventually, of course, they were *all* younger than Jack. He became the old but still very much respected man of international motorcycle racing.

He also had some wonderfully simple guidelines. Of that most confusing and complex of circuits, the 61 km of hills and curves around the Isle of Man: "Don't worry about gearing and all that stuff. Just ride as if you're running late for work." That shouldn't lull people into thinking Jack wasn't trying at IoM. He was fascinated by its challenge and collected 11 gold, silver and bronze replicas there for finishing within certain percentages of the race winner's time.

Jack was ninth in his first IoM appearance, the 500 TT in 1954. The weather was so bad it was stopped after only four laps (243 km). Like all the 500 races at the Island — the longest of all championship events — it was scheduled for seven laps. Nine years later, in 1963, after recording his 100 mph lap in practice, he was fifth in the 350 and ninth in the 500, despite being sick with flu and losing a lot of weight over the week of practice and racing. His best placing at the Island was fourth in the 1966 350 TT, just before his 42nd birthday.

But Ahearn was almost 50 in 1974 when he had his last race at the Island on a 350 Yamaha. He averaged 149.8 km/h. He returned the next year as sponsor of Sydney rider Robert Madden, son of another racer, Keo. Later, in 1987, Jack got into leathers again to be one of many riders celebrating 80 years of racing at IoM. With Jack aged 62, they did a Tourist Trophy Lap of Honour prior to the 500 TT.

Ahearn retained a practical, down-to-earth approach to his racing. Of tuning engines on dynomometers: "Bugger dynos. If the engine was nothing special, it would only pull a 22-tooth engine sprocket. If it was good it would pull 24 teeth. We didn't need a dyno to tell us that." On signing autographs: "The hardest thing to get in the pit area was clean rags," perhaps to mop up the oil that allegedly leaked constantly from British bikes. "I swapped autographs for clean rags."

Despite the large part played in motor racing by watches and accurate timing, Ahearn had a relaxed attitude to timekeeping. "You don't need a watch: If it's daytime, you're up. If it's dark, it's time for bed," he said. Perhaps that's why there was rarely anybody hanging over Ahearn's pit counter, waving a board to tell him how he and everyone else was going. "I tried to count the laps and kept going as hard as I could until they waved the flag."

He was equally practical about altering gearing on his bikes. "If you change sprockets all the time, nuts get loose. I'd tighten them up nice and hard at the beginning of the season, then peen them over." On the odd occasion that Jack wanted a different ratio,

Grand prix winner! Ahearn takes the chequered flag at Imatra in Finland, in 1964.

Riding tall . . . Ahearn at the Isle of Man TT, on a Norton. Note the Suzuki helmet logo and Jack's twin front brake.

Old mates . . . Jack Findlay (left), Jack Ahearn and works Jawa rider Frantisek Statsny (right) with Czech GP momentos, 1965.

he changed the back wheel for another with a different sprocket.

Still working on the if-it's-working-leave-it-alone principle, Jack said he left his carburettors on the same settings for most circuits. One of his most satisfying memories is of getting a Norton engine "that was so good, I didn't have to adjust the tappets for 23 meetings".

But he was impressed by Harry Hinton's knowledge of camshafts. "He had a different cam for just about every circuit. Harry surprised a lot of people in Europe with his technical approach." By comparison, Ahearn said if it was more complex than a different sprocket or a spark plug, he was stumped.

Jack's no-nonsense attitude gave him the time and perspective to enjoy his racing and the friendships. "A bunch of us, Guyla Marsovski, Dan Shorey and Jack Findlay, had a rule — the first one back to his pit after the race put on the coffee."

All of which belied the effort Ahearn put into his racing and the success he had. He was such an experienced professional that there was no longer any great tension or mystery about what was to be done. He was as professional, as competent and calm as an accountant approaching the day's column of figures. His letterhead, that was as much a part of the professional riders' equipment as his leathers and helmet, summarised Jack's achievements:

- runner-up world 500 championships, 1964. Point-scorer in world 500 championships in 1955, 1963 (tenth), 1965 (fifth) and 1966 (sixth).
- Australian Isle of Man TT representative 1954, 1955, 1958 and 1962
- Holder of Australian land speed record, 250 and 350cm^3
- Eight Australian championships, 20 state championships
- Nine wins at Bathurst: 1957 250, 350 and 500; 1959 500; 1960 350 and 500; 1961 500; 1967 250; 1969 500
- More than 200 wins throughout Australia
- International wins in numerous non-championship events, on circuits through Europe at places like Feldberg, Bordeaux and Zandvoort
- Sixth at a shortened Ulster TT in 1954, which thereby became ineligible for the world championships.

Ahearn at home in the mid-1950s, riding at Darley, Victoria. The crankcases of his Norton are Australian-made aluminium items.

Jack Ahearn's attitude generally was to treat himself as gently as he treated his machinery. But there's a crash that has not been counted by Jack in his career total. It's one of the most curious and amusing in motorcycle racing. It involved two Australians, Jack and Victorian Maurie Quincey, over their feelings for a third Aussie.

It was curious because Jack won the race, then crashed. It was amusing because he'd planned it all beforehand. So incensed was Jack at what he considered Maurie's lack of respect for Gordon Laing, that Jack decided he would crash if he had to, just to beat Maurie. Quincey and Ahearn had been very evenly matched over a number of meetings. Although they were both members of the 1954 Australian IoM team, they had fought some long, desperate duels. This no doubt was why Jack planned the battle at Feldberg and decided that he might have to crash for right to be done.

In the 500 TT at IoM in 1954, Ahearn finished ninth, one second ahead of Quincey after an hour and three quarters of racing. The person over whom they were later to battle, Gordon Laing, was sixth. At the shortened Ulster GP, Laing was third, Quincey fourth and Ahearn sixth. In a 500 race in Germany, Ahearn beat Quincey by 0.4 of a second.

On they went to Spa in Belgium. In the 350 race it was now Quincey's turn to reverse the results. In a race won by Ken Kavanagh, Quincey was ninth, Ahearn tenth and Keith Campbell, three years away from his world championship, 12th. In the 500 race, Kavanagh finished second to Geoff Duke, with Campbell fifth. Quincey had been well up in the early stages but dropped out with a split fuel tank. It was in the 350 race that Gordon Laing was killed.

Death was ever-present those days, as it was in car racing. Although there were fewer accidents, the consequences were almost always more severe. Riders reacted in different ways. Some, like Gregg Hansford, hated to visit a fellow rider in hospital. Some, like Ken Kavanagh, would step in to help widows with personal arrangements. Some purposely avoided becoming too friendly with fellow riders. After a cursory show of respect, most then shut such things from their mind and got on with the business of racing, sure that it wouldn't happen to them. Yet all had lost friends and fellow countrymen at home and abroad.

Quincey was a very orderly person. He packed up quickly from a meeting and prided himself in being one of the first set up at the next, no matter how far away. The meeting following Laing's death was at Assen in Holland, only six days later. Both Ahearn and Quincey were there and the battle continued. In the 500 race Ahearn was ninth and Quincey tenth.

But then came the big clash at Feldberg in Germany. By then Quincey had, in Jack Ahearn's eyes, slighted the memory of Gordon Laing by not going to his funeral. The race is remembered vividly by all who saw it.

Jack had thought of a contingency plan for the dash from the last corner to the curiously placed finishing line. To get around the corner after it you had to shut off the throttle before you got to the line. What Ahearn had sussed out was that you could keep the thing open wide all the way to the finishing line, if you took the escape road into the lake. If he and Maurie were close as they headed to the finish on the final lap and Jack then kept the throttle open all the way to the line, he'd probably win the day.

Everyone there reckoned it was one of the most wonderful sights that season, big Jack sitting up on his Norton as he rode into what suddenly became a wall of water. For a brief moment the square-jawed Jack, almost smiling at having won the battle, and his Norton were travelling so fast it looked as if the bike would skim across the surface. Of course it didn't. It sank rapidly and gracefully, as the wall of water subsided.

They say that the sight of "Never Crash" Ahearn struggling ashore, dripping wet in leathers, helmet, gloves and boots — his goggles looking like scuba diver's gear — was one of the highlights of 1954. But he hadn't forgotten his goal. As he waded ashore he announced defiantly "I beat him".

For all the intensity of that clash with Maurie Quincey, Ahearn still reckons he was the best Australian rider he raced against and that Surtees was the best of the Europeans.

A similar Ahearn stand on principle saw him hang a Swiss organiser out the second-storey win-

Ahearn riding a fully streamlined Norton at Mt Panorama, Bathurst in 1960. He won the 350 and 500 events.

dow of his office because he was tardy in paying prize money. Ahearn also told some Czechoslovakian race organisers that if they couldn't afford to pay the riders further down the grid, behind him, "they'd better give them my money. They need it more than I do." At which time he stamped out of the office. "To their credit, they saw the point and paid them. When I arrived to race next year they gave me my money for both years," Jack added.

The Ahearn goal of racing in Europe was very practical — to make a living out of motorcycle racing. It was a job, so earnings counted. Glory or winning championships was not the main aim. "From 1953 to 1973, I used stock model race bikes. They were slow but they were reliable. If there was a world championship event on somewhere and another meeting with £5 or £10 more money to be made, I'd go for the money.

"If I'd been ambitious I'd have stayed in England over the Christmas break each year and conned a works ride. But it was part of our commitment as an Australian IoM team rider, that we came home each year with our bikes and passed on what we'd learned. Yet I knew of some riders who would retire after a few laps at the Island, so they and their bikes were healthy for other racing. They used team selection only as a method of getting to Europe."

After each of his international seasons in Europe, Jack would spend six weeks and a lot of money on a sea voyage home. He would then race over the Christmas/New Year period and decide whether he'd stay in Australia for the next season or return to England and Europe.

The return to Australia may have cost Australian racers time and money, but they made some as well. Two of the few gratuities available in England, if you were good enough, were fuel for the race bike and free tyres. As part of his conservative policy in practice, Jack would top his bikes up with fuel, do a couple of laps and put them back in the van. The bikes' tanks were then drained into the transporter. Not much later, the bikes would be brought back out to have their tanks topped up. "We'd do that until the van's tank was full. Then we knew we were okay to get to the next meeting."

A similar principle existed for racing tyres, except that in this case the booty came home and was sold. It took careful planning to be able to conserve one tyre enough to be able to use it later after a replacement had been issued. When they reached Australia each tyre was worth a valuable £2.10.0 to the deprived local riders.

"It was a battle for survival in Europe. You had to be as cunning as an outhouse rat. If you blew up your 350, it was fair enough to run your 500 to collect the starting money. You had to use it gently and retire later in the race. It wasn't done to go tearing around on it beating other guys. But we had one keen guy over there in his first year who didn't follow the rules. He kept going and got a good result in a 350 race with a 500. I warned him that if he did it again I'd dob him in," Jack said.

One of the things that still haunts Jack Ahearn is "that so many Aussies got knocked off. They got a works ride then started riding faster, often over their ability and experience to justify it.

"Ernie Ring was good in Australia, got a works AJS, went to Belgium and was killed. Bob Brown ended up a good rider on Gileras and Hondas, but he was killed as well. Keith Campbell was good. I was with him at Cadours in the south of France when he was killed.

"He won the 350 race and I was second. In the 500 race we had stronger opposition, including Walter Zeller on a BMW. Keith was keen to make a break early on. So he charged away at the start, ignoring the sidecar race that had been on just before and made the track slippery. There was an oily patch about three metres long and a third of a metre wide. I was just behind Keith and moved over for it. But it was on the ideal line, so that's where Keith went.

"I was probably the happiest bloke around, never feeling that pressure to produce results, to go faster than I was comfortable with."

Ahearn waited a long time for an Australian world 500 champion, longer than for any other class. In the previous seven years he'd seen Australians take the championship in two grand prix classes — the 350 in 1957 and the 125 in 1961, so he probably thought he wouldn't be waiting long. Kel Carruthers tied up the 250 class only five years after the Ahearn commitment. In the 12-year period from 1957 to 1969 an Australian won every one of the original solo grand prix classes, except the 500.

But it took nearly twice as long as that from Ahearn's second place in 1964 to Gardner's win in 1987. The FIM medal hung around the Ahearn neck, assailed but never tarnished by all manner of Australian curses, for 23 years.

"I took it off the night Wayne won in Brazil. I don't know where it is now — around the house somewhere." Who would expect a practical, do-it-yourself motorcycle racer — who wouldn't adjust the tappets on his Norton as long as it was going properly — to know where he'd put the medal that he'd treasured for all those years?

JACK
FINDLAY

CHAPTER 9

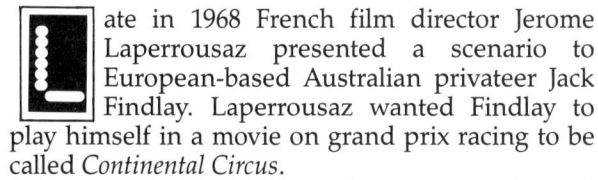

Late in 1968 French film director Jerome Laperrousaz presented a scenario to European-based Australian privateer Jack Findlay. Laperrousaz wanted Findlay to play himself in a movie on grand prix racing to be called *Continental Circus*.

Laperrousaz's theme was the extremes of grand prix racing, the comfortable lifestyle of the well-paid factory rider compared with the hand-to-mouth existence of the hard-up private entrant. He planned to follow the 1969 world 500 championship season and tell the story as it unfolded, documentary style. Laperrousaz chose his "co-stars" on the results of the 1968 world 500 title. He could not have found a better contrast.

The champion was Giacomo Agostini, a 26-year-old Italian bachelor with movie star looks, and the fast cars and boats to match his salary. He rode a 65 kW plus factory three-cylinder MV Agusta. Agostini was well liked in the paddock, and respected for the professional way he represented motorcycle racing.

The private entrant and 1968 runner-up was 34-year-old Findlay, whose single-cylinder McIntyre-Matchless (a machine he had owned, prepared and raced for six seasons) produced about 37 kW, or just over half the power of Agostini's MV.

Jack Findlay had wanted to be a grand prix motorcycle racer since the age of ten, when he found an action photograph of a racer. By 1968 Findlay was the embodiment of the successful privateer. He owned his tools of trade — a Bultaco 250, Aermacchi 350, the 500 Matchless, a van and a caravan — and little else.

Jack had earnest green eyes, spoke English, French and some Italian with the broad accent of a man born and raised in northern Victoria, and had a relaxed dry wit to match. He had arrived in Europe ten years earlier as an unknown in his own country and honed himself into a leading grand prix rider, particularly on the fast public road circuits which dominated the European calendar in the 1960s.

Findlay was to log another ten years of racing in Europe. His grand prix career began when Keith Campbell and Bob Brown were front-line GP racers, and closed the year Gregg Hansford arrived on the grand prix scene. Findlay's first 500 grand prix machine produced 37 kW, his last more than double that figure. Jack won three world 500 championship races, two on privately entered machines. Even at the end of 1988 he was the only Australian other than Wayne Gardner to win more than one race in this category.

Findlay was well known and respected in Europe in the 1960s. He lived in Paris from the end of 1962 until 1967, when he shifted base to Milan. He took a French racing licence in 1963 and immediately became France's best resident grand prix 500 rider.

Findlay's devotion to the Isle of Man TT and Ulster

Jack Findlay — professional motorcycle racer — aka "The Australian in Paris".

Grand Prix meetings put him on side with British enthusiasts, and the grand prix press liked Jack and admired his perseverance in the face of setbacks and injury. They described Findlay as one of the most likeable and dedicated of riders... One who struggled for a long time and who didn't receive the chances his skill and courage deserved... A rider's rider, solid and professional.

In the 1960s Findlay twice captured the coveted unofficial title of best-placed privateer in the world 500 championship. These were in 1966, when he was third overall to Agostini and Hailwood, and in 1968. Findlay had also been the leading private runner in the 1966 world 250 championship on a Bultaco. Yet his only invitation to ride works machinery was at the end of 1966 from Japan's Bridgestone, a maker of 50 and 125 cm^3 racers.

Findlay finally received a "works" 500 offer for 1969, in the sense that someone offered him a machine to race. But there was no large factory behind the offer. The bike was the Linto, named after its designer/builder Lino Tonti. The Linto was two 250 cm^3 single-cylinder Aermacchi engines bolted together to make a 500 parallel twin.

The Linto was a disaster for Findlay and German-based compatriot John Dodds. Someone said it proved the old adage that two good singles didn't make a good twin. The Linto had 25 per cent more power than the Matchless, but the Findlay and Dodds examples were unreliable to the point of heartbreak. Findlay slumped from finishing "in the points" in seven out of ten GPs on his own 500 machine in 1968, to scoring points in just one 500 GP in 1969 with the Linto.

Continental Circus, which opened simultaneously in eight cinemas in Paris in 1972, documented it all. Memorable images included an injured Findlay driving to the next meeting with one arm in a sling and his long-time ladyfriend Nanou changing the gears. Injured privateers still had to eat and pay their bills.

Findlay's career didn't fully recover from the Linto episode until 1971. In 1973 and 1974 he rode works machines for Suzuki and helped develop the company's successful square-four 500 racer. But Suzuki dumped Jack at the end of 1974, just as the 500-4 was overcoming its teething problems. Suzuki thought 39 was too old for a works rider, even when the man in question was its leading pointscorer (and fifth overall) in the 1974 world 500 championship.

Findlay's answer to Suzuki was a characteristic do-it-yourself effort. He bought a four-cylinder Yamaha TZ750, wrung more power from it on the test bench at friend Daniele Fontana's workshop, and beat Suzuki star Barry Sheene by one point to win the 1975 FIM Formula 750 prize (forerunner of the short-lived world F750 championship). Findlay used the same machine, with different cylinders and exhaust pipes, to finish in the top three in two 500 grands prix.

Jack rated 1975 his best year in racing. Many in the grand prix paddock were delighted to see him come up trumps after being sacked. Britain's Guild of Motoring Writers agreed, and voted him its Rider of the Year.

Jack was happier and felt a sense of achievement doing things his way. He had some of his greatest successes in the 1970s, and on the "wrong" side of 35, riding machines he built with Daniele Fontana, an Italian manufacturer of magnesium racing motorcycle brakes. Another motorcycle built and bench-tested in Fontana's 17th-century farmhouse near Milan brought Jack his first 500 grand prix victory in Northern Ireland in 1971.

But Findlay's major prize from two seasons on the Suzuki payroll was perhaps his most cherished. In 1973 he won the race he went to Europe to win — the Isle of Man Senior TT. It had taken 15 years and 31 race starts at the 61 km circuit to achieve his goal.

Jack Findlay retired from racing in 1978, but con-

Jack Findlay (left) receives the British Guild of Motoring Writers "Rider of the Year" award for 1975.

THE FAST LINE

"In the four-stroke era, you had to stay on the right line — and the line was only about this wide," said Jack Findlay, pointing to the width of his hand.

"It made such a difference in the fast bends. Take Monza, for example. Before they put the chicanes in for the cars, the very long start/finish straight took you flat out into the Curva Grande. Boy, if you could get around there on a single-cylinder four-stroke without shutting off, you were on your way. Only the good riders could do that.

"The same thing at Burnenville on the old Spa-Francorchamps circuit. The approach was downhill for about two-and-a-half kilometres. With tallest gearing a 500 single could pull maybe 230 km/h. You had tyres which today wouldn't be good enough for a 250 road bike... And you were trying to go around this big right-hander without shutting off!

"It was a real adventure, with the footrest touching the ground every now and then, and the bike drifting across the road. Every time you hit a bump it would jump out. And what was on the outside? It was houses, brick walls and a couple of straw bales leaned up against a telegraph post."

Findlay crashed once at Burnenville, in 1969, when he lost traction in sand on the inside of the corner. But he's around to tell the tale. Australia in 1953-1954 lost Ernie Ring and Gordon Laing in crashes at Spa-Francorchamps.

Eric Hinton, who, like Findlay, raced in the 1950s and 1960s, agreed the Curva Grande and Burnenville (commonly known among English-speaking riders as "the Cocoa Bends") were the most testing corners in Europe. "You needed big balls to get around those corners full-bore."

"Your speed around the Cocoas determined how fast you went down the Masta Straight, which was five kilometres long. So you had to make yourself as small as possible behind the fairing and try to keep your momentum up.

"The first part of the Cocoas was intimidating, because it was downhill. You were going pretty fast, with the bike skipping across the road on each bump. Then the road went uphill, and that washed off speed. If you weren't fast enough in the first part, you lost too much speed when the road started to climb. And you couldn't change back to third gear, because the bike was cranked over that far you couldn't get your foot under the gear lever," he said.

The first time Kel Carruthers practised at Spa on a 500 Norton he changed back one gear for Burnenville — and the others passed him. In his first race he took the corner in top gear, but peeking over the screen. The next year he was right up there with the gang, nose on the tank, engine on full noise and wanting more.

Carruthers draws some enlightening contrasts between racing in the 1950s and 1960s, and the 1980s. Changes to circuits, tyres and machines have changed the riding techniques required.

"When I rode in Europe, most of the circuits were public road circuits of ten, 12 and 14 kilometres a lap, and with surfaces ranging from good to bloody awful! Normally they were just high-speed circuits. Even if they had some slow corners, basically they were all quick," Kel explained.

"The big difference now is the tracks are smaller and slower, with a greater percentage of tight corners. There are lots of first and second-gear corners, where the difference between the best guys and the others isn't very great.

"The important thing on the old circuits was picking your line, being able to use all the road. If you had a 240 km/h motorbike, you had to be able to judge high-speed corners and make use of that speed. Now, with changes to circuits, bikes and tyres, there is a lot more braking involved and, especially with the 500s, it's how well you judge acceleration out of corners. You've got to get the bike to the stage where it's actually sliding, then be careful that you don't high-side."

Kel reckoned to outbrake another rider into a hairpin corner was not the done thing in his riding days. If you did, the other rider would tick you off in the pits afterwards, he said.

"Why pass the guy there and gain a fraction of a second when just up the road there were a couple of fast corners where you could gain a couple of seconds?"

Kel's opinion can be backed up scientifically. Paradoxically, slow corners produce a greater number of accidents than fast corners.

On fast corners, the wheels (and engine flywheels of bikes with the crankshaft set across the frame) of a motorcycle act as gyroscopes. It means a rider can more easily control a slide on a fast corner than in a slow corner. Moreover, the torque applied to the rear wheel is greater in a first-gear corner than a top-gear corner, so again the rider has a harder job controlling a rear-wheel slide in a slow corner.

Now consider two riders of unequal ability "contesting" corners. In a fast corner, the better rider gains the advantage with relative ease. He may have a 20 km/h advantage in cornering speed. But in the slow corner, where the difference in cornering speed might be only 3 km/h, the faster rider might have to take a risk to pass. Or the slower rider might take a risk trying to stay with the faster man.

Next time you watch a race, note where the single-bike accidents occur — usually on the slower corners or the corners leading onto and off the main straight.

tinued riding motorcycles fast until mid-1987, as a tyre tester for Michelin. He was head of the test squad which developed radial construction tyres for road-going machines — a major technical breakthrough.

Cyril John Findlay was born on February 3, 1935 at Mooroopna, near Shepparton, Victoria. At 15 he used his father's road licence to obtain a competition licence.

"That's how I became Jack Findlay, it was my father's name," he admitted. Findlay's racing achievements in Australia up to 1957 were not the stuff of legends. What level of skill did he reach?

"Mainly horizontal!" Jack quipped. "I fell off at every race circuit in Australia.

"I had a 350 Manx Norton and an unreliable hybrid Norton 500, built out of an old pre-1950 long-stroke Norton engine squeezed into a later model Norton Featherbed frame. The engine was set too far back in the frame, which made the front end too light and upset the handling. Combine that with full streamlining and questionable drum brakes and life became a real adventure at the end of Conrod Straight at Bathurst or Pit Corner at the old Fishermans Bend circuit," he said.

Findlay did, however, acquire two skills which would serve him well as a private entrant in Europe. In Melbourne he trained by day as an accountant with the Commonwealth Bank, and after hours as a race mechanic with road racer and later speedway rider John Board.

At the end of 1957 Findlay (now 22) took stock of his racing. "I realised I was falling off all the time because I didn't have enough experience. There was no way of getting experience quickly in Australia, because there were only about 12 road races a year — I was getting too old! The only way was to go to Europe and ride more often. Since I was ten years old I'd wanted to be a grand prix rider," Jack said.

"My goal was to be offered a works ride. I thought once I had a works ride, then I would see if I was good enough to be a world champion. But in the end my works ride never really happened."

Jack "Tiger" Findlay sailed to England with Harry Hinton Jnr and his wife Fay. They set up base in Birmingham in March 1958. Jack took jobs at the BSA motorcycle factory, then with Dunlop and later as a welder in a motor body factory, to subsidise his racing. His first machine in Europe was a new 350 Manx Norton. Jack's vivid memory of his first European season was trying to contest two classes with that one machine.

"I qualified 14th for the 350 German Grand Prix at Nurburgring. But just before the end of practice a tooth broke off the top bevel of the camshaft drive — a typical Norton fault. I'd also qualified the bike for the 500 class, and I needed the start money from both races.

"It meant I had to retire the bike early in the 350 GP to make sure I could start in the 500 race. Luckily the other riders didn't say anything," he said.

Each year for the next four years Findlay bought one new Norton — a 500 in 1959, a 350 in 1960 and so on — so he had two bikes, but one bike was always in its second season.

As in Australia, Jack's early results were not startling. He was still relatively inexperienced. Some of his contemporaries left Australia with a string of state and national titles on their letterheads.

Findlay did not score world championship points (awarded then only for top six placings) until July 1961, when he was fifth in the East German 500 GP at Sachsenring. In the next season and a half Findlay was "in the points" on just two more occasions.

In June 1962 Jack was an official Australian representative at the Isle of Man TT, along with his great mate Jack Ahearn and sidecar racer Bob "Orrie" Salter. But in September he seriously considered retiring from motorcycle racing, after his Norton 500 dropped a valve during the Italian Grand Prix at Monza.

"I was very downhearted at the end of the 1962 season and almost bankrupt. My 500 Norton was very fast, but kept dropping the head of its exhaust valve. At Monza I'd met a car racer who offered me a test drive back in England of his grand prix Lotus," Findlay said.

"At that time I had a contract with Shell in England. When Lew Ellis, the competition manager, heard about the car test he told me I was starting to make a name for myself in motorcycles, so it was a bit ridiculous to jump into the dark and drive a grand prix car."

Ellis, a powerbroker in motorcycle sport, then put a proposition which changed Findlay's career. Brilliant Scottish rider Bob McIntyre had been killed a few months earlier. McIntyre's special 500 Matchless, with a special frame he'd developed, was still for sale. Ellis offered Findlay assistance to buy the bike. In the next five years Jack Findlay and the McIntyre-Matchless became synonymous.

The end of 1962 also saw a significant change of address for Findlay, to Paris. A base in Europe made sense for a racer whose calendar included only two major meetings on the western side of the English Channel. Once in Paris, Findlay took a French competition licence. It was more convenient and the French made him feel welcome, a sharp contrast to the treatment he'd received from the Australian motorcycle governing body's starchy London-based agent.

France was short of front-line riders in the 1960s, so it adopted Findlay as "the Australian in Paris". Jack kept his base there until 1967, when he teamed with Daniele Fontana in Milan. He moved back to

Jack Findlay with the McIntyre-Matchless 500, which he raced from 1963 to 1968.

Findlay and the Matchless take to the streets of Northern Ireland in the 1968 North-West 200.

France in 1978, when Fontana died. Jack now lives in the Versailles district of Paris.

Jack also found a new partner, Nanou, who'd been attending grand prix races since the late 1950s. This attractive French woman also helped promote Jack as a rider — an area where Australians often fell down because they were embarrassed about promoting themselves. According to Australian racer Ross Hannan, Nanou had a forthright manner with race organisers.

"Nanou and Kel Carruthers' wife Jan helped other riders and stood up for them if they needed support. You couldn't have gone racing without people like that," Hannan said.

Findlay's new bike, home and ladyfriend seemed to turn his racing around. He won his first race on the McIntyre-Matchless, an international on the full Le Mans circuit, in March 1963. In 1963 alone it carried him to second place in the Italian 500 GP, eighth overall in the world 500 championship and 11 international race wins.

Jack raced his Matchless 500 for the next five years, the last three of which saw him firmly established as one of the top 500 private entrants.

Findlay had two notable incidents on the Matchless, both in 1967. He hit a pheasant while travelling at more than 210 km/h at Spa-Francorchamps during practice for the Belgian GP. Jack somehow rode two kilometres to the pits then collapsed. He nonetheless finished fourth and headed the private-entrants derby in the next day's grand prix. Jack claims English privateer Maurice Hawthorne later found the dead pheasant, cooked it and ate it for his pre-race dinner!

Three weeks later Jack had his biggest accident in five years with the Matchless when its gearbox seized during the Czech GP. He fractured his skull, but recovered to take fifth place in that year's world 500 championship.

"The Matchless was very good on the big, fast bends of grand prix circuits, but not so good on tight, short circuits," he said. "Bob Mac's frame was very small and a bit lighter than the other 500 singles. It also had a lot of weight on the front wheel and was very light in the back end, so you could drift the bike in fast corners, using opposite lock on the handlebars a bit like driving a racing car," Findlay explained.

"I believe the McIntyre-Matchless was the only single-cylinder motorcycle to average more than 200 km/h for a lap of the old 14 km Spa-Francorchamps circuit. Mike Hailwood on his super-tuned Manx Norton got around Spa in 1961 at about 198 km/h. A few years later with the Matchless I got around at 202 km/h. It was a good little compensation for a privateer whose bike was good for about 225 km/h flat out, downhill.

"At the end of '68 I thought it was time to sell the

Matchless. I'd raced the same bike for six years, so I wasn't making much progress!" he said, half-jokingly. Findlay's friend Daniele Fontana had tried to come up with a new 500 machine in 1967-1968.

"In 1967 Fontana built a three-cylinder 500 called the Cadori, which I test rode early in 1968 at Monza, when the temperature was zero. Each race in 1968 I'd start practice, then have to put it away and use the Matchless.

"But for 1969 I had an agreement to ride the new Linto 500 and Jerome Laperrousaz was making the movie. Little did I know 1969 was going to be a great disaster for me, with an unreliable bike and lots of crashes, but more so for all of motorcycling, because 11 top riders were killed in 15 months, including Bill Ivy and Santiago Herrero.

"So *Continental Circus* was not a very happy film, and not very good publicity for motorcycle racing." (The opening sequence was a series of horrific crashes.)

Findlay scored Suzuki's first-ever 500 GP at Ulster in 1971, riding a machine he built with Daniele Fontana.

Findlay (Jada-Suzuki, No 12) leads Agostini (MV, No 1) and Granath (Husquvarna, No 3) in the 1972 Swedish 500 GP.

The sad irony of the Linto episode was that its backer (Italian financier and car dealer Umberto Premoli) and designer (Lino Tonti) had set out to provide private entrants with an affordable 500 with the potential to win races. Hence the decision to build the engine from generally available Aermacchi 250 parts. There were 15 machines built. Findlay, as "works" rider, had a bike plus a spare engine.

Three grands prix into 1969, Premoli and Tonti must have twigged that all Findlay's problems with their bike (two DNFs and a third placing out of three GP starts) were recorded by Laperrousaz's cameras. There was no Linto for Jack at the Isle of Man or the Dutch GP. So he rode Aermacchi singles to third place in the 350 TT and fifth in the 500 GP at Assen.

Laperrousaz hired Tom Arter's Matchless, one of England's best known 500 race bikes, so Findlay could contest the Belgian GP. What followed could have been comic, if it hadn't happened at 220 km/h.

Jack tried to pass Linto rider Alberto Pagani on the inside in the famed Burneville Bends. But, just off the racing line, there was sand on the road. Jack's mount lost grip at both ends, did a 180-degree turn and went backwards into the scenery. The bike was wrecked and the rider added pain to his worst year in racing.

Findlay in 1970 returned to dependable single-cylinder Matchless power for the 500 class. Colin Seeley, a former sidecar racer, built the engines (using ex-AMC tooling), and designed and built the chassis. The Seeley brought Jack a couple of top-four grand prix places, but also convinced him the days of the four-stroke single were over in grand prix racing.

Jack needed a new engine. The choice in 1970 was between two roadster-based two-strokes — Kawasaki's three-cylinder H1 (or Mach III) and Suzuki's T500 twin. Findlay could have bought one of the over-the-counter Kawasaki H1R racers. Kiwi Ginger Molloy rode one to second place in that year's world title. But he chose the Suzuki engine, saying it was lighter, more compact, less complicated and produced peak power at lower rpm.

Jack's decision was also the best for his long-term career, because Suzuki from 1972 took increasing interest in European racing. By mid-1970 Jack had installed a modified Suzuki road bike engine in his Seeley frame. In the winter of 1970-1971 Findlay and Fontana realised a frame they'd built for Jack's Yamaha 350 would suit the Suzuki engine, so they built their own Suzuki-powered 500.

Findlay's image changed subtly in 1971. His bikes now carried the logos of trade sponsors, and his traditional pudding basin helmet gave way to a jet-style item, still in Jack's livery of sky blue with a ring of chequers and a white kangaroo motif. Jack shunned the new full-face helmets, saying he couldn't breathe in them.

Works rider at last . . . Findlay and the 1973 Suzuki 500 twin at Raatle in Holland.

The Milan-built Suzuki helped Findlay make history on August 14, 1971. He won the Ulster 500 GP on the Dundrod public road circuit. It was Findlay's first world championship race win and Suzuki's first GP win in the 500 class. Jack's engine was arguably the nearest to a roadster engine ever to win a world 500 championship round.

"Suzuki was already racing factory TR500s in America, but the only parts Suzuki would sell me in Europe were pistons. Suzuki Great Britain loaned me two pistons for the Ulster — I had to give them back after the race. We used converted road cylinders, not the factory T-port ones," he said.

In the winter of 1971-1972 Findlay and Fontana built a new, neater chassis using lighter-gauge tubing. They called this creation the Jada (from JAck and DAniele). It was purpose-built for circuits like Spa-Francorchamps. The engine was well forward in the chassis and the bike weighed in at the FIM minimum weight limit of 100 kg, despite its relatively heavy roadster-based engine. "The Jada was light and very small, the same size as my 350 Yamaha, so it was fast. Daniele and I did everything we could to save weight, using lots of titanium bolts. We held the engine in with circlips instead of nuts. The frame tubing was only half a millimetre in wall thickness, which explains why the front downtubes broke at the Isle of Man," he said.

The bit of Findlay pride, calling his new bike a Jada rather than a Suzuki, didn't stop importer Suzuki Italia giving him a "guest" ride at the 1972 Isle of Man meeting on its 75 kW works TR750 triple, one of the machines nicknamed the "flexi-fliers" by American team members. According to Jack, the TT organisers told him to "just take it easy", after it was timed through the speed trap at a record 255 km/h. Jack finished third in the Formula 750 TT, despite stopping twice in a five-lap (304 km) race to refuel.

"The Suzuki 750 was a pig of a bike. It was like riding a motocrosser. The front end spent most of the time in the air. But I liked it. All that horsepower was nice to use and the brakes were fabulous. The handling was better if I kept my weight on the footrests. That also made it easier to get my weight forward and keep the front end down through the rough sections," Findlay said.

Jack was running third in the Senior TT when the Jada's frame broke. It was a big disappointment. When he returned to Paris he had another setback. Thieves had taken $1200 from his caravan.

Suzuki Italia hired Findlay to contest the 1973

Findlay prepares the Suzuki 500 two at Raatle. Note the tent in background and the door of the ubiquitous Ford Transit van.

world 500 championship on a works water-cooled Suzuki 500 twin. He also rode a TR750 in the inaugural FIM F750 Championship, in the TT (where its gearbox failed) and, of all things, in a 1000 km endurance race at Imola.

The new 500 helped Findlay fulfil his long-held ambition of winning the Isle of Man Senior TT. Jack said at the time it was the proudest moment of his racing career. He finished fifth overall in the world championship and third in the F750 series, with a race victory in the Swedish round.

Findlay in 1974 realised his ambition of a full works contract when Suzuki signed him to ride its new 500 four. He was also given a new TR750 for the FIM F750 series. Findlay's long-sought works contract was no automatic ticket to success. Suzuki needed two seasons to develop the square-four 500 into a world-beater. The early engines were prone to breaking primary drives, seizing cylinders and breaking gearboxes, usually with painful consequences for the riders. Jack also found the engineers on the new project difficult to deal with. "They thought they knew it all," he said.

But the most painful part for Findlay was the end of the season. Jack was Suzuki's best-placed rider in two championships. He finished fifth in the world 500 championship (the sixth time he'd been in the top five since 1966) and third in the FIM F750 series, which fellow Aussie John Dodds won. During practice at the Isle of Man, Findlay pushed the under-developed 500 four to a lap of 170.5 km/h, which made him the third fastest man ever on the TT course. Yet Suzuki sacked him.

The fall-out from Suzuki's decision was felt by Daniele Fontana's neighbours. Over the winter of 1974-1975 they were treated to a new sound, the unmuffled cry of a four-cylinder two-stroke 750 Yamaha labouring on the test bench.

"Nobody in Europe would sell me a bike, so Kel Carruthers found me a Yamaha TZ750 in the USA. Daniele and I worked on the engine and suspension during the year. We started with 104 horsepower (77 kW) and had 125 hp (93 kW) by the end of the season. We improved the handling by increasing the rear suspension travel. To do that we built longer suspension units and laid them forward at an angle," Jack said.

Findlay's 750 let him down just once in his title-winning F750 season when it broke a connecting rod. Jack also raced the bike in the 500 grands prix, using converted Yamaha TZ250 cylinders and Milan-built exhaust pipes.

"Our home-built 500 Yamaha was good on fast circuits. I was third at Spa and in the Finnish GP. But it lacked the low-down torque to be any good on tight circuits."

Jacks's last big win — the 1977 Austrian 500 GP. He's flanked by Austria's Max Wiener (left) and Scotland's Alex George.

In 1976 Jack bought one of the new Suzuki RG500s, production versions of the motorcycle he had helped develop two years earlier. But his only rostrum positions of the season were second placings in the Swedish 500 GP and the British round of the F750 championship at Silverstone, on his Yamaha. The same year Honda hired him to ride in France's biggest motorcycle race, the Bol d'Or 24-Hour race. He finished fourth with veteran Briton Stan Woods. Findlay later described the experience as "nothing short of murder — like doing 12 grands prix in a day".

Findlay kept his Suzuki 500/Yamaha 750 combination for 1977, but with new Dutch-made frames. He had a brief moment of glory in the 1977 world 500 championship, winning a controversial Austrian GP at the fast, Armco-fence lined Salzburgring. A fatal accident in the preceding 350 GP had prompted the works 500 riders and some better-sponsored private entrants to withdraw to protest at poor safety standards.

The win gave 42-year-old Jack joint lead in the championship, with Sheene. Of course it was not to last. A week later Jack was 13th in the West German GP. A week later again (on May 15) he was lucky to be alive. Findlay's magnesium rear wheel broke up on a fast section of Italy's Imola circuit, triggering a huge accident.

"That crash was my only regret in motorcycle racing, and it pretty well finished my career," Jack explained. "I hit the road very hard. It twisted my body and stopped my heart. My brain passed the water layer and hit the skull, destroying part of it. For about three years I had trouble with depression.

"With my other accidents I was usually back riding within a week. I was in a very bad state after that one, but as a private entrant I couldn't afford not to race. All my money and ability to make money was tied up in my equipment. I went to the Isle of Man and slept 22 hours a day. They'd wake me up to go out and practice," he confessed.

Jack's racing career struggled along for another season of occasional mid-field world championship round finishes. This was despite his depression and the best efforts of some Italian criminals, who stole his van and bikes early in 1978. Findlay had to pay blackmail to retrieve his gear.

The last grand prix Jack Findlay finished was the 1978 Belgian 500 GP in the wet at his beloved Spa-Francorchamps. He was 15th, just ahead of a younger Australian, Greg Johnson. Perhaps it was fitting, it was the last time the 14 km Spa road circuit was used.

Jack contested the final 500 grand prix of the season at Nurburgring. He qualified 14th then broke down in the race, exactly as he had for the 350 GP there in 1958.

"In 20 years I hadn't made much progress," said the man whose grand prix career began with John Surtees as world champion and ended the day Kenny Roberts won America's first world road-racing crown.

Findlay had raced for 28 years, on machines ranging from hybrid Manx Nortons and six-year-old former works Mondial 250s, to a 50cm^3 Bridgestone, a works Honda endurance racer and a Yamaha TZ750. He'd lost several "best mates" from the grand prix paddock, to the point where he stopped making close friendships in racing.

Findlay's retirement from racing in 1978 left him with a problem. What does a 43-year-old Australian former motorcycle racer do for a living? Jack had never really planned for the day when he stopped racing and he figured his credentials wouldn't win him work in Australia. Fortunately, Michelin threw him a lifeline with its road-tyre test program.

Jack kept riding, found a new partner, Dominique, former wife of a French racer of the 1950s, and discovered tennis. He also rediscovered his accountancy skills, to help with the bookwork at Dominique's boutique. Jack promised Dominique he'd stop test riding if he had another accident. In April 1987, the week Michelin unveiled its radial road tyres to the world's motorcycle press, Jack Findlay had that accident on a public road near the Jerez circuit in Spain.

Findlay was well over the speed limit on the final leg of a test loop when a car driver turned absent-mindedly across his path. Jack's skill and, he reckons, the tyres, converted a potential quick death into a glancing blow.

"The car went into the ditch on one side of the road. The bike demolished a little bridge over a ditch on the other side, and I ended up in the middle of the road," Jack said.

"When I looked down my knee was hanging out through my leathers. Because I'd just discovered tennis, I got up and started running up and down the road to make sure my knee still worked! This was too much for the little Spanish driver. He grabbed me and tried to calm me down, because he thought I'd gone crazy.

"Fifty-two stitches and three weeks later my knee was okay and I was back on the tennis court. But I kept my promise to Dominique to retire from motor-cycling," Jack said.

Kel Carruthers flashes through Parliament Square, Ramsay, on his works Aermacchi 350. He retired on the last lap with broken valve gear while running second. (Heese)

Above: *Jack Ahearn (Manx Norton) at Quarter Bridge, during the 1965 IoM 500 TT. (Morley)* **Right:** *Barry Smith's works Derbi 50 silhouetted against the vast Hockenheim grandstands in 1969. (Heese)*

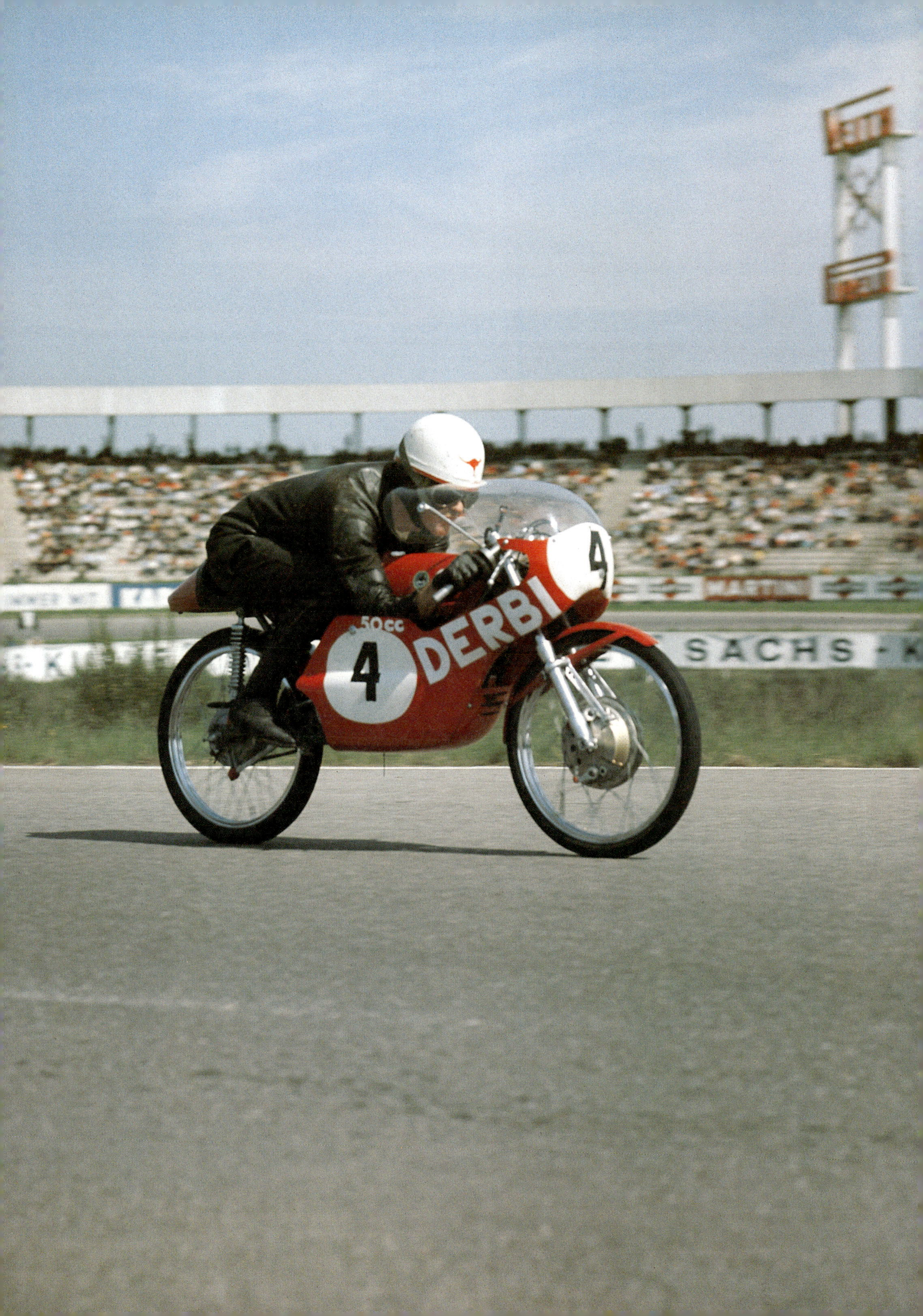
50cc
4
DERBI
4
MARTINI
SACHS

Above: *Works Suzuki riders Jack Findlay (No 4) and Barry Sheene earned their pay riding the prototype square-four 500s in the rain at the treacherous Salzburgring in 1974. (Heese)* **Right:** *John Dodds made his mark in the 1970s riding Yamaha 250s and 350s. At Brands Hatch he led world champion Giacomo Agostini's works MV Agusta 500. (Heese)*

48
HUFA

Right: *Casablanca-born Melburnian Vic Soussan, flat out on a Yamaha TZ350D in the 1977 Dutch GP at Assen. (Heese)* **Below:** *Gregg Hansford won ten GPs in 1978-79 on Kawasakis. Gregg's size is evident from this shot on the KR350 at Jarama in 1979. (Morley)*

Left: *New Zealand's Graeme Crosby and America's Wes Cooley fought out the 1980 Daytona Superbike race on their Yoshimura-Suzukis. Crosby won. (Morley)* **Below:** *Albury's Graeme Geddes began the 1981 grand prix season with a second place in the Argentine GP. But homesickness had set in by Assen, where he's pictured on a Bimota-Yamaha 350. (Heese)*

135

53
CHAMPION
CHAMPION
CHAMPION
REGINA CHAIN
Shell
61
TECHN. ABNAHME

Pre-race grid, 1981 German GP at Hockenheim. Graeme McGregor (left) and Jeff Sayle's mechanic Dave McGillivray warm up the Yamaha TZ350s, while Sayle autographs a fan's helmet. (Heese)

Right: *Paul Lewis qualified on the front row of the grid for the 1984 British 500 GP at Silverstone. But he crashed his Gary Flood prepared Suzuki RGB500 during the race. (Morley)* **Below:** *Jeff Sayle (Armstrong-Rotax, No 43) and Austria's August Auinger duel at Spa-Francorchamps in the 1981 Belgian 250 GP. (Morley)*

Graeme McGregor (Yamaha TZ250J) at Creg-ny-Baa, during the 1982 Isle of Man 250 TT. (Morley)

Wayne Gardner's 1988 US GP was more a rodeo ride than a race. Here he flicks through Laguna Seca's famed Corkscrew on his Honda NSR500, having just lapped America's Mike Baldwin, on his privately entered Honda RS500R V3. (Morley)

"Nice ride, Wayne", says second-placed Eddie Lawson after the 1988 Belgian 500 GP. It was Gardner's second victory in the space of eight days. Third-placed Randy Mamola (at right) still can't believe he's finished on the dais after a trying year on the Cagiva. (Martin)

Wayne Gardner thought he had the 1988 French 500 GP shot to pieces, until his Honda shot itself to pieces on the last lap. (Martin)

Australia's coming GP men . . . **Above:** *Kevin Magee in Yugoslavia in 1988.* (Martin) **Right:** *Michael Doohan, hurtling through Turn Three at Phillip Island on his Yamaha Superbike in December 1988.* (Lapka)

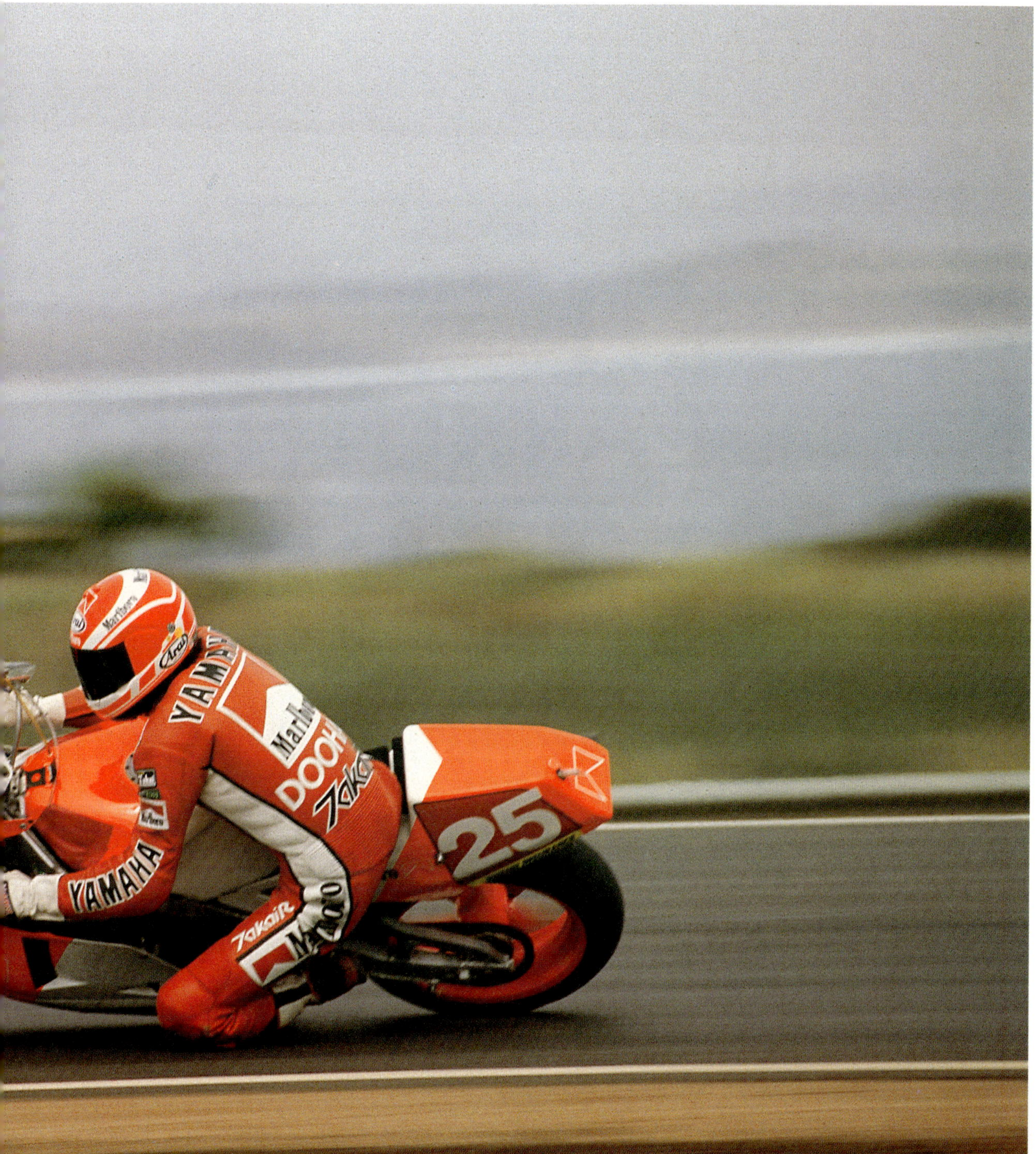
YAMAHA
25

KEL CARRUTHERS

CHAPTER 10

Opatija, Yugoslavia — September 14, 1969. Final round of the world 250 cm^3 championship, and the title is in the balance. Spain's Santiago Herrero (Ossa) has 83 points, Sweden's Kent Andersson (Yamaha) and Australia's Kel Carruthers (Benelli) each have 82. Whoever wins today will be world champion.

The three are nervous — more about the race conditions than the delicately poised championship. In Carruthers' view, it is a pretty dangerous situation. Opatija is not a race track. It is a town perched on the steep northern Yugoslavian coastline of the Adriatic Sea. The circuit is six kilometres of the town's streets, up and down hill, including two hairpins. It is damp and more rain threatens. Racing in the wet on any circuit can be a lottery, but town streets are worse. Opatija's roads have been resurfaced for this race — Yugoslavia's first world championship grand prix. The tar is slick and the road markings, just days old, are glossy.

The view from the grid is daunting. The road is straight for perhaps 200 metres, then curves left, flanked by a two-metre-high stone wall, and runs on to an uphill hairpin. Spectators are sitting along the top of the wall.

The Yugoslav tricolour drops. Carruthers, all of 31 years, 162 cm and 60 kg, heaves his four-cylinder Benelli forward. It is a large machine for a 250, particularly when compared with the single-cylinder two-stroke Ossa and the two-stroke Yamaha twin. But its small cylinders mean it is easy to start. Kel takes a few steps, jumps astride the bike, and flicks out the clutch lever. Four sculptured Italian exhaust megaphones answer in chorus. If the race is decided on sound quality alone, Carruthers will win. The exhaust howl builds to a scream as the 36 kW Benelli accelerates. The Australian leads into the "stone-wall" corner for the first of 21 laps.

Lap one. Herrero annexes the lead in the top section of the circuit and leads narrowly, tailed by Carruthers and his new Benelli team-mate Gilberto Parlotti. Herrero's left wrist is still in plaster from a crash two rounds earlier — it is win or nothing today. The other contender, Andersson, is back in fifth position. The drizzle returns on lap two. Andersson improves one place, but loses more time to the leading trio.

Lap seven. Herrero crashes right in front of Carruthers in a fast downhill bend. Kel is "scared silly", a race report later comments, and the experience tempers his riding for a few laps. Andersson closes, and on lap 14 he has caught and passed the two Benellis. Carruthers and Parlotti fight back.

Rain, slick tarmac, slicker road markings, and a rival pushing hard on a lighter, more nimble machine. Carruthers has never known such pressure.

Kel Carruthers runs the gauntlet of pit well-wishers after clinching the world 250 championship in Yugoslavia.

They battle for the next few laps, then Andersson's Yamaha goes into a frightening speed wobble, known as a "tankslapper", in front of the pits. Andersson loses ground, and Carruthers re-asserts his authority, while Parlotti plays the ideal team-mate, sitting half a second behind. Carruthers wins, Parlotti is second, and Andersson third, 6.9 seconds behind Carruthers after 126 km and 58 minutes of racing.

After four seasons in Europe Kel Carruthers had won Australia's third world road-racing championship. He rode back to the pits to find the Benelli team crying with joy over the make's first world championship since 1950.

Carruthers won his title in unusual circumstances. He had not planned to contest the 250 championship in 1969. He did not ride a Benelli 250 until the third of the 12 championship rounds, and he was not given the best Benelli machine until round ten. Only then did the Italian team brief the Australian to "try to win the title". In the last three rounds Kel turned a 21-point deficit into victory.

Rule changes, and team and machine troubles thwarted Carruthers' world championship hopes in 1970. The world governing body banned 250s with more than two cylinders. Benelli was hit by a strike

145

which hampered its ability to give Carruthers competitive 350 machinery. And Kel's own "production" Yamaha 250 suffered ignition trouble too many times. Still, he rode his privately entered Yamaha TD2 to second place in the 250 championship. Four times in the first seven grands prix, Carruthers led until late in the race, when the ignition contact breakers failed. Kel also ran second in the world 350 championship, riding a 1969-model works Benelli in three rounds, then his own Yamaha TR2.

But that wasn't the end of his superb career. Early in 1970, Kel had visited the United States to buy his Yamahas, and while he was there he won the 250 cm^3 international race at Daytona and took the lead in the 200-mile main event (for machines up to 750 cm^3) before his borrowed Yamaha 350 broke its crankshaft.

In 1971 Kel returned to the USA and proved his Carruthers-developed Yamaha 250 was nearly unbeatable. The 350 version beat larger-capacity BSA, Harley-Davidson, Honda and Triumph four-strokes, and embarrassed the early 750 Kawasaki and Suzuki two-strokes. In 1972, Carruthers founded Yamaha's American road-racing team, retiring from racing at the end of 1973 to concentrate on running the team.

Five years later Kel returned to Europe as team manager and chief mechanic for his star pupil, American Kenny Roberts. Carruthers-prepared machines have since won six of the last 11 world 500 cm^3 championships, three each with Roberts and Eddie Lawson. It is an incredible record, given the highly competitive 500 championship scene of the past decade.

Kel Carruthers was one of the most complete Antipodean road-racers ever to hit Europe. He left Australia in 1966, aged 28, with 16 years of competition experience, including 12 years road racing on machines ranging from 125 to 750 cm^3. He had several attributes which would serve him well in Europe: he could develop and prepare his own machines; he was well organised and a shrewd negotiator; and he rarely crashed, even when riding ten-tenths.

Champion Australian rider Eric Hinton's wife Kate summed up Kel Carruthers in one line. He was, she said, "a smart little cookie". Multiple world 500 champion Giacomo Agostini agreed. He often asked Carruthers technical questions in the field in the 1960s.

Kel's father, Jack, was a noted speedway sidecar racer with V-twin Vincent 1000 machines. He ran a motorcycle dealership and repair business in the Sydney suburb of Gladesville. Kelvin was Jack and Lil Carruthers' only child. He was born on January 3, 1938, and he grew up with motorcycles. At 15 he joined the business full-time.

Nobody made mini-bikes in the late 1940s and early 1950s, and no company sold budget-priced racing bikes. So, with his dad, Kel learned about competition motorcycles by taking road-going motorcycle parts and building racers. By the age of 12 Kel competed in open trials events and in clubmen dirt-track events soon after. At 15, Carruthers junior obtained a restricted road licence, to test-ride Australian Army Harley-Davidsons he helped service at Gladesville. Once Kel had a road licence, he could obtain an open competition licence for road races and scrambles.

But despite Kel's early start in racing, he did not seriously consider racing as a profession until after his 23rd birthday. In the late 1950s Kel was happy to compete as an amateur sportsman, riding perhaps a dozen road races and scrambles events each year, mostly in his home state. Kel's priorities were family — he was married to Jan in 1957 — and business.

Honda's entry into the Australian market changed Carruthers' racing horizons. Honda, at the end of 1960, built six replicas of its works four-cylinder 250 racer as promotional machines for export sales. Australian distributor Bennett and Wood received one, and gave it to Carruthers. He still has it.

The Honda's four cylinders, 16 valves, six gears, 31 kW power output and 14,000 rpm rev limit were impressive specifications in 1961. "It had a good motor, absolutely awful handling and virtually no brakes," Kel recalls. "But once you learned to ride it, it was okay."

Carruthers and the Honda 250-four dominated Australian 250 races, and most 350 races, for the next five years. At Honda's request he raced Australia-wide. The statistics of this period were staggering. He won 17 grands prix events at Bathurst and ten Australian titles. Between 1961 and 1965 he had 161 starts, for 115 wins, 27 second places and seven third places using two Hondas and a Norton.

Two years running, 1964 and 1965, Kel "rode the card" at Bathurst, winning the 125, 250, 350 and 500 unlimited grands prix. His mounts were a Honda 125 twin, the ex-factory Honda 250-four, and a Manx Norton 500, all prepared in the Gladesville workshop. At 1964's Easter meet, Kel entered the unlimited production race on a Norton 750 roadster and won that as well.

Five years of successful national competition riding three grand prix machines per meeting left Kel looking for a new challenge. He had planned to go to Europe in 1963, but his father convinced him to stay on until his children were older. When they did leave, Kel and wife Jan were well organised, and they had Jack's support. He sold the shop and went with his son. Then, before Kel left, he made extensive phone calls to contacts such as Honda team leader Jim Redman for background knowledge.

Jan Carruthers' experience as a secretary was also invaluable. She arranged correspondence lessons for the children, Sharon aged six and Paul five, and

Jack Carruthers, Bathurst race official Harry Bartrop and Kel, with the all-conquering Honda 250 four.

she also managed race entries and start money. That was aside from running a travelling home, helping with the bikes if needed, and handling stop watches and the pitboard when Kel was on the track.

Kel, in privateer terms, had strong financial backing thanks to his share of the sale of the family business. The sale meant that the whole Carruthers family could be in Europe for the first year. It cost 1,300 pounds for fares and freight to get the family and machines there.

His machines were a CR93 Honda 125 and two Manx Nortons. Carruthers knew he would need the three bikes to obtain starts and make the money needed to keep six people on the road. The Nortons were obvious choices, while the Jack Gates-owned Honda 125 twin was, Kel reckoned, "as good as any privateer 125 machine". He left his Honda 250-four at home, wisely reasoning it might earn him extra start money for a month or two, but would soon wear out if raced hard every week.

Kel and Jack flew to England early in 1966 to buy a van for the bikes, a ten-feet caravan for Kel's family, and a VW Campervan for Jack and Lil. The two Mrs Carruthers sailed to Naples on the liner SS *Iberia*.

Carruthers arrived in Europe at the very peak of the 1960s' grand prix racing. There were strong fields of works bikes in every solo class: Honda, Yamaha and Suzuki battled in the small capacity classes. Honda in 1966 mounted a challenge to MV in the 500 class. Private entrants were at best racing for minor placings.

And there were plenty of Australian privateers in

1966. Already there were the two Jacks, Ahearn and Findlay, Eric Hinton, Kevin Cass, Barry Smith and sidecar racer Barry Thompson. The freshman class of '66 includes Carruthers' chief rival in Australia, John Dodds, Malcolm Stanton and Len Atlee. Kel planned from the outset to stay in Europe for two years. He figured it would take that long to see if he could cut it.

The Carruthers campaign opened with six Italian meetings, mainly at seaside street circuits, in as many weeks, beginning at Riccione on the Adriatic Coast. His name appeared just once in world championship top-six results in 1966, when he placed fourth, just behind Jack Ahearn, in the Finnish 350 GP at Imatra. Highlight of Kel's first Isle of Man was eighth place in the Senior Tourist Trophy.

For all his organisation, experience and backup, Kel still recalls that his first year was difficult. Like many before and after, he had to make the adjustment from winning at home to fighting for top-ten placings in Europe.

"I didn't do as well as I expected. The racing wasn't that hard, but I found lots of guys had trick equipment, like five and six-speed gearboxes for their Nortons, and smaller, lower fuel tanks to use in short races," he said.

"You had to learn some long circuits, too — 10, 12, 14 kilometres. There were no private practice sessions at road circuits and not much official practice time. No one would help you with advice such as what gearing to run and such, except English rider John Cooper.

"My dad helped me with the bikes the first year. But most of the time until 1969 there was only Jan to help me. Sometimes you'd find a guy who'd take the wheels to the Dunlop tent to have the tyres changed. But when you were travelling you couldn't take the risk on anyone else driving, because everything you owned in Europe was with you — the van, bikes and caravan.

"My smartest move was at the beginning of 1967. I was one of the first good guys to get a first-rate Aermacchi 350 engine, which I put in a Rickman Metisse frame with Ceriani suspension. After that I was rarely beaten in a 350 race by another privateer."

In that year the Australian was the best-placed private entrant in the world 350 championship and one of the best in the 125 class. Kel finished in the top six in four of the seven of the 350 championship rounds run in Europe. His Honda 125 twin was the first private machine, and the first four-stroke, home in the Isle of Man 125 TT, and the Finnish and Ulster GPs.

Aermacchi gave Carruthers one of two special 350 cm^3 engines for 1968. He bolted it into a superb Italian Drixl chassis and he made the winner's rostrum the first time he rode the new Drixl-Aermacchi 350 in a grand prix. His push-rod single was third to Giacomo Agostini (MV-triple) and Renzo Pasolini (Benelli-four) in the West German GP, on the Nurburgring-South motorcycle circuit. But mid-season he switched back to the Rickman chassis, after some breakages with the Drixl. Finishing was his first priority.

Carruthers grew used to grand prix rostrums and garlands in 1968. He also took the Aermacchi to third place in the East German GP and second in the Ulster. The runner-up position in Northern Ireland meant Kel held second place in the 350 world championship, behind Agostini but ahead of factory riders from Benelli, Bultaco and East Germany's MZ. The final round was at Monza. Aermacchi loaned Kel a works 350, but he failed to finish in a very wet race. Pasolini, the Benelli works rider, finished second and took second place in the championship from Carruthers by one point.

Kel did, however, win a lucrative British 350 international series. And his little Honda was again the best private 125 machine at the Isle of Man. He finished third to the Yamaha V4 of Phil Read and Bill Ivy, in a race where Ivy rocked everyone with a 161.45 km/h lap. The works Yamaha 125s were fast in 1968.

That year also saw Kel Carruthers score points in five of the ten 500 championship rounds on his Norton. The top privateer in 500 series was, however, Australian compatriot Jack Findlay, who was second.

Aermacchi was impressed. It offered Carruthers three works machines for 1969: a 125 single-cylinder two-stroke, a special short-stroke 350 and 382 cm³ machine for the 500 class. The 382 combined the larger cylinder bore of the new short-stroke 350 engine with the long stroke of the production 350 version. Kel had achieved the privateer's goal — a works ride.

The new 350 Aermacchi was the pick of his three bikes. The short-stroke engine cured problems encountered with the earlier models, and the works Aermacchi frame was better than Kel had expected. He rated it on par with the Rickman. "The Aermacchi 125 was not bad for its day, but not as good as one cylinder from a Yamaha 250, for example," Kel said.

Carruthers opened the season in Italy with the usual series of round-the-houses internationals, and a special moment involving local hero Giacomo Agostini. Kel fell while leading Agostini in a 350 race. Agostini's MV hit Kel's Aermacchi and the world champion fell. An apologetic Carruthers helped Agostini remount and rejoin the race — motorcycle racing was different in 1969, and Kel knew the crowd had paid to see Agostini race.

The 1969 world championships opened on a rain-lashed May 4 at the new Jarama circuit, near Madrid. Carruthers finished second to Agostini in the 350 class and sixth in the 125 GP. A week later he was sixth in the West German 350 GP at Hockenheim, the Aermacchi perhaps hurting for top-speed on one of the fastest closed circuits in Europe.

There was no 350 class at the French Grand Prix, so Carruthers' next world championship meeting was the Isle of Man TT at the beginning of June. On the third day of TT practice, Carruthers recorded a 100 mph average lap on his 350 Aermacchi. The feat attracted the interest of the Benelli team.

Benelli had an urgent problem. It had one of the most powerful machines in the 250 class, but it had yet to log a single championship point in 1969. For the Isle of Man, Benelli hired reigning world 125 and 250 champion Phil Read to back up the fast but impetuous Pasolini. When Pasolini crashed in TT practice, Benelli promoted Read to its number one 16-valve 250-four and offered the second-string 8-valver to Carruthers as a one-off ride.

Kel was now in a privateer's idea of heaven. Two Italian companies wanted him to ride their machines at one meeting. He telephoned Aermacchi and asked permission to ride the Benelli 250. Aermacchi's prime concern was that Kel should not beat its works 250 rider, Angelo Bergamonti. Kel's reported response was classic irrefutable Carruthers logic: he said that if he didn't beat Bergamonti, somebody else would.

Carruthers discovered the Benelli 250-four engine was bigger and heavier than the 1961 Honda, because, he recalled, "It was made out of lots of little parts instead of a few large castings." But the frame and cycle parts were decidedly better. Kel took to the Benelli at once, using the style he'd developed early in his career of setting his weight to the inside of the machine in corners.

By the end of practice week Carruthers was second on the 250 practice leaderboard — the fastest man was on the injured list. But Kel's race instructions were to back up Read, who had the more powerful machine.

Carruthers had race position number one for the 250 TT — head of field and nobody to pass or chase. The weather was perfect for racing, and the sky and roads were clear as Kel pushed off down Glencrutchery Road for the first of six laps (365 km).

After one lap, Carruthers led by 12 seconds, with Read third behind Yamaha's Rod Gould. Carruthers went further ahead on lap two, while Read lost more ground to Gould. Read's position, behind Gould, made Benelli's race plan unworkable. The team signalled Carruthers: "Okay, 1st!" Carruthers raced on to win by nearly three minutes, setting the fastest lap at 159.35 km/h. Gould and Read did not finish.

Kel also finished second in the 125 TT on the works Aermacchi two-stroke, and he held second place to Agostini on the last lap of the 350 TT, when the Aermacchi broke a rocker arm.

The 250 TT win turned Carruthers' career around.

Aermacchi released Kel from his commitments and he flew to Italy and signed with Benelli, who intended he ride the second-string bike and back up Pasolini. Benelli's dream of a Pasolini victory was still achievable, because the 1969 championship would be decided on each rider's best seven results from the 12 rounds.

The plan worked for the next four races. Pasolini won the Dutch GP at Assen, from Carruthers and series leader Santiago Herrero. The Spaniard then surprised everyone by winning at the fast Spa-Francorchamps, from Gould and Carruthers. Carruthers' Benelli suffered wet electrics in the East German GP at Sachsenring. Pasolini won, Kel was fifth. Pasolini also won the Czech GP at Brno, from Gould and Carruthers, while Herrero's Ossa holed a piston, the first of five disappointments for the early season pace-setter. Herrero could have wrapped up the series by winning the Finnish GP. Instead he crashed, but remounted to take sixth place. Pasolini also crashed, breaking a collarbone. Kent Andersson won the race on his Yamaha. Carruthers finished fourth.

Benelli's only hope now was Carruthers. He was third on the points table, behind Herrero and Andersson. But he could win the championship if he won two of the remaining three races and finished second in the other. Benelli gave Carruthers its best machine for the Ulster GP. He dominated the race, beating Andersson by more than two minutes. Herrero crashed again and injured his wrist.

The Italian GP at Imola was a thriller, and confirmed Kel's opinions on the relative strengths of the machines. "The Benelli had a slight edge in top speed," he recalled. "But it was a big package and fairly heavy for a 250. The Yamaha was the best all-round bike. I confirmed that for myself the next year when I rode one. It was lighter than the Benelli, so it was easier to flick about. The Ossa lacked a little in top speed, but it accelerated very well — it was good on tight circuits."

Former works Yamaha team member Phil Read was a wild-card entry at Imola, on a privately entered Yamaha twin. He beat Carruthers by a bare

Kel Carruthers (Norton) leads Alberto Pagani (Linto) and Jack Findlay (Matchless) in the 1968 East German 500 GP.

two-tenths of a second. Andersson was nearly a minute behind. Herrero was fifth. The Italian result set up the all-or-nothing Herrero vs Andersson vs Carruthers final round at Opatija. Carruthers won that race and with it the championship.

Kel, Jan and the children flew back to Australia late in 1969 for four months' holiday and a few race appearances. At Sydney Airport they had a novel experience for Australians involved in motorcycling in the 1960s — a press conference. Kel's achievements had been recognised at home. He was a finalist in Australia's premier sports award, the ABC Sportsman of the Year, alongside world champion boxer Johnny Famechon, hurdles world record holder Pam Kilborn, tennis ace Rod Laver, Australian soccer captain John Warren and popular test cricketer Doug Walters. Only two other Australian motorcyclists have been finalists for this award: Tom Phillis and Wayne Gardner.

"I didn't think I'd be named Sportsman of the Year

Kel Carruthers (Benelli) leads Dieter Braun (MZ) in the 1969 Italian 250 GP at Imola.

Latin communications! Carruthers with the Benelli team in 1969.

because Rod Laver won the tennis Grand Slam that year! But I was given to understand I was in the top three in the national vote (by ABC sports executives and metropolitan newspaper sports editors)," Kel said. Laver, as Kel expected, won the award.

Carruthers' only concern over the Australian summer of 1969-1970 was what he would race in 1970. New world championship regulations for the 250 class limited engines to two cylinders, thus ruling out the Benelli. The Italians planned therefore to contest the 350 and possibly the 500 class. There were even reports of Benelli using its 250-four experience to build a 500 V8.

But in January 1970 came news which pulled the bottom out of Carruthers' world. The Benelli factory had been closed for six weeks by a strike. The small race department estimated that it would be June before Kel's new 350 would be ready.

The season after a world championship success is a vital one financially, and particularly in the years before 1980. A rider cashed in on his title and made up for the lean years with top-rate start money for international races and the grands prix.

But if international race organisers were paying top freight for a world champion, they expected a fully professional effort. Carruthers' observations from the 1969 season made his choice of alternative machines clear: a pair of Yamahas. The only place Kel could find Yamahas for sale was, at Rod Gould's suggestion, the United States. Kel bought a new TD2 250 from Yamaha America, and a used TR2 350 from Californian motorcycle dealer and later world motorcycle speed record holder Don Vesco.

Kel's contact with Vesco was the third great turning point in his motorcycle racing career. He said if Kel was coming to America to collect his bikes, then why not ride two Vesco-Yamahas at Daytona, America's richest motorcycle race meeting. Carruthers won the Daytona 250 cm³ international race, and proved the surprise of the 200-mile main race. Kel, riding a Yamaha 350, had just passed eventual race winner Dick Mann's works Honda 750-four when the Yamaha broke its crankshaft. "Don Vesco and I got talking at Daytona about what I would do after I finished racing in Europe. He said if I ever came back to America, I could operate out of his workshop and we'd run a race team between us," Kel recalled.

Carruthers began the 1970 world championship season in Europe riding his own Yamaha 250 and a 1969 works Benelli 350. His private team was typically professional. It included experienced grand prix mechanic Nobby Clark and a schoolteacher for the children. Jan Carruthers said they felt like the pick of the grand prix paddock with their new Mercedes-Benz 280 car and 16-foot caravan.

The first grand prix of 1970, at Nurburgring, was one of Australia's most successful. Carruthers won the 250 GP on his Yamaha, and rode the works Benelli to second place in the 350 class, behind Agostini. John Dodds won the 125 GP on an Aermacchi.

But Kel's first-up success in the 250 class clouded his one big disadvantage. He had a production Yamaha with a five-speed gearbox and magneto ignition. British rider Rod Gould had a semi-works Yamaha with a six-speed gearbox and electronic ignition. In the next seven 250 grands prix, Carruthers retired four times with ignition failure. It was the same story every time: Kel would be leading late in the race and the contact breakers would break. Gould, on the other hand, finished six of the seven races. When Kel finished, he was either first or a close second. Of the four races he and Gould both finished, the scoreline was two wins each.

Carruthers beat Gould by the huge margin of three-and-a-half minutes in the Isle of Man 250 TT. He was the first Australian to win a race two years running on the Isle. Gould then beat Carruthers by 15 seconds in a wet Belgian GP, and the Australian went on to win the Czech GP, which Gould failed to finish, and beat his rival by 37 seconds in the Ulster Grand Prix. Late in the season, a German company, Krober, made Kel an electronic ignition. But with three races to go it was, realistically, too late. Gould had a healthy points lead.

Like in 1969, Kel's victory in Northern Ireland gave him a chance to win the title. But this time he had to

Kel Carruthers won the IoM 250 TT two years running. In 1970 he won from Rod Gould (right) and Gunter Bartusch (left).

Kel Carruthers and Britain's Rod Gould (right) fought the 1970 world 250 title down to the wire.

win the Italian GP at Monza. It was the best race of the year, a tactical battle with three top riders on Yamaha twins slipstreaming one another. Carruthers and Gould crossed the line side-by-side, but the decision went to Gould by 0.03 of a second. Phil Read finished third, one second behind. Kel was understandably disappointed. He had won more 250 grands prix than the previous year, but lost the title.

Carruthers was also runner-up in the world 350

championship. The first two rounds saw him finish second on the Benelli to Agostini's MV. A broken drive sprocket then forced Kel to retire from the Isle of Man 350 TT in round three while holding second position. Soon after, Kel decided he was better off riding his own Yamaha 350, prepared by Nobby Clark and himself, than continuing as the second-string Benelli rider. Kel was right. He finished ahead of Benelli's Pasolini in the 350 championship.

During 1970, Kel and Jan decided that five years on the road in Europe was enough. They planned to take up Don Vesco's offer of a Carruthers-Vesco race team for one year, then return to Australia. The Carruthers family arrived in the United States in the middle of a motorcycle racing boom, with large purses and strong factory involvement. One 750 cm^3 race at Ontario, California, netted Kel US$8,400 for second place, behind John Cooper's works BSA 750. A win in the 250 class pushed his earnings for one day up to nearly US$15,000.

The American market was growing, so companies

Dutch photographer Jan Heese captured Kel Carruthers' leap at Ballaugh Bridge in the 1970 350 TT.

were out to promote their products through race success. Suzuki, Kawasaki, BSA-Triumph and Harley-Davidson had road-racing teams. Yamaha didn't have an official race team, but one of its Californian dealers set one up with a shrewd former world champion from Australia, Kel Carruthers.

America's road-racing calendar of eight national events suited his family, who set up home near Don Vesco's shop. Kel now had time to develop and refine his machines, incorporating ideas he and Vesco conceived: with the 350 he shifted the engine forward 7.5 cm in the frame and lengthened the swinging arm, to improve handling.

Carruthers had a great year in 1971. He took out the Daytona 250 international for the second time and won six of the other seven 250 cm³ national events. Kel also won the AMA 750 cm³ national road-race at the Road Atlanta circuit, Georgia, on his 42 kW 126 kg Yamaha 350. It was Yamaha's first victory in an AMA Grand National road-race.

"That year in America I made more money from

Kel, Jan, Paul and Sharon Carruthers celebrate Kel's second successive Daytona 250 cm³ international victory in 1971.

CARRUTHERS AS MECHANIC

During his riding career, Kel Carruthers gained a reputation as one of the world's great motorcyclists. And after retiring from riding in 1973, the Australian former world champion proved that a long-term career can be carved out of sport.

Carruthers took his skills on the track with his machines, and turned to looking after Yamaha teams. The champion rider became a winning mechanic and manager. Between 1978 and 1988, bikes he prepared won six world 500 titles.

Three-times world champion Kenny Roberts knows why: Roberts worked directly with Carruthers for more than a decade and the American still compares notes with Kel, even though the Australian works for one Yamaha team and Roberts owns a rival team. "Kel is one of the best people to have in the paddock," says Roberts. "He's a guy who gets things done. There have been times Yamaha thought it didn't need someone like that. And I kept saying, Kel does things nobody knows.

"When I raced I didn't have to worry about whether the bike had enough gas in it and the chain was adjusted right and all that stuff, because Kel had been through it all.

"If you ever have a piece of aluminium lying in the middle of the workshop, and you want to race that aluminium, then Kel Carruthers is the guy to do it. Because in an hour he'll have wheels on it and a motor in it!"

Eddie Lawson agreed. He won three world 500 championships in five years on Carruthers-prepared machines. "Kel really downplays himself, because he's really quite a fabricator. And as an organiser, he's the best. I was glad he was on my side," Lawson said.

"Whenever we had a problem, we'd rely on Kel. He would make a part on the lathe or the mill; he'd just whittle it out, then the factory would make it — instead of the other way around. Not many people knew that.

"In 1987 we started the year with a motorcycle that just didn't work at all. We had bigger problems than people realised. But Kel brought that bike up to competitive standard by the end of the season. He was instrumental in the Marlboro-Yamaha team's success," Lawson said.

"When it came to organising, Kel would tell everyone what to do. He'd give them a certain job — and it worked like clockwork."

Warren Willing, former manager of Australia's Marlboro-Yamaha Dealer Team, tells a story from the 1987 Japanese Grand Prix which endorses Lawson's point. "The radar-trap speeds from practice showed the Yamaha 500 was down 5 km/h on top speed to the new Honda. A factory engineer came to tell Kel and said, 'Kel-san, can you please fix?' They'd been working on the bike for six months, and they wanted him to 'fix' it overnight!" Warren said.

Willing says Carruthers was an inspiration to him. "I met Kel in the States in the 1970s, when I was racing. He gave me an insight into another side of racing — that is, what you could do with success. Kel showed me there was more to a career than racing for a few years then fading away," Warren said.

"In the 1970s I'd visit Kel and Jan whenever I was in the States, maybe five or six times a year. And I'd stay from a few days to a month on each occasion. They always made me feel like part of the family.

"Kel showed me things other than ways to make motorcycles go fast: the way he organised his workshop, as well as the preparation of a number of bikes, for example, so he minimised human error and could trace problems quickly.

"I looked at the way Kel's post-racing career developed and made that my goal," Willing said.

Carruthers as team manager preparing a Yamaha TZ250 for Daytona in 1976. Kenny Roberts won on another of Kel's 250s.

Yamaha 350s prepared by Kel Carruthers often embarrassed larger capacity machines in America. Here Carruthers (73) hassles Don Emde's Suzuki 750 at Daytona in 1973. Kel's bikes finished one-two.

eight major meetings than I'd made in three or four years in Europe," Kel said. "I just happened to get lucky, I guess. When I went to the States I didn't plan to stay more than a year. Like a lot of people, you go where your job is. And, at that time, the place to be was America because that's where the money was.

"At the end of the year Kawasaki and Yamaha wanted to sign me. So I signed a contract with Yamaha and stayed in America," Kel said.

It wasn't the most lucrative contract to begin with. Kel had to dip into his own savings to help the 1972 Yamaha race budget. But in the long-term it offered Carruthers far more than an earlier idea of going home to Australia and buying a motel. Carruthers raced for another two seasons. In 1972 he won four of the six 250 national events. Kel also tutored the talented young Americans in the team, of which Kenny Roberts was the best prospect.

The following year, Kel Carruthers was appointed manager of Yamaha America's road-racing team. The team's 350s continued to trouble the 750 opposition and Kel continued riding. He finished second to Yamaha's Finnish ace Jarno Saarinen in the Daytona 200-miles, second by half a wheel to New Zealander Geoff Perry (Suzuki 750) at Atlanta, Georgia, and won the AMA National road-race at Talladaga, Alabama. He prepared the winning Daytona bike and still has it in his workshop. During 1973, Kel's riding became secondary to his role as team manager, so he retired from racing at age 35. His first post-racing task was to assist with development work on Yamaha's new 750 racer.

Carruthers has worked for Yamaha ever since: in the United States until the end of 1977, then in the world championship scene. In the late 1970s Kel handled the chequebook for the Kenny Roberts effort, as well as supervising the machines. He still travels on an Australian passport and has helped visiting Australian racers whenever possible.

In 1988, Carruthers became one of only two motorcyclists — the other being speedway champion Arthur "Bluey" Wilkinson — to be formally inducted into the Bicentennial Sport Australia Hall of Fame. Such an honour recognised Kel Carruthers' great achievements and placed him among Australia's 200 top sports stars.

BARRY SMITH

CHAPTER 11

If Barry Smith had been Spanish, Dutch or possibly German, he would have been a hero. But, being an Australian on small capacity bikes rather than the better accepted big capacity machines, his considerable achievements in Europe and at the Isle of Man have been largely ignored.

Smith was born at Macclesfield in England, but came to Australia as a child and grew up in Victoria. That didn't help his recognition in Australia. But his major problem was that he rode some of the smallest, least macho bikes and won the least glamorous championships. He was also involved in two successful stints of record-breaking, with some of his world records still standing.

The Australian perception of 50 and 125 cm^3 racing is that it's barely worth bothering about, but in Spain they're the most keenly followed classes. Apart from Suzuki and then Honda concentrating on the class for the early years of their move into Europe in the 1960s, the 50 cm^3 class (which was enlarged to 80 cm^3 in 1984) has been the province of amazingly quick and sophisticated German, Spanish and Italian machines.

It's also commonly held that these tiddlers are the easiest things with which to win, if your bike has the most power. Most riders say they're the bikes on which the rider's skill has least influence, but Barry Smith thinks otherwise. He bases his claim on far more experience than those who would deny it.

"Having the least power of any racing bikes, you have to be more accurate in judging your cornering speed. If you come in too slowly, you'll lose ground. Winding on the throttle then won't do you any good; they take too long to react. If you come into the corner too fast, you'll either wash off speed and lose ground, or crash. Either mistake loses you places and races.

"The 125 MBA that Jack Walters bought for me in 1979 used to slide both ends if I pushed it at Silverstone. In earlier days we rode them on the throttle only, whereas now you tend to break them loose coming into the corner, then adjust things with the throttle to keep the wheel spinning and sliding," Smith said.

Smith used this bike to win the Belgian GP in 1979, claiming, "I'd never had so many slides in my life." It was the year of the boycott of Spa by many riders because of last-minute resurfacing. New bitumen with oil seeping through it was a diabolical combination that many riders preferred to avoid.

Before the FIM restricted 125s to twin cylinders and 50s to one cylinder and six gears, they were extremely difficult to ride. They had an almost endless number of gears, driven by engines revving faster than any reciprocating engine before or since. Warren Willing tells of how Honda used to set up its five-cylinder 125 machine in 1965-1966:

Barry Smith was born in England, began racing in Australia in 1958, and headed for Europe in the 1960s.

"It was far too difficult to adjust carburation at the racetrack, so they just sent along a pile of engines, each set up slightly differently. They'd install them in the bike, one by one, until they found the engine that would rev freely past 20,000 rpm. That was the one they raced with."

Smith adds: "To produce the power and speed they did, they worked within a very small power band, sometimes as little as 600 revs at up to 16,000 revs. The first Derbi factory racers had 14 gears. The later German Kreidlers had 12 speeds. The Kreidlers were like a bicycle, with a three-speed hand shift combining with a four-speed foot shift. The riders rarely knew what gear they were in. They just kept revving the thing to the red line, then changing gears until they ran out of gears, revs or road."

Yet these tiny machines with an engine capacity the size of an average hen's egg, and less than half a decent lawn mower, could top 100 mph. "On the Masta Straight at Spa, my Derbi was timed at 184 km/h," Smith said. To achieve that sort of speed, the machines were extremely narrow — the widest part of the whole unit with the rider fully tucked-in was his helmet. They also had a fearfully small tyre contact patch of little more than half a hand width.

Smith was an ideal size for such a machine, just 1.65 metres tall and 60 kg. His weight was the exact minimum for 50 cm³ racing. But Smith's Derbi teammate Angel Nieto was even lighter and he had to carry weights to bring him up to the minimum.

Smith had a lesser ambition than some of the Aussies who headed to Europe. His goal was merely to race at the Isle of Man. He not only achieved that, he *won* at the Island four times and won two world championships as well. He was also third twice in the 50 cm³ world championships and won four world championship and six non-championship grands prix. In two bursts of 24-hour record-breaking in Europe and Australia, he was one of a number of riders who set nearly 200 Australian and world speed records. He won 60 international road races and 150 national events and was European Hillclimb champion in 1965. He retired in 1983 after 25 years of extensive racing in Australia and Europe and was delighted at exceeding his expectations.

To increase his income in his early years in Europe, Smith raced as a sidecar passenger for more than two years. He rode successfully in production endurance races from six to 24 hours in Australia and Europe. Smith returned to Australia after the 1969 season and campaigned extensively until 1978. Then he went back to Europe, almost ten years after he'd left, with a bike conceived and developed in his Melbourne workshop, and won again at the daunting Isle of Man circuit. It was a repeat of what the great Mike Hailwood had done a year earlier. Hailwood last won at IoM in 1967 (impressively, winning the 250, 350 and 500 TTs) then returned 11 years later in 1978 to win the TTF1 race.

In the TT Formula Three class introduced in 1977 to give two- and four-stroke engines an equal chance, Smith was just as dominant as Hailwood had been in his era. Of the two options available in TTF3, the most successful until then had been the 400 cm³ four-stroke. But Smith not only reckoned a 250 two-stroke would be superior, he said: "Along with guys in Australia like Warren Willing and Tony Hatton, I knew how to get the best out of them."

The main challenge was not in the engine itself, but adapting it to the compulsory 28 mm carburettors from a production Yamaha. He spent months working on that in his Glen Waverley workshop, as well as on constant checking with the FIM to clarify the rules.

The combination of a race-modified production Yamaha engine in a TZ grand prix frame was a

Barry Smith (Derbi) and Dutchman Jan De Vries (Kreidler) duel in the 1969 French GP at Le Mans.

winner. It was a nice European finale to a very successful career, interspersed by nine years of 125 grand prix and production racing in Australia, during which he won the Australian 125 championship when 38 years old.

Barry Smith gave the blossoming Spanish firm Derbi, now one of the strongest contenders in the 80 and 125 classes, its first world championship grand prix and IoM TT win. It led to an interesting situation the following year after he had beaten the second most successful motorcycle racer of all time, Spaniard Angel Nieto, into third place in the 50 cm^3 world championship in 1968. With three races remaining in the 1969 championship, the title fight was a three-way battle between Smith, Nieto and Dutchman Aalt Toerson.

That same year, when most of the continental factories were cutting their expenditure on racing and the Japanese were also slowing up after their first foray into Europe, Smith was one of just six riders in the world contracted to a factory. There was Giacomo Agostini on MV Agusta, Kel Carruthers on Aermacchi and then Benelli, Renzo Pasolini with Benelli, Santiago Herrero on Ossa, and Angel Nieto and Smith with Derbi.

That was classy company for the two Australians — in with the two most successful GP racers of all time, Ago and Nieto, the former with 122 GP wins and 15 world championships, the latter with 90 wins and 13 world championships.

Smith started racing at Bacchus Marsh, in Victoria, in 1958. During a return visit to England he'd attended the 1957 Isle of Man meeting as a spectator and been enormously impressed by the two British riders Bob McIntyre (the first rider to do a 100 mph lap, that year) and John Surtees. Smith's response was, "I want to do that." It was also the year Keith Campbell became the first Australian to win a world championship.

Next year Smith was "doing it", despite the recent deaths overseas of Keith Campbell and Roger Barker. Working for a motorcycle dealership at Footscray, he asked if he could borrow one of the less popular road machines of the time, a 650 sprung hub Triumph. Not many people asked to borrow sprung hub Triumphs, for anything, so he was given permission providing he fixed any damage. "I was second production bike in a novice unlimited race to a BMW," Smith said.

Smith was later to appreciate the good grounding of racing in Australia. "There's a greater variety in the type of circuits in Australia, so we tend to learn new circuits easily. In England racers at that time seemed more complacent, letting races settle down before they really got going.

"Riders in Australia were really aggressive, getting the bike out of shape. They were wilder, more crazy. When they went to Europe, they either got results or crashed, because they needed results to eat and get to the next meeting. They had plenty of incentive to win prize money," Smith added.

His first foray to Europe was in 1963, when he was just 23 years old. Smith quickly learned that racing in Europe is for money and career. "I was leading in my third race, on a street circuit on cobblestones in northern Spain, at Valadolid. I was still leading as we came into the last corner. Then Franco Farne on a works Ducati kicked me off my bike."

But it fired Smith up, rather than dispirited him. "I'd been working in England and got some time off to do a couple of races in Spain. After taking third in the first one, I decided to stay for the five-race series. The racing went well and I learned plenty. But when I turned up late for my job, I was fired."

It didn't matter too much, for he went to Derbi in 1966 and started life, aged 26, as a successful, well paid, professional motorcycle race rider.

Smith showed his determination and keenness by being a sidecar passenger "to make money, which I needed". He got £20 a race with English 1962 sidecar TT winner Chris Vincent (himself a sometime 50 cm^3 solo rider) for two years and then German George Auerbacher for "two or three rides" in 1967. He only rode for Vincent on the Continent. Other passengers were used in England. Another Aussie who chaired for Auerbacher was Robert Hinton.

Life on a chair was not easy. "Chris used to push me out with his boot, making sure I stayed cranked out as far as possible through left hand corners. His keenness for me to be out as far as possible was because the sidecar wheel would often be up to 30 cm off the ground while the whole thing was sliding sideways. But sometimes he demanded I stay tucked in, to gain extra speed through the air. They didn't have any power to spare.

"Up the fast but narrow back straight at Spa, he kept saying 'Stay in closer, get your head down'. We did this several times until eventually we saved more than a second a lap through the reduced aerodynamic drag just on that part of the track."

After using a 250 Italian Aermacchi with some factory support to win the European Hillclimb championship in 1965 and being allowed to buy Derbis at a special price, Smith became a factory Derbi rider in 1966. He stayed with the company until the end of 1969, giving Derbi its first world championship round victory at the IoM TT. Nieto gave Derbi its first world championship.

Smith's signing-on fee is quaintly amusing by today's standards. "I got £1000 when I signed on, they doubled any prize money I won and, most importantly, they gave me one peseta for every kilometre I covered in my van. That was when one pound equalled about 1600 pesetas." That meant about one penny reimbursement for every six kilometres travelled, which wasn't exactly throwing

Barry Smith astride his home-built Yamaha 250 after winning the 1979 IoM TT F3 race. Bendigo sponsor Jack Walters is at Smith's right.

money around. Wayne Gardner would be amused.

Yet Barry Smith did well out of it. "I made £10,000 clear profit in 1969, after covering 60,000 kilometres in my van and racing at about 30 meetings on 50, 125 and 250 machines." And they lived well. "Derbi owned hotels, as well as building motorcycles. Unlike today's riders, we stayed in top quality hotels, especially in Spain." Smith says that in those days, "where most riders were privateers, they were treated really well by promoters, almost like factory riders. We were also treated well behind the Iron Curtain, with plenty of social functions and prize-givings."

But Smith served the Derbi factory in other ways, unofficially helping them overcome critical shortages of materials, brought about by General Franco's regime. "It was mainly the lack of good materials, rather than design or workmanship, that caused their mechanical problems in races," Smith said. When riding for Derbi, Smith crossed the border 13 times near Barcelona bringing in Reynolds 531 tubing for frames, aluminium ingots and tyres. "I spoke Spanish and was on first name terms with the customs officers. There was never a problem because they recognised that this was all about Spanish pride."

Smith won at IoM in 1968 and got married at Liverpool a couple of months later. By the time he went campaigning in 1969, his wife Sue was pregnant. After some initial success racing a production Suzuki T20 Hustler, Smith took one to the Isle of Man. He was 11th in the 250TT on a production Suzuki that was so relatively quiet he got the nickname Whispering Smith. Smith then went to the 24-Hour race at the Spanish Montjuich Park circuit where he was second with co-rider Irishman Chris Goosen on a Suzuki Hustler. A street circuit, in Barcelona, it was not for the unskilled. It was unusually hilly and had poor run-off areas in case of a fall.

It was the trip back to Britain that became even more memorable than their hard-won placing. "There was Ralph Bryans, Ireland's 1966 world champion, Tommy Robb, Goosen and me in a van. We were all worn out and sleeping where we could. There'd been a bit of drama at one stage when a truck came close to us back in England but nobody thought anything of it. Except that when we pulled up in Wales, Tommy was screaming 'Where's the wardrobe and the stove?' The whole side of the van was missing, torn off by the truck, with us so tired we didn't even realise it had happened.

Suzuki got enthusiastic about Smith's results on the Hustler and became keen to notch up some records. He was part of a team of riders who took eight Suzukis (four 250 Hustlers, four 315 cm^3) to Monza's banked track for a 24-hour record-breaking spree. "We set 177 speed and distance records, many of which still stand," Smith said.

If the Spanish had shown less favouritism to their fellow countryman Nieto, the next year, 1969, could have rewritten the records of Australian success in world championship racing. We might have had two world champions that year, Barry Smith on a 50, as well as Kel Carruthers in the 250 class on the factory Benelli.

"There were two rounds remaining in the championship, which looked like a fight between Aalt Toersen on a German Kreidler, Nieto and me. I had a 23-second lead going into the last lap at Imola, the second-last race. But then my Derbi broke its piston. Luckily I was far enough around on the lap, with a mainly downhill run to the finish, to be able to roll to the finishing line," Smith said.

"On I went, praying that I'd get to the line before second-placed Paul Lodewijkx of Holland caught me. That didn't happen, though. He came charging past but then, within sight of the finishing line in the last corner, he shot off the track! I coasted past him, delighted to be back in front but he recovered, just in time to pip me again, just two metres from the flag!"

Into the final round at Opatija in Yugoslavia, Toersen had a total of 93 points, although he was only allowed to count 75 from his best six results. Smith had 69 points and Nieto 64. Any of the three could win the championship.

"Because of some strong competition earlier in the season, Derbi was now worried about winning the championship, ahead of German Kreidler. They made me two offers, one of which made me realise that I'd never rate the same treament as Nieto in a Spanish team," Smith said.

"I was fastest in qualifying, so Derbi offered me 10,000 pesetas not to kick Nieto off in the first corner. And there was further offer: 'If Nieto can win, there's £1200 in it for you if you let him.' Well it didn't come to that. I broke down, so at best could finish second in the championship. But Nieto kept going, behind Lodewijkx, who didn't make a mistake, and won.

"So Nieto passed me in the championship, finishing on 76 points in six rounds, the number he was allowed to count. With Toersen only allowed to count his best six, he finished with 75 countable, although he had far more than anybody else, 93 overall. That gave Angel his first championship and meant I missed the chance of being 50 cm^3 world champion."

It was a curious result, with the two riders who won most races (both Toersen and Lodewijkx won three) finishing second and fourth in the champion-ship, while the two who won two each, Nieto and Smith, ended up first and third.

You may see tiddler racing as gentle, formation racing, more like chess than the wild action of 500 class competition. It's certainly cerebral, but held on circuits just as tough and unforgiving as the bigger bikes: Smith was first on the then 7.7 km Assen circuit and the 14.1 km of Spa. He was second on the cobblestones and through the villages of Brno, where anybody who ever did a fast lap on two wheels is a hero. He was third at Hockenheim and sixth at Le Mans.

There's an interesting tale about his win in the Dutch TT, an enormously popular meeting held over nearly a full week of racing, that draws more than 200,000 people. "For less weight and drag I wore skin-tight leathers and ended up on this occasion 2 kg below the class weight limit. So I had to carry weights in my pocket to bring me up to the minimum. But I also knew the weigh-in was the other side of the track and they were unlikely to put us to the trouble. Anyway, the works Kreidler was light, with lots of it made from very light materials."

If you made an error on some of these tracks, you were not only likely to be injured, you were lucky on some occasions to survive the treatment. "I crashed and dislocated my shoulder at the old Brno circuit, the one that went over cobblestones and through villages. I'd soldered a brake nipple on to a cable on my 125 but done it badly. The first time I braked hard it pulled out and I lost my front brakes. The front wheel hit a kerb and catapulted me into a cabbage field.

"That happened on the first lap, but it was after the finish of the race that medical attention arrived. They decided to fix the dislocation right there. Initial attempts didn't work too well, so two guys rigged up a sling to give them some pull. Kiwi Hugh Anderson had crashed at the same corner and was

Barry Smith made his name as a GP rider on a 50 cm³ Derbi, but he also rode the firm's 125. This is Barcelona 1968.

horrified to find them with two feet planted on my shoulder and ribs and two guys pulling as hard as they could. By now I'd passed out with the pain but he told them to stop. They didn't understand and he actually had to knock them out of the way to convince them. They tore the ligaments so badly I was eight weeks with my arm in plaster."

Riding in the same team as the legendary Angel Nieto meant Smith got to know him well. Nieto was regarded in Europe as only a slightly lesser god than the even more handsome Giacomo Agostini. "Angel was handsome and a nice fellow, very down-to-earth. He was known to the Spanish as Nin(y)o, which means little boy, or child. He was very emotional. If I beat him, he'd sit on the steps of his caravan and cry. But he was every bit as good a rider as his record suggests."

That was when Barry Smith decided that if he were to have lesser chance of winning a world championship, he had better be well paid for the sacrifice. "I asked them for twice as much money as previously. Really I was tired of it, the English winters, the constant travelling around," Smith said. "Derbi wanted Nieto to win the championship again in 1970, which they got. They wanted me as a second string, which would have been all right if they'd compensated me for it. They were happy to pay me the same as in 1969, but I wouldn't agree to that, so I came back to Australia."

That was when he opened the motorcycle shop at Glen Waverley which gave him the time and facilities to reach his greatest achievements in racing, nearly ten years later. For three years, 1972-1974, he rode a Milledge Bros Yamaha 125 and DS7 against Ron Toombs' factory bikes. He also rode

The spindly lines of the 50 cm³ Derbi are shown to good effect at Assen in 1969. Smith won the race.

"I've never had so many slides in my life," said Barry Smith after winning the 1979 Belgian 125 GP on an oil-soaked Spa circuit.

production bikes, taking the 250 class win the last time the class was run in the Castrol 6 Hour race at Amaroo Park in 1974.

He did the Castrol 2 Hour race at Calder three years in a row on 750 Yamahas and took three first places in the 350 class. He had four first places in the 250 class in the Adelaide Advertiser 3 Hour.

The urge to go back to Europe started when, sitting in his office at his Melbourne motorcycle business, he looked at the race times at the Isle of Man in the late 1970s. "They weren't going much faster than they had done in my day. I thought F3's the class for me. Like Warren Willing and Tony Hatton, I knew how to tune a two-stroke. Over there most of them favoured the 400 four-stroke option, but I reckoned a 250 two-stroke would be better. The potential problem with it, which had probably stopped other people using it, was to get a race engine to work with the compulsory small bore carburettors off a production machine.

"Doing all the work on the dyno workshop at Glen Waverley in Melbourne, I started off with a production DS7 engine, ported virtually to grand prix TZ shape, with TZ expansion chambers. And we got it all working with the production 28 mm carburettors. We did lots of testing and then shipped it off to England.

"It was 15 km/h faster than the opposition, which meant it was pretty easy to win with. I won by four minutes and set a new lap record at 99.37 mph (160 km/h), three miles an hour (5 km/h) faster than previously," Smith said. That meant 45.8 seconds carved off the lap record, which Smith successfully cut further in the next two years. In 1980 the speed was raised to 100.94 mph (162.5 km/h) and in 1981 to 101.31 mph (163.1 km/h). After just 11 km of a 243 km race, Smith was leading by 14 seconds. Most impressive was that his race average speed of 97.82 mph (157.5 km/h) would have placed him fourth in the bigger capacity TTF2 class.

"They protested against it, but there was no problem. It was totally legal, just something they hadn't thought of or been able to do." That same bike won three years on the trot, raising the lap record every time.

But while Smith was annihilating the F3 field three years in a row at IoM, he failed the hat-trick in the F3 world championships. He won in 1979 and 1981, but missed in 1980. Each of those years was just two rounds, IoM and Ulster.

In 1980, he'd wanted to win both the championship rounds, as well as the British Grand Prix. The whole plot came apart in a 125 race, at Zandvoort. "Bruno Kneubuhler and I were dicing for fifth place. It was a fast corner, from top back to fifth gear and sitting up slightly. He slid and then caught it but I got out wide on pebbles and went off at about 200 km/h, feet-first into a barrier. I broke some bones in my foot, splintered a bone in my leg and hurt my vertebrae," Smith recalled.

"I got permission from the doctor at Silverstone to practice there, but had a freak accident. I'd qualified 13th and came in at the end of a wet session only to crash on a wet yellow line in pit lane.

"I didn't hurt my foot but the bike was bent, so I was a non-starter. Then it was off to Ulster, for the second of the two rounds in the world F3 championship. I wasn't too sharp, still getting around on crutches. So for the race there I tried to hide my problems by riding through the pit area to the dummy grid. Everything should have been all right, I was more than three seconds faster than the opposition. But some fine stones picked up by the tyres got into the carburettor bellmouth and soon went into the engine. It locked up. Ron Haslam won the race and the championship."

In his next and what turned out to be his final year in Europe, 1981, Smith was back at IoM. Again he won the TTF3 race. Then he went on to the 500 race, in difficult conditions. He was sharing the pit bay with another Aussie, Kenny Blake. "It was wet over the Mountain but dry in other parts. We were both on slicks and it was pretty dodgy. Eventually I pulled in and retired."

But Blake had just been offered some endurance race riding with Honda. "He was keen to reinforce their judgment, also he'd had a fuel leak on the start line and been delayed. I watched him pit but then fly back out, his bike snaking into the distance under acceleration. He never came back."

That made Smith decide to return to Australia and not go back to Europe. He competed here until 1983, giving him 25 years of enjoyment and success in motorcycle racing until he retired at 43.

JOHN DODDS

CHAPTER 12

Summer days in Fairfield, west of Sydney, are hot and dry. They are days for minimal exertion, to sit in the shade staying cool, either by jumping into something cold and wet, drinking it, or sucking on it.

None of that had meant much to 14-year-old John Dodds, who was already mad keen on motorcycle racing, along with some other slightly older kids in the neighbourhood, like Len Atlee, Jim Airey and Gordon Guasco. They were a talented foursome, with all but Dodds becoming an Australian champion and all competing with distinction at world championship level, Airey and Guasco in the unforgiving world of speedway.

The trouble was that their "track", some bushland at Bossley Park, was ten kilometres away. Dodds had no licence, there was nobody to drive him there and the local police were on the lookout for any quick flit on unregistered bikes. So there was only one way to get there. To push. A drum of fuel was strapped to the seat, a spare tyre slung around his neck. Ten kilometres there, a day of hot, dusty and hard racing, then ten kilometres home.

If you've ever pushed a motorcycle — even a 1934 250 Velocette two-stroke as this was — with your body and muscles working totally off-centre, you'll know that 100 metres is tiring. Ten kilometres is heroic. It was a far greater achievement than riding his pushbike to Taronga Park Zoo, as Dodds had done some years earlier.

When Dodds left for Europe in 1966 he said he wanted to be world champion. "But I didn't make it, so I failed, didn't I?" Yes, technically he failed. But barely. He was knocking on the door for a works ride when he was injured on the starting grid at Paul Ricard at the start of the French 350 Grand Prix in 1975. If the world governing body of motorcycle racing, the FIM in Geneva, had decided to call its Formula 750 championship a "world" championship from its inception in 1973, instead of in 1977, Dodds would have been world champion.

Instead he was the 1974 FIM Formula 750 champion, after being runner-up in its first year to Barry Sheene, who was on his upward climb to two 500 championships in 1976-1977. They were two very different personalities, although the outgoing Sheene and the quiet Dodds teamed up to get some eating money by turning a vending machine upside down at Nurburgring when they were both a touch short of the necessary cash for a meal. Two Australians finished within six points of Sheene in the F750 championship in 1973, Dodds four behind and Jack Findlay just two points more in arrears. The remarkable aspect was that Dodds had split the works Suzukis riding a 350 Yamaha.

When Dodds won the championship in 1974, it was the shortest series in its seven-year existence, just three rounds. Behind him was Frenchman

John Dodds, with daughter Jasmine, toasts 1970s success with a soft drink. He did it tough in the late 1960s.

Patrick Pons and Jack Findlay. The following year, over nine rounds, Findlay beat Sheene by just a point, with Pons third.

Winning the FIM F750 championship was Dodds' best result in championship terms, although he won four GPs in three different classes, one 125, two 250 and one 350. Dodds was third in the 250 championship in 1973, after being sixth the previous year. In 1973 and 1974 he was fourth in the 350 class and at other times had finished fourth and sixth in the class. That's four times he was in the first four of the world grand prix championship. In two of his wins he beat Dieter Braun, the West German double world grand prix champion. He also won dozens of non-championship international races, the races privateers needed to enter to earn the money to live.

All of this was as a privateer, for Dodds missed out on the works ride which would have meant a better chance of winning a championship. Trying to get a factory ride can be financially and physically dangerous for the ambitious privateer. He can end

167

up crashing by riding too hard to achieve the results that will get him out of his bind. And it can break his budget as he forces over-taxed machinery too hard, blows it up and then misses out on prize money.

Dodds' move on to a Linto in 1969 nearly ended his racing career. The dreadfully unreliable machine lost him a lot of prize money, cost him a fortune to run and was almost worthless when he came to get rid of it. The only two finishes he got on the Linto in 1969 were a third at Imola (with Australian Terry Dennehy behind him on a Drixl-framed CB450 Honda) and fourth at Hockenheim, behind another Aussie, Jack Findlay, also on a Linto.

Dodds says it was a mistake to buy the 500 Linto for the 1969 season. The bike's motor was cobbled together from two 250 Aermacchis. "I should have bought another 250 Yamaha and continued winning money," he said.

Dodds' campaign in Europe was hectic. Without a works ride he campaigned in five classes with championship wins in all but the 500. He had many notable performances that satisfied him, such as out-qualifying Agostini's 350 MV at Hockenheim in a classy field that included Finnish rider Teppi Lansivuori and world champions Phil Read and Walter Villa. He beat the most successful 250 rider of all time, five times world champion Toni Mang, who retired during the 1988 season aged 38. This clash was ten years earlier at Hockenheim on a new 250 Yamaha. He remembers Mang as a hard rider, determined to win at all costs.

Dodds was only really hurt in one accident in 1975, although it had a significant effect on his career. It came sufficiently late to lose him the chance of a works ride and detune him towards his retirement. But he was ominously close to some other horrors.

He was in the race that killed both Renzo Pasolini and Jarno Saarinen, probably the worst accident in the history of motorcycle racing for the number of people involved and its far-reaching effects on circuit safety. It happened on the first lap of the 250 race at Monza in 1973. The race itself was abandoned and the 500 race cancelled. Championship motorcycle racing didn't return to Monza for another eight

Dodds rode a Norton 500 when he first went to Europe in 1966, but he achieved his best results in the 1970s on Yamahas.

Dodds was third in the 1973 world 250 championship on his privately entered Yamaha.

years. Until 1973 Monza had hosted all but two Italian GPs since 1949.

Predicting trouble, Dodds tried to have the race delayed while they cleared up spilled oil. But the organisers took no notice. Dodds had placed fourth in the preceding 350 race behind Agostini, Lansivuori and Swede Kent Andersson. He'd seen Italian Benelli rider Walter Villa — later a four-time world champion — drop oil during the race as he tried to get his stricken machine back to the pits. But Saarinen, who was concentrating on defending his 250 title and breaking into the 500 class, and Pasolini were unaware of it, not having run in the 350 race.

"I got off my 350 and went to the office, asking them at least to delay the start of the 250 race. But it went as scheduled," Dodds said. He warned Pasolini and Saarinen of the track conditions but the latter had won the first three races of the season and was in no mood to hang around. "Naturally I wasn't in too much of a rush to get away," Dodds said.

The devastation looked more like war than racing. "Pasolini seized and forced Saarinen wide. He hit a barrier and bounced back in front of the field, perhaps with no more than a broken leg. But because the Armco was close to the track edge, he bounced back into the path of the following riders.

"Straw bales and bikes caught fire as 15 riders became involved in the one massive crash. It was chaos, with fire, debris and people littered everywhere but, seemingly, no officials. There was certainly no signalling when Dieter Braun, Chas Mortimer, a couple of others and I arrived, the first bunch not to be involved."

That prematurely finished the career of one of the greatest natural talents in motorcycle racing. Saarinen had toted up 15 GP wins in three classes in three years, won the 250 world championship in 1972 and been runner-up on a Yamaha to Agostini's MV Agusta in the 350 championship in 1971 and 1972. He was a charismatic star at a time when there were few works bikes and his personality and tremendous ability had finally scored a works ride with Yamaha.

Dodds was also a survivor of one of Isle of Man's horror years when seven people were killed, although he never concentrated on nor did well at the Island.

He averaged more than 190 km/h around the old, fast but dangerous Spa-Francorchamps circuit in Belgium on a single cylinder Norton with just over one third the power (54 bhp) of today's V4 two-stroke Hondas and Yamahas. But even that old thumper had a top speed of 225 km/h, while spraying its rider and those following with oil.

Dodds' first grand prix win was in the most difficult and unlikely circumstances on a second-string machine in the fog at the old, 22.85 km Nurburgring in 1970. He had still been up at 4 am working on the dreaded Linto. The way for a privateer to increase his popularity with promoters, which ensured a start and determined the amount of money he got, was to have two machines. "But few of us could afford two competitive machines, so we had one

After a disastrous run with the Italian Linto 500, Dodds tried the Koenig flat-four two-stroke. Riders behind are Theo Louwes, Martin Carney and Ron Chandler. Tubbergen, Holland.

starting money special and one that we concentrated on," Dodds said. "Carruthers was the only person I knew who had two really competitive bikes, a real luxury."

Dodds' cheapie was a 125 cm³ Italian Aermacchi, the stand-by that was to support his major effort in the 500 class on the Linto. It was a cold, foggy day in the dense greenery of the lush Eiffel Mountains area, although most of what Dodds had seen was the all-too-familiar internals of the Linto. So out he went on the Aermacchi to face the fog, not expecting much after a miserable and tiring night. "Every lap the fog had moved to somewhere different. It was almost impossible to know where you were going," he said. But things went well, as they sometimes do when you're not expecting anything, and he won the first of his four GPs. Ironically it was in a class that he didn't rate, because Dodds reckoned a race result on anything smaller than a 250 is more influenced by the power of the bike than the skill of the rider.

It was at the infamous Nurburgring that Dodds first met his wife. He'd been given a "bonus" — a free new chain by English chain-maker Renolds in recognition of being second privateer on the grid behind the works MVs. "I was really looking forward to the race," Dodds said. "But the chain broke on the second lap. So I retired to a hospitality tent, got sloshed and met this lovely German girl, Evelyn." She lived near where they still live with their two children, in Lindenfels, east of the autobahn connecting Stuttgart and Frankfurt.

But in 1974 he refused to race at the original Nurburgring, along with an impressive number of riders, Angel Nieto, Dieter Braun, Agostini, Sheene, Phil Read, Kent Andersson, Bruno Kneubuhler, Michel Rougerie, Walter Villa, Patrick Pons, Teppi Lansivuori, Olivier Chevallier and Jack Findlay. The track was considered too narrow and dangerous, with trees right up to the track edge and no run-off areas.

Among many other dangerous tracks, Dodds raced over the 14 km worn, shiny, frightening cobblestones of the villages around Brno in Czechoslovakia. It's now gone, even touring cars refusing to race there. But on one memorable occasion Dodds decided on a big risk to make up

Leif Gustafson (25), Patrick Pons (3), John Dodds (7) and Othello Buscherini (52) duel on their Yamahas at Opatija, Yugoslavia in 1975. Not a forgiving circuit.

time. He speared through a village in a terrifying, once-only attempt at a fast time. "It was a section where good riders usually changed down one gear. Cautious ones went back two for the charge through the town, footpaths on one side, the unyielding brick and stone walls of houses on the other. I gritted my teeth, tucked down and hoped, tearing through in top gear, without lifting off very much.

"I got through but it was terrifying, very marginal". At the end of the day a spectator came into John's tent, his face incredulous as he told of watching this mad rider go through the village, sliding one way then another without changing back a gear but very nearly splattering himself on both sides of the roadway. "It's lucky you saw it," I told him. "Remember it because you'll never see it again."

Dodds began road racing after being a bicycle skid kid, then he tried short circuit dirt-track racing at places like the Bossley Park bush. At one early road race meeting at Hume Weir on January 27, 1963, while Kel Carruthers was finishing second to the Rhodesian world champion Jim Redman, Dodds dominated what was then regarded as the nursery class. He was first in both races of the 500 C grade and second in the 350.

By late 1965, after two years of rapid learning and lapping, he was competing against Carruthers. All Australia's best riders were, but with little success. Ron Toombs (who raced overseas in Malaysia and America), scrambler and speedway star Ken Rumble (who was doing just as well at road racing), and Melbourne's racer and tuner Ron Angel had been competing against Carruthers all year. They were up against a steamroller of 125 and 250 Hondas, a Norton, the money to run them and Carruthers' ability and experience. Despite the best that Dodds or anybody else could do, Carruthers was stacking up trophies and wins faster than his opponents could beat their heads against nearby brick walls.

The year before, Carruthers had won all four solo events at Bathurst. In 1965 they put on another, apparently just for him, because he then won all five. At Winton for the Victorian TT he won seven races. He dominated the Australian TT at Longford and he won five out of five at Lakeside. He crashed on oil while leading at Oran Park, but that was rare imperfection.

John Dodds (2) won the 1974 Spanish 250 GP at Montjuich Park, a street circuit in Barcelona.

When Carruthers and Dodds came to the prestigious Tom Phillis Memorial race, Carruthers had not been beaten in a race he'd finished for more than a year. In fact he wasn't beaten again until he left for overseas in January to take on the world. But John Dodds achieved what was then a lofty goal, beating Carruthers that September 26 at Winton in a tough race-long duel. The closest Dodds came to winning an Australian championship was in the 1965 Australian 500 TT at Longford, Tasmania. Carruthers won from Dodds, both on Nortons. Carruthers said: "Dodds was the best guy I had to beat in Australia in my last year."

Dodds packed his leathers, helmet and hopes for Europe at the beginning of 1966. He went with less money and probably less planning than Carruthers and quickly discovered that, even if he did reckon he could be world champion, not a lot of the promoters agreed with him. Dodds found it difficult to get starts, which equalled start money, which equalled food. Once at Spa, Carruthers' wife Jan found Dodds so run down with malnutrition, she berated him. He was on the verge of collapse. "How can you race if you can barely stand up?" she asked him.

A Norton was hardly the latest hot equipment, despite Jack Ahearn's second place in the 1964 championship. Of the traditional British marques in a dying industry, Matchless was also hanging in, especially Aussie Jack Findlay's, but they were really only racing to come in behind the works bikes.

Dodds' first landing point was England, but he quickly discovered more bad news than good. "They were only paying starting money to two riders, John Cooper and Derek Minter. So, in preference to going to work, I went racing in Europe," Dodds explained. At the end of that first season he owed a friend £15. So he cashed in the return boat ticket that his mother had insisted he buy before he left. That was after paying back an uncle the £650 he'd lent him to buy a Norton.

"We were so green, wasting almost two years finding out how to make it all work. Nobody who had been over told us anything. We had to make all the same mistakes again," Dodds said.

After the disaster of the Linto, the other major stumbling block to Dodds' career was his accident on the grid at Paul Ricard in 1975. He'd qualified fourth, on the front row next to Johnny Ceccotto's near-works Yamaha and the factory Yamahas of Hideo Kanaya and Giacomo Agostini. "The grid there is about 100 metres long. I was hit during the push start by a rider from the rear of the grid. He must have been doing at least 120 km/h. I was thrown into the air, badly injuring my right leg. It wasn't helped when I crashed two months later.

"In fact, for a long time it took away one of my best assets. I was always good under brakes but it took me a long time to recover my confidence and physical condition," Dodds added.

He was in Europe in 1978 when Kenny Roberts and Gregg Hansford arrived from America and Australia respectively. Both had far more experience of slick racing tyres than those resident in Europe. Dodds never rode with a front slick tyre, only a rear when they were introduced in 1975. "By 1976 slicks were the only way to go, although the front tyre was not up to the ability of the rear. I crashed a lot that year," Dodds said.

"By 1978 my motivation was not so good. I was making new mistakes. It was obvious I wouldn't get a works ride at that stage, yet I was taking greater risks to go even slower. So I retired."

When you get your first set of free leathers (from Furygan) three years before you retire, you know you've had to battle. "For most of my career, I was lucky to get some free spark plugs, a chain or some oil. Sponsors were rare." Yet Dodds reckons it was so satisfying that he'd do it all again. He has a pile of funny stories about the things he and others had to do to survive. "We forged dates on out-of-date green cards, smuggled girls into the pits in Transit vans, then brought them in again later after they'd been ejected." He was chased by police in Czechoslovakia and East Germany. It seems if you've been a struggling motorcycle race rider in Europe, you've been hassled by the police at some stage. His wife Evelyn loved every moment of it and still misses the travel and the social life it involved.

Dodds though is harder, more professional about the sport on which he once concentrated his life. Along with an old rival Dieter Braun he was invited to do a comparative test for the large and influential magazine *Das Motorrad*. But he refused. "When you retire, it's total. The same as when you're racing. I don't want to get on and start playing around." So Dodds will not do a parade, a demonstration or a historic run, although he did remain involved in racing for a few years after his retirement.

He ran a team concentrating on the German championships. One of his proteges was current 250 runner Reinhold Roth. With Dodds' guidance, he, Ernst Gschwander and another German rider won one 500 title, three 350s and two 250s. "But I got out of it and the tuning business in 1983. Those wanting tuners are often the slowest riders. Extra power is readily available — it's in the throttle," Dodds said.

The bigger the bikes, the more he rates the riders. "On a 250, the rider is responsible for around half of the overall performance of the bike and rider. The rest is dependent on the power of the machine, about which the rider can do nothing," he asserts.

"On a 350, perhaps two thirds of its overall performance comes from the rider. On a 500 it's around 70 per cent." Dodds reckons the engine power is 90 per cent of the equation on a 50 cm^3 bike (no longer a current formula) and 75 per cent on a

The general availability of Yamaha's 250 and 350 production bikes brought more riders into the sport in the 1970s. But Dodds proved one of the period's best.

125. Because of that, he doesn't rate riders of bikes smaller than 250 cm^3, a class that he says at the moment "has 20 madmen, all on works bikes and all desperate for a win, prepared to do almost anything to achieve it".

That's a generally accepted formula, although small bike expert Barry Smith presents an alternative viewpoint. "To be quick on a small bike, you have to judge cornering speeds very precisely. If you come in too fast, you'll wash off too much speed or crash. If you're too slow, they don't have the power to adjust, as you can to some extent with the enormous power of a modern 500."

Dodds has a poignant memory of racing in East Germany at the famed Sachsenring, which used to attract at least 250,000 spectators to any international meeting. It was the 250 race in 1971, with some top riders like Phil Read, Jarno Saarinen, Braun, Rod Gould and Barry Sheene. Dodds had broken a crankshaft, so he saw the whole drama from the pits. "They didn't have sidecar races at Sachsenring because the West Germans dominated sidecar racing. West German Dieter Braun got away last.

"Remember that crowd control was by army officers with guns. Braun had been steadily reining them all in. As they appeared in sight of the finish on the last lap — but still quite a distance away on the 8.6 km track — Braun was still a long way behind Rod Gould. But Braun pulled a miracle. He was out on the dirt, refusing to brake, until he pipped Gould by 0.5 second and won. There was silence for a while among the officials and the enormous crowd. There must have been around 90,000 in the area

John Dodds (12) pushes off in the 1973 Finnish 350 GP at Imatra, against works MV riders Agostini (1) and Read (5).

around the start-finish line, apart from those lining the track. Eventually they played the West German anthem. The crowd then stood and began singing along with it.

"You could see the young soldiers' fingers tighten on the triggers. They didn't know what to do, but they were vastly outnumbered and wisely decided to do nothing. Evelyn cried, along with a fair few others." World championship motorcycle racing only survived one more year at the East German circuit.

"What I like about racing today", said Dodds, "is that because of better circuit safety the fastest rider doesn't have to be the bravest, just the best. Yet of all the circuits I've raced on, including allegedly dangerous ones like Karlskoga (Sweden), Brno (Czechoslovakia), Imatra (Finland), Opatija (Yugoslavia), Nurburgring (Germany), Sachsenring (East Germany) and Spa (Belgium), it was one of the safest, Assen in Holland, that seemed to have the worst accident record."

Dodds now does nothing more exciting than battle with the fast-flowing traffic on the German autobahns as he races around building up the market for French Motul oils, as used by Kevin Magee and Wayne Rainey in the Lucky Strike Yamahas. His wife runs Blumen Dodds, a flower shop in a small village near their home.

He says Gardner and Carruthers were the two best Australian riders because "they achieved their ambition of becoming world champions and they're still alive".

Dodds may have missed out on a world championship, but there is no doubting the courage and determination he showed as a battling, and perhaps unlucky, privateer Aussie racer in Europe. He'd come a long way from pushing his motorbike 20 kilometres each Sunday.

GREGG HANSFORD

CHAPTER 13

"GREGG Hansford came close to Freddie Spencer in pure talent, but lacked the desire to smoke everybody. He just had fun doing what he did and had the talent to do it. I think he had more fun in the pits than Spencer ever did racing." The author of these words is "King" Kenny Roberts, three times world 500 champion.

In his book *Techniques of Motor Cycle Road Racing*, Roberts compares the talents of Hansford, whom he raced against frequently on 250s and 750s, Wayne Gardner, Kork Ballington, Freddie Spencer and Eddie Lawson. He puts Spencer on top in the ability to win races, with Hansford number two, followed by Ballington, with Lawson fourth. But on determination to win, in a race against each other, he reckons the result might be Spencer, Lawson, Gardner and Hansford.

It's high praise of someone who never won a world championship, but who's remembered by many onlookers as one of the great natural talents, one of the very best never to be world champion. In Hansford's two full seasons in Europe (1978-1979), he won ten world championship grands prix in two classes, almost always on tracks on which he was racing for the first time. He was twice runner-up in the 250 class and twice third in the 350. His tall, broad build was a handicap against the lighter and more compact riders, especially in the 250 class.

Hansford's success was achieved despite the blond Queenslander constantly wishing he was back home. If anything held him back in Europe, it was that he didn't want to be there.

By the time he left Australia, most observers thought it was only a matter of time before he would return as world champion. More than any other departing Australian motorcycle racer, it was Gregg Hansford who was most expected to reach the top. His success was regarded as almost inevitable. If winning championships depended solely on talent, that probably would have been the case.

For eight years Hansford held an unwanted unofficial record. He had won the most grands prix of any rider in the world championships without becoming champion. It was a title Randy Mamola took from him during 1987.

Like many other top Australian riders, Hansford started on dirt tracks and then motocross, excelling at the latter before he turned to road racing. He had the complete range of skills. He was relaxed about high speeds at places like the banked oval at Daytona and the faster grand prix tracks, but was also a demon on short, tight corners. As Roberts notes: "Gregg was as good on brakes as anyone I've ever seen."

Hansford made his overseas debut in America in 1974 on an F750 Yamaha at the famed tri-oval at Daytona, in Florida. This was followed by a race

Gregg Hansford in reflective mood in America in the mid-1970s.

later in the year at Ontario, California. He was one of the first Australians to race at Daytona. His first race in Europe was at Circuit Paul Ricard in 1975, and the first thing about the team that impressed the Europeans was that the Australian H2R Kawasaki was the lightest 750 at the weigh-in.

Team Kawasaki Australia did numerous forays overseas until it tackled the grand prix series in 1978. Always on the big and awesomely powerful F750s, they returned to Ontario in 1975, and went to Daytona regularly, plus races at Venezuela, Imola and Indonesia. In 1977 they campaigned 250s as well. Various minor problems held back the results promised by qualifying, but it didn't stop the Europeans recognising Hansford's talent.

The authoritative motorcycle sport annual *Motocourse* rated Hansford as number five rider in the world in 1977, behind Barry Sheene and Kenny Roberts, before he'd done his first grand prix! The authors had him ahead of Johnny Ceccotto, who had already been world 350 champion, Kork Ballington, Marco Lucchinelli, Christian Sarron and Franco Uncini, who were all destined to become world champions.

After two years of grand prix campaigning in 250 and 350 machines that were theoretically too small for his tall, broad build, it was obvious he should be rewarded with bigger machinery. If he could do so well on bikes he dwarfed, how well would he go on 500s, the fastest grand prix bikes of all?

Hansford was held in enormous esteem within Kawasaki and by many Australian fans. He was what most young Australians wanted to be — tall, athletic, blond and handsome. Even his opponents liked him. Kenny Roberts once said he wouldn't pull an elbow-barging desperate move to get past Hansford, but he would on Barry Sheene. Hansford's easy-going nature belied his seriousness when he went racing. Even now he remembers lap times, grid positions, records and other details that many riders have long forgotten. Hidden beneath his warm, friendly smile was a very analytical and professional racer. The relaxed exterior probably came because his enormous natural talent let him do so easily what others had to work harder at.

A riders' revolt at the end of the 1979 season meant that he sat out a grand prix season in 1980. Confusion over whether there would be one or two championship series and who would ride for whom saw Hansford stay loyal to Kawasaki and his fellow striking riders, to the detriment of his career.

He was reluctant to leave Kawasaki and his mentor Neville Doyle. And he was staunchly loyal to riders such as Roberts and Randy Mamola, who supported the still-born World Series movement. It was a cause that incited strong passions. Like the grand prix car drivers before them, the motorcycle racers had become fed up with poor circuit safety, ridiculous prize money, lack-lustre organisation and poor promotion in the official world championships. In 1980 they were still racing at the original and very unforgiving 22.8 km Nurburgring Nordschleife, which the F1 car drivers had abandoned after Niki Lauda's near-fatal crash there in 1976.

The World Series was mooted during 1979, when the world's leading riders proposed their own race series. When the series finally failed, Hansford was the only leading rider left without a grand prix ride for 1980. In the middle of the dispute, when two series seemed possible, he'd been offered a ride in the world championships with Yamaha. But, committed to the renegade movement, he refused the ride, as had Randy Mamola.

When he finally got on a 500 in 1981, two things went wrong. He was involved in two freak accidents, and the bike never looked like doing the job he and Kawasaki expected of it. Kawasaki's race department had far less money and fewer people than its three Japanese rivals. On top of this the engineers were reluctant to make changes recommended by the riders. The bike's wheelbase was too long, which made it slow changing direction, and it was down on power.

In an exploratory ride on it at Nurburgring in 1980, Hansford broke the screen controlling a violent tank-slapper that all but threw him off. Kork Ballington, four times world champion and Hansford's Kawasaki team-mate, could only manage a best result of fifth place on the 500. This was in Finland in 1980.

There was almost a complete redesign of the bike for 1981, so Hansford left Australia with high hopes at the beginning of the year. His prospects seemed much better than when he'd been second and third in the world championships on smaller bikes. But within four months his two-wheeled career was finished.

He qualified fastest for the season opener, the Imola 200 at Easter. But things soon went wrong. Running wide through the fastest bend to lap some slower riders, he hit a damp patch and fell off, in a horrific high-speed crash. He had a fractured tibia and was sidelined for eight weeks. In that time he missed five championship meetings, during which the 500 title chase became a battle between Marco Lucchinelli (who went on to win it for Suzuki), Barry Sheene, Kenny Roberts, Randy Mamola and Graeme Crosby.

In his comeback race, the rain-affected Dutch GP at Assen, Hansford was 14th. The next race was at the demanding Spa-Francorchamps circuit in Belgium on July 5. He called into the pits with a

Hansford took Europe by storm in 1978, winning seven GPs, four in the 250 class and three on the Kawasaki KR350.

handling problem, which wasn't helped by intermittent rain. Gregg got off the bike, convinced that nothing could be done. But Neville Doyle and the Kawasaki crew worked on the handling problem, changed the front wheel and asked him to continue.

To change the front wheel on the Kawasaki the disc-brake calipers had to be removed and the pistons pushed back. It required half a dozen pumps of the brake lever to push the piston back into position and the pads onto the disc. Neither the mechanics nor Hansford did this. He arrived at the end of the main straight doing perhaps 270 km/h, grabbed the front brake lever and had nothing. It went straight into the handlebar. But that didn't seem too great a problem because part of the old circuit made a welcome escape road straight ahead. Unfortunately, a marshall had parked his car across the road what seemed like a safe distance from the corner. It wasn't a safe distance for somebody with only a back brake working. Still doing around 70 km/h, Hansford hit the car with the same leg that was injured at Imola.

Not only did he break his femur, he had more serious problems with blood clots in his thigh. It took more than five years and many operations to fix. Hansford's career was prematurely ended at just 29 years of age. It was a dreadful waste of potential. His early appearances in Europe had the locals genuinely amazed.

Hansford and Kawasaki's Neville Doyle were better at racing than they were at arranging the documentation necessary for the bikes. For the 1975 meeting at Circuit Paul Ricard, they shipped the

Gregg Hansford with his new Yamaha TZ700, ready for his Daytona debut in 1974. Warren Willing is at the right.

bikes to Rome without any of the paperwork necessary to clear them through customs. Not surprisingly, they couldn't manage to convince the Italians to let the bikes in, so eventually they shipped them to Paris. Their fate there seemed similar, until one man took pity and let them through on a personal promise to re-export the bikes. Gregg and a helper drove south overnight, virtually to Marseilles.

On another occasion, Hansford was destined for the 1977 Imola 200 after competing at Daytona. He'd finished fourth in the 200-mile race and run out of petrol when contesting the lead with Roberts in the 250 race. After more organisational problems, they finally arrived at Imola with less than 30 minutes of final qualifying remaining. After his fifth lap in his first visit to the track, he was, unbelievably, fifth-fastest and on the front row of the grid. Gunther Wiesinger, an Austrian motorcycle journalist, remembers the team didn't have time to change tyres. Hansford finished sixth in the first leg behind a trio of works Yamahas, but failed to finish in the second.

If that was dramatic, the opening to his 1978 campaign was quite sensational. It started with a win in the 250 international race at Daytona, followed by his first grand prix, the 350 at Venezuela. In that, he

The bike that promised much and didn't deliver – the 1981 Kawasaki KR500.

was pulling away from the field at around a second a lap, when an oil seal broke in the gearbox, forcing his retirement. He had also had oil seal trouble in the 250 race at Venezuela.

In the second heat at his next meeting, the Imola 200 for F750 machines, Hansford's brilliance under brakes caused Kenny Roberts — by his own admission — to crash. Roberts started from the rear of the grid because he had blown his engine in the first heat. By the third lap, on a drying track, he was close to Hansford in fourth place. Roberts claims his faster bike tempted him to try to outbrake Gregg into the chicane at the end of the back straight. Roberts pulled out of Hansford's slipstream, but saw immediately he was in trouble. He hit the back of Hansford's bike and crashed.

The next race was even more remarkable. The organisers of the Spanish Grand Prix at Jarama had refused to let Hansford and Roberts start because they were not on the official FIM grading list. After more than a day of arguing, they were left with only the final day of practice. Roberts was fastest qualifier, 0.1 second ahead of Hansford. In the race, Gregg said he "followed Kenny for a few laps because I couldn't remember where the track went," then passed him and went on to win.

Then it was back to the undulating Brands Hatch circuit, south of London, for another world F750 championship round. Kawasaki Britain was so pessimistic about its chances it didn't even contest the meeting. Hansford crashed early in the first heat, but worked his way back to fourth place behind the Yamahas of Roberts, Steve Baker and Johnny Ceccotto.

In the second heat, the enormity of Hansford's achievement on the under-powered Kawasaki became obvious. He was duelling for the lead with Roberts on a works Yamaha. They started lapping back markers, most of whom were on private Yamahas. One such lapped rider, Englishman Derek Chatterton, had sufficient straight-line speed advantage over Hansford to repass him down the straight. Hansford had to tuck behind him for a tow, a tactic that came unstuck when Chatterton braked 50 metres earlier than Hansford expected. He ran into the back of him, crashed and broke his shoulder.

The 350 GP at Salzburgring in Austria gave a classic demonstration of Hansford's pre-race cool. Staying in a glorious five-star hotel nearby, he woke less than half an hour before the race start. But he led the first lap of the race and finished seventh, despite his painful shoulder injury caused by the Brands Hatch crash. This was where the organisation, experience and dedication of Hansford's Kawasaki team-mate Kork Ballington came to the fore. He won. And he won both the 250 and 350 championships in the two years Hansford was in

Europe, although few people rated Ballington as talented as Hansford.

In the next world championship round, at the tight bumpy little track at Nogaro in France, Hansford won both the 250 and 350 races. But it doesn't always pay to win. At the next grand prix, the Italian GP at Mugello, Kawasaki's team manager Ken Suzuki got some new parts, but only enough for one rider's bike. According to journalist Gunther Wiesinger: "Suzuki thought that, as Hansford had been going so well, he'd give the parts to Kork to help him." Which they did. Ballington won both races, with Hansford second.

Wiesinger and British journalist Mick Woollett both say Hansford had more talent than Ballington. But the South African and his mechanic brother had more experience in Europe and were more consistent. Hansford and Doyle had almost doubled their problems by contesting the grands prix and the F750 championship. The two series were usually held at different race tracks. Adding to their problems was the slowness of the 750 Kawasaki compared with the works Yamahas. Gregg was hurting himself trying to make up the difference. For example, at the fast Oesterreichring, he crashed in the first heat, but with rather remarkable presence of mind. "The bike was about to high-side me into the Armco, so I held the throttle open and let the bike spin out," Gregg said. Later that day he was fifth in the second heat.

His best 750 result of the season was at Hockenheim where he finished third overall and set fastest lap in the rain-affected first heat. But the best finish should have been at Assen. He won the first heat and led the second until the last lap, when he crashed due to a worn front tyre.

Hansford's crowd-pulling appeal as the only Kawasaki 750 rider in a horde of Yamahas was well recognised by the Dutch organisers. The two heats were scheduled to be 16 laps each. That would have forced the thirstier Kawasaki to pit for fuel, but not the Yamahas. When Doyle and Hansford pointed this out to the organisers, they made the first heat 17 laps, forcing everyone to refuel, and the second one 15 laps, a non-stop race for everyone.

In these days of large teams and lots of helpers, it's incredible to think that Neville Doyle in 1978 was managing the team and fettling the bikes alone for three championship classes. About the first help he had was when Aussie rider Jeff Sayle wasn't allowed to start in Holland, so his mechanic, Mick Smith, helped Doyle.

Of the 15 remaining 250 and 350 races at eight meetings, Hansford had a double victory in

Organisers of the 1978 F750 race at Assen altered the race distances to give Hansford's Kawasaki an even chance. He won the first heat.

Hansford and Doyle confer in pit row at Le Mans in 1979 – the end of a trying year.

Sweden, and in the last round at Yugoslavia, when Ballington had both titles virtually sewn up. At the same time, Ballington had seven wins. Three non-finishes in the middle of the series cost Hansford dearly. He lost second place in the championship by one point to Takazumi Katayama on a Yamaha.

Between-season tyre testing on the KR750 was no happier. Gregg wrote off two bikes in two weeks in Australia, testing new Michelin front slicks. Kawasaki was busy at the same time, building him a new four-cylinder 750. It vibrated so much Gregg couldn't race it.

Although Hansford and Ballington finished in the same positions in both championships in 1979, Gregg didn't do as well. Where he'd won seven GPs in the first year, he won only three the next, all of them in the 350 class. Tyres and early season problems with reliability were the two culprits. By the third grand prix of the season, he switched from Michelin to Dunlop, after crashing twice in the rain in practice in Germany and then finishing 12th in the Austrian GP.

The tyre switch was very significant. Hansford and Doyle's racing efforts had been funded by Kawasaki Australia, but later Michelin put money into the team. The teams' switch to Dunlop, not only cost a source of tyres, but also valuable funds.

Some of the 1979 F750 races clashed with GPs, but Gregg won a heat at Nogaro and was second overall at Brands Hatch. However, the most influential meeting for Hansford's career was one he didn't race at — the 1979 Belgian Grand Prix. The Belgian Government had invested millions of dollars to rebuild the Spa-Francorchamps circuit to better suit the demands of modern car and motorcycle racing. The circuit was shortened from 14.1 km to 6.9 km. The new circuit used the existing pits and retained the famous La Source hairpin. Problems began when workmen moved in to lay the new racing surface. The winter of 1978-1979 was so cold that the workers mixed diesel fuel with the bitumen.

The leading riders were so alarmed by the slippery surface they met at a local hotel and voted to boycott the meeting. The less financial private entrants and all the sidecars stayed and raced. The people who led the boycott, including Kenny Roberts, Barry Sheene, Will Hartog, Virginio Ferrari, Gregg Hansford and Randy Mamola, and the then editor of *Motocourse*, Barry Coleman, became the prime movers in the World Series movement. Their aim was to run an independent race series.

The possibility of two series running in 1980 gave the Japanese factories a problem. They wanted to contest both series, but Roberts and a number of riders were adamant they would ride only in the World Series. That gave Gregg Hansford a chance of becoming a works 500 Yamaha rider. It was very tempting, with most of his mates and major rivals contesting the 500 class while he was stuck on 250s and 350s. Yamaha was committed to Roberts, whatever decision he made. So it needed a 500 rider for the world championship. It offered Mamola and then Hansford contracts to contest the 1980 world 500 championships.

Gunther Wiesinger saw this as Hansford's big chance: "Yamaha was prepared to give bikes to Kenny for the World Series and to Gregg for the world championships. But Kenny and Gregg threw me out when I tried to stop him signing for the World Series." he said.

Roberts confirmed the Yamaha opportunity: "My contract with Yamaha applied to whatever series I chose. Yamaha wanted Gregg to run in the world championships, but he refused it. When everybody was forced to go back to the world championships, that put me back in number one spot in the grand prix team and the previous offers to Randy and Gregg were closed."

World Series didn't happen and didn't do Hansford any good, but it did improve conditions including doubling the grand prix prize money.

★ ★ ★ ★ ★

Gregory John Hansford was born in 1952 to a well-off Brisbane family. He showed early potential. One of his more competitive early road race bikes was bought for him by his mother. It was a fast, but not so sweet handling, H1R 500 Kawasaki. He made good use of it at Surfers by having a big duel with one of the then guns of local road racing, Ron Toombs. But for the next three years he showed plenty of dedication, racing three different types of Yamahas and maintaining them himself.

In 1973, when he was just 21 years old, he won the Australian Unlimited and 500 titles and was third in the 250. That year he won the 500 race at Bathurst on a 350 Yamaha, helped by the NSW A-grade riders boycotting the meeting over a disagreement on prize money.

Then came the hairy-chested Yamahas, awesome four-cylinder, 750 machines made by virtually combining two 350 engines. They pushed out up to 125 horsepower and were capable of more than 300 km/h. The bikes were intimidating for some young racers, but not GJH. He got two and shipped one immediately to Daytona, where he raced using Warren Willing as mechanic. Willing didn't yet have his Yamaha so went along to help and learn. During the race Gregg retired with ignition trouble.

Just after Daytona, Willing and Hansford battled in one of the all-time classic races at Bathurst. They finished within a second of each other, with 8.85 seconds carved from the lap record. Hansford lost that battle, but he won the Australian Unlimited Championships again and was second to Tony Hatton in the 250.

The next year, 1975, he joined Ron Toombs and Murray Sayle in Team Kawasaki Australia (TKA), initially as a guest rider in his old Chesterfield leathers. He broke both wrists in a fall at Bathurst, leaving Warren Willing to win again. He retained his Unlimited title that year and contested the Marlboro series in New Zealand, coming up against a rising international star out of America, Pat Hennen. They had some good battles until Hansford fell in the fourth round. He finished third in the series.

Hansford and Kawasaki KR750 versus the Yamaha TZ750s of Boet van Dulmen and Skip Aksland.

In 1976, Yamaha set up a dealer team for Warren Willing. Hansford had a disappointing ninth place in the Unlimited Championship round at Bathurst, then a crash at Sandown. As he was now out of championship contention, he did not contest the final round in Western Australia. While Willing was wrapping up his first Unlimited title, Hansford was racing in Indonesia.

In 1977 Gregg won his fourth Unlimited championship and his first 250, from TKA team-mate Murray Sayle. Hansford and the Sayle brothers had some classic battles in the 1977-1978 Marlboro Series in New Zealand, until Gregg fell during a 250 race and broke his shoulder. Despite that, Hansford had such an enormous local reputation and had so impressed on his overseas trips, he was practically forced to consider a full European campaign.

The rest is history. As we've seen, Gregg gained an impressive list of results overseas. He was also recognised as a man who loved his racing. The only question is why he didn't do better. Kenny Roberts singled Hansford out in the first chapter of *Techniques Of Motor Cycle Road Racing*: "There are (riders) who miss out on winning because they are not so determined and dedicated. Gregg Hansford had such a lot of ability, but he didn't really have the drive or the pure dedication to win the world championship. When he did have it, he didn't have the equipment to do the job."

But then again, he had a lot of fun.

WARREN WILLING

Australian motorcycle road racing enjoyed a boom year in 1976. Kawasaki and Yamaha both employed full-time professionals to race locally and equipped them with factory 750 racers. Team Kawasaki Australia's number one was Gregg Hansford. Yamaha's answer to TKA was the national Yamaha Dealer Team. It had only one rider, Warren Willing, but he made it one of the most professional in the history of Australian racing.

Hansford and Willing represented a new breed when they burst onto the national scene in the early 1970s. They were a promoter's dream. And they rode the biggest capacity pure-bred racing machines in the world — Formula 750. Hansford's H2R 750 and KR750 were the "Green Meanies", while Willing was the "Red Rocket" on his Yamaha, a bike timed at more than 290 km/h at Bathurst in 1976.

Gregg Hansford won four Australian Unlimited Championships, two on Yamahas, two on Kawasakis, and all with his favourite "02" number.

Hansford made it to the top in Australia a little before Willing. But Warren put himself on the same stage on Easter Sunday 1974, when he downed Hansford in one of the greatest races ever seen on Mount Panorama. Willing won at Bathurst again in 1975 and finished second to works Yamaha rider Ikujiro Takai in 1976. On Easter Saturday 1976 Willing recorded the first 100 mph motorcycle lap of the Bathurst circuit.

Willing, Hansford and Murray Sayle (Kawasaki H2R 750) fought out the Australian Unlimited Road-Racing Championship that year. Willing won the title, ending a Hansford clean sweep which began in 1973. Warren now had two options — race in Australia in 1977 on a new factory Yamaha, or spend his own money and head to Europe. Warren had no hesitation in packing his bags.

A serious accident in 1979 ended Willing's riding career. But his impact on Australian racing has been as great in the 1980s, as a team manager and development man, as his riding was in the 1970s. Warren's lucid thinking on racing meant we could leave him to tell most of the story.

"Ninety per cent of the time in Australia, my bike went to the line in better shape than Gregg's. But in Europe that advantage only got you to fifth place. Looking back, I had three problems in Europe. First, I was trying to split my concentration between racing and the machine. Second, I was a bit hard on my own performances and detuned myself. I was used to finishing first or second in Australia, so coming fifth or sixth was a big shock. People keep telling you that fifth place in a world F750 round is a good result, but you haven't got that perspective. Third, my riding became tentative because I had greater responsibilities overseas. I had my girlfriend (now wife) Wendy with me and my mechanic George Vukmanovich. I was the breadwinner for the three of us.

"In March 1974 I went to the Daytona 200 Mile race in Florida as mechanic for Gregg, who had a new Yamaha TZ700.

"I came home really enthused and talked Adams and Sons, my sponsor, into buying me a Yamaha 700. It was worth $3400. Vince Tesoriero found some money to run it from Levis, the clothing company. Bathurst was my first race on it. The money I won there meant I could take the bike to the United States later in the year, and to the Indonesian GP. I was ninth in the AMA national at Laguna Seca and fifth in another at Ontario, near Los Angeles.

"In 1975 I modified the bike for Daytona. Hurley Wilvert, an American rider, had developed some frame modifications and improvements such as laying the rear suspension units forward to increase the suspension travel. I built up some heavier crankshafts to use at fast circuits. I finished fifth at Daytona, then came home and won Bathurst again.

"In August I went to the States again to do Laguna Seca. A guy on a 250 crashed during practice and brought me down. I hurt my back and damaged the bike. I stayed on with Kel until October to do Ontario, where I tied for sixth place with Tepi Lansivouri on the works Suzuki.

"I was planning to go to Europe in 1976. I'd arranged for George Vukmanovich, who had been Hurley Wilvert's mechanic, to go with me. I built a new monoshock frame for my 750 with Peter Campbell and Chris Dowde in Sydney. Kel had offered me three more bikes — a 250, 350 and spare 750. I was trying to put a deal together with Levis up until the minute I left for the States. But it fell through, then George's hip collapsed and he had to go into hospital. So I prepared two 750s in San Diego, went to Daytona and just wore myself out trying to do all the work by myself. All week I seemed to have the best engine in the worst frame. I ended up falling off in the race.

"From Daytona I went back to the West Coast and shipped the bike off to the next F750 championship round in Venezuela. At least I thought I'd shipped it off! I arrived in Caracas. But my bike didn't. It hadn't been loaded in Los Angeles because the ground staff had smelled fuel in the explosion-proof foam in the tank. That just topped things off after the sponsorship falling through and Daytona!

"At Bathurst I finished second to Ikujiro Takai on my own bike. After the meeting I spoke with McCulloch, the NSW distributor, and direct with Yamaha, at an office it had established in Sydney. We did a sponsorship deal with Levis and formed the Yamaha Dealer Team. George came out from the States to join me. We did 13 races and had one breakdown with the Agostini bike.

"Yamaha had offered me a new works 750 to race in Australia in 1977 and a trip to Japan to test it as a bonus for winning the Australian championship. But I'd made enough money to revive my plans of going to Europe. I told Yamaha of my plans and received $5000 in lieu of the trip to Japan.

"I sent the Agostini bike back to Australia after the Marlboro Series and ordered a Yamaha TZ750D in California for Daytona," Willing said.

Warren, Wendy and George Vukmanovich went on to Europe. They travelled in a Mercedes-Benz van and caravan. Warren was supposed to have a special new Yamaha 250, but the frame builder failed to complete the chassis. Willing's refusal to race at meetings where he had no guarantee of starting money meant he only contested 15 meetings in the season — a mixture of internationals, world F750 championship rounds and grands prix.

Willing's two grand prix starts perhaps typified his year.

"Five days before the French GP, a replacement for the 250 I'd been promised turned up at Amsterdam.

Warren Willing, on the ex-Agostini Yamaha OW29 750, and New Zealander John Woodley (Suzuki RG500) at Sydney's Oran Park in 1976.

George and I did an all-nighter to convert the 750 to a 500, then we drove non-stop down to Circuit Paul Ricard, near Marseilles, in a van that did 85 km/h flat out. The 250 practice was first. On the first lap the bike seized. I took the 500 out while George rebuilt the 250, then ran the new engine in the next 250 session. Then it rained in the third and final 250 session, which made qualifying impossible. I didn't bother going out, so I hadn't qualified — and that was the race I went there for! In the 500 race I finished 13th, just ahead of John Woodley.

"The next grand prix was the Dutch, at Assen. It was the best race I rode in the whole season. I used the 750 as a 500 again. I really liked the circuit and it suited the characteristics of the bike — as long as the track was dry. I qualified 11th, ahead of Agostini, who was on a works Yamaha 500.

"Unfortunately it rained at the start of the race and the converted engine was too peaky to ride in the rain. I slipped back through the field to virtually last, then rode back up to finish 14th as the track dried out. Several people told me afterwards it was the best they'd seen me ride over there."

Willing finished in the F750 points for the third time in the season at Zolder, then suffered his second crash of the year in the F750 race at Assen, when his front wheel fractured and sent the tyre flat. He did two races in California, including one more world F750 round. He was 11th overall in the world championship. Warren and Wendy then came home via New Zealand, where he was third in the Marlboro Series, behind the Sayle brothers.

Warren was now at a career crossroads. Crowds and promotions were falling in Australia, so sponsorships were harder to justify. He made an agreement with English sponsor Sid Griffiths to buy and prepare a 750 in Australia, ship it to Europe and ride it in three F750 races. Before Warren left for Europe he gave one of his most sensational rides at Bathurst in the rain. The race was the Easter Saturday preliminary to the Australian Grand Prix. Warren streeted a field which included works Yamaha rider Hideo Kanaya and Mike Hailwood, who was then building up to his superb Isle of Man comeback. In the first four laps, Willing pulled away from the field at the rate of eight seconds a lap!

Willing's short overseas trip produced an eighth place overall in the Imola 200, a DNF at Paul Ricard and seventh place overall at Brands Hatch. Warren returned to Australia via Japan, where he won a Yamaha-backed international race at Sugo. His brother-in-law, Murray Sayle, was second.

The Willings and mechanic Alan Adams went away in 1979 with a plan. Warren would race for one year, then manage a team for Sid Griffiths. But the plan went astray from the start.

"I was really involved in development work by then. I had all the ideas to do the engines, but I wanted to do it all tomorrow. So Alan and I worked ourselves into the ground. We built up a 750 which was a rocket for Paul Ricard. During practice it was over-revving in top gear on Mistral Straight with the

Warren Willing's best ride in Europe in 1977 was in the Dutch GP. He converted his Yamaha TZ750 (No 24) to a 500 for the race.

tallest available gearing. On race day I fell off the 250 and hurt my hand and the 750 seized on the first lap because we were still learning about the new power-jet carburettors.

"We arrived back in England feeling stuffed, and had a couple of days more work because Sid had promised bikes to Mick Grant and Steve Baker for the Easter Trans-Atlantic Match Races. So we spent Easter building and rebuilding bikes. I did a meeting at Mettet in Belgium, then Alan and I set out to do a whole lot more work before the North-West 200, which is run on a ten-mile circuit in Northern Ireland. I had no interest in doing street circuit meetings, but Sid asked me to do it as a favour.

"Things went wrong from the start, as if I wasn't meant to be at that race. We worked 24 hours straight to finish preparing the bikes, then we loaded them and rushed off to catch the ferry, which almost went without us. We practised on the Thursday and had more troubles — the 250 seized and the 750 session was damp. I qualified well, but wasn't able to test the new Dunlop dry-weather tyres, which had been specially made for the high speeds at that circuit. There was a rest day, then we raced on the Saturday, May 26.

"There was a race for 750s in the morning. I had not expected to start in that race, but I decided to start to try out the new tyre. While we were warming the bike up the fuel tank split, so there was another panic. Ron Haslam loaned me a spare tank. I started from the back of the grid. The tyre felt okay and the engine was fast. I passed half the field before we reached the University at Coleraine, near the end of the first lap.

"There was an S-bend at the university. I was in a group of riders. Coming out of the second bend in those esses I saw Kevin Stowe up ahead, travelling slowly on the right-hand side of the road, which was the racing line. So I pulled over to the left. An Irish rider, Frank Kennedy, was behind me on a Suzuki. When I pulled to the left, he must have thought I was slowing, because he went around the outside of me and ran straight into the back of Stowe's bike.

"Stowe's bike burst into flames and the wreckage from their two bikes knocked me over. I ended up on the edge of the road with my left leg a mess. The week leading up to that moment had been so chaotic, the first thing I felt was a strange sense of relief — like something I'd expected had finally happened," Warren said.

Doctors in Belfast are used to treating shockingly damaged limbs. The staff at Coleraine Hospital made a prompt and fairly game decision to save Willing's lower left leg. It was touch and go for many weeks, with the risk of infection ever-present. Frank Kennedy was less fortunate. He died as a result of injuries received that day. Kevin Stowe's injuries forced him to retire from racing.

Eighteen operations and ten years later, Warren Willing holds a respected position in motorcycle team management.

187

THE LAST PRIVATEERS

CHAPTER 14

JEFF SAYLE AND GRAEME McGREGOR

Early in 1983, as Jeff Sayle packed for his sixth season in Europe, he predicted he and Graeme McGregor could be the last Australian private entrants to do a full season in Europe. Jeff's prediction that the great Australian privateer tradition would fade away in the face of spiralling costs in Europe and comfortable race contracts at home was very close to spot on. In the next five years the only Australians who attempted a full European season away from home were two sidecar drivers, for whom there were no contracts at home.

Jeff Sayle's experiences highlighted what a precarious business racing in Europe could be without a works contract. Here was a rider who went within 1.8 seconds, 0.76s and 2.7 seconds of winning world championship grands prix, finished fifth in a world championship and made the winner's podium of a grand prix five times. He lapped the Isle of Man at 109 mph in his first year at the circuit and in 1979 finished third behind Kenny Roberts and Barry Sheene in Britain's prestigious Race of the Year. Yet at the end of six seasons, the last an unmitigated disaster due to a miscalculation by a frame designer, Jeff Sayle came home broke.

Grand prix mechanics tend to be keen students of rider form, and they know the ins and outs of why 11th in a particular race was a good result. Two of Australia's more experienced wrenches, Lionel Angel and Mick Smith, reckon Jeff Sayle should have been a works rider.

Sayle is candid about his years in Europe. "I went all right, but like everything in life, when you get more experience you can look back and see the areas where you'd have done things differently. I could have been a bit more organised and serious about it. I could have won a couple of grands prix. Going to Armstrong in 1981 after finishing fifth in the world 350 championship on a privately entered Yamaha didn't help. But racing for the world championship was what I wanted to do, and I did that. At least I tried, whereas other people can only say they could have but they didn't. Five years after I finished in Europe, it had become too expensive to race there for a season as a private entrant."

Jeffrey Sayle and elder brother Murray grew up in Australia's second oldest city, Parramatta. They went to the same high school as Warren Willing. Jeff showed talent in almost every sport he tried, particularly soccer and motorcycle racing. He had a knack of tucking himself away so well on every bike he rode that it looked as though machines were specially built for him. Jeff started racing on his ride-to-work Yamaha DT250, then progressed through

Graeme McGregor (39) and Jeff Sayle (33) duel for sixth place in the 1979 Dutch 350 GP.

Yamaha RD model road bikes to a Yamaha TZ350 racer.

At Bathurst in 1975 Jeff Sayle had a great duel with brother Murray in the 350 race. Jeff lost because he became excited about winning and didn't change down enough gears for the last corner. But he won his first national title that same year, aged 20. Jeff had his first ride at Daytona in 1976, and crashed the Yamaha TZ750 he'd been loaned for the meeting.

In 1977 Jeff packed in his job as a draftsman and went racing full time with a new Yamaha TZ750D and a Suzuki RG500 supplied by extrovert Gold Coast motorcycle dealer Donny Pask. He also found a regular mechanic in Mick Smith, whose previous charge, Rob Hinton, had just retired. Sayle's story in the next 12 months read: first in the Australian 500 championship, a close second to Gregg Hansford in the Australian Unlimited Championship, first in the Rothmans Formula 750 Series in Sydney, second in two major races in Indonesia and first in the New Zealand Marlboro International Series. The Marlboro Series win capped off a year of Jeff Sayle/Gregg Hansford duels.

When Hansford left for Europe, so did Sayle. Mick Smith quit his job as a diesel engine fitter in the NSW railways to go with him. The duo's only sponsorship came via English journalist Andrew

McKinnon, who convinced insurance broker and part-time racer Jeremy Montgomery-Swan to give them a van. He also put them up in a basement flat when they were in London. Montgomery-Swan was killed in a race crash in Northern Ireland in August 1978. It was later revealed he had an interesting definition of insurance broking — to collect money for insurance policies and pocket it.

The 1978 season was a suitably tough first season, but Jeffrey surprised a few critics by sticking it out. "If you wait until you have all the gear lined up, you'll never leave Australia. We didn't have a caravan. There was just Mick and me, a grotty van and a Yamaha 750 which my mother half paid for. When I got to Europe I was homesick and missed my girlfriend (now wife Zita), but I was there and I had to race. By the end of the year I was able to pay back my mum and find some support for '79," Sayle said.

Sayle and Smith had compatriot Graeme McGregor for company for their first five meetings. When McGregor returned to Australia, Montgomery-Swan bought his Yamaha 350 so Sayle could compete in a second class. The first season produced results any first-timer would be proud of. Jeff's performance in the Imola 200, where he lost sixth place with a bungled refuelling stop, led Italian motorcycle magazine *Moto Sprint* to name him in a list of six riders to watch in the remainder of 1978 (McGregor was also in that six).

Sayle went on to win the Newcomer's Award at Ireland's North-West 200 meeting by finishing fifth in the 750 race. He also finished eighth in the Isle of Man 1000 TT, with a best lap of more than 176 km/h (109 mph). At the time, only one newcomer had lapped the Isle of Man at a higher speed. Jeff's best results in world championship competition were a fine sixth overall in the F750 championship round at Brands Hatch in England and tenth overall in the Belgian world F750 round at Nivelles. Jeff Sayle capped the year by returning to Australia and winning the inaugural Swann Insurance Series from brother Murray.

The entire Sayle racing troupe went to Europe in 1979 — Jeff and fiancee Zita, Murray and wife Rhonda, and Mick Smith. For much of the season they shared Jeff's truck and caravan. Smith departed mid-season to join Suzuki Great Britain, leaving Jeff's preparation to a variety of Australian mechanics. His equipment was a new Yamaha TZ350, his own 1978 model Yamaha 750 and Murray's 1978 model 250. Jeff's season seemed to build as he went along. He finished just outside the points in his first two 350 grands prix, then took fifth place in the Italian 350 GP. Murray was sixth.

Jeff again found form on public road circuits. He was third in the North-West 200, fifth in the Isle of Man 250 TT after suffering fuel starvation in the last 15 km, and fourth in the 1000 TT, despite troubles

Jeff Sayle seemed equally at home on 250s and 750s in Australia in the 1970s. Here he is on a Yamaha TZ750 at Sandown in 1979.

with a harder-than-expected rear tyre and making two fuel stops compared with one by most other riders. Both TT races were memorable. Sayle was running second in the 250 TT, until he had a comparatively slow mid-race refuelling stop due to the tiny filler hole on Murray's lightweight K&K Yamaha 250. This allowed compatriot Graeme McGregor to catch up. The next two-and-a-half laps of the 61 km circuit saw Sayle and McGregor engage in a duel for second, until blocked fuel filters caused fuel starvation on Jeff's mount.

Jeff said he didn't enjoy the 1000 TT at all, particularly when his rear tyre broke traction and the rear of his machine tried to overtake the front in the middle of a flat-out bend. "The bike was only just off vertical and the back started coming around — you don't need that at the Isle of Man," he said.

The Sayle brothers thought they had the refuelling game sorted out for the race, but instead produced some comedy for the grandstand patrons. Jeff's main worry was to completely fill the TZ750's standard-issue 24-litre tank. Murray used a piece of wood for a front-wheel ramp, so the machine would be level for refuelling. This was fine until Jeff tried to roll forward over the wood. His feet came off the ground, he fell over and the bike landed on top of him. Jeff delivered a restrained: "Get it off me!" Rhonda Sayle later described the incident in terms akin to two little boys in a playground... "And then Jeffrey had to ask Murray to put him back on his bike." Jeff remounted and overtook Graeme McGregor on the last lap to finish fourth.

Jeff Sayle's next grand prix start produced another duel with McGregor. They finished side-by-side for sixth place in the Dutch 350 GP. The timekeepers gave them identical race times but the judge's verdict finally went to McGregor. Just who was sixth over the line that day is still the subject of friendly disagreement. Eight days later, Jeff was seventh in the Belgian 250 GP.

Sayle's best GP ride of the season was at Silverstone on his Yamaha 350. He qualified tenth fastest on a machine which was stock standard, save for some carburettor sorting by Warren Willing, who had only just been released from hospital in Northern Ireland. Sayle made a steady start, but by the time McGregor crashed out of the lead on lap 11, Jeff had arrived to join a leading bunch of Kork Ballington and Gregg Hansford (Kawasakis) and Swiss Michel Frutschi (Yamaha).

Ballington pulled out a narrow lead and Frutschi dropped back, leaving Hansford and Sayle, the former 750 rivals in Australia, battling for second. In the end it was only Hansford's super-late braking which kept Sayle at bay. A scant two seconds covered the first three placings, with 0.3 second between the two Australians. Sayle finished eighth in the rain-affected final 350 grand prix of the season at Le Mans, to claim tenth place in the 350 world championship.

The end-of-season international races in Britain gave Sayle more chances to impress on his 350 and 750, which now sported Warren Willing-developed tuning parts. He scored a third, a fourth and a fifth riding the 750 for the Rest of the World team in the AGV Nations Cup. He capped the year with two standout rides in the Race of the Year meeting at Oulton Park. Jeff finished a close second to world 250/350 champion Kork Ballington in the 350 race and a close third in the Race of the Year behind the two biggest names of the day — Yamaha's Kenny Roberts and Suzuki's Barry Sheene.

English pharmacist and motorcycle race sponsor George Beale backed Graeme McGregor and Jeff Sayle for 1980, McGregor directly and Sayle in conjunction with a business associate, Ruth Randle. Melbourne mechanic Dave McGillivray looked after Sayle's machine.

Jeff's target was the world 350 championship. His results that year on a standard Yamaha TZ350 never received the recognition at home they deserved. Sayle finished eighth in the Italian GP, 11th in the French GP at Paul Ricard, fourth in the Dutch GP, retired from the British GP after qualifying ninth, third in the Czech GP and seventh in the West German GP, his first meeting on the Nurburgring. Jeff Sayle was fifth in the championship, behind Jon Ekerold's Bimota-Yamaha, two works Kawasakis of Toni Mang and Jean-Francois Balde, and another Bimota-Yamaha of former world 350 champion Johnny Ceccotto.

Sayle later told Brian Cowan of *Revs Motorcycle News*: "There were times in Australia when I won against moderate opposition, without too much effort, because I was on a good bike and was well backed, and received top publicity. During 1980 I rode better than I ever had, and got next to no recognition, particularly in Australia."

In Britain during 1980 Jeff won five international 350 races and finished eighth in the Isle of Man 350 TT. He also set a 350 lap record at Donington Park which may well stand for all time, because the 350 class has been discontinued. Sayle also had top-five results early in the British season on a new Yamaha TZ500, before the machine had to be parked due to a potentially dangerous gearbox fault. Jeff's one ride in a 500 grand prix produced an 11th place at Assen, behind seven works machines.

Sayle's 1981 grand prix fortunes were tied to his position in a new team. Ruth Randle joined forces with specialist British racing manufacturer Armstrong to run a team. The team's 250 machines had tradesman-like Armstrong frames and Austrian Rotax rotary disc-valve tandem-twin engines. The riders were Jeff Sayle and Briton Steve Tonkin.

The year opened with Sayle taking fifth place in the Daytona 250 international and another fifth on a Yamaha in the Argentinian 350 GP. Jeff was fourth in the Isle of Man 250 TT (which Tonkin won) and fifth in the Dutch 250 GP. But as the season progressed the British team's lack of engine development showed. Sayle finished just outside the points in the Italian, San Marino and British 250 GPs. His only other grand prix points came from seventh place in the British 350 GP. The season proved too much for mechanic Dave McGillivray. Tired of constantly fixing silly faults with Rotax engines and gearboxes,

Jeff Sayle, Toni Mang, Mick Grant and Jean-Francoise Balde duel in the Dutch 350 GP in 1981.

he returned to Australia and became mechanic for Mick Hone Superbike team rider Rob Phillis.

For 1982 Armstrong developed its own rotary disc-valve 350 engine, a strange move given the world 350 championship was in its last year. The idea of building a 350 engine, then down-sizing it to a 250 didn't make a lot of sense either. According to Sayle, the team was taken aback when it went to Argentina for the first round of the world championship. Armstrong's new twin-cylinder 350 was bigger than Honda's new three-cylinder 500. Jeff qualified seventh fastest in Argentina, but failed to finish.

Sayle's next few races were highly encouraging, helped, he said, by the fact that the Armstrong 250 was really the well-sorted 1981 machine. The opposition was still sorting the new Yamaha TZ250H model, which had variable exhaust-port timing. Jeff was ninth in the Austrian 350 GP, then took a pair of third places in the 250 and 350 races at the French GP at Nogaro.

Jeff's 250 race was sensational. He was nearly last off the grid, but cut through the field on a damp track to take the lead after 15 of the 35 laps. Six laps from the end, young French Yamaha rider Jean-Louis Tournadre took the lead, only to be challenged by veteran compatriot Jean-Francois Balde (Kawasaki), who tried such a desperate move on the last lap that Sayle hung back, expecting both Frenchmen to crash. They didn't and Sayle finished third, just 0.76 of a second behind the winner. Balde then won the 350 race, from Belgian Didier de Radigues and Sayle. Jeff's 350 result was the best finish by an all-British grand prix machine in more than a decade.

The next two grands prix, in Spain and Italy, resulted in an eighth place and a did-not-finish for Sayle. And then came the Dutch GP in front of 140,000 fans at Assen. Jeff qualified sixth-fastest. The 15-lap race was run in typically fickle Assen weather. It began in dry conditions. Sayle was second after two laps and took the race lead from French Kawasaki rider Jean-Louis Guignabodet on lap five. By lap seven Jeff Sayle had set fastest lap, in response to pit signals that world champion Toni Mang was in third place and closing after a poor start on his Kawasaki.

And then it began to sprinkle rain. Sayle continued to lead. But as the rain became heavier, Mang's experience and the gallantry of Guignabodet and Tournadre began to tell. Jeff held them off until the last lap, as the four riders fought wheel-to-wheel in slippery conditions. Mang annexed the lead on the final lap. Then Tournadre dived past to grab second place with a game late-braking move before the last corner. Sayle finished third, in a race where 3.2 seconds covered the first four places.

Jeff Sayle was now third in the world 250 championship, behind Tournadre and Mang. He

Formation flying in the 1982 Dutch 350 GP. Sayle led the 250 race on the same day until the last lap.

even had a side-bet running with New Zealander Graeme Crosby (who was competing in the 500 class) on who would be the first to notch a grand prix victory. But Jeff could see the Yamahas and other Rotax-powered machines improving and Armstrong-Rotax development stagnating. For example, Graeme McGregor finished second in the Belgian 250 GP on a Waddon-Rotax, which had more power than the Armstrong-Rotax, but an inferior chassis.

Sayle went to Armstrong management and made an astute prediction. "Armstrong had a policy of stopping development work on the current machines halfway through the season to concentrate on the next year's bikes. I told them if they didn't do some work on my current bike I wouldn't be in the championship top ten by the end of the series." Jeff's prediction was pretty close. He recorded just two more finishes in the remainder of the season — in Belgium, where he was 14th, and Yugoslavia, where he placed seventh. By the end of the season he slipped from third to ninth in the world 250 championship.

Outside the 250/350 grands prix, Jeff's season highlights were setting a 250 lap record for the Brands Hatch long circuit which stood for more than five years and being sounded-out for a works Suzuki 500 ride at the Belgian GP. Unfortunately, the executive with the final say didn't attend the meeting.

At the end of 1982 Jeff Sayle and Graeme McGregor tested an engine they quite reasonably thought would make them grand prix winners in 1983. It was a rotary disc-valve parallel-twin 250 made by Austrian racer/engineer Harald Bartol in his workshop at Strasswalchen, near Salzburg. The test sessions were on Frenchman Patrick Fernandez' machine, which had a 1978-model Bimota chassis. Bartol's engine was the quickest in the 250 class, but it needed a new chassis. The engine was already reliable — it finished all but one of its GP starts in 1982 and had taken Fernandez to fifth placings in two of the last three GPs of the 1982 season.

The plan for 1983 was ambitious. Bartol was to build a "works" machine for Sayle, four customer bikes, one of which was for McGregor, and six customer engines. Bartol had a friend in the Austrian motorcycle industry design the chassis in his spare time. That chassis, and the sheer magnitude of building four or five motorcycles from scratch, told the Jeffrey Sayle story in 1983. To top it off, Jeff had virtually no sponsorship to buy a transporter and cover running expenses.

Sayle flew to Austria in February 1983 to help build the machines, along with Graeme McGregor and Bartol's long-time mechanic Alistair Taylor. Ten days after Jeff arrived in Strasswalchen, he complained of stomach pains. Bartol drove him to a local hospital. Two hours later Sayle's appendix had been removed and he faced a large hospital bill. It was that sort of year.

Sayle missed the first three grands prix because his bike wasn't finished. He turned out for the fourth GP, at Hockenheim, only to have the swinging arm fracture. He failed to qualify. The next grand prix, at Salzburgring, Bartol's home track, saw Sayle again fail to qualify due to handling problems. The machine wanted to bounce across the road in corners. Jeff tried hanging off the bike in one practice session at Rjelka in Yugoslavia. The bike bucked and left him clinging to the side as though he'd been shipwrecked.

The problem centred on rear suspension linkage of the Bartol chassis. The designer had used a rocker-arm system, which Suzuki used at the time on its 500s. But instead of positioning the pushrod and suspension unit vertically in the chassis, he'd cantered the whole system forward, towards the engine. Warren Willing reckoned it looked wrong from 18,000 km away. Late in July, Melbourne engineer Bob Martin went to the British GP at Silverstone as mechanic for Chris Oldfield. Martin looked at the frame and said the linkage system wouldn't work properly until the pushrod and suspension unit were vertical.

Fine idea, lost in the translation – Jeff's 1983 Bartol 250.

Failure to qualify in Britain finished Jeff Sayle's funds. Murray Sayle negotiated a ride for Jeff in the Australian Castrol 6 Hour race. The riding fee was an air-ticket back to Sydney. About a month after Jeff had arrived home, he noticed an interesting result in Murray's air-mail copy of Britain's *Motor Cycle News*. August "Gustl" Auigner, who rode an MBA 125 prepared by Harald Bartol, had finished second and set fastest lap in a European 250 championship round at Brno in Czechoslovakia. His machine was listed as a Bartol. Jeff phoned Harald to check which chassis Auigner had used. The plan when he left Strasswalchen was to put the Bartol engine in a Yamaha frame. Harald said no, he hadn't used a Yamaha frame, he'd removed the rear suspension linkage so the pushrod and unit were vertical. Jeffrey Sayle at that moment felt sick in the stomach, much like he did six months earlier when his appendix was inflamed. "Oh shit," he told Bartol.

"That's exactly what I said," came the Austrian's reply.

Jeff Sayle found a job with long-time friend Mark Briggs at his fibreglass business, and worked his way up to a supervisory role. Before long his racing machine experience was sought for testing and guest rides — even though he hadn't started in a race since the end of 1982. Sydney sponsor Dick Hunter bought Jeffrey Sayle a new Yamaha TZ250 for 1984. Murray Sayle prepared the bike, and Jeff rode it to victory in the Australian 250 championship. Hunter supplied a new machine each year for the next four years, and each season Jeff won a title — Australian Grands Prix in 1985 and 1987, Australian road-racing championships in 1986 and 1988. He also set a 250 lap record at Surfers Paradise on the day the circuit closed.

Sayle became Australia's benchmark 250 rider for ambitious riders to try to beat, and an object lesson in how experience and nous in racing can match youthful verve. Those who could stay with him across the top of Mount Panorama at Bathurst would return to the pits expressing admiration at his smooth riding. In August 1986 Jeff Sayle achieved another first. He was expert commentator on Australia's first direct world championship grand prix telecast from Europe.

The inside story on the 1983 Bartol – leaning the rear suspension unit and pushrod towards the engine was a recipe for disaster.

GRAEME McGREGOR

Graeme McGregor knew Australia's road-racing circuits very well. He learned them with his nose a few centimetres above the tarmac as a sidecar passenger. Graeme made a relatively late debut as a solo rider. It was the end of 1975 and he'd just turned 24. As if to make up for lost time, Graeme McGregor made an impact as soon as he switched. He won his graded races at Bathurst at Easter 1976 in lap record time, won the Australian 350 championship in 1977, and made his European race debut at Easter 1978.

McGregor made a splash in international races, too. He set fastest lap in his second start in England, was named by the Italian press as a rider to watch after his 1978 debut at Imola, and in 1979 won the Newcomer's Award at the Isle of Man TT by finishing second in the 250 race. For a while it seemed the more difficult the course, the more surprising Graeme's performance would be.

But McGregor's early successes were not picked up by major teams. And when they were, it was a case of wrong time or wrong team. At the end of 1980, for example, Graeme said he cost himself a place in the Honda Britain team because he gave an honest rather than a gung-ho assessment of what he could do.

Graeme McGregor became tagged as a 250/350 rider, which might have been fine had he been based in Europe, but in Britain 750 and 1000 rides were the ones that really paid. Graeme says in hindsight he stayed on smaller bikes too long. There were times in 1980, 1981 and 1985 when he looked set to become a regular big-bike runner, only to strike mechanical failure or somebody else's oil spill. McGregor had some notable grand prix rides, including dais finishes in the British and Belgian 250 GPs in 1981-1982. However, the results which gave Graeme a unique place in the history of Australian international motorcycle racing occurred on June 7, 1984, when he became the only Australian to win two Isle of Man TT races at one meeting and one of the few men to win two TTs in a day.

Graeme McGregor grew up in Sydney's southwestern suburbs, but learned to ride motorcycles quickly with his mates on a windy road along the southern shore of Sydney Harbour.

He spent five years as a sidecar passenger, almost all of it with a tall red-haired driver named Steve Bayliss, whose father Stan had raced solo and sidecars for nearly 40 years.

Steve Bayliss and Graeme McGregor won the Australian 650 cm³ Sidecar Road-Racing Championship in 1973, 1974, 1975 and twice won the 650 cm³ sidecar class at Bathurst on a Honda-powered outfit.

Steve Bayliss said "Macca" was the best passenger he had in his career, and recounted an incident

Graeme McGregor – a cheerful disposition and plenty of determination. Recognised it could be a tough business.

which showed McGregor's presence of mind and determination. They were racing at Symmons Plains, Tasmania. The first corner after the start at Symmons Plains is a textbook hairpin bend. Bayliss led from the start, but braked for the hairpin a fraction before McGregor expected. Graeme was thrown forward, off the platform, onto the road. Bayliss' reaction was to yell to him to let go. "But Macca realised if he did that, he would be run over by our outfit and the whole field. He hung on until I got around the corner and onto the grass verge. Then he let go and went under the outfit. I turned around to see if Macca was okay. He just jumped back into the chair and said 'Let's go.' So I took off and we won the race!"

At the end of 1975 McGregor bought a second-hand Yamaha TZ350 and went solo racing. By rights he should have been a C-Grade rider for the Easter 1976 Bathurst meeting, but meeting secretary Jan Blizzard sensed McGregor's ability was well above his grading and had him up-graded for the meeting.

Mrs Blizzard was right. McGregor won both the 350 cm³ and 1300 cm³ B-Grade races from Sydney-based New Zealander Rick Perry. Graeme slashed more than six seconds from the 350 B-Grade lap record and three seconds from the previous best 1300 B-Grade time. His best lap time in the 350 B-Grade event was more than a second quicker than

Sydney's Oran Park, 1972. Steve "Barney" Bayliss and Graeme "Macca" McGregor, with Steve's dad's Honda outfit.

the previous year's lap record in the 350 grand prix event. Years later, McGregor nominated that 1976 350 B-Grade race as one of his favourite races. "My bike was slow in the straight, but we were really honking through the Mountain. Remember we were racing on vague-handling Yamahas with twin upright shocks and treaded tyres. Rick became a Team Kawasaki Australia rider within a year of that race."

McGregor worked night shifts driving heavy earthmoving equipment to finance his racing. He won the six-round Australian 350 Road-Racing Championship in 1977 and finished second to leading English private entrant Chas Mortimer in the 1977-1978 New Zealand Marlboro 350 Series. Encouraged by Mortimer and English journalist Andrew McKinnon, Graeme planned a five-meeting trip to England and Europe around Easter 1978. He couldn't go for any longer because he had finally obtained sponsorship to race in Australia. McGregor freighted a new Yamaha TZ350E to England and struggled onto his plane with enough parts as luggage to convert it to a 250 for the 250 support races at the Imola 200 and Paul Ricard 200 meetings.

McGregor teamed up in London with Jeff Sayle and mechanic Mick Smith. They contested support races for the Easter Trans-Atlantic Match-Race Series, racing at Brands Hatch on Good Friday, Mallory Park on the Sunday and Oulton Park on the Monday.

"The first thing we learned about English racing was they gave you very little practice. I had one 20-minute session to learn Brands Hatch and gear the bike. I was seventh in the 350 heat race and tenth in the final," McGregor said.

"Mallory Park was interesting. It snowed the night before the race. In the morning, before practice, we were warned there was ice on one corner, but the officials laid down salt. It was so cold you couldn't warm the bike up in the pits." McGregor qualified fastest but had to use a new rear tyre for the race, because the one he'd qualified on was coming apart at the splice. "It was a 20-lap race, so I took it easy until the tyre bedded in. I caught the guy running third. When the chequered flag came out I was right behind the two leaders, Tony Rutter and Charlie Williams." (They were later to be his rivals at the Isle of Man).

"The next day I scrambled through to finish fifth at Oulton Park, after starting from grid position 29. I headed off to Imola with Jeff and Mick, having earned a princely $170 prize money in three meetings."

McGregor, Sayle and Smith spent the next 36 hours travelling from Cheshire in England to Imola in Italy in Sayle's Transit van. After representations from two journalists, McGregor was given the chance to qualify for the 160 km 250 race. He was sixth fastest in the official practice session on the Thursday and qualified 11th fastest, in a virtual grand prix field.

"It rained early on race day, stopped for a while, then rained again on the warm-up lap. The race organisers very sensibly gave everyone ten minutes to change tyres and another warm-up lap. I made a good start and began passing people, mainly through the fast left-hander after the pit straight. Unfortunately, I didn't have a pitboard. I went through a long period in the middle of the race when I thought I was the only rider still out there. Finally I saw the spray of another bike up ahead, so I gave chase. It turned out to be an Italian rider who was running fifth. A little later a bike loomed up beside me. It was Kork Ballington on the works Kawasaki. I figured he must be leading and was coming up to lap me, so I moved over and let him through! Then I realised what was happening. I caught Ballington and the Italian on the last lap, but they both out-sprinted me to the line, so I finished seventh, behind Kenny Roberts, Gregg Hansford, three Italians and Ballington, and won $350. After the race an official agent for the Paul Ricard meeting offered me a start in the 250 race there. Gregg Hansford negotiated a guaranteed fee for me against whatever prize money I might win," McGregor said.

"The one-mile straight at Paul Ricard made me realise just how slow the standard 123 kg Yamaha TZ250 was against Gregg's works Kawasaki and the special lightweight Yamaha Kel Carruthers had built for Kenny Roberts. Many of the mid-fielders had fast bikes, too. Throughout my racing, I always reckoned if I was beaten because someone out-rode me, I had no complaints, but it annoyed me to be beaten by blokes who were slower in the corners but had faster bikes. I qualified 17th and finished 16th in a field of 56. The only enjoyable part was a dice with Vic Soussan and two other blokes."

The trio headed back to England through a snow storm. They rounded out Graeme's trip by sampling London and its pubs. Sayle's sponsor bought McGregor's bike. Graeme flew back to Australia and a comparatively dismal home season. His only memorable results were beating Chas Mortimer to win an end-of-season international race at Surfers Paradise and winning the 350 class at the first meeting on the Macarthur Park street circuit in Canberra. But McGregor had achieved two objectives in Europe — he knew what to expect for 1979 and he'd been noticed. And by making a short trip, he'd achieved good results before factors like living out of a Transit van could detune his riding.

Jeff Sayle in a letter home said: "Macca was very impressive when he was here, a pity he had to go back, but I think some people noticed his performances." Giancarlo Galavotti, a reporter for Italian motorcycle newspaper *Moto Sprint*, was impressed

How it started for McGregor . . . acted as moving ballast for Steve Bayliss.

Isle of Man TT winner after six years of trying . . . Graeme McGregor at Parliament Square, Ramsay, on the EMC-Rotax 250.

with both McGregor and Sayle. The week after the Imola meeting, *Moto Sprint* named them in a list of six riders to watch in 1978. Two others on the list were Dale Singleton, who went on to win the Daytona 200 twice, and Randy Mamola, who has since set a record for the number of grands prix won without winning a world championship.

On March 24, 1979, Graeme McGregor walked into the arrivals hall at London's Heathrow Airport carrying a suitcase, new leathers with "Australia" boldly stitched across the back, his helmet, boots, gloves, tools, a few Yamaha racing parts and a spare front tyre. He caught a train to Derby, to watch a race meeting at Donington Park. At the end of the year Graeme McGregor went home with the Isle of Man TT Newcomer's Award, trophies for second and fifth places in TT races, the winner's trophy for a British international 250 series, the prestigious Grovewood Award and a sponsorship commitment to contest four classes in 1980.

McGregor's 1979 season began inauspiciously with a trip to Circuit Paul Ricard in the back of Warren Willing's truck and a ride on a borrowed bitza Yamaha 250. He finished 12th. His lucky break occurred two weeks later, on April 22.

Jeff Sayle was contesting the Brands Hatch round of the world F750 championship. Jeff loaned Graeme his new Yamaha TZ350 to bed in and race in the supporting 350 event. The bike was slow to fire in both the heat and the final, but McGregor rode through the field to finish second in both races.

Midlands pharmacist and race sponsor George Beale had noticed Macca's ride at Mallory on Easter Sunday 1978. A few days after the Brands Hatch race, Graeme received word via journalist Andrew McKinnon that Beale had two new Yamahas for him to ride. Beale was just the sponsor McGregor needed at the time. Graeme had never fancied himself as a businessman and wheeler-dealer. He now had Beale to arrange the machines, starts and start money, while he concentrated on racing. By the end of May, Graeme McGregor had scored his first international race win in England in a 350 race at Brands Hatch short circuit and scored his first points in the British international 250 series.

McGregor went to the Isle of Man TT determined to do well first time. He really attacked the 61 km course, scratching on the tight corners. In later years he became a classic TT rider — one who made going fast look easy by flowing through the faster sections. Graeme's first TT race produced a best lap of just over 109 mph on his 350, which put him in the same league as America's Pat Hennen and Jeff Sayle (in 1978) and fellow 1979 "debutant" New Zealand's Graeme Crosby for the fastest lap by a circuit newcomer. McGregor was running eighth in the 500 TT when his Yamaha broke its crankshaft. Even though he rode the last lap-and-a-half on one cylinder, he still finished 22nd.

The two-day lay-off before the 250 TT saw Graeme team up with former Chas Mortimer mechanic Lionel Angel, who helped with his bike preparation for the race and acted as pitcrew. The race was over six laps. Sayle and McGregor started together. Sayle gained 26 seconds on McGregor in the first three laps. When they pitted for fuel, Sayle held second place and McGregor fifth. At this point Angel pulled two key tactical moves. The first was to use two refuelling guns, one in each filler hole of McGregor's enlarged fuel tank. Murray Sayle could only use one with the smaller filler hole on brother Jeff's mount. Angel didn't fill McGregor's tank. As soon as he saw Sayle push off, he yelled "That's enough" to McGregor, shut the filler caps and pushed him back into the race.

"I figured if Macca could get back out on the road with Jeffrey he could stay with him," Angel explained. The next two-and-a-half laps produced a classic dice. Sayle could out-accelerate McGregor from corners, but the porting on brother Murray's engine meant it would rev past 11,000 rpm. So on long straights, McGregor could slipstream Sayle and repass him. Their combined pace meant they both bettered the 250 lap record on lap five and climbed from equal fourth after the pit stop to second and third on the final lap. On the fifth lap they passed each other four times within sight of the Keppel pub at Creg-ny-Baa. McGregor led into view around the bumpy left-hander at Kate's Cottage. Sayle passed him on the undulating downhill straight which followed, then ran wide on the exit from the tight right-hander in front of the pub. McGregor cut underneath him, waving his boot to his mate as he went. Sayle again had the edge on acceleration on the next straight, but McGregor had the top-end advantage as they headed off out of view towards Brandish Corner. On the last lap McGregor drew ahead to secure second place, while Sayle struggled home suffering fuel starvation.

McGregor put in another hard ride in the 1000 TT, recording a best lap of more than 111 mph (178.89 km/h to be exact) on his 350. He finished fifth, behind Alex George, Mike Hailwood, Chestershire TT ace Charlie Williams and Jeff Sayle.

Graeme's ability in debut performances continued when he rode his first grand prix event at Assen. He duelled with Sayle to take sixth place in the Dutch 350 GP. McGregor qualified second-fastest and finished fifth in the Belgian 250 GP, after a gamble in running wet-weather tyres on the controversial super-slick surface backfired. Graeme qualified on the front row for the British 350 GP and led the race for 11 laps before falling off. He made amends by finishing fourth in the 250 GP. Graeme also finished third in the non-championship Ulster 250 GP at Dundrod.

By the end of the season McGregor had won two more international races in England and beaten series favourite Charlie Williams to win a British 250 international series. In September 1979, Graeme went to Imola to watch his George Beale team-mate and now firm friend Roger Marshall ride in the AGV Nations Cup, a teams event for F750 riders. British captain Barry Sheene crashed during practice and was unable to race, so McGregor was drafted to ride Marshall's spare bike for the Brits. The British team finished last, but Graeme McGregor in his last three races of the day scored seventh, eighth and ninth placings, racing against F750 regulars.

If there was a theme to Graeme McGregor's career for the next few years it was that all efforts to

McGregor's finest GP moment – duelling with multiple world champ Toni Mang (1) in the 1982 Belgian 250 GP. Closing is Didier de Radigues (9).

establish himself as a big-bike rider, the area which was most lucrative in Britain, fell flat. For 1980 George Beale rented a farmhouse near Donington Park for the Sayle/McGregor entourage. He planned a mainly British assault for Graeme, with a new Peckett & McNabb-framed Honda TT Formula One bike, a new Yamaha TZ500, as well as 250 and 350 Yamahas. Graeme surprised himself with his early races on the TZ500 — he finished second to works Suzuki rider Randy Mamola at his third start on the bike and third the next time out to two works Suzukis. But both Beale team Yamaha TZ500s had to be parked after that due to a gearbox fault. The TT F1 machine also showed promise. Graeme was second to team-mate Roger Marshall in the opening round of the British TT Formula One Series. At the Isle of Man he did a practice lap at 112 mph on the machine, which he likened to racing an armchair. But the TT produced huge disappointment the second time around. Graeme failed to finish in all four starts. He led the TTF1 race for a lap before his clutch cable broke. It left Graeme little choice. "There was no way I was going to continue in a race at the Island with no clutch," he said.

Two months into the season, McGregor gained a third new machine, a Cotton-Rotax 250. The 1980 Cotton was the first machine in Britain to use the new Austrian-made Rotax rotary disc-valve tandem-twin engine. McGregor and mechanic Phil Leslie had the English development model. "The first thing we found was that it lost power when it got hot because the water pump didn't spin fast enough," McGregor said. "We also found the primary drive ratio didn't spin the gearbox fast enough. Dealing with Rotax was really difficult in 1980, the factory reps just wouldn't listen to your comments. At one point I asked for a different internal gearbox ratio to give a better spread of ratios. But the factory rep said, 'Our Dutch rider doesn't think you need it.' Two months later you'd go to a meeting and the same Dutch rider would have the new ratio you suggested."

McGregor's 1980 season in Britain produced just three international race wins, one on the Cotton, one on a Yamaha TZ350 and one on the TTF1 P&M Honda. Fortunes were also mixed in the grands prix which Graeme contested. He finished ninth in the Dutch 350 GP (when McGregor's gofer was one W.M. Gardner) but was forced to retire the Cotton with overheating troubles after qualifying eighth for the Belgian 250 GP.

When the Cotton 250 ran, it made a slightly better machine than a private entrant's Yamaha. Take the British 250 GP. Graeme was running third behind Kork Ballington and Toni Mang on their Kawasakis, but just ahead of Thierry Espie (Yamaha), Edi Stollinger (Kawasaki) and Steve Tonkin (Cotton). "By the last lap I had them covered and I was thinking about making the winner's podium and spraying champagne — then the engine seized! I let the clutch out again and it fired, so I rode home to finish seventh — and just about threw the bike on the ground," Graeme said.

There was, however, one major consolation at that Silverstone meeting. Graeme met Lincolnshire schoolteacher Sandra Tuxworth, sister of racer Neil Tuxworth. Graeme and Sandra McGregor now have a son Ross and live in a house they've restored near Louth in Lincolnshire.

Graeme wrapped up the grand prix season by finishing fourth in the 250 class in his one and only meeting at the old Nurburgring. It was the last time the circuit was used for the West German GP. Graeme McGregor and George Beale met soon after with the management of Honda Britain to discuss a race contract for 1981 to ride works TT Formula One machines. "During the meeting I was asked if I could beat Graeme Crosby, who was Suzuki's number one rider. I said I would do my best, but they wanted a yes. I didn't see how I could give them an assurance like that when I hadn't seen the bikes I was going to race. The same thing happened when I was on the short list for a Suzuki ride at the end of 1982. There's no such thing as a definite in racing because the machine can turn out to be a heap."

McGregor's missed opportunity with Honda was partly made up for with some rides on Kawasakis in 1981. For the Isle of Man he was offered Kawasaki Britain's former Kork Ballington works KR250 and one of the Graeme Crosby-backed Moriwaki team's TT Formula One machines, because regular pilot Wayne Gardner did not contest the TT. It was a case of lucky for some...

"I thought the Moriwaki-Kawasaki was a nice machine, much better than the P&M Honda. Wayne had ridden the bike at Daytona and in the British TTF1 races and finished every time. I took off for my first lap of practice and went two miles before the gearbox locked up. It threw me down the road and broke a bone in my arm. I still did a 112 mph lap on it later in practice week, but it stopped in the race. The 500 TT was dreadful. I backed right off after my 500 Yamaha aquaplaned from one side of the road to the other at 160 mph near Greeba Castle. Kenny Blake was killed in that race when the iffy conditions caught him out."

Graeme's Kawasaki 250 ride produced his first TT lap record and another disappointment. He led the race after two laps. On his second lap he cut nearly half a minute off the 250 lap record, for an average speed of more than 109 mph. On the third lap the Kawasaki's ignition failed.

McGregor was offered the Kawasaki KR250 again for the British GP. He qualified fourth fastest behind Toni Mang, Roland Freymond and Martin Wimmer. "Freymond started really quickly on the Ad Majora but Toni Mang and I caught him on our Kawasakis. Toni got himself past Freymond, but I got stuck with him. Freymond and I finished side by side, but I felt I was second. I received the garland for second, then someone in Freymond's team protested and the positions were reversed. I had two more rides on the Kawasaki. I won at Mallory Park and set a new lap record, and qualified fastest at Brands Hatch, before the weather wrong-footed us with tyres. Things were looking promising for 1982, then the Kawasaki Britain management decided to pull out of racing."

McGregor finished the season with some impressive results on his Yamaha TZ350. He was fifth in the Dutch 350 GP and seventh in two other 350 GP appearances, to finish tenth overall in the world 350 championship. Back in Britain, Graeme rattled off three consecutive 350 international wins (beginning with the Ulster GP) and set three 350 class lap records.

Graeme opened his 1982 season in the same vein. He says of the Argentinian 350 GP: "As far as satisfaction goes, that was my best grand prix ride. I was on a standard Yamaha running with Carlos Lavado, Patrick Fernandez, Eric Saul and Jean-Francois Balde, who all had trick bikes. Finally I

Belgium 1982 . . . climbing out of Eau Rouge Corner on the Waddon-Rotax 250.

pushed too hard and crashed. In the French GP I had to retire while battling with Alan North for fourth place, because one carburettor came off."

The Isle of Man TT produced the now annual bout of disappointment. Graeme led the 350 TT by half a minute, before his machine stopped with a burned piston. But out of the TT came an offer to test another Rotax-engined 250, known as the Waddon-Ehrlich. Waddon was a British company hoping to sell production racers in opposition to Yamaha. The Ehrlich was Austrian-born Dr Joe Ehrlich, who had built EMC two-stroke racers in the early 1960s. Graeme hoped Ehrlich's background would improve communications with Rotax.

The first time Graeme raced the bike, he won an international race at Donington Park, and backed the result by finishing sixth in the Dutch 250 GP.

McGregor requested some changes to the machine before the Belgian GP, so Ehrlich returned to England and made some new parts. The upshot was McGregor's highest-ever grand prix finish. He qualified second fastest and took the lead after one-and-a-half laps. Toni Mang passed him soon after, but could not shake the determined Australian.

"There was a lot of thinking involved in that race. Toni could pull out ground on me at one of the corners on the new section of the circuit, but I could pick that ground up at the bus-stop chicane. I reckoned if I could stay with him until the last lap, my bike would out-accelerate his Kawasaki between the last hairpin and the finishing line. But one lap, going into the chicane, Didier de Radigues came past me out of control. We both made it into the chicane, but it meant I didn't pull back the ground I needed on Toni that lap, so he slipped away. Didier and I diced for a while, but he had a broken collar-bone from a crash in the Dutch GP and finally settled for third. I was happy to make the podium at the end with second place and a best lap 0.3 seconds slower than Toni," McGregor said.

McGregor's next target was the British GP. He warmed up by winning a 250 international in lap record time at Snetterton in England and making a brief appearance on a Yamaha TZ750. "By this time I had a name as a small-bike rider, which I wanted to shake off. For Snetterton we dusted off one of George's Yamaha TZ750s. The bike felt good and I qualified fastest for the Race of Aces, ahead of Wayne, Roger and the usual big-bike front runners. But the handling just got worse as the day went on, until it was a monster. The bike had stood idle for two years. During that time the gas had leaked out of the rear suspension unit, meaning it had no damping control after a few laps.

"We went off to Silverstone with high hopes for the Waddon. It was progressing well, apart from the frame design, which made it want to bury its head in corners. During one practice session the front slid away. I remember sliding across the road and into the grass, thinking I'd be okay. But the bike was ahead of me. It knocked a haybale away from one of the wooden poles holding the catch fencing. These poles were suposed to be old and brittle. But there were some new ones, which Franco Uncini as riders' rep had asked the organisers to put saw cuts in. Of course they didn't, so instead of the pole breaking, it broke my leg. I went to hospital, where I was soon joined by Barry Sheene, Jack Middelburg and Gary Padgett."

Graeme McGregor began 1983 in Austria, working with Alistair Taylor to build a Bartol 250 racer. The end product did not provide happy memories for Graeme. "Harald Bartol had a mate, Herbie, who worked at KTM. Herbie had Toni Mang's Kawasaki 250 over the winter, so he could copy the frame. But he thought he could do it better. I was very disappointed, especially when we'd spent two-and-a-half months building the bike that was supposed to win us a world championship. Instead it ruined Jeff's career and didn't exactly help mine. I had to ride a slow Yamaha, which I crashed in Italy trying to keep up with the lads."

The year was saved for Graeme by the Isle of Man TT meeting and his rides on a Ducati 600 TT Formula Two machine. He retired from the 350 TT while in contention for the race lead, due to a failing front brake on his Yamaha. In the 250 TT his "slow" Yamaha was good enough for second place, behind Ireland's Con Law on Dr Ehrlich's EMC. McGregor led the TT Formula Two race until half distance, when a faulty rear tyre on his bike and a new race record by veteran TT runner Tony Rutter reversed their positions. Graeme finished third in the TTF2 race at the Ulster GP, to claim third place in the World TT Formula Two Championship, and he won the British TTF2 Championship on the Ducati, giving Australia a double, because Wayne Gardner won the British TTF1 crown.

The Bartol experience and the escalating cost of contesting the grands prix calendar led McGregor and manager Beale to look for other goals in 1984. "It was no longer possible to finish in the top ten in grands prix on a tight budget with standard bikes, the way Jeffrey Sayle and I had done," Graeme said. Joe Ehrlich hired Graeme to ride his EMC 250, and one of George Beale's friends, Arnie Fletcher, built a new Yamaha 350 for the world TTF2 championship.

Graeme McGregor (8) and jovial Swiss Jacques Cornu (6) duel in the Austrian 350 GP in 1982. Frenchman Roger Sibille is behind.

Both machines used Spondon aluminium chassis.

Graeme McGregor made his Daytona debut on the EMC. He finished second in the 250 international to Wayne Rainey, who had just switched to a Team Roberts Yamaha 250 after winning the US Superbike Championship. McGregor then spent four or five British meetings sorting the chassis of the EMC 250 to give the machine some traction out of corners. The bike was sorted for the IoM TT. Graeme was second-fastest in practice in both classes. Scheduled race day for the 250 TT and the TTF2 event dawned wet and foggy. When the fog failed to shift by lunchtime, the races were postponed until the following day, June 7.

Thursday, June 7, was a perfect day for racing. It was fine and warm. Graeme's EMC fired immediately at the start, but was slow to take throttle. After an agonising ten seconds, it chimed, and the most lucrative few hours in Graeme McGregor's racing career began. After one lap a four-second margin covered Phil Mellor, Charlie Williams, Graeme McGregor and Ireland's Mr TT Joey Dunlop. On lap two McGregor set a new lap record to annex the race

McGregor's only Daytona bid, in 1984, netted him second place in the 250 cm³ international behind America's Wayne Rainey.

lead. Dunlop fought back at mid-race after making a quicker pit stop. (McGregor's bike was again slow to take throttle.) They were neck and neck through lap four, then McGregor forged ahead, upping his own lap record speed to 178.7 km/h (111 mph). Dunlop retired on the last lap, officially out of fuel. On the last lap the course commentators were openly wishing Graeme would have no mechanical troubles. He didn't.

McGregor won by more than a minute from Williams, a pleasing finish, because he'd long respected the Cheshire rider as a rival. "The EMC engine really steamed up the Mountain Mile. The only problem I had was the rev counter kept falling off on the fourth lap. Despite what Dr Joe thinks, I do look at it occasionally," he quipped after the race.

Graeme barely had time to fit a new visor and tear-offs to his helmet before he lined up for another four laps in the TT Formula Two race, the first round of the TTF2 world championship. He led from start to finish, setting new lap and race records. Tony Rutter, the king of TTF2 Ducati riders, was second. McGregor's day's work was three hours and 27 minutes of racing, during which he covered ten laps of the TT course (607 km) at an average speed of more than 175 km/h. He received $9000 in prize money.

KEN BLAKE

Ken Blake was one of the heroes of Australian domestic racing in the 1970s. He was killed at the Isle of Man on June 9, 1981. So many people felt strongly about perpetuating his name that they formed the Ken Blake Foundation which presents a grant each year to a promising Australian rider.

Ken Blake started road-racing in 1966 and scored his first national success in 1969-1970, winning back-to-back Australian Unlimited TTs at Surfers Paradise and Phillip Island on a Triumph prepared by Les and Deane Jesser of Adelaide. Soon after the 1970 Australian TT, Blake switched to Kawasaki two-stroke racers prepared in Melbourne by Ron Angel. At Easter 1970 Blake rode a Kawasaki H1R 500 to victory in the Bathurst Unlimited race and cut five seconds from the lap record. The Kawasaki 500 was fast, but not well mannered. Blake had a heavy fall at Hume Weir that same year when the Kawasaki's engine seized. But he won another Australian TT on it in 1971, this time at Symmons Plains, Tasmania, in the 500 class.

The next few years saw many successes, mostly on Yamahas sponsored by Bendigo motel owner Jack Walters and prepared by Ron Angel. Blake won the 125 and 250 races at Bathurst in 1973 (the 125 on Clem Daniel's Special), and the newly instituted Australian 250 Championship series the same year. In 1974 he won the Australian 350 and 500 Championships and was runner-up to Gregg Hansford in the Unlimited series. And then there was Blake's most famous 1970s racing machine ride in Australia. Ken, riding a new Suzuki RG500, beat world champion Giacomo Agostini's works MV Agusta to win the Australian 500 TT at Laverton Airbase.

Production racing proved just as fruitful for Ken Blake in the 1970s. He won the Castrol Six Hour race solo on a Kawasaki 900 in 1973, with Len Atlee on a Kawasaki 900 in 1974 and with Joe Eastmure on a BMW 1000 in 1977. On top of that he won the 1975 Unlimited Production race at Bathurst on the new 863 cm^3 Ducati. He rode solo and finished second in the 1975 and 1976 Castrol 6 Hour races.

Ken raced a Yamaha TZ750 at Daytona in 1975 and 1976. The association between Ken Blake and Angel/Walters faded in '76, and for a while so did any chance of Ken Blake competing in Europe.

But then, in New Zealand, Ken met Englishman Chas Mortimer, a former works Yamaha 125 rider. Ken headed for Europe in 1978, thanks to his 1977 Castrol 6 Hour prize money and Mortimer's invitation to share his transporter.

The association with Mortimer saved Blake much of the traditional first-year Europe blues. Remember, too, Ken was a very experienced rider when he went to Europe; he was 32 and had been racing for 12 years. The benefits of teaming with Mortimer were three-fold. Mortimer arranged Blake's race starts, so he contested 32 meetings in his first season. Second, Mortimer provided a 1977 Yamaha TZ250 which Ken rode in the 250, 350 and sometimes the 500 class, by switching between 250 and 350 cylinders and exhaust pipes. Third, the business-like Englishman had the full set-up — a transporter, caravan and an excellent Australian mechanic, Lionel Angel (no relation to Ron Angel).

Blake scored his first victory in Europe, within a month of arriving, on the Tulln-Langenlebarn airfield in Austria. He won the international 350 race from two private entrants, Ireland's Tom Herron and West Germany's Reinholt Roth (who was second in the world championship in 1987).

Blake's next two major achievements were in the French GP, in May 1978 at the bumpy Nogaro circuit — getting a start in and then finishing 10th in the 500 race on a 350 machine.

Blake was on the same arrangement with Mortimer for 1979, except for a change of mechanic. He rode a Yamaha TZ350. The highlights of Ken's year were the TT, the Belgian GP and the Bol d'Or 24-Hour race. He finished all three starts in the Isle of Man, taking eighth place in both the 500 TT and the 1000 TT on his 350, and 12th in the 250 TT.

The 1979 Belgian GP was a controversial meeting. The track was so slippery that the works riders and well-heeled private entrants staged a boycott. Ken Blake gave an inspired performance on his Yamaha 350, beating off a field of 500 Suzukis to finish second to New Zealander Dennis Ireland (on a Suzuki). Blake set the fastest lap in the race with a time a second-and-a-half faster than pole position holder Johnny Ceccotto managed on his works 500 Yamaha before the boycott was called.

Blake's 1979 Bol d'Or effort brought him to the attention of the Honda France works endurance team for the 1980 endurance championship. His other highlight for 1980 was recording his best finish at the Isle of Man — fourth in the 250 TT.

Ken Blake looked forward to 1981 with some security, thanks to the Honda France contract. But his chance to become a household name in France ended at the Isle of Man. Blake recorded a TT practice lap of 179.5 km/h (111.5 mph) on his 350. Few men had gone faster on machines of that capacity.

During the 500 TT Ken's bike struck an unexpected wet patch. The bike aquaplaned off the road and he was killed instantly.

Brian Cowan, who covered many of Blake's great races in Australia, said in an obituary in *Revs Motorcycle News*: "Kenny Blake was more than a talented road-racer, a good conversationalist, a friendly socialiser... he was a very complete person, and gently at ease with that completeness."

McGregor had won at the TT at his sixth attempt. But his hopes of winning the world TTF2 title nose-dived in the next round, held on the streets of Vila Real in Portugal. Graeme qualified fastest and had just set fastest lap to stretch his race lead when one carburettor blew off the engine. "The TTF2 Yamaha had a reed-valve engine, so in theory any back-pressure should simply close the reeds. Obviously Lady Luck hadn't read the theory, but those sorts of things seem to happen to me," he said. "And I spoiled any remaining championship hopes by falling off at the third round in Ulster."

Suzuki Great Britain hired Graeme McGregor for 1985, to ride the TTF1 race version of its new oil-cooled GSX-R750 roadster. It seemed his chance on big bikes had finally come. "Suzuki hired me on the grounds that I could give Honda's Joey Dunlop a run for his money. But the first-year GSX-R race motor wasn't exactly the fastest or most reliable engine. But the engine wasn't our problem in the TT, it was the suspension.

"White Power in Holland took a rear suspension unit from the road bike and made up a racing unit which had one-and-a-half to two inches (3.8 to 5 cm) more travel. During practice Mick Grant had a problem on Bray Hill. The suspension bottomed and the bike started tank-slapping. I had the same drama on the first lap of the TTF1 race. The bike went into a tank-slapper at Greeba Castle. I couldn't turn when I wanted to turn... I missed the telephone box, but fired the bike into the wall and bounced back onto the road." He was lucky to escape with a broken collarbone.

McGregor finished ninth in the next TTF1 championship round at Assen, in a half-wet race where tyre choice was all-important, then finished second to Dunlop in 35 degree heat at Vila Real. The fourth round was at Montjuich Park. Fifteen laps into the 42-lap race, the Suzuki mechanics were smiling. Their man McGregor was in a leading threesome with Dunlop and local ace Juan Garriga (Ducati) and looked to be doing it easily. Then fourth-placed Andy McGladdery's Suzuki blew up and left an oil spill. "At that moment I was looking to repass Joey and lift the pace, because I didn't want to get tangled up in a dice with Garriga. Next thing I hit the oil from McGladdery's bike and went down so fast I didn't know what happened. Garriga, Tony Rutter and three others crashed. Tony was badly hurt. Joey got through and won the race."

McGregor finished third in the Ulster TTF1 round and fourth in the final round at Hockenheim, to claim third place in the world TTF1 championship. Graeme was the only Suzuki rider to win a round in the British TTF1 Championship, Honda's Roger Marshall won six rounds. "But at the end of the season Denys Rohan didn't renew my contract. That was very disappointing, because in 1986 the Suzuki was much more powerful. At Hockenheim in 1985 Joey's Honda was geared for 192 mph in top and my Suzuki for 174 mph, which shows what we were up against.

"Suzuki told me so late about dropping me for 1986 that most other rides were filled. I rode Bimotas and Ducatis for Steve Wynne. Jerez was the only circuit where the bikes were really competitive. I won the TTF2 race there and split the works Suzukis to finish second in the TTF1. There was virtually no straight at Jerez, so you had the Ducati heeled over and the throttle flat for most of the lap." He finished third in the world TTF2 championship. His mother Janet collected the FIM bronze medal from Kel Carruthers in a ceremony at Sydney's Oran Park.

McGregor's other major outings for 1986 were painful. He shared Anders Anderson's Suzuki in the Bol d'Or 24-Hour race. The team's three riders qualified within 0.2 seconds of each other, but Graeme was felled during the evening when the engine broke a connecting rod as he shut off from 270 km/h at the end of the main straight. Graeme crashed in the oil from his own bike and badly damaged two fingers when they became jammed under the bike. He flew off to Japan to ride a former Joey Dunlop Honda in a race at Suzuka, qualified fastest and crashed on the first lap. Graeme tore a hole in his ankle and had to spend six weeks in hospital when he returned home to Louth. "Still, it's all good fun," he said.

Problems with potential race deals coming apart at the last minute meant Graeme McGregor's racing for the next two seasons was confined largely to the Isle of Man and riding some uncompetitive machines in the Suzuka 8 Hour. In 1987 he was the first 350 rider home in a combined 250/350 TT. In 1988 Graeme stood in for Suzuki at the last minute in the Formula Three Production TT, riding a new Suzuki 250 road bike. He finished second.

Graeme McGregor was the fourth major Australian international to settle in Europe, joining Ken Kavanagh, who lives in Bergamo (Italy), Jack Findlay in Paris and John Dodds, in Lindfelds, West Germany. Kavanagh was the first Australian to win a TT and Findlay was the first Australian to win the 500 TT. So Graeme is in good company, even though he didn't set out to be known mainly as a TT rider.

"When I came to Europe to race I didn't think there was such a thing as a specialist TT rider. I came to do the grands prix, but there's only so much you can do with over-the-counter racing machinery. The best bike I rode was the ex-works Kawasaki KR250. I liked the challenge of the TT and the old Nurburgring, especially the TT, where you set off at intervals and only see a few riders during the race. Memory of the circuit is so important. After a few years you know every manhole cover and the gear for every corner," Graeme concluded.

TOKYO EXPRESS

CHAPTER 15

Curiously, Australia's greatest era in 500cm^3 grand prix racing, the 1980s, started as its worst. It was the decade when Wayne Gardner brought grand prix motorcycle racing into the homes of ordinary, non-enthusiast Australians. Telecasts of the GP bike races so enthused people that they created one of the highest viewer responses outside an Olympic Games. Some was just sincere appreciation by a generally preyed-upon minority, motorcycle riders. But much of it was appreciation of the action and of the Aussie in the middle of it.

The eighties began with some hope. Riders in Europe in 1980 included Sayle brothers Murray and Jeff, Graeme McGregor, Greg Pretty, John Pace, Kenny Blake, Peter Campbell/Richard Goodwin (sidecar), Graeme Geddes (for five races), Wayne Gardner (for a look-see), Gregg Hansford (for two races), Graeme Crosby and Barry Smith.

The freckle-faced Albury rider Geddes, who was Australian 250 and 500 champion in 1979, scored world championship points in the 1980s, along with nine other riders or drivers. Three were on sidecars. Peter Campbell, with a mixture of clever engineering to overcome lack of budget, and with the determination to overcome the physical handicap of polio, was the first. Then there was Doug Chivas, scoring a lone point in 1988, after an unsuccessful season in 1985. His long term and Australian Grand Prix-winning passenger Margaret Halliday missed out on the honours.

Their replacements as the dominant sidecar combination in Australia, long-term friends Andre Bosman and Dave Kellett, scored points in three GPs, in a campaign that allegedly cost them $100,000.

Prior to the more acclaimed performances in the 500 class of Wayne Gardner and Kevin Magee — Paul Lewis before them — were two less well remembered riders. Graeme McGregor won two Isle of Man TTs in 1984, becoming only the fifth Australian to win a Tourist Trophy. By 1988 he was the only rider from outside Europe still racing at IoM. The other was Jeff Sayle, who'd gone to Europe in 1978, the same year as McGregor.

Sayle's failure was typical of so many Australians. Halfway through the 1982 World 250 Championship, he was lying third on his English Armstrong which had an Austrian Rotax engine. When his opposition continued development but Armstrong stopped, he dropped to ninth. He went very close to a GP win on several occasions. He led the 1982 Dutch GP and set fastest lap but slipped to third when it rained. On another occasion, the French 250 GP at Nogaro, he was just three quarters of a second behind the winner. Yet he was third!

More Australian success in the 1980s came right at the start, when Barry Smith won his third TT F3 race, his fourth TT. As one half of the F3 World Championship, that gave him his second world title. His win almost coincided with Ken Blake's death at IoM. Smith and he were sharing the same garage, when Blake crashed in the 500 race.

Other Australian successes included the middle of the three Willing brothers, lanky Len, who won at Selangor in Malaysia in 1982 and Gardner who has also won there.

But the 1980s started dismally in the 500 class; 1981 was only the second year — consecutively — in which no Australian scored a championship point since the world championships started in 1949. It even happened again in 1982, if you don't count the mercurially quick Kiwi Graeme Crosby as an Aussie. Croz did so much of his racing in Australia and was so popular because of his laid-back humour and natural talent, that Australians adopted him as their own.

But it was the diminutive, bespectacled Paul Lewis who put Australians back in the 500cm^3 record book in this period. He scored one point for tenth place at Silverstone. That was 1983, the same year Wayne Gardner convinced Honda Great Britain to allow him to spend around £10,000 of his own money doing a few GPs in Europe. He was working so well for Honda in Britain they didn't want him to leave. If it had been left to them Wayne Gardner may never have raced in a grand prix. But he was confident enough to spend his own money backing his ambition that year.

Graeme Geddes (Bimota-Yamaha, No 20) cuts inside Swiss rider Weibel during the 1981 Belgian 250 GP.

"Welcome aboard Wayne!" Jeff Sayle and his then British sponsor, Ruth Randle, greet Gardner at Daytona in 1981.

Graeme McGregor, Australia's last regular IoM competitor, on his way to second place in the 1983 250 TT.

Wayne Gardner has grown to be one of the gutsiest and best riders of the mean, fearsome 500s. Wayne did it, of course, with Honda, which had been out of grand prix racing from 1968 to 1979. At first Honda tried pouring expertise and money at a project no other manufacturer would have bothered with. That was trying to lift the power deficiency of a four-stroke engine to equal that of a two-stroke, firing twice as often.

The NR oval-pistoned engine was a disaster as a 500 GP bike, but with dogged perseverance it became both reliable and fast as a 750 in 1987. Its historic first win, after almost ten years of development, was by an Australian, Mal Campbell, in the 1987 Swann Insurance International Series. When the NR500 four-stroke didn't win, Honda built a three-cylinder two-stroke machine, which won races in its first season and a world championship, for Freddie Spencer, in its second.

And Wayne had his wins against the best efforts of another Australian, the 1969 world 250 champion Kel Carruthers. Carruthers helped start the American dominance of 500 racing which Gardner, Kevin Magee and now Michael Doohan are doing their best to end. In 1978, nine years after his own world championship, Carruthers brought American national champion Kenny Roberts to Europe with him.

Carruthers, a former Ryde, Sydney, businessman, guided the inexperienced Roberts through the intricacies of racing and surviving in the multinational complexity of Europe. They not only won the title at their first attempt, they won it three years in succession, a feat not equalled since.

Then the American champions started taking turns. For 1983 it was the God-fearing but motorcycle-taming Freddie Spencer, who was followed by three more Americans in the championship, Kenny Roberts, Randy Mamola and Eddie Lawson. In 1984, two-time AMA Superbike champion Eddie Lawson shot to the top of the heap. Then it was back to Spencer in 1985, returning to Lawson in 1986.

Enough of that, said Wollongong Wayne, who overcame the American dominance to take the '87 title. Then Lawson, Yamaha and Carruthers struck again. Lawson won the title for the third time in 1988 and in the process won more 500 GPs than anybody except his team patron Giacomo Agostini and the late Mike Hailwood. That put Carruthers — a brilliant tuner — as the force behind six world 500 championships in the 11 years since he returned to Europe. Carruthers' influence on world championship racing, since he headed to Europe more than 20 years ago, has been enormous.

Only two of the several hundred people contending Australia's first world motorcycle championship GP at Phillip Island had previous experience at the brilliantly laid-out, weather-battered island —

Rothmans Honda's Jerry Burgess and Marlboro Agostini's Kel Carruthers. They not only both raced there before it slid into disuse, Carruthers once won the entire solo program there.

So the decade has been about Australians coming back into the 500 class in the same numbers as in the days of Ken Kavanagh, Jack Ahearn, Jack Findlay and others. They're doing it with similar success, but one big advantage — factory backing. They have spannermen, team managers, publicists, spare bikes and engines. They have tyres galore, big retainers, handsome bonuses and endorsement contracts. And works machinery, the denied dream of many Aussie strugglers, the achievement of a privileged few.

The 500 class is the factory-supported class, equivalent to F1 car racing. It's where privateers now have no chance. Even the 250 class has become extremely difficult for private entrants. Once the 500 privateer had one or two MV Agustas he knew he couldn't beat and, at various times, a small number of other machines. Now he has about 15 factory bikes lining up for each grand prix. His privately owned, out-of-date bike is no match for them, even if he had better tyres, engineering, riding talent and money.

The only chance is to form a team, to lease two of the latest Hondas or Yamahas (if you have the reputation for them to be made available) and run them for your one talented rider. The bikes alone account for around US$500,000, not because they are so exotic in materials and technology, but because the enormous development costs are spread over only a few machines. The price is material cost, plus big hunks of research and development expenditure.

So things are now done differently. Whereas a private owner once bought his bike, went racing and assumed financial control for the exercise, now all teams, private and factory, are underwritten by sponsors.

This has led to Australia having its greatest ever number of riders on current factory bikes. Three are full-time (Magee on Yamaha, Gardner and Doohan on Hondas) and two part-time (Dowson on Yamaha and Campbell on a Honda).

Two vital things had changed by the 1980s — the racetracks themselves, then the types of machine and riding technique needed for the new type of racing. Gone were the long, flowing tracks of old, with high-speed corners taken flat out in top gear. In their place were tracks where riders raced up to relatively low-speed corners, braked like madmen trying to avoid a precipice, then squeezed on the power as they exited.

The bikes protested, their frames and rear swing arms often distorting under the force. The tyres were being put through hell, at roughly similar temperatures. The riders decided that if they were going to spend all this time accelerating out of second, third and fourth gear corners in a brief, frantic rush up to the next one, they might as well enjoy the experience and try to minimise the time doing it.

So they now hang off the bikes, leaving them more upright than they'd otherwise be. Their knees become a measure of lean, warning them not to go further when their kneepads are being shaved away by the track surface. They can also work as an emergency prop, holding the bike up when one wheel lets go unexpectedly.

If riders crashed during the first 60 years of motorcycle racing, it was because they misjudged their speed or braking into a bend, became involved in someone else's accident or fell on something slippery, like water or oil.

Things changed in the mid-1970s. A crash is now more likely to occur while 120 kW (160 horsepower) is forced through a tortured frame and rear tyre, the back wheel sliding and spinning while the whole device powers its way, sideways, towards the track edge. Just a fraction too much throttle or a fraction too early and the back whips around in a violent tail-overtaking-front manoeuvre. Whether he tries to ride through it, or quickly corrects it by getting off the throttle, the rider has every chance of being in the classic 1980s-style accident, a high-side. The forces are so great, the rider is kicked out of the seat. Rarely does a rider not crash once a full-blooded high-sider is underway. He's usually tossed over the front, possibly then caught and pummelled by the machine after he's come down from an unpleasantly high orbit.

The different characteristics of the modern 500 GP machine and the techniques involved in riding are what distinguish this era from all others. The rider who can commit himself to sliding and wheel spinning his machine out of corners on opposite lock but with his feet on the footpegs, is the rider who can succeed in the 500 class. Those who can't do this don't win races.

So the decade that started with not one Australian scoring points in the world 500 championship proceeds with the first Australian 500 champion. Fourteen GPs had been won by Wayne Gardner and one by Kevin Magee up to the end of 1988, the year Gardner passed Gregg Hansford as the Australian with the most world championship GP wins. They brought the number of world championship GPs won by 11 Australians to 58.

In 1988 Australians did themselves proud, helped a little by the grand prix pointscoring system being altered to award points down to 15th place. And the inaugural World Superbike championship was the instrument for seven Australians to score world championship points.

In all in 1988, we had three riders — Wayne Gardner, Kevin Magee and Mal Campbell — score points in the 500 championship. In the sidecar class, Australian champions and long-time friends Andre Bosman and Dave Kellett, as well as former champion Doug Chivas, scored points, although the latter just squeezed in with one point in Sweden after several times not qualifying. Bosman battled with the usual handicap, lack of money leading to lack of power and tyres, but he and his mechanic Trevor Otto learned plenty.

Otto had been scheduled to leave for Europe in 1980 with fellow South Australian Greg Pretty but his place was taken at the last minute by another South Australian, former Suzuki 500 rider turned spannerman Jeremy Burgess. He not only fettled Wayne Gardner's V4 Honda in his championship-winning and losing years but also Freddie Spencer's 250, under Erv Kanemoto, in 1985. For 1989 he switched from repairing bikes bent by Yatsushiro to fettling an all Anzac part of the Rothmans Honda Team, looking after Michael Doohan.

In Superbikes Robbie Phillis and Mal Campbell went to Europe and Japan and thereby finished sixth and ninth respectively in the championship. Michael Doohan won both rounds at Oran Park, something nobody else did in the nine-meeting series. He finished 12th out of 68 pointscorers from just one race. Honda Australia's number two rider Rob Scolyer had a best place of fourth in one heat in New Zealand. He scored in both Australian and both NZ heats. Michael Doohan's local Marlboro-Yamaha Dealer team-mate, Michael Dowson, did better, at Oran Park, where he finished second to the scintillating Doohan in both races.

In the same period, Australians have had great success in the world endurance championship race, the Suzuka 8 Hour in Japan. Since its inception in 1978, this has become one of the major races on the international calendar. Until the Japanese authorities started limiting attendance, crowds of up to 300,000 made it by far the best attended race since the days of Solitude, old Nurburgring and Sachsenring in East Germany.

Four Australians have been among the winners in five of its 11 years. Both Kevin Magee and Wayne Gardner have won it twice, to make it an Australian monopoly (along with their co-riders) since 1985. But many more have tried. In its second year, 1979, Tony Hatton and Michael Cole won it, after Hatton had been third with Graeme Crosby in its first year. In 1980 Crosby won it, followed by Gregg Hansford who was second with co-rider Eddie Lawson.

Wayne Gardner tackled it with John Pace in 1981, but they retired after 60 laps on what the Japanese labelled the Moriwaki Monster. Crosby went two laps less. Pace returned for a finish the following year. He was 13th, immediately in front of Honda's pairing of Andrew Johnson and Greg Pretty, now a commercial airline pilot.

In 1983 Crosby was back for the fifth time in six races. He was 13th, with the nuggetty Robbie Phillis (no relation to Tom). Mick Cole and Tasmanian Scott Stephens failed to finish. The awesome Andrew Johnson was back the following year with his then Honda Australia co-rider Malcolm Campbell. They were sixth, performing better than Gardner, Crosby, Len Willing and Robbie Phillis, all of whom retired early in the race.

The 1985 race saw a truly heroic ride by Gardner. It was hellishly hot and his co-rider Tokuno was slow. Every time Gardner got back on the bike, he had to ride like a demon to catch up. Finally he did a double stint, out of blazing heat into the darkness of the last hour. It was a brilliant physical and mental effort that the Japanese acknowledged with a fervour that became the basis of his hero status in Japan.

The next year was easier for Gardner, with Dominique Sarron backing him up better. The heroes that year were Marlboro Dealer team-mates Michael Dowson and Kevin Magee. They qualified ridiculously well on a bike that Kenny Roberts said was a heap of crap. They then rode way above the bike's ability to come home second. It was a portent for future years.

Magee did a 1985-style Gardner performance to win it in 1987, although the machine wasn't great and the Japanese team management was woeful. He was a lot faster than German grand prix rider Martin Wimmer and had only one set of new tyres in the race, when he started. On top of that, he had a TT F1 win in Japan and a third (that was really a second given away under team orders) in the Portuguese Grand Prix at Jarama in Spain. That earned Magee the honour of being the first rider in the history of the world championships to have been on the dais for three different world championship series in one year (Endurance, F1 and GP 500). It was inevitable that he would have his pick of a top race team for 1988.

When Magee returned to Suzuka only 12 months later in the middle of a tough season, he had won a grand prix but had also had his confidence shaken by a series of crashes. He'd been knocked unconscious at Spa, as well as taking several other nasty tumbles from his GP 500 Yamaha. So he played a back-up hand in the race to his Lucky Strike team-mate Wayne Rainey. They won again, although there was plenty of strong Australian opposition. For the second year in a row Gardner felt he was let down by his co-rider. He retired with a blown engine.

Kevin Magee (No 40) qualified sixth in his GP debut at Suzuka in 1987. During the race he led Sarron, Chili and Ito.

Magee's third place in his third GP start — the 1987 Portuguese GP at Jarama — left no doubt. He was good.

A virtual novice measured by his time in top-level motorcycle racing, Michael Doohan was brilliant, working his way up to third in the seventh hour, behind grand prix experts Magee/Rainey and Kevin Schwantz. Then, with just ten minutes remaining, his Yamaha had electrical trouble and stopped. With his Japanese co-rider Macchi, he was originally classified a non-finisher, but eventually was re-classified ninth. Michael Dowson was eighth. He had a couple of crashes but had been one of four leaders in the second hour. Phillis achieved his best result to be fifth.

Not a bad Australian result, four in the top ten in a very important race now graced by some of the best grand prix and endurance race riders. Crosby, Peter Goddard and Len Willing were among the Antipodeans battling heat, exhaustion and then darkness that year.

Not surprisingly, this level of achievement has been well recognised in Japan. There have been an increasing number of works-assisted races at Sugo in Japan for Magee, Dowson, Doohan and Rob Phillis.

In one of the nursery racing categories based on 250 production Yamaha two-strokes, Australians Ian "Buster" Saunders and Russell "Rusty" Howard have made it Australia's for the past two years. In the one race world final of an international series, Saunders won in 1987, followed by Howard in 1988. New Zealander Iain Pero and Graeme Muir have both been second and Matt Blair third.

After stirring up the local racing scene, the daring and battered Steve Trinder and younger brother Craig have taken off for racing in America. Iain Pero did likewise, for what he found a tough year, in 1987.

Malcolm Campbell was second fastest qualifier for the Le Mans 24 hour on the revolutionary NR750 and was close to the race lead until it struck engine trouble. The enormous Crosby talent backed up the Carruthers and Hansford onslaughts, by winning the Daytona 200 miler that later diminished in importance, as Suzuka has grown.

Paul Lewis was the best-scoring of five Aussie pointscorers in the 1987 world Endurance championships, two points ahead of Kevin Magee who contested only the Suzuka 8 Hour. Others to score were Rob Phillis, Michael Dowson and Michael Doohan.

Despite South Australian optical technician Martin Renfrey attempting a number of grands prix in the 250 class, he scored no points and learned that a quick bike in Australia is no match at all for a factory bike or even a good private bike in Europe.

The lesson of the 1980s was that Australian riders did not need to go to Europe to win a works ride, as they had for the previous three decades. Kevin Magee and Michael Doohan brought themselves to the attention of GP team managers with impressive performances at Suzuka and Sugo. The old Continental Circus had been replaced by the Tokyo Express.

Suzuka pit row, 1983. Michael Cole and Scott Stephens battled to sort their Beet Racing Kawasaki for the 8 Hour.

WAYNE GARDNER

CHAPTER 16

Two things stand out in the rise of Wayne Michael Gardner to the top of the premier class in grand prix motorcycle racing.

He left for Europe earlier in his road-racing career than people like Carruthers, Hansford and Crosby. When they left, they were dominant locally, and Australian fans expected them to become world champions. When Gardner left, he was just one of a number of top talents in Australia, including people like John Pace and Graeme Geddes. He was good, but yet to show just how good.

Gardner distinguished himself in his first year in Britain with an unusually long-term approach to his racing career. He signed with a business manager. It was an unusual decision by one so young and so recently arrived from Australia, but it proved to be the right one. His first season overseas won him a factory supported ride.

From early in his career he was dedicated to climbing to the top. Others like Hansford and Crosby wanted that too, but were perhaps just a little less disappointed when they lost, feeling less of the need to prove themselves. Even now, acknowledged as one of the best riders in the world, it hurts Gardner to lose. And while he's out on the track, pushing and winning, Wayne Gardner Enterprises is a growing profitable business.

It takes guts for a 21-year-old sportsman, newly arrived in England, to walk into a businessman's office and push across most of the money he has in the world, which wasn't much.

"That much is for the airfare home. Put that aside. The rest is for you to look after. I want you to look after me." Not many people think they need that help, certainly not so soon. Few think they have much more to learn. Which is why Wayne Gardner's 1988 championship-losing season was so good. It wasn't one that wins sporting awards. But ask Wayne Gardner what 1988 was like, the year he returned the world title to Eddie Lawson, and he will tell you it was rich in experience and satisfaction.

"It was a year when I learned so much about myself. I had to fight lack of results and I had to fight to get the machine to work better. I thought I knew plenty about frames and suspensions, but I didn't. Not by comparison with what I learned in 1988. And I learned so much about myself. I think I rode every bit as well in 1988 when I lost the championship as the previous year when I won it."

Gardner's team manager from 1986 to 1988, South Australian Jerry Burgess says Gardner only crashes if he's not concentrating. "He's so good, he never crashes if his mind is fully on the job." And when the good riders crash, they almost always know why. Where the crash is a blur of trouble and sweaty fear for the average person, the motorcycle race champion will be able to tell you what went wrong.

Wayne Gardner beams after his first GP win at Jarama in 1986. Injury to Freddie Spencer meant he was now team leader.

He knows why he crashed and how he'll avoid it next time.

In 1988 Gardner learned that the title is nice, but it's not everything. So he learned to satisfy himself with his performances, not the public. The real champion knows when he did well and when he was lucky. He's happiest when he performed to his best, no matter what the result.

All this from a man who lost the title that had taken up more of his life than anything else. It was something he'd been heading towards, subconsciously at first but then with grim determination, since 1973, when he was 14. It took him until he was 29 and he's still far from finished.

It was also from a man who has seldom been happier, even after returning to Wollongong with just a few friends and business acquaintances instead of the hero's welcome-home parade of 12 months earlier.

Wayne Gardner became world motorcycle champion late in 1987. Wayne Gardner learned about himself and became a fully rounded person in 1988.

Gardner is the complete sportsman/businessman. He delegates and he succeeds. Unlike most motorcycle racers, what happens out on the track with Gardner is just part of the package. He's one of the few people who can race at the very top level while pursuing and organising business deals.

The businessman approached by the 21-year-old Gardner was Harris Barnett, a former employee of Mark McCormack. They're still together, and they are a formidable combination. Gardner talks to Harris Barnett, telling him his aims and demands for the next season, what he wants from Honda and other sponsors. Harris, not Gardner, then talks to Honda. Honda doesn't like Harris Barnett, but Gardner doesn't care. He even thinks it might be an advantage.

All this is hard work. Don't ever tell someone like Wayne Gardner, "You're lucky." It's not appreciated. If he started listing the work he's put in, all the plans, the travel, the thought, the negotiating, as well as the riding, you'd be asleep before he finished chapter one.

The big difference between Wayne Gardner and every other Australian who has tried his hand at international motorcycle racing was summed up by one answer at Sydney Airport on his return in October, 1988. "Will you be going to your town house back in Wollongong" a journalist asked. "I don't own any property in Australia, I'm a resident of Monaco," he said.

It was nothing more than a pocketful of redundancy pay that prompted Gardner to go overseas in 1980. Although he took his helmet and leathers, the idea was just to have a look around. He spent just about everything he had on the airfare, so he lived very cheaply for the month he travelled in England and the Isle of Man. Hitch-hiking was the regular mode of travel.

He did eventually have one race, at Donington Park in the English Midlands. After jumping away fairly enthusiastically at the start, he then scared himself almost as much as the other competitors, so slowed to a safer pace and finished tenth.

After that, it was back to Australia, where it had all begun. Gardner had the advantage of a lot of country kids — plenty of land to play with, which usually meant that they grew up driving cars and riding motorcycles at a much younger age than their city cousins.

This was the case with Gardner, who was runner-up in the Australian Minibike titles in 1974, when he was 15. It was the closest Gardner has been to winning an Australian championship. That was after he kicked off his career with a hefty investment of $5 for his first bike, plus another $10 from Dad for a rather necessary rear wheel and a boxful of parts. What this gave Gardner was lots of practice and the confidence to slide a bike sideways and steer it with the throttle. It's now the accepted technique for making a grand prix 500 go quickly. As Gardner and a brace of Americans have shown in the past ten years, racing on dirt is the best training for this rather delicate operation.

Another advantage of living in Wollongong was the motorcycle enthusiasts/dealers living there: Kevin Fraser, Kevin Cass (who raced in Europe), Karl and Willi Praml. All helped him with bikes in the early stages of his career. It was Kevin Fraser who lent Gardner a 125 motocross machine, which he took to Lithgow in 1974. Compared with what he'd raced previously, this was a thoroughbred machine. It was also a tall one. Gardner could barely reach the ground when he was on it, which prompted his mother Shirley to suggest he shouldn't be using it. But when he won six races on the day, she thought perhaps she was wrong.

The scrap at Oran Park in late 1976 between Warren Willing, Gregg Hansford and New Zealander John Woodley was the inspiration for Gardner to want to go road racing. Within a couple of months, he was riding at Oran Park himself, at a closed club meeting with Wollongong Motorcycle Club. He dished out some punishment to a YZ125 Yamaha motocross bike, which eventually responded by blowing up.

He improved things by getting a bigger-engined machine made to do the job, a second-hand Yamaha grand prix bike, a TZ250. He acquired the bike after pleading with a friend for a ride on his to see what it was like. This was when road racing began to become serious for Wayne Gardner, for it meant a racing licence and lots of travel to circuits in other states. With such a machine he automatically started off as a C-Grader. But he didn't stay there for long.

At the Lakeside circuit near Brisbane in May 1977, he won his first prize money, a modest $25. To Gardner it was gold. It was only when he was assured that a faithful copy could be taken of this cheque that he was prepared to bank it. Imagine winning money for doing what you most enjoyed doing. Later that year, less than a year since getting his road-racing licence, he was promoted to B-Grade.

Promotion through the grades is carefully watched by an expert grading committee. You first need results to merit consideration of a higher grading, but also a standard of control and attitude that will ensure you're not a danger to yourself or anyone else. A quick but crazy rider is more likely to be spoken to than promoted.

That only served to keep Gardner chasing goals. According to him, that's one of the most critical aspects of his racing; "setting an achievable goal each year and then meeting it". The beginning of 1978 saw a further step upward, to a new TZ350 bike, in a bigger class. With a B-Grade licence he could now race against some of the top riders, which he first did in the 350 Australian Championship round at Oran Park in April. He was tenth.

Only four months later he was promoted to A-Grade. That put him among an elite of perhaps 50 of Australia's top riders, of whom around 30 raced regularly. He was not quite 19 years old.

Although Gardner's career was now progressing quickly, his work as a fitter and turner with Tubemakers wasn't. He was often tired when he got to race meetings after driving up to a thousand kilometres on a Friday night. And he wasn't in much better shape when he got back to work on the Monday after a taxing weekend fixing and racing his motorbike. If he got to work. Eventually Tubemakers decided it could do without his talents.

Gardner's other problems in 1979 were two other talented young riders, John Pace from Sydney and Graham Geddes from Albury, both of whom also went on to race in England. Their bikes were often faster than Gardner's 350, although all were being noticed and building up their reputations.

So it was that Gardner and Pace teamed up on a Z650 Kawasaki for the 750 class of the 1979 Castrol 6 Hour production race at Amaroo Park. They stormed through to win the class, Gardner at his first attempt, Pace at his second.

As he continued to campaign the GP Yamaha, Gardner was offered other rides in major events. For the one-off Coca-Cola 800 race at Oran Park in early 1980, he was teamed with experienced Queenslander Dave Robbins on an 860 NCR Ducati. For all its legendary handling in dry conditions, its power deficit would have kept it well back from the leaders,

Gardner and the 1987 Honda V4 looked championship material from the opening race, at Suzuka.

especially the experimental 1000cm³ Kawasaki of Gregg Hansford. But in the rain Gardner and the Ducati excelled. On lap two, after wondering what he was doing threatening Hansford, one of his early idols, for the race lead, he stopped wondering and went past. Gardner led only for as long as it took the Ducati's electrics to ingest enough moisture to cause its retirement.

But progress continued in the burgeoning career. Former car race team mechanic and team manager Peter Molloy had been commissioned by Mentor Motorcycles' Billy Hill to build up a Superbike based on a CB900 Honda. Wayne Gardner caught Molloy's eye and got the ride. Molloy had looked after some top racing drivers, among them Warwick Brown, Neil Allen and John Harvey. Molloy said at the time that Wayne Gardner had enormous talent and would make it to the top. Wayne says of Molloy: "He taught me what professionalism, proper presentation, was all about. I started to realise there was more to success than just winning races."

Gardner ran the Molloy Superbike in the Arai 500 km race at Bathurst, a circuit he now says is one of three in the world he would not race on. "The walls and safety fences are too close to the track for the fast speeds possible there." That race was won by Victorian Michael Cole for Team Honda Australia.

It wasn't long before Gardner's Honda dealer-backed Superbike started to beat, and therefore embarrass, the factory entry. It happened the next month at Oran Park, in the first of three rounds for a Bel-Ray Oils series. Again it was wet. Again Wayne Gardner rode beautifully, but unlike the Ducati, the Honda kept going. Gardner had two wins.

He then headed for England to see what the racing was like. It obviously didn't appeal much, for he went to Isle of Man and has always refused to race there. Then he went to Donington, got a ride in place of an injured rider, but only impressed by being accused of trying too hard.

In round two of the Bel-Ray series, Gardner won again. Again Team Honda was embarrassed.

Back in Australia later that year, he got a plum ride as second rider to the fiercely determined Andrew Johnson on a Honda CB 1100R, a purpose-built, limited-edition production race bike. Johnson and Gardner shared the bike in the Castrol 6 Hour.

Gardner went into the race as the junior partner to the hard-charging, no-compromise AJ. But he didn't do a thing wrong, setting up the race win in his opening stint of three hours.

That was followed by the final round of the Bel-Ray series. It looked as if Gardner would win the series, but team tactics among the official Honda riders saw him denied a series victory. The race was being led by Dennis Neill, with Cole second, ahead of Gardner's ailing machine. Neill slowed to let Cole through for the place he needed to win the series from Gardner.

Gardner's tears of joy at winning the world championship in Brazil in 1987 were nothing compared with his tears of anger and disappointment that day. He saw it as an injustice. Honda had plotted with its riders to beat him. It had taken two people and a team plan to take what he saw as his legitimate title. He now says it was a good lesson in toughening up to the hard realities of professional racing.

The Swann Insurance International Series' fourth and final round at Sandown in 1980 was combined with what turned out to be a dramatic final round to the Australian championships. A keen observer was Mamoru Moriwaki, head of a Japanese tuning firm that sells after-market performance equipment. He needed a rider for a move into England and had been rather impressed by Albury rider Steve Trinder. Trinder had given Kiwi Graeme Crosby a fearful time, from the opening round at Oran Park onwards. There wasn't much subtlety or safety margin in Trinder's riding, as shown by a nasty crash at Adelaide raceway, in which he broke his leg.

So Moriwaki was open to other convincing performances at Sandown. Graeme Geddes had a field day, winning the 250, 350 and 500 championship races. Gardner had run in the Swann Series but then put his big, heavy, four-stroke Superbike away for the day. There was no point in running it against thoroughbred grand prix machinery. The Mentor Superbike's creator Peter Molloy was comfortably ensconced in a well-catered part of the Sandown grandstand, surveying the wet track.

Suddenly he saw Gardner wheeling the big bike on to the grid. He'd seen the rain moving in and reckoned that it would be fairly useful in such conditions. Indeed, it was useful enough to win the race, the first win by a four-stroke in an Australian solo championship event since Ken Blake won on a Triumph ten years earlier. It was also good enough for Moriwaki to talk to Gardner about racing for him in England. The Moriwaki agent was Graeme Crosby. He was later to say ruefully, "It cost me $20,000 to get Wayne a Honda contract."

Gardner had a potential embarrassment of riches. Molloy had teed up a deal that would give Gardner $20,000 for a season in Australia in 1981. Now Moriwaki was offering good money in England.

So in February 1981 Gardner headed for England, via America. First stop was Daytona in Florida in March, now one of the most important meetings outside the world championships. It was an impressive performance, fourth in the 160 km Superbike race behind Wes Cooley, Graeme Crosby and Freddie Spencer. Select company indeed.

His first race in Britain, at Cadwell Park, was even more impressive. Although he only qualified seventh, he won the race, beating Graeme Crosby, Ron Haslam, Roger Marshall and Dave Potter, all experienced and well respected riders. Gardner was second to Potter in the second heat.

Although Ron Haslam went on to take the title, Gardner was capable of winning it with one round remaining. But he was brought down by another rider at Mallory Park and injured his wrist. Wayne followed up his Cadwell win by giving English grand prix hero Barry Sheene a very hard time at Donington. Sheene was on a 500 grand prix Yamaha, Gardner the Moriwaki Kawasaki Superbike. The latter shouldn't have got near the GP bike, but he dogged Sheene throughout the race. It was only a desperate late-braking manoeuvre that saw Sheene squeeze through to a narrow win.

Gardner didn't win anything else until a Streetbike race at Brands Hatch on October 25, although he finished fourth in that championship and third in the Superbike series. He interspersed that with the 200 km race at Suzuka, in Japan, in June and the Castrol 6 Hour at Amaroo Park in October. He crashed out of the latter on a wet track but had his first of three wins in the Swann Insurance Series in November/December on a Moriwaki F1 bike.

It was an impressive opening campaign, with enough there to entice teams to chase his services. Gardner wasn't so certain, but when he received offers from Honda, Suzuki and Yamaha for 1982, he soon started to believe it. They fitted in well with the planned wind-down of the Moriwaki activity. So when he came back to Australia for the Swann

GRAEME GEDDES   A Flash of Brilliance

Graeme Geddes personified one of the central themes of this book — that factors other than riding skill have a huge influence on success in international motorcycle racing. The freckle-faced Albury rider had a brilliant start to the 1981 grand prix season, but suffered classic first-season blues, much the same as Kevin Magee in 1988.

Geddes was a domestic road-race contemporary of Wayne Gardner. They debuted on tarmac in the same year and first clashed as C-graders at Brisbane's Lakeside Raceway in April 1977.

Geddes began junior dirt-track racing in Victoria at the age of 12. By 16 he decided to give up a sponsored ride on a speedway-style 500 four-stroke dirt-track slider and switch to road racing. The dirt-track team, he said, lacked professionalism. Graeme debuted as a road-racer at Phillip Island on New Year's weekend 1976-77, aged 16 years and four months. He led his first race until a minor mechanical failure intervened.

His career blossomed within 12 months, thanks to his obvious talent and assistance from Melbourne businessman and tuner Ron Angel and Bendigo motel owner and sponsor Jack Walters.

Before 1977 was out he began winning A-Grade races on a new Angel/Walters Racing Yamaha TZ350. He was third in the Australian 350 and 500 titles in 1978 on the machine. For 1979 Angel built up two Bimota-Yamahas, a 250 and a 350. Geddes won the Australian 250 and 500 championships, the 250 title from Team Kawasaki's Rick Perry, and the 500 championship from Andrew Johnson and fellow Albury resident Rob Phillis. Graeme also won the Australian 350 GP at Bathurst.

Geddes and Angel headed to Europe in June 1980 for a reconnoitre. They took one Bimota chassis, and two engines — 250 and 350. Wayne Gardner started in the same 350 race at Donington on June 22. Geddes muffed his start and was last away, but cut through the 35-rider field to finish eighth.

Angel had trouble obtaining a start for Geddes in the Dutch 350 GP. By the time a start was arranged, Graeme had missed the only dry qualifying session. He was fifth fastest in the wet, but the time translated to 25th overall. In the race, Geddes started well and was 14th after two laps, when his clutch failed.

The Belgian GP in 1980 was held at Zolder, a new circuit for grand prix regulars as well as Australian visitors. Geddes qualified 15th in the 250 class. He again made a good start and held seventh place for much of the way through the race. In the last few laps two riders just ahead of Geddes suffered mechanical failures, promoting the 19-year-old Australian to a fine fifth place. Angel and Geddes had one more date before they were due back in Australia — a round of the British 250 international series at Snetterton. Geddes won the race easily.

Geddes wrapped up the season by retaining his Australian 250 title with three wins and two second places from five starts. The final round of the 1980 Australian titles at Sandown Park produced Graeme Geddes' best results in Australia. Riding on a wet track he won the 250 and 350 title rounds on his Bimota-Yamaha 250 and the 500 round on a Yamaha TZ500.

Ron Angel planned a full European season for 1981, concentrating on the 250 and 350 grands prix, but with forays into the 500 class.

Riding-wise, Geddes was well equipped for Europe. He rode in a series of controlled rear-wheel slides, a style which suited 1980s tyres and circuits. He was fast, but knew his limits and thought about his racing. In 1978-1980 for example, he went 18 months without a single crash.

But there was one factor the team didn't plan for: homesickness. Geddes was a shy 20-year-old and came from a large inland country town. Yet he headed off to spend a season based outside Amsterdam, and to travel with two men who were roughly twice his age — Ron Angel and unrelated mechanic Lionel Angel.

Geddes opened the 1981 season brilliantly at the Argentinian GP, despite contracting influenza in Buenos Aires. He qualified third fastest for the 250 GP, then muffed his start through nerves. But he recovered and set fastest lap on his way to finishing second. Geddes qualified sixth fastest in the 350 class and ran in the first three early on in the race, before the combination of the steamy weather, the flu and his hard 250 ride sapped his strength. He finished eighth.

The Austrian 350 GP produced another strong finish. Graeme was fourth, behind three of the top four 350 riders of the day — Patrick Fernandez, Toni Mang and defending world champion Jon Ekerold. The third grand prix of the season was the German GP at Hockenheim. Graeme qualified in the top ten in the 250 and 350 classes. One of the riders he outqualified in the 250 class was Eddie Lawson.

Geddes finished 11th in the German 250 GP, one place behind compatriot Graeme McGregor. But the 350 GP saw the first setback of Geddes' season. Four laps into the race, Graeme held fourth place. Then Fernandez crashed at one of the chicanes. The fibreglass tank on the Frenchman's Bimota shattered. Geddes crashed on spilled petrol. From that point on, he recorded only one more top ten finish in a grand prix.

Lionel Angel said later: "In hindsight, Graeme was too young for a full season and, like everyone, he did it hard in his first year. He needed to do a few GPs for a few years, then make the big effort."

Series he was confused as to which team he should pick. They interpreted the slowness to reply as holding out for more money, so increased their offers. That helped the decision-making process!

Finally he signed with Honda Great Britain to do three major series, the world and British TT F1 championships on a 1000 Honda and a Streetbike series on a CB1100R. It was a busy and memorable year. In just one fortnight, from April 4 to 18, he raced eight separate rounds of three championships at five different circuits!

And he warmed to the task. Later in the year, in June and July, he won at three different tracks in three different countries. He won at Penang in Malaysia, then the Suzuka 200 km race in Japan and the F1 race on the road circuit at Vila Real in Portugal. Englishman Roger Marshall took the ride that Gardner had been offered with Suzuki, making altogether too much good use of it from Gardner's viewpoint. Marshall won two of the series that Honda would have liked Gardner to win.

Once again he returned to the Castrol 6 Hour at the unforgiving Amaroo Park track. It was a race that had boosted Gardner's reputation early in his career and he remained loyal to it for longer, eventually, than made sense. But it was *the* race in Australia and was the most reported. It also carried most weight in England.

The race in 1982 was a beauty. He was teamed with fellow South Coast resident Wayne Clarke. Gardner rode with consummate confidence, hauling in time to put them back in the lead after Clarke had pitted early. In the last hour he furiously chased sparring partner (and 1979 6 Hour class-winning co-rider) John Pace. He caught Pace and went under him just ten minutes from the end. After some further arguing, Gardner went on to win by just six seconds. Coincidentally, he was to lose a 6 Hour by the same margin two years later.

But what really made his year was a ride on an RS500 V3 Honda grand prix bike in the Malaysian Grand Prix. He was second in the first heat and crashed in the second, but he loved its precision, agility and speed. From then on, the goal was to ride grand prix bikes. Although he'd ridden grand prix 250 and 350 Yamahas in Australia, this was something different. This, Gardner suddenly realised, was where his future lay.

There were more 500 grand prix bikes around then than now, and more races for them. Gardner stayed with Honda GB to ride in two series for grand prix machinery, while Ron Haslam pushed off to race in world championship grands prix. Gardner was again doing three British series, the third with a four-stroke Honda. Roger Marshall moved across from Suzuki to Honda.

By June, Gardner had won an impressive number of races and was leading both grand prix series. His eyes opened to wider horizons, to the Dutch GP on June 25. It was an appointment with fate, bringing Gardner to one of three occasions on which he very seriously contemplated giving up racing. It was his first world championship grand prix.

Gardner qualified modestly, 16th out of 36 starters. As has been seen many times on television, he arrived at a section of track (now cut from the Assen circuit) just as world champion Franco Uncini made a desperate lunge to the side of the track after having fallen.

He crawled right into Gardner's path, heading off to the grass on the left-hand side of the track. Gardner's bike hit Uncini's helmet, tearing it off and fracturing his skull, among other injuries. Gardner was also tossed off but that was of minor consequence by comparison with his horror at what had happened to Uncini. The initial feeling was that he'd be permanently brain damaged, but he recovered fully and eventually raced again, a year later.

It was Gardner's Honda GB team-mate Roger Marshall who encouraged him to keep racing. He did continue, but a series of crashes and disappointing results didn't do much for his confidence. Where he'd won three of four races in the Shell Masters 500 series before Holland, he didn't win another, although he did win a race at Snetterton on July 24, one week before his next grand prix.

That was at Silverstone, in a race stopped in some confusion by a fatal accident. Gardner qualified well, ninth ahead of the all-time most successful 250 GP rider, Toni Mang. But Gardner's bike gave trouble and he slipped to 16th in the race. He was compensated with a win in the TT F1 race there.

Gardner also slipped in his series pointscores. He was beaten in all of them, despite having won an impressive number of races. That was the mental battering. But he had some physical punishment coming up.

At Donington Park in the Midlands in September 1983, he broke two fingers and cracked a collarbone. Nursing those injuries, he flew to Australia for the Castrol 6 Hour. He took a big toss in early testing, broke bones in two knuckles and lost a lot of skin off his hand. He was so sore and generally wounded that he couldn't ride, especially as he wanted to be fit enough for his final British meeting of the year a week later at Brands Hatch on October 22. But the only good thing at Brands Hatch was that he wasn't more badly hurt when he was helped into a wall by another rider. He broke an ankle, bruised his ribs and hurt his back.

It was therefore a sore and sorry Wayne Gardner at season's end who reckoned he'd put in a lot, not had the commensurate results and was battered as well. He seriously considered whether this was a good way to earn a living.

Gardner paid his own way to several GPs in 1984. Rewards included fourth place in the Italian GP and third in Sweden.

What did cheer him up was that British enthusiasts voted him *Motor Cycle News* Man of the Year in the magazine's annual poll. As Mike Hailwood, Giacomo Agostini, John Surtees and Phil Read had also won the poll, he felt perhaps there was a purpose and a reward for all the commitment and hard work. He was pleasantly surprised to win it ahead of confirmed British heroes Barry Sheene and Ron Haslam.

Watching the opening 500 grand prix of the 1984 season, televised from South Africa, fired him up again to get into the action. Gardner reckoned there were riders there he could beat. So he badgered Honda for a ride in round two at Misano in Italy. Honda was happy to make bikes and people available, but had no budget. Gardner had to pay all the bills. So he was determined to make this appearance, only his third world championship grand prix, really count.

In the first session, he was nothing short of stunning. The only person faster than Gardner was the reigning 500 champion and grand prix legend, "Fast" Freddie Spencer. Gardner went faster in the second qualifying, but so too did a couple of other riders, including Eddie Lawson.

Gardner finished third-fastest, albeit 1.8 seconds slower than Spencer, who was a second clear of Lawson. Uncini was fifth, Sheene 13th. He ran well in the race, working his way up from sixth a few laps from the end to finish a meritorious fourth. The expense was considerable: £2800. But the results made it worthwhile.

Gardner sat out the next five GPs but made good use of the time. Making a superb comeback from the disasters of the latter half of 1983, he dominated two of the three British championships but won all three of them. He won eight of the nine rounds of the TT F1 series, four of the five rounds of the Shell Oils 500 championship, but only one of five rounds in the Masters. The Masters and the Shell Oils 500 championship were both won on a grand prix Honda V3.

This sort of steamroller encouraged Honda GB to fund visits to some of the GPs nearer home. So off he went to Holland, now with the Uncini section no longer part of the racetrack and shortened from 7.7 km to 6.1 km. It was quite a race, with the lead between Raymond Roche and Randy Mamola changing eight times in the second last lap.

Gardner qualified eighth, but improved on that to finish fifth. He made every chance count in 1984. He started in just five of the 12 GPs in the series, yet finished seventh in the pointscore. He scored points in every race he contested, with a best of third place in Sweden. Honda had been so encouraged by his performance, it had lent him a works engine for Sweden. Being on the podium at his seventh GP was impressive, on top of the qualifying times he'd done. And he'd stayed upright through it all.

Once again he came back to Australia, for the Castrol 6 Hour and, for the first time since winning it in 1981, the Swann Insurance Series. Although his 1000 Honda for the 6 Hour was seen as an unlikely winner, Gardner got the best out of it, to fight to the end with Marlboro's local Yamaha Dealer Team riders, Michael Dowson and Richard Scott. Dowson rode like a demon, his chin almost digging a dent in the tank of the light RZ500 Yamaha V4 two-stroke.

Although Dowson and Scott went on to win by three seconds from Gardner, he had lost nearly five seconds early in the race when he knocked off the ignition kill button without realising it. The Swann Series was even better for Gardner, giving him his second series win. He capped that by winning again in 1985. So in ten years, he's won it three times and is still the only person to have won more than once.

Obviously Gardner should have been right for a full grand prix season for 1985. But it nearly didn't happen. He ended up in another dispiriting crumbling of his chances and wondered whether he shouldn't pack up and go home.

Former racer Roberto Gallina — who had guided Marco Lucchinelli and Franco Uncini to their world championships in 1981-1982 — offered Gardner an attractive package, which included the use of a motor home, a flat in Italy and a car, as well as two Suzuki GP bikes. Gardner eventually decided to stay with Honda because he wasn't sure how competitive the Suzukis would be. Honda GB was sure it had a computer manufacturer which would fund a full season. But that didn't happen and suddenly it looked as if all the promise was about to dissolve in an abortive season. There was no way Gardner was vaguely interested in doing another season in Britain. There was no challenge in that. The options included going to America to race Superbikes (where he'd have made lots of money) or going back to Wollongong.

Happily Honda Japan recognised that such alternatives were wasteful of Gardner's talents, so a last-minute rescue plan was drawn up. Only Freddie Spencer would have one of the new V4s, riding for Rothmans Honda. He was to be backed up by Randy Mamola, on a V3. Gardner and Ron Haslam were slotted into a Honda GB team with V3 machinery, also sponsored by Rothmans. All of this was announced just three weeks before the first grand prix, but only one week before his first appearance for the team at the non-championship two plus four meeting at Suzuka. The event was an important car/motorcycle meeting at which Honda was very keen to do well. Suzuka is owned by Hondaland, so Honda's losses there are viewed with even more disappointment than normal.

A quick, private briefing made it very clear to Gardner-san that he was expected to win on the NS500 GP bike and four-stroke RVF750 in the F1. What was also made clear was that there would be a large number of Honda chiefs at the track who would love to see another Honda win. The task was made a bit easier by the machinery. He loves the RVF750, rating it the best, most manageable bike he's raced.

Gardner not only won both races, he set lap records in both. Although he didn't know it at the time, it was the beginning of a run of perfect results in Japan that ran through until September the following year. It brought him an ever-increasing number of Japanese fans, many of whom were desperately keen to help the Gardner coffers by buying all manner of souvenirs.

With Lawson and Spencer combining more experience and better machinery, Gardner could really only hope to do well behind them as he watched and learned, hopefully for a more competitive season in 1986. His major task, which he achieved, was to be the most successful of the Honda V3 riders ahead of Haslam and Mamola. Although that is basically what he did, there were some highlights. He qualified third for the Spanish Grand Prix at Jarama, with just one second separating the three fastest qualifiers, Lawson, Spencer and Gardner.

In the race, he was run off the track by another rider. The bike toppled over at the end of the excursion, so by the time he regained the track Gardner was 28th. He then rode flat out and pulled back to an impressive fourth place. Curiously in the light of later tension between Gardner and Lawson, Eddie complimented him, telling him he had what it takes to reach the top. Gardner said at the time: "Eddie's a friend. I get on well with him."

At the tight Bugatti circuit at Le Mans, which cuts out the long Mulsanne Straight of the endurance race circuit, Gardner was sensational on the V3. The Bugatti circuit suited the lesser, more progressive power of the V3.

After qualifying fourth, Gardner did the unthinkable. He passed Spencer on the first lap as Gardner moved up to second place. On lap four, Gardner hit the lead, with Spencer hot on his heels. Two laps later Spencer went past and Gardner now trailed him. On lap eight, Spencer was baulked briefly and Gardner again shot to the lead. This time he managed to capitalise on it and pull away. It looked as if Spencer had no answer, but unfortunately, Gardner's rear tyre started throwing off chunks of rubber and he was out.

The compensation from a rushed trip to Japan was a win in a most important race, the Suzuka 8 Hour. It was Gardner's first win in a round of a world championship, in this case the world endurance championship. This encouraged Honda to promise him a V4 for Silverstone. Gardner had already wrestled the more powerful V4 to a win at Suzuka on June 9, so he knew he wasn't in for an easy ride. That ride came about partially as a Honda incentive, against expressed interest by Giacomo Agostini for Gardner to join Marlboro Yamaha for 1986. A streaming wet track at Silverstone made things even harder. Like a number of riders, Gardner was forced into the pits with his fullface helmet visor misted up.

That non-finish was expensive in the season pointscore, as was the next round in Sweden. Gardner qualified sixth on his V3 behind Spencer, but ahead of Lawson. Better than that he worked his way up to second in the race but his bike ran out of fuel on the last lap!

He finished equal fourth in the championship, tied with his Honda GB team-mate Ron Haslam. But the points from Sweden would have brought him up to third in the championship ahead of Christian Sarron. Finishing behind only Spencer and Lawson would have been a very satisfying result, although he still had little to complain about. Gardner scored in eight races, Haslam in ten. Both had one second place but Gardner had four thirds, to Haslam's two.

Again it was a year onward and upward for Wayne Gardner — a happy and successful acceptance of increased responsibility and pressure. Back he came for what turned out to be a wet Castrol 6 Hour at Oran Park. It was disastrous for Gardner. As he later realised, he shouldn't have come. Such an intense season is hardly ideal preparation for an event your opponents see as one of the biggest of the year, when you view it as low-key fun. It's a recipe for being beaten at best, and possibly getting into trouble. Both things happened. He had two crashes in dreadfully slippery conditions. The second one was almost farcical. He slid off harmlessly on to a near-lake of an infield. Trying to walk beside his kg Honda as he powered it out, he and the bike slithered and slid. Finally, with neither the bike nor Gardner making any sensible progress, he threw it on its side and walked away. "That was the last one," he said correctly and very understandably.

Offers again came flooding in, almost as heavily as the Oran Park rain. Agostini wanted him for Marlboro Yamaha, Roberto Gallina for his HB Suzukis, the Castiglione Brothers, as ever, wanted him for their Cagivas and the great Kenny Roberts would have been only too happy to have him. Not only would he have been happy, he was offering top incentive — around $750,000. Honda and Rothmans weren't even near that figure initially. But eventually the on-going Honda/Gardner relationship entitled the factory to a discount. For around $600,000, 20 per cent less than the sum offered by Roberts, Gardner agreed once again to straddle Hondas and wear the Rothmans colours.

Gardner's results at the non-championship Japanese Grand Prix convinced Honda of what he had been trying to get across all year — that he deserved a V4 for 1986.

He then went to Kuala Lumpur to race in the Selangor GP. There he added further success, as well as an enormous boost to his confidence. He beat Eddie Lawson. At the end of that year he said: "I've got Lawson's measure, he'll never be champion again." That obviously wasn't right — he underestimated Eddie. But Gardner was now eligible to do so. He had the confidence, the ability and the machinery.

After getting Honda to agree to the most important stricture of all, that he have equal machinery with Freddie Spencer in 1986, Gardner readily accepted a training program on the V4. This came at the Swann Insurance Series in Australia, against Briton Rob McElnea and local Honda rider Mal Campbell. There was some great racing.

In the wet at Oran Park, the wild wheel-spinning power of the V4 was hardly the best thing against Campbell's V3. Gardner's Dunlop tyres were hardly the goods either, against Campbell's Michelins. Gardner won one race in round two at Oran Park, after having won both heats at Calder. But the other was a thriller. Campbell and Gardner banged into each other a couple of times, but eventually it was Campbell first, over Gardner.

For the final-round showdown the next weekend at Surfers, both were grimly determined. Gardner was not amused. Campbell was inspired. The latter got a works V3 engine with an extra ten horsepower, loaned by the factory and flown in for the weekend. Again Gardner won the first heat. But each was sizing up the other, while Rob McElnea, on the fairly manageable Suzuki, kept them both honest.

French GP, 1985 . . . Wayne Gardner (Honda NS500 V3) led Freddie Spencer (NSR500 V4) until his rear tyre chunked.

There was enormous tension as they lined up for the final heat. Gardner's Dunlops weren't helping forward progress much, sliding sideways and wheelspinning. But they did help a very game, skilful and determined young man provide some of the most spectacular footage ever seen on television.

The sight of Gardner's Honda laying a new track of rubber on the circuit under, appropriately, the Dunlop Bridge, at more than 200 km/h was quite incredible. While it was doing this, lap after lap, Gardner, McElnea and Campbell were swapping places, diving under and over each other in a brilliant display of motorcycle racing. It's still selling well as an ABC video! Finally Gardner crashed spectacularly (as seen in Swan Lager commercials), and Campbell won. Motorcycle racing won more fans and the Gardner legend was building.

He'd been very busy in 1985, and very successful; 18 wins from 33 starts. Lots of racing, good results and no nasty injuries. But even he, in his most optimistic mood, could not have believed how the next season would start. The apprentice went to round one of the 1986 championship, at Jarama in Spain, as number two to Spencer. "You do it, I'll watch and follow," was the general idea. There was pressure on Spencer, but plenty also on Gardner.

Against the odds so early in the season, Gardner won. He was the first Australian to snag a 500 GP since Jack Findlay won in Austria in May 1977. Gardner had broken through, won his first championship grand prix. Spencer retired with tendonitis in his right arm that was to become a two-year serial. The win probably sent Gardner into the wrong race strategy for the year, but it was a welcome and delicious moment.

He was leading the championship, although it didn't take long for things to go wrong. Gardner was probably alone in wanting Spencer to be at round two at Monza, but the Honda Team leader was absent. And Gardner was hit by another rider on the starting grid. He lost more than a lap in the pits, rode around courageously but scored no points. He did, though, show the Gardner determination that took him on to his championship the next year.

It was to be a tough, satisfying season for Gardner. When he and Spencer first crossed paths in the pits at Spain, the greeting wasn't much more than a grunt. Spencer turned up, but only briefly, in Austria. Gardner was virtually on his own.

When Gardner raced poorly at Spa in Belgium, not only did Eddie Lawson pull further away in the championship lead, but Randy Mamola, the runaway winner in dreadfully wet conditions, took over second in the championship. But Gardner had already added the Dutch GP (in front of the year's biggest crowd) to his win in the opening race. Then when he added the British Grand Prix, he reckoned he'd won the three most satisfying and significant races of the year.

For all that Gardner was able to look back and be disappointed at being hit at Monza, disappointed with his riding in Yugoslavia and Spa. It was a good, gutsy, learning year. With his second place in the 500 world championship, Gardner joined Jack Ahearn, Jack Findlay and Graeme Crosby as Australasian runners-up in the fastest, most prestigious class in world championship grand prix motorcycle racing. But it was not enough for Gardner. "All I have to do now is go one better," he said back in Australia.

Wayne Gardner's skill is acknowledged. He gives 100 per cent to his racing, not only on the track, but all the time. He knows how to relax and when to get on with the job. He will try to psych his opponents out before the race, in conferences or on the starting grid. He's a very shrewd tactician.

But Gardner felt Honda didn't show the recognition he deserved in end-of-season negotiations, considering it was bidding for the best Honda rider in 1986. It got to the stage where Gardner really thought he would end up at Kenny Roberts' Lucky Strike Yamaha team. He didn't much appreciate the Japanese way of negotiating. But Gardner and Harris Barnett proved equal to the boardroom battle. Sitting in London, they refused to move until Honda got somewhere near to Roberts' offer, which was at least a million dollars. Laughing about it later, Gardner confidants told of a big-budget poker game done by international phone calls.

They had won, for they knew that to be in Japan without a reasonable offer on the table was to be disadvantaged. To go there after one had been made had the advantage in their court. The Japanese would not have liked, but would have respected, their opponents' tactics.

Silverstone 1986. Gardner (Honda V4) and de Radigues (Honda V3). Determined Wayne plus revised engine equals victory.

Gardner won four of the first six GPs in 1987. Mamola and Lawson helped spray the champers at Rijeka.

In 1987, as was closely observed by an increasing number of Gardner's race fans in Australia, he fought and slid, planned and competed his way to becoming world 500 motorcycle racing champion. He loved it and he'd earned it. He cried when he won, as might one who'd worked as hard as he had. Happily, Australia's first 500 world champion was a deserving title-holder. He fought hard, fast but intelligently, with Eddie Lawson, Randy Mamola and anyone else who wanted the title.

From the second round, he always looked in control, as if he would win the title. He led the pointscore from then and was never overtaken. A slip in the last two rounds could have seen him overtaken but a feature of Gardner's riding is that he rarely slips. In the most frantic race situations, he's planning the race end, how to catch his opponents out unexpectedly.

He won seven of the 15 GPs in 1987, employing brilliant tactics on several occasions. Most spectacularly, he did it during the enthralling dice with Randy Mamola at Salzburgring. It was an awe-inspiring encounter — literally. Gardner and Mamola (Lucky Strike Yamaha) banged into each other twice at more than 270 km/h up the back straight. They swapped the lead numerous times on perhaps the most dangerous of the current circuits. But all the time, Gardner was thinking of how to win. He had the reserve capacity to think about other things, switching his riding (almost) on to automatic pilot. He finally made his break by slowing just a fraction for a couple of laps through a right-left flick. It was a section where it forced

Mamola to slow a little as well, losing some momentum. Then Gardner hit it, flying through and catching Mamola off-guard. It broke the vital tow, the slipstream of the leader clearing the air for the bike behind. The margin after 40 minutes of racing was 2.37 seconds.

Mamola's three wins in 1987 took him clear of Gregg Hansford, as the rider who has won most world championship GPs and not a championship. A similar but not so spectacular dust-up with Mamola at Rijeka in Yugoslavia, a circuit where Gardner has gone perilously close to crashing on several corners over several years, saw them finish in the same order only 3.57 seconds apart.

Gardner could also calculate when it was not worth taking too much risk, when it was better to settle for some certain points rather than risk crashing and getting none. On that basis, he soldiered on to a single point — scoring tenth place at Hockenheim, after his bike took sick while in command. As Gardner slipped helplessly backwards through the field, Lawson inherited an easy win, his only one in the first six races. But Lawson came on strongly in the latter part of the season, winning half — four out of eight — of the remaining races. That came from the increasing competitiveness of the Marlboro Yamaha and Gardner's good sense in being prepared, where necessary, to drop a few points.

Some close finishes between Lawson and Gardner, 2.2 seconds in Sweden, 2.13 in Czechoslovakia and 5.19 seconds in Brazil came from Gardner building a big lead in the first half of the race and Lawson then pegging him back.

It was a fast, gutsy, intelligent and well controlled season by Gardner. He had some luck but there was lots of application. He rode like a champion and looked like one. Australia was delighted.

At the end of that draining championship year he wanted to concentrate on trying to win the championship three years in a row, as Kenny Roberts had done in 1978-1980. There was never any real chance of him changing camps for 1988. Gardner, Rothmans and Honda had a mutual interest in sticking together.

The big surprise was how much work a champion does when he's champion. Wayne Gardner was big news. Australia took him to its bosom, from schools who wanted him to inspire pupils, to sports shows and awards, an endless round of radio, newspaper and television interviews, promotions and business deals. It was impossible to do them all.

So he was jubilant but jaded when he went racing in 1988. He'd been a bit off-hand testing the new Honda, into which he'd had a lot of input. He signed it off as being up to the job, when it soon proved to be well short. So, for the first time since 1983, he went backwards in results.

A lot of the pre-season testing was done at Calder, near Melbourne. Despite the addition of a slight rise on the simple road layout and attached banked circuit, it is a circuit that tests acceleration and braking but not much of rider ability and handling. The 1988 Honda accelerated better but did not handle or brake well.

Brilliantly daring and determined riding in the opening round at Suzuka in Japan saw Gardner second to one of the bright new prospects, young American Kevin Schwartz. After cold wet weather all through the qualifying races, few bikes were ideally set up for the dry race conditions. Schwartz's down-on-power but good all-round package Suzuki won the day. In a last do or die effort Gardner's Honda gave him a heart-stopping moment in a fourth gear 200 plus km/h corner. It was only because a wall had been removed and no helicopter was on its landing pad, that Gardner managed to stay upright.

The Yamaha camp was despondent, convinced that they couldn't match the Honda power or, at least on some circuits, the Suzuki package. Neither Honda nor Yamaha were too happy at being beaten by the least powerful bike in the field. But things were soon to change. The first world championship GP at Laguna Seca in America showed up the Honda's handling problems. Gardner was prepared to risk a little more, compensating for the problems, so he was still the best of the Honda brigade. But as the season progressed, he realised the futility — and danger — of trying to match the Yamahas without any improvement in the Honda.

When he became dispirited about the situation and spoke out, Honda didn't like it. Such off-track troubles were a classic case of misunderstanding between East and West. Gardner didn't know whether Honda was reacting, trying to fix the problems, nor did he know, if that was so, when improvements could be expected. It was almost inevitable that somebody with the fight and hunger to be champion would become frustrated when he was so handicapped. But it wasn't well understood in the Honda corridors of power. It's not a lot of fun spending many millions of dollars on racing, to have your image tarnished.

Lawson let the first half of 1987 slip but then came on strongly. Gardner did the same in 1988. His first GP win was not until round eight at Assen. But then he won the next two. If Lawson made an error, perhaps Gardner could still retain his title. But Lawson and Gardner are both too good to throw away a big lead. Lawson knew it in 1987 and Gardner knew it in 1988, although he kept hoping and always kept up the pressure.

If there was one cruel blow in a year where finally, he won four GPs, it was at the French GP at the fast Paul Ricard circuit near Marseilles. Although other motorcycle races had been as good, it was perhaps the best motor race to have been seen live on Australian television.

Gardner, Lawson, Schwartz and Christian Sarron were into it, racing brilliantly. They passed and repassed each other, underneath and around the outside in corners. They slip-streamed their way past each other, at 300 km/h. Then Gardner again slowed them a touch through the corners on to the straight and bolted. Against all the previous evidence, it suddenly looked as if he could — and would — win.

But the Honda engine had major problems and Gardner slowed. If it was cruel that he was robbed of a win, he was lucky that it hung together long enough to get him to the line in fourth place.

It was a tough, character-forming year, as they say when a sportsman doesn't get the results for which he was shooting. He became the full professional, tough, game, confident and very competent. He was *only* runner-up, so he had a quiet off-season in Australia. There were dramatic movements of riders like Lawson and Freddie Spencer (who'd retired after pre-1988 season testing), Australian Michael Doohan got a guernsey to wear the Rothmans Honda colours and Gardner's Jerry Burgess moved across to look after him, along with Dave Cullen, who'd been mechanic for Shunji Yatsushiro.

And there was Phillip Island. At last an Australian world championship grand prix, with Australia's champion at his peak, itching to attack on that great circuit. He's never won at Bathurst, nor has he won a pre-championship Australian Grand Prix, but Gardner has little else to prove on the track. Certainly, these days no-one would dare accuse him of a lack of obvious riding talent and determination.

Wayne Gardner samples the fruits of success at Monaco.

AUTHORS' "DOZEN"

Peter Campbell (1979-81)... popular, practical and ultimately unlucky.

Vic Soussan (1973-79)... cosmopolitan road-racer and sometime fisherman.

Tony Hatton (1977-79)... thinking man's endurance racer, won Suzuka in '79.

Gordon Laing (1952-54)... killed before he could shine on works Norton.

Greg Johnson (1978-79)... no starts, little help, but strong F750 runner.

Kevin Cass (1965-67)... went for three months, stayed three years, sabotaged at TT.

Kevin (and Jake) Magee (1987) . . . grand prix winner with warm country smile.

Kenny Blake (1978-81) . . . nature's gentleman, national treasure lost at Isle of Man.

Ray Quincey (1978) . . . triple Australian champ 1976, paralysed in Europe.

Murray Sayle (1979-80) and Graeme Crosby (1977-82) . . . droll, under-recognised introvert leads laugh-a-minute Kiwi extrovert.

Mal Stanton (1965-69) . . . familiar story – talent but no money.

Ross Hannan & Phil O'Brien (1968-70) . . . mates since 1955, pushed off together in 1970 500 TT.

Barry Thompson (1964-66) . . . won lottery, raced BMW to top five in GPs.

INTERNATIONAL 1912-1988

As this is the first attempt at compiling a complete record, details are sketchy and scattered, and in some cases, missing. Remember that this is an attempt to be precise about many people who find it difficult to send their entries to a meeting on time; their riding is usually more precise than their record-keeping. The authors welcome any information that expands or corrects the following.

Further complication comes from riders not always running their lives as precisely as historians would wish. Rather than do complete seasons, some darted back and forth in sporadic forays, some went to look at a race or a country with their leathers, helmet and boots with them "just in case". Injuries, love affairs, lack of money and/or machinery often caused plans to change.

The Honour Roll is set out in chronological order. Where available, each entry includes the following information: year or years spent racing overseas, rider's name, place of origin, classes raced and countries in which races were held. The entries in bold type denote world champions.

Abbreviations
GP — competitor won a grand prix
IoM Win — competitor won at the Isle of Man
WCP — competitor scored world championship points

1912-1914 BAILEY, S.L. (Lesley), Newcastle, 350, 500 Douglas — IoM, record breaking at Brooklands
1913 REGLESS, H., 500 — IoM
1924 MOYLE, A.J., 350, 500 — IoM
1924-1925 STUART, J.A., 350, 500 — IoM
1925-1931 WILLIAMS, Stewart, Sydney, 250, 350 — IoM
1927 MELROSE, Aub, 350 — IoM
1927-1934 SIMCOCK, Arthur, 250, 350, 500 — IoM, Britain, Europe
1927 STEWART, L., 500 — IoM
1931-1932 BREWSTER, Dave, 350, 500 — IoM
1932-1933 PRINGLE, Jim H., Victoria, 350, 500 — IoM, Britain
1933 WEATHERBY, Cec, Sydney, 250, 350, 500 — IoM, Britain, Europe
1933 HANNAFORD, George, Bathurst — IoM
1934 BALGARNIE, W., 350, 500 — IoM
1935 HORTON, K.N., 250 — IoM
1939 MUSSETT, Frank, 350, 500 — IoM, Britain
1948-1950 McPHERSON, Eric, Sydney, 350, 500, IoM, Britain, Europe — **WCP**
1949-1951 HINTON, Harry, Sydney, 350, 500 — IoM, Britain, Europe — **WCP**
1949-1950, 1952 MORRISON, George, 350, 500 — IoM, Britain, Europe, USA
1951-1958 CAMPBELL, Keith, Melbourne, 350, 500 — IoM, Britain, Europe — GP, WCP
1951-1960 KAVANAGH, Thomas Kenrick, Melbourne, 125, 250, 350, 500 — IoM, Britain, Europe — **GP, WCP, IoM Win**

1951-1955 McALPINE, Tony, Sydney, 350, 500, 1000 — IoM, Britain, Europe — **WCP**
1951 McCONNELL, R.D., 350 — IoM
1952-1954 LAING, Gordon, 350, 500 — IoM, Britain, Europe — **WCP**
1952-1953 RING, Ernie, 350, 500 — IoM, Britain, Europe — **WCP**
1952-1956 TINKER, Len, Victoria, 250, 350
1952-1956 TINKER, Neil, Victoria, 125, 250
1953-1954 BOULTER, Laurie, 350, 500 — Britain, IoM
1953-1957 BRYEN, Keith, Sydney, 350, 500 — IoM, Britain, Europe — **WCP**
1953 MACK, Bernie, Victoria, sidecar driver — Europe
1953 SCOTT, George, WA, 350, 500
1953 WALKER, Geoff, J., Tasmania, 350, 500 — IoM
1953-1956 WILLIS, Sid, Sydney, 250, 350, 500 — IoM, Europe
1954, 1955, 1958, 1961, 1966, 1974 AHEARN, Jack, Lithgow, 250, 350, 500 — IoM, Britain, Europe — **GP, WCP**
1954-1956 MITCHELL, Bob, Melbourne, sidecar driver — Britain, IoM, Europe — **WCP**
1954-1955 GEORGE, Max, sidecar passenger — Britain, IoM, Europe — **WCP**
1954-1955 QUINCEY, Maurie, Melbourne, 350, 500 — IoM, Britain, Europe — **WCP**
1955-1960 BROWN, Bob, Sydney, 250, 350, 500 — IoM Britain, Europe — **WCP**
1955, 1958 BURT, Allen, Sydney, 350, 500 — IoM
1955 COX, F.W., 350 — IoM
1955, 1957-1958 FORREST, Jack, Sydney, 250, 500 — IoM, Britain, Europe
1955-1958 THOMPSON, Richard Golden (Richie), Sydney, 350, 500 — IoM — **WCP**
1956-1959, 1965-1969 HINTON, Eric, Sydney, 250, 350, 500 — IoM, Britain, Europe — **WCP**
1956 HODGKINSON, Barry, 350, 500 — IoM
1956 LANG, Arthur Ronald, Victoria, sidecar driver
1956 MAXWELL, D.G., sidecar passenger
1957 BARKER, Roger, Mudgee, 350, 500 — IoM, Britain, Europe — **WCP**
1957-1959 HINTON, Harry W. (Junior), Sydney, 350, 500 — IoM, Britain, Europe
1958 DUNN, Clarrie, A., 350, 500 — IoM
1958-1978 FINDLAY, Jack, Mooroopna (near Shepparton), 50, 125, 250, 350, 500, 750, Endurance — IoM, Britain, Europe — **WCP, GP, IoM Win**
1958 JOHNSON, Neil, Victoria
1958-1962 PHILLIS, Tom, Sydney, 125, 250, 350, 500 — IoM, Britain, Europe — WCP, GP
1958 THOMPSETT, Jim, 350, 500 — IoM
1959-1961 MILES, Ron, Melbourne, 350, 500 — IoM, Britain, Europe — **WCP**
1959 URQUHART, Lindsay, Melbourne, sidecar driver — Europe
1959 FOSTER, Ray, sidecar passenger
1960s RAE, Tommy, WA
1960s LUCK, Trevor, NSW sidecars
1960s LAING, Paul, sidecar driver
1960-1961 FOSTER, Ray, sidecar driver (same as above)
1960 FOSTER, Jean, sidecar passenger
1960-1961 BENNETT, Malcolm, sidecar passenger

HONOUR ROLL

1960-1962 SALTER, Bob (Orrie), sidecar driver — IoM
1960 SMITH, Graham, 350, 500 — IoM
1960-1961 WEST, Bob, 350, 500
1961 POUND, Trevor, Melbourne, 350, 500 — IoM, Britain
1962-1966 FRY, Dennis, Sydney, 350, 500 — IoM
1962 SCHUPPAN, Dene, Adelaide, 125, 250
1962-1969, 1979-1981 SMITH, Barry, Melbourne, 50, 125, 250, F3, sidecar passenger — IoM, Britain, Europe — **GP, WCP, IoM Win**
1963 BOSWERGER, Bill, Ballarat, sidecar driver — Britain, Europe
1963 FAIRBROTHER, Chas, 350, 500
1963-1970 ROBINSON, Ron, Victoria, 125, 250, 350, 500 — IoM
1963 SHAW, Raymond, 350, 500 — IoM
1963 WATERS, Colin, 350, 500
1964 JOHNSON, David, 350, 500
1964-1966 THOMPSON, Barry, Melbourne, sidecar driver — **WCP**
1964-1965 BRADLEY, Richard, Bendigo, sidecar passenger — **WCP**
1964-1965 TURNER, John, Victoria, sidecar driver
1965-1967 CASS, Kevin, Wollongong, 125, 250 — IoM, Britain, Europe — **WCP**
1965 COOMBER, Brian, ACT — IoM (Manx GP)
1965-1969 GILL, Thomas, Perth, 350, 500 — IoM
1965, 1969-1970 HANNAN, Ross, Sydney, 250, 500 — IoM, Europe — **WCP**
1965 HINTON, Robert, Sydney, sidecar passenger — Europe
1965 JOHNSON, Dave, 350, 500 — IoM
1965 LESLIE, John, 125
1965-1967 RICHARDS, Peter, Adelaide, 350, 500 — IoM, Britain, Europe
1965-1968 SAUNDERS, Jack, Sydney, 350, 500 — IoM, Europe
1965-1969 STANTON, Malcolm, Melbourne, 350, 500 — IoM, Britain, Europe — **WCP**
1966-1967 ATLEE, Len, Sydney, 250, 500 — IoM, Britain, Europe — **WCP**
1966-1970, 1971-1973 CARRUTHERS, Kel, Ryde, Sydney, 125, 250, 350, 500 — IoM, Britain, Europe, USA — WCP, GP, IoM Win
1966-1978 DODDS, John, Sydney, 125, 250, 350, 500, 750 — IoM, Britain, Europe — **WCP, GP**
1966-1975 EICKELBERG, Paul, West Germany/Melbourne, 250, 350, 500 — Britain, Europe — **WCP**
1966-1975 SMITH, Brian, 125, 250, 350 — IoM, Europe — **WCP**
1966 WILSON, Ron, 350, 500
1968-1969 BAUSKIS, John, 125, 250
1968-1975 DENNEHY, Terry, 350, 500 — IoM, Britain, Europe — **WCP**
1968-1969 O'BRIEN, Phil, Sydney, 250, 350, 500 — **WCP**
1969-1970 MacDONALD, Terry, 350, 500
1970s TINGATE, Rod, Melbourne, 350 — Europe
1971 JONES, Peter, Melbourne, 250, 500 — IoM, Europe
1970-1972 STANLEY, Dave, Sydney, 125, 500 — Europe
1972-1979 SOUSSAN, Vic, Melbourne, 250, 350 — IoM, Britain, Europe — **WCP**
1973-1974 DUBOIS, Steven, Sydney, 125, 250 — Europe
1974-1981 HANSFORD, Gregg, Brisbane, 250, 350, 500, 750, Endurance — USA, Britain, Europe, Japan, South America — **WCP, GP**
1974-1976 KENNY, Les, Sydney, 250, 350, 500, 750 — IoM, Britain, Europe, USA
1974, 1977, 1979-1980 SAYLE, Murray, Sydney, 250, 350, 750 — Britain, Europe, USA — **WCP**
1974 TOOMBS, Ron, Sydney, 750 — USA, Malaysia, Indonesia
1974, 1977-1979 WILLING, Warren, Sydney, 250, 350, 500, 750 — Britain, Europe, Japan, America — **WCP 750**
1975 HEDLEY, Ross
1975-1976, 1978-1981 BLAKE, Kenny, Adelaide/Melbourne, 250, 350, 500, 750, Endurance — IoM, Britain, Europe, USA, Central America — **WCP**
1975 READ, Duncan, Sydney, 750 — Britain
1976 BAYLISS, Stanley, Sydney, sidecar driver — Britain
1976 CAMPBELL, Alec, sidecar driver — IoM
1976 GLEESON, Kevin, sidecar passenger — IoM
1976, 1978-1983 SAYLE, Jeffrey, Sydney, 250, 350, 500, 750 — IoM, Britain, Europe, USA, South America — **WCP**
1977-1979 HATTON, Tony, Sydney, Endurance — Japan, Europe
1978-1979 JOHNSON, Greg, Melbourne, 750 — Britain, Europe — **WCP 750**
1978-1988 McGREGOR, Graeme, Sydney, 250, 350, 500, 750, TT F1, TT F2, Production, Endurance, sidecar passenger — IoM, Britain, Europe, Japan, Indonesia, USA, South America — **WCP, IoM Win**
1978 QUINCEY, Ray, Melbourne, 250, 350 — Europe
1979-1981 CAMPBELL, Peter, Sydney, sidecar driver — IoM, Europe, Indonesia — **WCP**
1979-1981 GOODWIN, Richard, Wanganui, N.Z., sidecar passenger — IoM, Europe — **WCP**
1979-1983 COLE, Mick, Melbourne, Endurance, Production — Japan, Britain
1979 COBURN, Vaughan, Sydney, 250, 350 — Britain, IoM
1979-1980 PRETTY, Greg, Adelaide, 750 — IoM, Britain, Europe, Japan, Indonesia
1979-1980 WALDEN, Rick, Sydney, 750 — Britain, Europe — **WCP 750**
1979 WILLING, Len, Sydney, 250, 350, 500, Endurance — Britain, Japan, Malaysia
1980-1988 GARDNER, Wayne, Wollongong, 500, TT F1, Endurance, Production — Britain, USA, Europe, South America, Japan — WCP, GP
1980-1981 GEDDES, Graeme, Albury, 250, 350, 500 — Europe, Britain, South America — **WCP**
1980, 1981, 1983, 1984 PACE, John, 250, 350, 500, Endurance — IoM, Britain, Europe, Japan
1981-1984 JOHNSON, Andrew, Melbourne, 500, Endurance — Malaysia, Japan
1983-1988 LEWIS, Paul, Melbourne, 500, Endurance — Europe, America — **WCP**
1983 OLDFIELD, Chris, Melbourne, 250 — Britain
1983-1988 TRINDER, Steve, Albury, 500, Superbike, Super stock, Production — USA
1984-1988 CAMPBELL, Malcolm, Launceston, TT F1/Prototype, 500 — Europe, Japan — **WCP**
1985, 1988 CHIVAS, Doug, Sydney, sidecar driver — Europe — **WCP**

1985, 1988 HALLIDAY, Margaret, sidecar passenger — Europe

1985 MUIR, Graeme, Melbourne, Yamaha 250 Production world final — Holland

1986-1988 DOWSON, Michael, Bunbury/Brisbane, Endurance, Superbikes — Japan

1986 MORRIS, Graeme, Newcastle, Yamaha 250 Production world final — France

1986-1987 MUIR, Peter, West Wyalong, TT F2, Endurance — IoM, Europe

1986, 1988 PHILLIS, Robbie, Albury, TT F1, Superbikes, Endurance — Britain, Europe, Japan, Australia — **WCP**

1986-1987 SAUNDERS, Ian, Wangaratta, **Yamaha Production 250 world final (1st)** — France, Italy

1987 BLAIR, Matt, Yamaha 250 Production world final — Italy

1987-1988 MAGEE, Kevin, Horsham, 500, TT F1 — Britain, Europe, South America, Japan — **WCP, GP**

1988 BOSMAN, Andre, Adelaide, sidecar driver — Europe — **WCP**

1988 KELLETT, Dave, Adelaide, sidecar passenger — Europe — **WCP**

1988 DOOHAN, Michael, Gold Coast, TT F1 — Japan — **WCP**

1988 HODGSON, Grant, Melbourne, **Suzuki GSX-R750 Production world final (1st)** — Spain

1988 HOWARD, Russell (Rusty), Hobart, **Yamaha 250 Production world final (1st)** — Britain

1988 RENFREY, Martin, Adelaide, 250 — Europe

1988 RICHARDS, John, Yamaha 250 Production world final — Britain

Australia's first world championship placegetter, Eric McPherson, rode a works AJS 350 in the 1950 Ulster GP.

THE AUSTRALIAN POST-WAR HONOUR ROLL

1948 *Isle of Man Team:* Eric McPherson

1949 *Isle of Man Team:* Harry Hinton, Eric McPherson
Works rides: Hinton and George Morrison — Norton;
Championship placings: McPherson equal third in inaugural world 350 championship on AJS
Best race results: McPherson fourth in Ulster 350 GP; Hinton ninth in IoM 500 TT;

1950 *Isle of Man Team:* Harry Hinton, Eric McPherson, George Morrison
Works rides: Hinton, Morrison — Norton; McPherson — AJS
Best race results: Hinton third in Dutch 500 GP; third in Ulster and Italian 350 GPs. McPherson fourth in Ulster 350 GP

1951 *Isle of Man Team:* Harry Hinton, Ken Kavanagh, Tony McAlpine
Works rides: Hinton and Kavanagh — Norton
Championship placings: Kavanagh fourth in world 350 championship on Manx and works Nortons
Best race results: Kavanagh second in Ulster 500 GP; second in Ulster and Italian 350 GPs

1952 *Isle of Man Team:* Ken Kavanagh, Tony McAlpine, Ernie Ring
Works rides: Kavanagh — Norton
Championship placings: Kavanagh fifth in world 500 and 350 championships
Best results: Kavanagh first in Ulster 350 GP (Cladys Circuit)

1953 *Isle of Man Team:* Ken Kavanagh, Tony McAlpine, Ernie Ring, George Scott
Works rides: Kavanagh — Norton; Ring — AJS
Championship placings: Kavanagh third in world 500 championship and fourth in 350
Best race results: Kavanagh first in Ulster 500 GP (Dundrod)
Ring killed during Belgian 500 GP
Geoff Walker killed at IoM

1954 *Isle of Man Team:* Jack Ahearn, Laurie Boulter, Maurie Quincey
Works rides: Ken Kavanagh — Moto Guzzi; Gordon Laing — Norton
Championship placings: Kavanagh third in world 500 championship and fourth in 350
Best race results: Kavanagh first in Belgian 350 GP
Boulter killed in road accident in Isle of Man
Laing killed during Belgian 350 GP

1955 *Isle of Man Team:* Jack Ahearn, Bob Brown, Maurie Quincey
Works rides: Ken Kavanagh — Guzzi; Quincey — Norton
Championship placings: Kavanagh fourth in world 350 championship
Best race results: Kavanagh first in Dutch 350 GP; Keith Campbell third in Belgian 350 GP on Manx Norton, and first in non-championship Czech 500 and Finnish 350 GPs. Bob Mitchell/Max George third in Dutch Sidecar GP on a Manx Norton

1956 *Isle of Man Team:* Keith Bryen, Eric Hinton, Barry Hodgkinson. (Jack Ahearn, Bob Brown, Keith Campbell and Tony McAlpine under six months' suspension following riders' strike at 1955 Dutch 350 GP)
Works rides: Campbell — Guzzi
Championship placings: Bob Mitchell/Eric Bliss (GB) fourth in world sidecar championship on Manx Norton
Best race results: Ken Kavanagh first in Isle of Man 350 TT; Mitchell third in Belgian Sidecar GP and fourth in IoM TT; Campbell wins non-championship Swedish 350 GP on a Manx Norton

1957 *Isle of Man Team:* Roger Barker, Bob Brown, Eric Hinton
Works rides: Brown — Gilera; Keith Campbell — Guzzi; Keith Bryen — AJS and Guzzi
Championship placings: Campbell wins world 350 championship; Bryen fourth in 350 championship (Manx Norton and Guzzi)
Best race results: Campbell first in Dutch, Belgian and Ulster 350 GPs; Bryen second in Ulster 350 GP
Barker died from heat exhaustion during a race at Thuringia, East Germany

1958 *Isle of Man Team:* Jack Ahearn, Bob Brown, Eric Hinton
Works rides: Ahearn debuted Matchless G50 500 at IoM (Gilera and Moto Guzzi withdrew from grand prix competition on September 26, 1957 — affected Brown, Keith Bryen and Keith Campbell)
Best race results: Campbell second in Belgian 500 GP and third in Belgian and Dutch 350 on Manx Nortons; Brown third in Isle of Man 500 TT on Norton
Campbell killed at Cadours, France

1959 *Isle of Man Team:* Bob Brown, Eric Hinton, Ron Miles, Tom Phillis
Championship placings: Brown third in world 500 and 350 championships on Manx Nortons

Best race results; Brown second in Dutch 500 GP and Ulster 350 GP; Brown first in Formula 1 race (for non-works racing machinery) at Dutch TT; Hinton first in non-championship Czech 500 GP
Harry Hinton Jnr died following race crash at Imola

1960 *Isle of Man Team:* Bob Brown, Ron Miles, Tom Phillis
Works rides: Brown and Phillis — Honda
Championship placings: Brown fourth (posthumously) in world 500 championship on Manx Norton
Best race results: Brown second in Dutch 500 GP; Phillis second in Ulster 250 GP on works Honda
Brown killed during practice for West German GP at Solitude

1961 Isle of Man Team: Jack Findlay, Ron Miles, Tom Phillis
Works rides: Phillis — Honda
Championship placings: Phillis wins world 125 championship and second in 250
Best race results: Phillis first in Spanish, French, Dutch and Argentine 125 GPs, and French and Argentine 250 GPs
Miles killed at Ulster GP

1962 *Isle of Man Team:* Jack Ahearn, Jack Findlay
Works rides: Tom Phillis — Honda
Championship placings: Phillis fourth (posthumously) in world 250 championship
Best race results: Phillis third in Spanish and French 250 GPs and Isle of Man 250 TT
Phillis killed during Isle of Man 350 TT

1963 *Isle of Man Team:* Jack Ahearn, Dennis Fry, Ron Robinson
Best race results: Jack Findlay second in Italian 500 GP on the McIntyre-Matchless

1964 *Isle of Man Team:* Jack Ahearn, Dennis Fry, Barry Smith
Works rides: Ahearn — Suzuki 250-4
Championship placings: Ahearn second in world 500 championship on Manx Norton
Best race results: Ahearn first in Finnish 500 GP

1965 *Isle of Man Team:* Jack Ahearn, Peter Richards, Malcolm Stanton
Works rides: Ahearn — Suzuki 250-4; Kevin Cass — Cotton
Championship placings: Ahearn fifth in world 500 championship on Manx Norton; Barry Smith first in European Hillclimb Championship on an Aermacchi 250

Best race results: Ahearn fourth in East German 500 GP; Smith third in French 250 GP on a Bultaco

1966 *Isle of Man Team:* John Dodds, Kel Carruthers, Malcolm Stanton
Works rides: Barry Smith — Derbi 50
Championship placings: Jack Findlay third in world 500 championship on the McIntyre-Matchless
Best race results: Findlay second East German 500 GP

1967 *Isle of Man Team:* Len Atlee, Malcolm Stanton, Brian Smith
Works rides: Barry Smith — Derbi 50
Championship placings: Jack Findlay fifth in world 500 championship on the McIntyre-Matchless; Smith fifth in world 50 championship on works Derbi
Best race results: Findlay third in West German, East German and Ulster 500 GPs; Smith third in Dutch 50 GP

1968 *Isle of Man Team:* John Dodds
Works rides: Barry Smith — Derbi 50
Championship placings: Jack Findlay second in world 500 championship; Kel Carruthers third in 350 championship; Smith third in 50 championship
Best race results: Smith first in Isle of Man 50 TT; Findlay second in Spanish, Dutch, Belgian and Czech 500 GPs; Carruthers second in Ulster 350 GP

1969 *Isle of Man Team:* Kel Carruthers, Tommy Gill, Phil O'Brien
Works rides: Carruthers — Aermacchi (125, 350 and 500) and later Benelli (250); Barry Smith — Derbi 50; Jack Findlay — Linto 500
Championship placings: Carruthers wins world 250 championship; Smith third in 50 championship
Best race results: Carruthers first in Isle of Man 250 TT, Ulster and Yugoslav 250 GPs, and second in Isle of Man 125 TT, Italian 250 GP and Spanish 350 GP; Smith first in Dutch and Belgian 50 GPs

1970 *Isle of Man Team:* Kel Carruthers, Jack Findlay, Ross Hannan
Works rides: Carruthers — Benelli 350 (three races)
Championship placings: Carruthers second in world 250 championship on a Yamaha, second in 350 championship on Benelli and Yamaha
Best race results: Carruthers first in Isle of Man 250 TT, West German, Czech and

Ulster 250 GPs, and Daytona (USA) 250 international 250; John Dodds first in West German 125 GP on an Aermacchi

1971 *Isle of Man Team:* Peter Jones
Championship placings: John Dodds fourth in world 250 championship on a Yamaha; Jack Findlay fifth in 500 championship on a Suzuki twin
Best race results: Findlay first in Ulster 500 GP; Dodds second in Belgian, Finnish and Italian 250 GPs; Kel Carruthers first in AMA Road Atlanta National road race

1972 *Championship placings:* John Dodds sixth in world 250 championship on a Yamaha; Jack Findlay eighth in world 500 championship on Jada-Suzuki
Best race results: Findlay second in Yugoslav 500 GP on Jada-Suzuki; Dodds third in Austrian 250 GP on a Yamaha

1973 *Works rides:* Jack Findlay — Suzuki 500-2 and 750-3; Kel Carruthers — Yamaha 350 (USA)
Championship placings: John Dodds second in FIM F750 series on a Yamaha 350; third in world 250 championship and fourth in 350 championship on Yamahas; Findlay fifth in world 500 championship and third in FIM F750 series
Best race results: Findlay first in Isle of Man 500 TT and Swedish F750 round; Dodds first in Spanish 250 GP and Spanish F750 round; Carruthers second in Daytona 200 Miles and first in AMA Talladega National road race

1974 *Works rides:* Jack Findlay — Suzuki 500-4 and 750-3
Championship placings: John Dodds first in FIM F750 series and fourth in world 350 championship; Findlay third in F750 series and fifth in world 500 championship
Best race results: Dodds first in Spanish 250 GP and Finnish 350 GP, and Spanish F750 round; Findlay fourth in Austrian, Italian and Finnish 500 GPs

1975 *Championship placings:* Jack Findlay wins FIM F750 series on a Yamaha 750
Best race results: Findlay second in the Dutch F750 round, third in Belgian and Finnish 500 GPs on a Yamaha; Warren Willing fifth in Daytona 200 Miles (US round of F750 championship)

1976 *Championship placings:* John Dodds fifth in world 350 championship on a Yamaha
Best race results: Dodds third in Austrian and Italian 350 GPs and Dutch 250 GP; Jack Findlay second in Swedish 500 GP (Suzuki) and British round of F750 championship (Yamaha) and fourth in Bol d'Or 24 Hour (Honda)
Les Kenny killed during Isle of Man 250 TT

1977 *Best race results:* Jack Findlay first in Austrian 500 GP on a Suzuki; Gregg Hansford first in Canadian round of World FIM F750 championship and fourth in Daytona 200 Miles (US round) on a Kawasaki; Vic Soussan third in French 250 GP on a Yamaha

1978 *Works rides:* Gregg Hansford — Kawasaki 250, 350 and 750
Championship placings: Hansford second in world 250 championship and third in 350 championship
Best race results: Hansford first in Spanish, French, Swedish and Yugoslav 250 GPs, French, Swedish and Yugoslav 350 GPs, and Daytona 250 international, fifth in Daytona 200 Miles

1979 *Works rides:* Gregg Hansford — Kawasaki 250, 350 and 750; Tony Hatton/Michael Cole/Kenny Blake — Honda endurance racers
Championship placings: Hansford second in world 250 championship and third in 350; Barry Smith first in World TT Formula Three championship on a Yamaha
Best race results: Hansford first in Italian, Dutch and Finnish 350 GPs; Smith first in Isle of Man TT F3 and Ulster TT F3 races and Belgian 125 GP; Hatton and Cole first in Suzuka 8 Hour; Jeff Sayle third in Britain's Race of the Year on a Yamaha 750

1980 *Works rides:* Gregg Hansford/Jim Budd — Kawasaki endurance racers; Kenny Blake — Honda endurance racer
Championship placings: Jeff Sayle fifth in world 350 championship on a Yamaha
Best race results: Barry Smith first in Isle of Man TT F3 race on a Yamaha; Hansford second in Suzuka 8 Hour; Sayle third Czech 350 GP

1981 *Works rides:* Gregg Hansford — Kawasaki 500; Kenny Blake — Honda endurance team
Championship placings: Barry Smith first in world TT F3 championship on a Yamaha
Best race results: Smith first in Isle of Man and Ulster TT F3 races; Graeme Geddes second in Argentinian 250 GP on a Bimota-Yamaha
Blake killed during Isle of Man 500 TT

1982 *Best race results:* Wayne Gardner first in Portuguese round of world TT F1 championship; Graeme McGregor second in Belgian 250 GP on Waddon-Rotax; Jeff Sayle third in French and Dutch 250 GPs and French 350 GP on Armstrong-Rotax and Armstrong

1983 *Championship placings:* Graeme McGregor third in world TT F2 championship and first in British TT F2 championship on a Ducati; Wayne Gardner first in British TT F1 championship on a Honda
Best race results: McGregor second in Isle of Man TT F2 race; Gardner fourth in Dutch TT F1 race; John Pace second in British round of FIM European 500 championship

1984 *Works GP rides:* Wayne Gardner — Honda 500 engine (late in season)
Best race results: Gardner third in Swedish 500 GP and fourth in Italian 500 GP: Graeme McGregor first in Isle of Man 250 TT and IoM TT F2 world championship round

1985 *Works GP rides:* Wayne Gardner — Honda V3 500; Paul Lewis — Suzuki 500
Championship placings: Gardner fourth in world 500 championship
Best race results: Gardner first in Suzuka 8 Hour, second in San Marino 500 GP, and third in South African, Italian, Yugoslav and Dutch 500 GPs

1986 *Works GP rides:* Wayne Gardner — Honda V4 500; Paul Lewis — Suzuki 500
Championship placings: Gardner second in world 500 championship; Graeme McGregor third in world TT F2 championship on a Ducati
Best race results: Gardner first in Spanish, Dutch and British 500 GPs, first in Suzuka 8 Hour; Mike Dowson/Kevin Magee second in Suzuka 8 Hour on a Yamaha; McGregor first in Spanish TT F2 round on a Ducati

1987 *Works GP rides:* Wayne Gardner — Honda 500; Kevin Magee — Yamaha 500
Championship placings: Gardner wins world 500 championship
Best race results: Gardner first in Spanish, Italian, Austrian, Yugoslav, Swedish, Czech and Brazilian 500 GPs; Magee first in Suzuka 8 Hour and Japanese round of world TT F1 championship, and third in Portuguese 500 GP

1988 *Works GP rides:* Wayne Gardner — Honda 500; Kevin Magee — Yamaha 500
Championship placings: Gardner second in world 500 championship; Magee fifth in 500 championship
Best race results: Gardner first in Dutch, Belgian, Yugoslav and Czech 500 GPs; Magee first in Spanish 500 GP and Suzuka 8 Hour; Michael Doohan first in World Superbike Championship round at Oran Park and first in one heat at Sugo

1989 *Works rides:* Wayne Gardner, Michael Doohan, Mal Campbell (AGP) — Honda; Kevin Magee, Michael Dowson (AGP) — Yamaha.

Note: Best race results category is not intended to be an exhaustive listing of each year's achievements.

AUSTRALIAN FIRSTS

- Ken Kavanagh was the first rider from outside Europe to win a world championship grand prix (Ulster 350 Grand Prix, 1952 on a Norton).
- Kavanagh was also the first rider to race the Moto Guzzi 500 V8 (Imola Gold Cup, 1956).
- Keith Campbell was the first rider from outside Europe to win a world championship (world 350 championship 1957 on a Moto Guzzi), and the last to race the Guzzi V8.
- Bob Brown was the first Westerner to score world championship points on a Japanese machine (fourth in Isle of Man 250 TT, 1960, on a Honda).
- Tom Phillis was the first Westerner contracted to ride for Honda at world championship level (Isle of Man TT, 1960) and the first rider to win a world championship grand prix on a Japanese machine (Spanish 125 Grand Prix, 1961 on a Honda).
- Eric Hinton scored Kawasaki's first international race win (Mettet, Belgium in 1966).
- Barry Smith scored Spanish factory Derbi's first world championship grand prix victory (Isle of Man 50 TT, 1968)
- Kel Carruthers was the first rider from outside North America to win at Daytona (250 cm^3 international, 1970) and the first to win an AMA National road race (Atlanta, Georgia national, 1971). Carruthers' victory at Atlanta was Yamaha's first in an AMA 750 cm^3 National event. Carruthers was later founding manager of Yamaha's American road-race team.
- Jack Findlay was the first rider to win a 500 grand prix on a Suzuki (Ulster GP 1971) and the first to win the Isle of Man 500 TT on a Suzuki (1973).
- Wayne Gardner was the first rider from outside Europe and the United States to win the world 500 championship (1987).

ACKNOWLEDGMENTS

The authors wish to thank the following people and publications...

Revs Motorcycle News and *Two Wheels* Magazine, for permission to reproduce passages from Don Cox's feature stories on Australian international riders. *Australian Motor Cycle News* "The First 30 Years", for details on Australian TT winners 1948-72.

Eric Hinton for his excellent memory of the 1950s and 1960s and for help in checking the manuscript. Jeff and Murray Sayle, and Warren Willing, for help with 1970s and 1980s technical details and with the manuscript.

Kim White of EMAP National Publications Archives, for assistance with photographic research and prompt answers to our enquiries.

Bennie Pinners for invaluable help with statistics and information tables.

Dennis Quinlan for help checking IoM TT teams and entries.

George Campbell, Tom Phillis Snr and the former Mrs Betty Phillis, for their comments and encouragement.

In addition to the riders profiled, we also extend our thanks to Geoff Duke, John Surtees, Luigi Taveri, Vic Willoughby, Mick Woollett, Gunther Wiesinger, Kenny Roberts, Eddie Lawson, Barry Sheene, Wes Brown, Arthur Blizzard, Alan Wallis, Allen Burt, Bill Jeffers, Maurie Pearson, Ron Kessing, Jan Carruthers, Kate Hinton, Tony Hatton, Tony McAlpine, Ross Hannan, Phil O'Brien, Maurie Quincey, Vic Soussan, and Peter Jones (motorcycle historian) for their background information and comments.

Don Morley, Jan Heese, Mick Woollett, Greg McBean, John Lapka and Projects Pictorial helped with photographs. Thanks also to Jamie McIlwraith for help with local photo research.

Research on the world championships would of course be much harder without the work of the Marlboro and Rothmans press services, and Maurice Bula in compiling world championship record books.

A special thanks to Tony Love, John Fenton-Smith, Claire Walls and Jane Tenney of John Ferguson Publishing, for helping make it happen. And to Colin Menzies, for his sympathetic editing. And all the riders and mechanics who gave of their time to answer our questions. We hope we've done justice to your efforts over the last 40 years.

Thank you all, Don Cox & Will Hagon
Sydney, March 1989

PICTURE CREDITS

Colour photographs by Jan Heese, Don Morley, Lou Martin and John Lapka.
Black and white photographs:
EMAP Archives, 12, 16, 17, 27, 30, 32 (bottom), 33 (top), 34, 38, 42, 43, 44, 48, 50, 51, 55 (top) 56, 61, 67, 68 (bottom), 79, 83 (bottom), 88 (bottom), 89, 90, 91, 92, 93, 94 (top), 99 (bottom), 101, 102, 105, 106 (bottom), 110, 119, 124 (top), 150 (top & bottom), 156, 157, 160, 166, 167, 169, 183, 188, 195.
Jan Heese: 118, 125, 126, 127, 149, 151 (bottom), 152 158, 162, 169, 170, 171, 174, 178, 181, 187, 191, 207.
Don Morley: 97, 198, 201, 203, 208 (top & bottom), 211, 212, 215, 217, 221, 223, 224, 225.
Mick Woollett: 58, 107, 113 (top), 120, 124 (bottom), 144, 145, 151, 153.
Revs Motorcycle News: 26, 28, 30 (bottom), 53, 120, 123 (top), 189, 213, 228 (bottom centre), 229 (top centre).
Leo Vogelzang: Contents page and 192, 193, 194, 199, 202, 206, 214.
Rob Lewis: 176, 184, 190.
Greg McBean: 228 (centre), 229 (top right, and centre left).
Bill Salmond (Island Photographics): 9, 30 (top).
Isle of Man Examiner: 24 (bottom), 60.
S.R. Keig Collection: 32, (top), 33 (bottom).
Charles Rice: 35 (bottom).
Keith L. Ward: 99 (top), 116.
Barry Marshall: 197.
John Ulrich: 177.
Nick Hartgerink: 227.
Projects Pictorial: 180, 228 (bottom left).
Bill Meyer: 154, 186.
Jim Greening: 155, 168.
Don Cox: 18, 182, 228 (top, and centre left).
John Lapka: 229 (top left).
Youngs Photo Press Agency: 21.
G.V. Kneale: 86.
T. Evans: 147.
Noel Colon: 94 (bottom).
Graham Monro: 196.
Nigel Snowden: 173.
Rowland White: 123 (bottom).
Jarda Sejki: 109.
Dave "Fredman": 179.
John Schaepman: 10.
V.L. Fischer: 24 (top left).
Kurt Schmidtpeter: 24 (top right).
Bryan Gunther: 36.
Alec Fisher: 85.
Photographer unknown: 15, 35 (top), 37, 47, 54, 65, 68 (top), 70, 71, 72, 76, 77, 80, 82, 83 (top), 87, 88 (top), 95, 104, 106, 113 (bottom), 114, 115.

INDEX

Numerals in italics indicate an illustration of the subject mentioned; bold face indicates both illustrations and text references of the subject mentioned.

A

Adams, Alan, 186
Agostini, Giacomo, 44, 55, 109, 119, *133*, 146, 148, 151, 152, 159, 163, 168, 169, 170, 186, 204, 209, 221, 222
Agusta, Domenico, 51, 107
Ahearn, Jack, *14*, *15*, 20, 36, 37, 39, 41, 49, 60, 62, 69, 75, 76, 85, 86, 95, 96, 100, **106-117**, *130*, 147, 172, 209, 224
Allan, Neil, 217
AMA Grand National, 153, 155, 209
Ambrosini, Dario, 33
Amm, Ray, 45, 46, 49, 50, 55, 63, 74
Anderson, Bob, 84
Anderson, Fergus, 29, 37, 44, 46, 48, 49, 50
Anderson, Hugh, 162
Andersson, Kent, 145, 149, 150, 169, 170
Angel, Ron, 171, 189, 204, 219
Argentinian GP, 103, 201, 219
Armstrong, Reg, 46, 47, 48, 49, 85, 192
Atlee, Len, 41, 147, 204
Auerbacher, George, 41, 159
Australian-Cycle Council of Australia (ACCA), 29, 78
Australian GP, 22, 53, 194, 227
Australian TT, 38, 72, 96, 204
Austrian GP, 37, 110, *127*, 180, 182, 192, 219

B

Bailey, S.L., 17
Baker, Steve, 180, 187
Balde, Jean-Francois, 191, 192, 201
Ballington, Kork, 177, 178, 180, 181, 182, 191, 197, 200
Baltisberger, Hans, 38, 88
Bandolira, Carlo, 32, 51
Barker, Roger, 38, 62, 159
Barnett, Harris, 216, 224
Bartol, Harald, 193, 194, 202
Bartrop, Harry, 29
Bartusch, Gunter, 151
Bathurst, 16, 29, 30, 33, 34, 39, 41, 45, 60, 73, 79, 85, 95, 114, 122, 146, 183, 184, 185, 189, 194, 195, 204, 227
Bayliss, Steve "Barney", 195, *196*, *197*
Beale, George, 198, 199, 200, 202
Belgian GP, Spa-Francorchamps, 11, 17, 19, 32, 40, 41, 49, 50, 57, 58, 62, 63, 66, 67, 69, 71, 79, 83, 91, 102, 103, 109, 123, 124, 127, 128, 151, 158, *164*, 182, 191, 193, 195, 199, *199*, 200, 201, 204, 219
Bell, Artie, 32, 48
Benelli, 148, 149, 150, 152, 159
Bennett, Dave, 55
Bennett and Wood, 27, 146

Benstead, Tommy, 27
Bergamonti, Angelo, 148
Blair, Matt, 212
Blake, Ken, 16, 165, 200, **204**, 207
Bliss, Eric, 71, *78*, *79*
Boddice, Bill, 78
Bosman, Andre, 22, 207, 210
Boulter, Laurie, 49, 55
Braun, Dieter, *150*, 167, 169, 170, 172, 174
Brett, Jack, 46
Briggs, Mark, 194
British GP, 195
Brown, Bob, *14*, *15*, 19, *24*, 36, 38, 39, 53, 55, 57, 62, 67, 69, **82-91**, 94, 96, 98, *99*, 100, 117, 119
Brown, Warwick, 217
Bryans, Ralph, 161
Bryen, Keith, *24*, 36, 38, 49, 60, 62, **63**, 64, *65*, 67, *68*, 73, 83, 88
Burgess, Jeremy (Jerry), 209, 210, 215
Burt, Allen, *24*, 84, 85, *85*, 86, *86*, *87*, 88, 90, 96
Byrnes, Bat, 29

C

Campbell, George, 59, 60
Campbell, Keith, 13, *14*, *15*, 16, 17, 19, 20, 34, 36, 37, 38, 49, 50, **56-69**, 75, 76, 83, 84, 85, 86, 88, 94, 96, 115, 117, 119, 159
Campbell, Malcolm, 209, 210, 211, 212, 223, 224
Campbell, Peter, *18*, 185, 207
Carcano, Ing Giulio, 49, 64, 66
Carey, Ted, 85
Carruthers, Kel, 16, 17, 19, 20, 23, 25, 41, 55, 57, 89, 91, 95, 100, 103, 117, 121, 127, *129*, **144-155**, 159, 161, 171, 172, 175, 185, 197, 205, 209, 215
Cass, Kevin, 41, 147, 216
Castrol 6 Hour, 109, 112, 164, 194, 204, 217, 218, 220, 221, 222
Ceccotto, Johnny, 172, 177, 180, 191, 204
Chatterton, Derek, 180
Chevallier, Olivier, 170
Chivas, Doug, 22, 210
Clark, Nobby, 150
Clark, Wayne, 220
Cole, Michael, 210, 211, *213*, 217, 218
Coleman, Rod, 45, 46, 85
Continental Circus, 30, 61, 119, 120, 124
Cooley, Wes, 218
Cooper, John, 152, 172
Craig, Joe, 30, 32, 45, 48
Crosby, Graeme, 13, 57, 84, *135*, 178, 193, 198, 200, 207, 210, 211, 212, 215, 218, 224
Crowe, George, *14*, 15
Czechoslovakian GP, Brno, 22, 37, 41, 58, 62, 88, 123, 149, 151, 191

D

Dale, Dickie, *14*, *15*, 35, 37, 44, 49, 63, 64, 66, 84, 86, 98
Daniel, Clem, 85, 88, 90, 91, 103, 204

Daniell, Harold, 23, 30, 32, 40
Daytona, 40, 146, 150, 153, 155, 177, 180, 183, 185, 189, 191, 198, 200, 203, 212, 218
Dearden, Reg, 69, 111
Degner, Ernst, 39, 101, 102, 103
Dennehy, Terry, 168
Dennis Island, 204
De Vries, Jan, 158
Diener, Les, 60
Dodds, 16, 17, 41, 119, 120, 127, *133*, 147, 151, **166-175**, 205
Doohan, Michael, 13, 19, *143*, 209, 210, 212, 227
Doran and Petch, 45
Dowde, Chris, 185
Dowson, Michael, 211, 212
Doyle, Neville, 178, 179, 181, 182
Duke, Geoff, 19, *31*, 32, 33, 36, 37, 43, 44, *44*, 45, 46, 47, 48, 49, 55, 61, 62, 63, 67, 69, 83, 84, 85, 88, 89, 90, *90*, 91, 97, 110, 115
Dunlop, Joey, 203
Dutch GP, 11, 32, 39, 45, 50, *52*, 58, 62, 63, 64, 67, 77, 79, 84, 100, 109, 124, 149, 178, 186, 190, 192, 199, 200, 201, 207, 219, 220, 224
Dutch Sidecar GP, 71
Dutch TT riders strike, 22, 36, 86

E

East German GP, 11, 35, 39, 63, 109, 122, 149
Edmonds, Bob, 61
Ehrlich, Dr Joe, 201, 203
Ekerold, Jon, 191
Emde, Don, 155
Ennett, Derek, 55
Espie, Thierry, 200
European Champion, 11
European Grand Prix, 11

F

Farne, Franco, 159
Federation Internationale des Clubs Motorcyclistes (FICM), 11
Federation Internationale Motorcyclistes (FIM), 11, 13
Fernandez, Patrick, 219
Ferrant, Derek, 49
Ferrari, Virginio, 182
FIM F750 Prize, 13, 16, 25, 127, 167
Findlay, Jack, 13, 16, 17, 20, 22, 25, 39, 41, 84, 94, 96, 110, 114, **118-128**, *130*, *132*, 147, 148, *149*, 167, 168, 170, 172, 209, 224
Finnish GP, 62, 108, *113*, 127, 147, 149
Fletcher, Arnie, 202
Fontana, Daniele, 120, 122, 124, 127
Foster, Bob, 37
Forrest, Jack, 60, 85, 95, 111
Fox, Laurie, 72
Fraser, Kevin, 216
Frend, Ted, 32
French GP, 11, 17, 102, 103, 192, 201, 204
French, Jack, 44, 71
Freymond, Roland, 200
Frith, Freddie, 13, 111

Frutschi, Michel, 191
Fugger, Doug, *14, 15*, 80

G
Gallina, Roberto, 221, 223
Gardner, Wayne, 13, 19, 22, 25, 41, 57, 107, 117, 119, *140-141*, 161, 175, 177, 200, 207, *208*, 210, 211, **214-227**
Garriga, Juan, 205
Geddes, Graeme, *135*, 207, *207*, 215, 217, **219**
George, Alex, *127*, 199
George, Max, 73, *73, 74,* 75, *76, 77,* 78, 79
German GP, 193, 219
Goddard, Peter, 212
Goodwin, Richard, *18*, 207
Gould, Rod, 148, 149, 150, 151, *151*, 174
Graham, Les, 13, 33, 46
Grands Prix, see individual country names
Grant, Mick, 187, 205
Griffiths, Sid, 186
Gschwander, Ernst, 172
Guignabodet, Jean-Louis, 192
Guthrie, 11

H
Hailwood, Mike, 35, 36, 52, 84, 89, 93, 100, 101, 102, 103, 104, 105, 108, 109, 119, 123, 158, 186, 199; Stan, 35, 53, 209, 221
Hansford, Gregg, 16, 20, 22, 115, 119, *134*, 172, **176-184**, 189, 191, 197, 204, 207, 210, 215, 216, 217, 226
Harris, Pip, 77
Hartle, John, 57, 64, 90, 110
Hartog, Will, 182
Hartwell Motorcycle Club, 44, 46, 50, 55, 71, 73, 98
Harvey, John, 217
Haslam, Ron, 165, 187, 218, 220, 221, 222
Hass, Werner, 49
Hatton, Tony, 158, 164, 183, 210
Hazel and Moore, 29, 111
Hennen, Pat, 183, 198
Herrero, Santiago, 124, 149, 159
Herron, Tom, 204
Hillebrand, Fritz, 78, 79
Hinton, Harry, 19, **26-41**, 44, 45, 59, *60*, 61, 114; Eric, 13, *24*, 25, 27, 28, *31*, **34-41**, 53, 59, 69, 71, 76, 88, 93, 94, 96, 98, 100, 121, 147; Harry Jnr, 27, 28, *34,* 35, *35, 36,* 38, 39, 55, 122; Robert, 29, 35, 41, 159, 189; Peter, 41; Tony, 41
Hirst, Lloyd, 59
Hocking, Gary, 35, 84, 90, 101, 102, 103, 104
Hocking, Jim, 71, 72, 73
Hodgkinson, Barry, 36, 63, 95
Honda Motorcycle Company, 98
Howard, Russell, 212
Hunt, Tim, 11
Hunter, Dick, 194
Hunter, Ron, 44

I
Indonesian GP, 185
Internationals, Imola, 34, 38, 45, 63, 103, 127, 178, 180, 186, 195, 196
Isle of Man Touring Trophy (IoM TT), 11, 13, 16, 17, 19, 23, 25, 29, 30, 34, 38, 39, 40, 43, 44, 49, *50,* 53, *53,* 60, 61, 63, 66, 71, 78, *80,* 83, 84, 85, 86, 89, 93, 96, 98, *99,* 102, 107, 110, 112, 114, 119, 120, 122, 124, 125, 147, 148, 151, 152, 158, 159, 165, 190, 195, 201, 202, 203, 207
Italian GP, 11, 19, 32, 38, 43, 45, 63, 103, 122, 123, 149, 151, 169, 181, 190, 191,
Ivy, Bill, 124, 148

J
Jamieson, Sam, 36
Jemison, Tom, 29
Jenkinson, Denis, 13
Jenson, Sid, 32, 40
Johnson, Andrew, 210, 219
Johnson, Greg, 128

K
Kanaya, Hideo, 172, 186
Kanemoto, Erv, 210
Kassner, Horst, 38, 88
Katayama, Takazumi, 182
Kavanagh, Ken, 16, 19, 25, 33, 37, **42-55**, 62, 64, 69, 71, 72, 73, 75, 115, 205, 209
Kellett, Dave, 207, 210
Kennedy, Frank, 187
Kenny, Les, 16
Kessing, Ron, 84, 85, 86
King, Alistair, 89
King, Norm, 71
Kneubuhler, Bruno, 170
Kosmicki, Leo, 13

L
Laing, Gordon, 49, 61, 62, 115, 116, 121
Lancefield, Steve, 30
Lansivuori, Teppi, 168, 169, 170, 185
Lavado, Carlos, 201
Lawson, Eddie, 146, 154, 177, 209, 210, 215, 219, 221, 222, 223, 224, *225, 225,* 226, 227
Leadbetter, Don, 96
Lewis, Bob, 102, 103, *138*
Lewis, Paul, 51, *138*, 207, 212
Liberati, Libero, 67, *68,* 69, 83
Lockett, Johnny, 32, 33
Lodewijkx, Paul, 161
Lomas, Bill, 46, 50, 63, 64
Longford, 25
Lorenzetti, Enrico, 43, 48, 50
Lucchinelli, Marco, 177, 178, 221

M
Mack, Bernie, 72, 80
Madden, Robert, 112
Magee, Kevin, 13, 19, *142*, 175, 207, 209, 210, 211, *211,* 212, *212,* 219

Mamola, Randy, 177, 178, 182, 198, 200, 209, 221, 222, 224, 225, *225,* 226
Mang, Toni, 168, 191, 192, *199,* 200, 201, 219, 220
Mann, Dick, 150
Marshall, Roger, 200, 205, 218, 220
Marsovski, Guyla, *108*, 114
Martin, Bob, 193
Martin, Louis, 49
Masetti, Umberto, 45, 46, 55
McAlpine, Tony, *21,* 30, 33, 36, 44, 45, 62
McCandless, Rex, 30
McCormack, Mark, 216
McElnea, Rob, 44, 223, 224
McGillivray, Dave, 191
McGregor, Graeme, 16, 25, *136-137, 139,* 189, 190, 191, 193, **195-205**, 207, *208,* 219
McIntyre, Bob, 23, 35, 57, 61, 66, 71, 83, 89, 93, 101, 102, 103, 104, 122, 159
McPherson, Eric, 13, 17, 29, 30, 32, *33,* 40, 60
Meier, Georg, 45
Mellor, Phil, 203
Middelburg, Jack, 202
Middlemiss, Glenn, 51
Miles, Ron, 53, 96, 98, 100, 103
Miller, Sammy, 37
Milne, Jack, 29, 41
Minter, Derek, 39, 104, 110, 172
Mitchell, Bob, 20, **70-81**, 94, 109
Molloy, Ginger, 110, 124
Molloy, Peter, 217, 218
Montanari, Alano, 67, 83
Morrison, George, *16,* 29, 30, *32,* **40**
Mortimer, Chas, 169, 196, 198, 204
Motor Cycle Racing Club of N.S.W., 29
Muir, Graeme, 212
Mussett, Frank, 29

N
Neill, Dennis, 218
Nieto, Angel, 157, 159, 161, 163, 170

O
O'Brien, Phil, 95
Oldfield, Chris, 51, 193
Oliver, Eric, 13, 72, 75, 77, 78
Olympic Motorcycle Club, 61
Osborne, 27
Otto, Trevor, 210

P
Pace, Johm, 207, 217, 220
Padgett, Gary, 202
Pagani, Alberto, 124, *149*
Pagani, Nello, 13, 23
Parlotti, Gilberto, 145
Pasolini, Renzo, 148, 152, 159, 168, 169
Pero, Iain, 212
Perris, Frank, 109
Perry, Geoff, 155, 219
Perry, Rick, 195
Persi, Roberto, 83
Phillip Island, 25, 39, 44, 53, 79, 80, 94, 96, 204, 219, 204, 227

239

Phillis, Rob, 95, 192, 210, 211, 212, 219
Phillis, Tom, 13, 16, 17, 19, 22, 39, 53, 84, 91, **92-105**; Memorial Race, 172
Pons, Patrick, 167, *170*
Portuguese GP, *212*
Potter, Dave, 218
Pound, Trevor, 95
Praml, Karl and Willi, 216
Pretty, Greg, 207, 210
Price, John, 215

Q
Quincey, Eric, 38
Quincey, Maurice *17*, *24*, 38, 44, 45, 49, 60, 62, 85, 95, 111, 112, 115, 116
Quincey, Ray, 16

R
Rainey, Wayne, 175, 203, 211, 212
Rattan, Keith, 43
Read, Phil, 41, 107, 108, 148, 149, 151, 168, 170, 174, 221
Redman, Jim, 35, 90, 91, 94, 100, 101, 103, 104, 105, 109, 110, 171
Regless, H., 17
Renfrey, Martin, 212
Renson, Ralph, 90
Ring, Ernie, 44, 45, 60, 117, 121
Robb, Tommy, 36, 104, 161
Robbins, Dave, 217
Roberts, Kenny, 41, 146, 154, 155, 172, 177, 178, 180, 189, 191, 197, 209, 211, 223, 224, 226
Roche, Raymond, 221
Roth, Reinholt, 204
Rougerie, Michael, 170
Ruffo, Bruno, 13
Rumble, Ken, 95, 103, 171
Rutter, Tony, 196, 202, 203, 205

S
Saarinen, Jarno, 155, 168, 169, 174
Salter, Bob "Orrie", 122
Samspon, Col, 44, 71
Sandford, Cecil, 69
Sarron, Christian, 177, 222
Saul, Eric, 201
Saunders, Ian "Buster", 212
Sayle, Jeffrey, 22, *136-137*, *138*, 181, 186, **189-194**, **196-202**, 207, *208*
Sayle, Murray, 183, 184, 185, 186, 189, 190, 194, 198, 207

Schimazaki, 102
Schwartz, Kevin, 212, 226, 227
Scolyer, Rob, 210
Seeley, Colin, 124
Senior, Art, 29
Serron, Christina, 227
Sheene, Barry, 23, 120, *132*, 167, 170, 174, 177, 178, 182, 189, 191, 202, 221
Shorey, Dan, 114
Sidecar technique, **74**
Simcock, Arthur, 11, 17, 78
Sinclair, Frank, 72
Slaughter, Les, 85
Smith, Barry, 13, 16, 19, 22, 25, *131*, 147, **156-165**, 174, 207
Smith, Cyril, 73, 75, 77, 78, 79
Smith, Mick, 41, 181, 189, 190, 196
Soussan, Vic, *134*
Spanish GP, 11, 43, 48, 93, 101, 148, 161, *171*, 180, 211, *215*, 222
Spencer, "Fast" Freddie, 177, 209, 210, 218, 221, 222, 223, 224, 227
Stanton, Malcolm, 41, *109*, 147
Stastny, Franta, 39, 90
Stephens, Scott, 211, *213*
Stollinger, Edi, 200
Stowe, Kevin, 187
Surtees, John, 30, 45, 50, 51, 57, 66, 69, 83, 89, 90, *90*, 98, 103, 116, 128, 159, 221
Suzuki, Ken, 181
Swedish GP, 11, 37, 45, 67, 89, 128
Swiss GP, 11, 32, 35, 48, 75

T
Takahashi, 103
Takai, Ikujiro, 185
Tanaka, 103
Taniguchi, 100
Taveri, Luigi, 20, 39, 62, 98, 100, 101, 102, 103
Taylor, Alistair, 193, 202
Team Kawasaki Australia (TKA), 183, 184, 196
Techniques of Motor Cycle Road Racing, 177, 184
Tesoriero, Vince, 185
Thompson, Richie, 36, 37, 85, 88, 96
Tinkler, Len, 61
Tobin, Leo, 27
Toerson, Aalt, 159, 161
Tonkin, Steve, 191, 200
Toombs, Ron, 163, 171, 183
Tournadre, Jean-Louis, 192

Trinder, Craig, 212
Trinder, Steve, 51, 212, 218
TT Formula One (TT F1), 13, 158, 200, 202, 205, 211, 220, 221
Two (TT F2), 13, 203, 205
Three (TT F3), 13, 16, 158, 207

U
Ubbaili, Carlo, 90, 100
Ulster GP, 11, 13, 27, 30, 32, 34, 43, 45, 46, 49, 55, 62, *68*, 69, 84, 88, 90, 100, 103, 108, 109, 114, 119, 125, 147, 148, 149, 151, 165, 199, 201, 202
Uncini, Franco, 177, 202, 220, 221
Urqhart, Lindsay, 80

V
Van Praag, Lionel, 17
Venturi, Remo, 90, 91
Vesco, Don, 150, 151, 152, 153
Victorian GP, Phillip Island, 98, 100, 103
Villa, Walter, 169, 170
Vincent, Chris, 159
Vukmanovich, George, 185, 186

W
Walker, Geoff, 46
Walker, Lennie, 39
Walters, Jack, 80, 157, 204, 219
West, Bob, 100
West German GP, 11, 37, 46, 50, 77, 79, 84, 88, 91, 100, 122, 128, 148, 191, 193, 200, 219
Wiener, Max, 127
Wilkinson, Arthur "Bluey", 155
Willetts, Ben, 78
Williams, Charlie, 196, 199, 203
Willing, Len, 207, 211, 212
Willing, Warren, 16, 154, 158, 164, 183, **184-187**, 189, 191, 193, 198, 216
Willoughby, Vic, 30
Wimmer, Martin, 200, 211
Wise, Alex, 39
Woodley, John, 186, *186*
Woodruffe, 79
Woods, Stan, 128
Woollett, Mick, 71, 84, 94, 101
World Series, 22, 182
World Superbike Championship, 13, 210
Wynne, Steve, 205

Z
Zeller, Walter, 45, 117

240